# INDEPENDENT ADMINISTRATIVE AUTHORITIES

# INDEPENDENT ADMINISTRATIVE AUTHORITIES

*Edited by*

ROBERTO CARANTA, MADS ANDENAS
AND DUNCAN FAIRGRIEVE

BIICL
BRITISH INSTITUTE OF
INTERNATIONAL AND
COMPARATIVE LAW
www.biicl.org

Published and Distributed by
The British Institute of International and Comparative Law
Charles Clore House, 17 Russell Square, London WC1B 5JP



*British Library Cataloguing in Publication Data*
A Catalogue record of this book is available from the British Library

ISBN 0–903067–49–8



Typeset by Cambrian Typesetters
Frimley, Surrey
Printed in Great Britain by Biddles Ltd
King's Lynn

# PREFACE

Independent administrative authorities have become a permanent feature of the institutional landscape over past decades. Tested in the United States of America, they have been adopted in one form or another in most European States. The need for institutions with both impartiality and technical expertise has inexorably led to an increase in number and scope of independent administrative authorities.

The place which these bodies occupy in the different national constitutional arrangements is still a matter for debate. In spite of the fundamental nature of these bodies, there is a need for further doctrinal analysis. The aim of this book is to bring together a comparative law analysis of the current developments of independent administrative authorities, highlighting common trends and examining remaining differences.

The chapters of this book cover both the United States and European jurisdictions, and a specific paper is devoted to the European Union. The analysis of the national models has broadly followed a framework of questions set out in an Annexe at the end of this volume. A number of different questions are covered, including regulatory powers, judicial review, and the liability of independent administrative authorities.

One theme which runs through many of the contributions is the issue of legitimacy. This is a consequence of the conflict between independence and accountability. In some ways, independent administrative authorities are at odds with the traditional notion of separation of powers which still lies at the heart of constitutional thinking. This tension is articulated in different ways in the countries studied. This has perhaps been less perceptible in those jurisdictions—such as the Netherlands and the United Kingdom—where the constitution is considered flexible enough to make room for institutional innovation. Elsewhere, the picture is somewhat different: the United States has developed a functional approach to the separation of powers which is not without its critics. In France, the rule-making power has been limited and judicial review has been reinforced. In Spain, independence is weak enough to minimize conflicts with more traditional powers. In Germany, ministerial supervision mandated by the *Grundgesetz* is simply waived *de facto*. In Italy, recourse is made to different Constitutional provisions in order to gain legitimacy for independent administrative authorities.

The overall impression is that classical constitutional thinking—and its emphasis on specific forms of separation of powers—is stretched almost to breaking point. The traditional arrangement of executive powers are at odds not only with the reality of the current institutional architecture but also with the overriding objective to protect fundamental rights from encroachment by the executive.

In the past, many constitutions have entrenched fundamental rights against legislative encroachment by means of constitutional judicial review mechanisms. In several continental countries, the division between constitutional review and administrative review (with separate jurisdictions and procedures), have resulted in less focus being placed on the actions of the executive. Ministerial accountability through the parliamentary process is, however, poorly suited to provide protection of fundamental rights against abuses of the executive. The Spanish and Italian reports point out that independent administrative authorities play an important role when fundamental rights are concerned. Traditional constitutional arrangements have often failed to provide the tools for the effective protection of fundamental rights and—more generally—failed to shelter regulation and adjudication from the unchecked rule of the majority. It would not make sense to stick rigidly to these traditional constitutional arrangements in developing the new European constitutional order.

Separation of powers deserves to be given fresh thought. This book ends with a chapter challenging some timeworn and traditional assumptions about separation of legislative, executive and judiciary powers. Independent administrative authorities offer food for thought. This is an encouragement to engage in further thinking.

The work undertaken for this book was the result of a wider project under the direction of Professor Giandomenico Falcon on *Il diritto amministrativo dei Paesi europei tra omogeneizzazione comunitaria e diversità culturali*. The editors are very grateful for the support of this project through grants from the Italian MIUR and from a number of Italian universities. The project on independent administrative authorities also benefited from additional grants from the *Dipartimento di Scienze giuridiche 'Filippo Serafin'* of the *Università degli Studi di Torino*.

Once again, many thanks go to Olivia Skinner and Dr Simona Rodriquez.

*London, 5 July 2004*

ROBERTO CARANTA
MADS ANDENAS
DUNCAN FAIRGRIEVE

# TABLE OF CONTENTS

# 1. AN ANALYSIS OF THE CONSTITUTIONAL POSITION OF THE US INDEPENDENT AGENCIES

*Saskia Lavrijssen*[1]

## I. INTRODUCTION

This chapter discusses how the position of independent administrative agencies, with broad regulatory powers, can be reconciled with the US Constitution and how the legitimacy of their regulatory actions can be ensured. The experiences with the problems of legitimacy of US administrative agencies might well contribute to the resolution of questions that arise as regards the constitutional position of (independent) regulatory agencies in the EC Member States.

The US constitution is based on the principle of Separation of Powers, reflected in Articles I, II, and III of the Constitution.[2] Pursuant to Article I all legislative powers granted in the Constitution are vested in Congress. Pursuant to Article II the Executive Power shall be vested in a President. Article III vests the Judicial Power of the United States in one Supreme Court, and in such inferior Courts as the Congress may from time to time ordain and establish. The framers of the Constitution had the conviction that the centralized accumulation of power in any person or single group of persons meant tyranny: the division and separation of powers, both vertically (along the axis of federal, state, and local authority) and horizontally (along the axis of legislative, executive and judicial authority) meant liberty.[3] It was thus essential that no department, branch or level of government would have the power to achieve dominance on its own.[4]

Except for the institution of these named three branches, the US Constitution does not provide any further information on how central government should be organized nor on the question of how 'legislative', 'executive', and 'judicial' should be defined.[5] Neither does the

[1] Researcher and lecturer, Department of European and International Public Law, Tilburg University, The Netherlands. The author thanks Professor D Gifford, Faculty of law, University of Minnesota and Dr S van Bijsterveld, Senior Lecturer, Faculty of Law, Tilburg University, for their comments on an earlier draft of this chapter.

[2] LH Tribe, *American Constitutional Law* (3rd edn Foundation Press, 2000) 7.

[3] Ibid.

[4] Ibid.

[5] Ibid 137 and PL Strauss 'The Fourth Branch' (1984) Columbia Law Review 597–602.

Constitution explicitly mention the power of Congress to found administrative agencies.[6]

It might seem that the position and the powers of the administrative agencies contravene the Separation of Powers principle in three ways. First, Congress has founded agencies, headed by officers that do not serve at the will of the President, meaning that the latter is restricted in removing them from office. These agencies are commonly referred to as the independent or regulatory agencies. These agencies can be distinguished from executive agencies. The officers of the latter type of administrative agencies serve at the will of the President. In the opinion of critics of the administrative state the position and the powers of the independent administrative agencies contradict with the Separation of Powers principle of the Constitution.[7] Indeed, it can be questioned whether Congress can legitimately place agencies with a mandate to execute the law outside the control of the President.

Secondly, when Congress adopts acts it usually delegates broad regulatory powers to administrative agencies to implement the acts. It is not uncommon for Congress to leave it up to the agency to take important policy decisions on which Congress itself could reach no consensus. This means that non-elected officials may have the power to create new rights and obligations for the citizens. It can be questioned whether the practice of Congress to delegate broad rulemaking powers to the agencies does not contravene Article I, which vests all legislative power within Congress.

Thirdly, administrative agencies combine powers previously distributed among the President, Congress and the Judiciary. For instance, the Securities and Exchange Commission (SEC) formulates law by writing rules that spell out what disclosures must be made in a stock prospectus. The SEC then enforces these rules by prosecuting those who violate its regulations through disciplinary actions against broker-dealers or through stop order proceedings against corporate issuers. Finally, the SEC also acts as a judge and jury in deciding whether its rules have been violated. In exercising the latter function it conducts adjudicatory hearings to determine guilt and mete out punishment.[8]

The tremendous growth of administrative agencies with broad regulatory powers in the twentieth century has raised many policy and coordination problems in government. These developments led Brownlow to make his famous statement that the administrative agencies are a 'headless fourth branch of government', acting irresponsibly and not being

[6] This contribution will only deal with independent agencies and executive agencies. Para 2 describes the distinction between these two types of agencies.

[7] PP Swire, 'Incorporation of Independent Agencies into the Executive Branch' (1985) 94 Yale Law Review 1766.

[8] E Gellhorn and RM Levin, *Administrative Law and Process* (4th edn St Paul 1997) 9–10.

coordinated by the President.[9] This paper will analyse to what extent the position and the powers of (independent) administrative agencies conflict with the Separation of Powers principle. The paper mainly explores how the US Supreme Court has dealt with constitutional problems relating to administrative agencies and their powers. From this analysis, it will be concluded that the case law of the US Supreme Court, supports the view that the powers of Congress, the President and the Judiciary can be combined and that there is room for Congress to adapt the government structure to the necessities of new governmental policy. A more functional Separation of Powers approach will be advocated that is both legal and more practical in order to assess the constitutional position of administrative agencies.[10]

After having concluded that from a more functional Separation of Powers perspective the position and powers of the US (independent) administrative agencies may well be reconciled with the structure of the US Constitution, the paper discusses to whom institutions administrative agencies are accountable. It is described how the actions of administrative agencies are checked and balanced by the President, Congress and the Judiciary. Furthermore, the paper illustrates the President, Congress and the Judiciary are not the only three players that control the agencies' activities. Since the agencies have to follow administrative procedures in which the public may participate, interest groups influence the agencies' activities as well. From this overview it can be concluded that administrative agencies represent anything but a 'headless fourth branch'. The analysis shows the process of checks and balances is not static, and adapts to changing economic and political circumstances.

## II. THE ROLE AND THE CONCEPT OF INDEPENDENT AGENCIES

### *A. Organization, terminology and constitutional position (questions 1, 2, 3, 12, and 13)*

There are many different administrative agencies within the US administration.[11] Generally, the administrative agencies can be classified in four categories. First, there are the executive departments mentioned in the Constitution, which are attached to the cabinet officers who control

[9] *Report of the Committee with studies of Administrative Management in the Federal Government* (1937) 39–43.

[10] Strauss 'The Fourth Branch' 574.

[11] See for a clear description of the organization of US administrative agencies, R Pierce, SA Shapiro, and PR Verkuil, *Administrative Law and Process* (3rd edn Foundation Press, 1999) 92–6.

them.[12] These administrative organizations have the most important policy and budgetary responsibilities. Important examples are the Departments of Defense, State, Justice, Agriculture and Health, and Human Services (HHS). Secondly, there are sub-agencies that are within these departments, but that are often organizationally distinct, such as the Food and Drug Administration (FDA) in HHS. Thirdly, there are also agencies that are separate from the executive departments, but that are nonetheless 'executive'. Here the Environmental Protection Agency (EPA) and the Office of Management and Budget (OMB) are prominent examples. Finally, there are agencies designated 'independent' by Congress and they are also referred to as 'regulatory agencies'. A lot of the latter agencies were founded during the New Deal period. Prominent agencies are: The Federal Communications Commission (FCC), The Federal Trade Commission (FTC), the National Labor Relations Board (NLRB) and the Securities and Exchanges Commission (SEC). This paper will mainly deal with the distinction between 'executive' and 'independent' agencies. If the word 'administrative' agency is used, both the independent and the executive agencies are meant.

An important difference between independent and executive agencies is related to the President's restricted power to remove officials of the independent agency. Unlike the officials of executive agencies, who are subject to dismissal at the will of the President, the President can remove the officers of independent agencies only 'for cause'. For instance, pursuant to the Federal Trade Commission Act the President may remove the Commissioners of the FTC only 'for inefficiency, neglect of duty or malfeasance in office'. Since the Supreme Court has never said what 'for cause' means, there is no controlling judicial decision on how 'independent' the independent agencies actually are. According to some authors, the 'for cause clause' ensures that a President will not be able to discipline an official for purely political reasons, or for no reasons at all.[13] Lessig and Sunstein argue, that it would be possible to interpret the relevant statutes as allowing a large degree of removal and supervisory power to remain in the President, enabling the latter to remove the agencies' officials for political reasons under some circumstances.[14] According to Lessig and Sunstein the statutory words might even allow the discharge of commissioners who have frequently or on important occasions acted in ways inconsistent with the President's wishes with respect to what is required by sound policy.

There are several other ways in which independent agencies can be

[12] Pursuant to US Constitution Art II, s 2, the President may require the Opinion, in writing, of the principal Officer, in each of the Executive Departments, upon any subject relating to the duties of their respective Offices.

[13] PR Verkuil, 'The purposes and limits of independent agencies' (1988) Duke LJ 260.

[14] L Lessig and C Sunstein, 'The President and the Administration' (1994) 94 Colum L Rev 110–11.

legally or structurally distinguished from executive agencies.[15] Like the heads of executive agencies, the officials of independent agencies are appointed by the President and confirmed by the Senate. However, the terms of the officials of the independent agencies may exceed the 4-year term of the President, reducing the influence of the President on the agency. In addition, the members of the independent commissions are required by statute to be selected on a bipartisan basis. Unlike the appointment of executive officials, the President is restricted to naming only a majority of the members of his own party: the remainder must be from the other party or registered independents. Sometimes independent agencies possess additional characteristics, although these do not have to be decisive for their independent status.[16] For instance, whereas executive agencies tend to be shaped around single administrators, independent agencies may be organized as commissions consisting of five or seven members. This makes their deliberations and decisions the product of collegial decision-making, which is a process that has its closest analogue in the appellate judicial setting.[17]

From this analysis it follows that 'independence' in US constitutional law means less susceptible to presidential control. Indeed, less susceptible indicates the President still has quite some power to influence the independent agencies' actions. Although related, independence and impartiality are two different concepts. Since independence only relates to the amount of presidential control, it is a narrower concept than impartiality. Impartiality means that an agency should justify its decisions on objective grounds without being influenced by private and political interests. Administrative law imposes strict impartiality requirements on the agencies as regards the exercise of their adjudicatory powers in order to ensure procedural fairness and to prevent abuse (see paragraph VII).

### *B. Are independent agencies really different from executive agencies?*

Although, from a legal perspective, independent agencies are to some extent independent from political control, it might be questioned whether those agencies enjoy a constitutional or legal position which is very different from executive agencies.[18]

The President has the power to appoint, with the advice and consent of the Senate, the agency officials of both the independent and the executive agencies. It is generally agreed, that President Reagan was able to achieve

[15] Pierce et al op cit 94–5.

[16] T Zwart, 'Independent Regulatory Agencies in the US' in L Verhey and T Zwart (eds), *Agencies in European and Comparative Perspective* (Intersentia 2003) 4.

[17] Pierce et al op cit 95.

[18] S Breyer, WH Stewart, CR Sunstein, and ML Spitzer, *Administrative Law and Regulatory Policy* (Aspen Law 2002) 118–20.

significant policy changes by appointing agency heads who shared his objective of reducing the burden of regulation on business.[19] The political effects of the power to appoint officials have not been limited to executive agencies, since President Reagan could implement his policies through the officials of independent agencies as well.

Although the President might remove the officers of independent agencies, only 'for cause', unlike the officials of executive agencies, the distinction between those two categories of agencies should not be overemphasized.[20] The fixed terms of office and removal for cause obligations do not pose serious obstacles to the President's ability to influence regulatory policy through the appointments process, because a newly elected President almost always has the opportunity to make key appointments early in his administration. Moreover, if the President formally requests an administrator's resignation, it is not unreal that the officer will actually resign.[21] In addition, the President can influence the independent agency's policy by way of his power to appoint the chairs of the independent commissions. Although the chair can only be removed from the agency for cause, he holds the chairmanship at the will of the President, making him susceptible to the President's policy views. Since the chair of the agency is responsible for the management of agency's operations, a change in leadership often results in policy changes.

Furthermore, from a strictly legal point of view it is not clear to what extent the President is really prevented from dictating policy to independent agencies. After all, the President has the constitutional duty to 'Take care that the Laws Be Faithfully Executed.'[22] This duty requires the President to maintain significant, ongoing relationships with all agencies for law administration.[23] According to Strauss 'the principle of unitary responsibility' does not allow for relationships in which the President is permitted so little capacity to engage in oversight that the public could no longer rationally believe in that responsibility.[24] To the extent permitted by the boundaries of the law, the President is believed to have the power to review the agencies actions by imposing on the agencies the duty to engage in economic analysis before exercising their rulemaking powers. For instance, President Reagan's Executive Order No 12,291[25] required agencies to adopt rules only if they were both cost-beneficial and benefit-maximizing. Although this Order was formally not applicable to the independent agencies, the executive orders were widely followed by them. President Reagan made clear that he had left out the independent agencies to avoid political controversies, not because he believed he lacked authority to apply the order to

[19] Gellhorn and Levin op cit 50.
[20] Ibid 57.
[21] Ibid 58.
[22] US Constitution, Art II, s 3.
[23] Lessig and Sunstein art cit 107–14.
[24] Strauss 'The Fourth Branch' 644.
[25] (1980) 46 Fed Reg 13193.

the independent agencies.[26] In addition to the power to impose the duty to engage in economic analysis, it must be assumed that the President has a general power to coordinate the agencies' actions in order to ensure that overlapping policies of the different agencies do not conflict.

It follows that the President cannot be prevented from giving policy guidance to the agencies to the extent permitted by the law. However, it would seem irreconcilable with the independent agency's primary decision-making power that the President would substitute the agency's policy judgements with his own judgement. This, however, does not clearly distinguish the position of an independent agency from an executive agency, for in a sense the President is also prevented from dictating policy to units within the executive branch. Although there is no authoritative answer to the question, paragraph 5 discusses whether, and in what sense the President can order executive branch officials to take decisions following the will of the President. For instance, despite the fact that the Federal Aviation Administration (FAA) is part of the department of Transportation, it is questionable whether the President could directly overrule the FAA's decision to grant a licence to fly, for Congress has delegated the authority to licence to the administrator and not to the President.[27] Whether or not the President is allowed to substitute the agencies' views, it is certain that his directions should remain within the legal boundaries of the statutes.

Both the President and Congress have many formal and informal instruments to influence the activities of independent and executive agencies. Furthermore, it is important to note that both independent and administrative agencies are subject to the same procedural requirements of the APA (paragraph 6) and that the scope of judicial review of the agencies' actions is the same for all the agencies (paragraph 7). Therefore, it can be concluded that the differences between independent and executive agencies should not be exaggerated.[28] Nevertheless, in practice, independent agencies may be more responsive to Congress and the President treats independent agencies more independently than executive agencies. For instance, the Office of Management and Budget (OMB) may treat the independent agencies' budget requests or legislative recommendations with greater respect than those of the executive agencies.[29] Moreover, several Presidents, with the exception of President Clinton, have been reluctant to allow OMB to over-

[26] Strauss 'The Fourth Branch' 662.

[27] S Breyer, WH Stewart, CR Sunstein, and ML Spitzer *Administrative Law and Regulatory Policy* (Aspen Law 2002) 118.

[28] GP Miller, 'Introduction: the debate over independent agencies in light of empirical evidence, Nineteenth Annual Administrative Law Issue, Symposium: The Independence of Independent Agencies' (1988) Duke LJ 218–19 and SB Foote 'Independent agencies under attack: a sceptical view of the importance of the debate' (1988) Duke LJ 232–7.

[29] Breyer et al op cit 118.

see the process of regulation by independent agencies, even when such Presidents made serious efforts to oversee and coordinate national policy. Presidential control of the agencies' actions, as well as the OMB's reviewing role, will be discussed in more detail in paragraph 5.

### *C. History, tasks, and powers of independent agencies (questions 14 and 16)*

Independent agencies have been active in the United States for more than a hundred years.

For instance, the International Commerce Commission (ICC), which had the task to regulate the railways, was founded in 1887. The Federal Trade Commission (FTC) was created in 1914 and was modelled after the ICC for the latter's independent power and authority.[30] With the creation of the FTC, it was clear that the ICC would serve as the template for a multitude of new independent regulatory commissions in the early twentieth century.[31]

Many of the independent agencies were founded in the course of Roosevelt's New Deal, expanding the role of central government in economic affairs and in promoting social and economic rights for the citizens. The mandate of the administrative agencies to regulate private market behaviour can be justified on several grounds. For instance, some agencies have the power to regulate market behaviour in order to solve market failures, like the need to control monopoly power (Federal Energy Regulatory Commission [FERC]) or the need to compensate for inadequate information (Securities and Exchanges Commission). Other agencies have the power to redistribute resources from one group to another (National Labor Relations Board), or have the power to promote non-market or collective values such as the environment ord public broadcasting (Environmental Protection Agency and the Federal Communications Commission).[32] Although, many of the federal independent agencies have the task of regulating private market parties, like the FERC and the FCC, some of the independent agencies have the task of promoting citizens' rights. For instance, The Equal Employment Opportunity Commission promotes equal opportunity in employment through administrative and judicial enforcement of the federal civil rights laws and through education and technical assistance. The Federal Election Commission administers and enforces the federal statutes governing the financing of federal elections.

The reasons why Congress has insulated to some extent independent agencies from political control cannot easily be explained, because the

[30] MJ Breger and GJ Edles, 'Established by practice: the theory and operation of independent federal agencies' (2000) American Bar Association 1132.

[31] Ibid 1132.

[32] See for an overview of the legitimate grounds for regulation, Breyer et al op cit 4–13.

legislative history on the creation of independent agencies does not always reveal why Congress preferred one organizational format over another.[33] Although there is no coherent theory on the creation of independent agencies, several authors have supplied a rationale for the foundation of independent agencies.[34] It is plausible that Congress confers this status upon agencies for two reasons. The first reason is that some agencies should function impartially, since political forces could negatively affect how they carry out their tasks. This argument was, for instance, put forward during the debates leading to the adoption of the FTC Act. The FTC has the power to direct cessation of unfair methods of competition in commerce, after adjudicatory hearings. The assurance of impartiality and the absence of political controls are very important for proper execution of the statutory scheme and the apolitical judgements to be reached.[35] In addition, to the impartiality argument, the expertise argument justifies the existence of independent agencies. The application of statutes, such as the statutes regulating the capital and communications markets, requires a high degree of technical expertise. Therefore, it is thought that objective experts and not the politicians should apply these statutes.

Independent agencies typically possess a combination of rulemaking and adjudicatory powers. By virtue of adjudicatory powers agencies may determine individual duties and rights, for instance by granting licences, issuing violation orders or imposing penalties. Here the power of the FCC to grant licences to operate broadcasting stations may serve as an example. By virtue of rulemaking powers agencies may formulate rules of general applicability. For instance, the FCC has the power to make such regulations as it may deem necessary to prevent interference between radio stations and to carry out the provisions of the Communications Act 1934. Paragraph 6 discusses more deeply the distinction between adjudication and rulemaking, and in particular the procedural requirements that apply to the agencies' adjudicatory or rulemaking powers.

### *D. Jurisdiction (question 5)*

In addition to the federal agencies, many commissions with regulatory powers operate at the state level. The question whether the federal agency or the state commission has the power to regulate a certain activity is mainly a matter of statutory interpretation. The organic acts determine the

[33] Verkuil 'The purposes and limits of independent agencies' and Foote art cit 232.

[34] AL Peters 'Independent agencies: Government's scourge or salvation' (1988) Duke LJ, 286 and Verkuil 'The purposes and limits of independent agencies' 260.

[35] According to Strauss the apolitical nature of the FTC's tasks made the Supreme Court decide in *Humprey's executor* (295 US 602 (1935) that Congress could legitimately restrict the President's removal power, Strauss 'The Fourth Branch' 613.

federal agencies' jurisdiction, which may extend to both interstate and intrastate activities.[36] By virtue of the Supremacy Clause, federal agency rules pre-empt conflicting rules of state authorities.[37] Moreover, state rules are pre-empted in case where it was the intention of Congress to exclude state regulation. The very existence of a federal regulatory agency may signify a congressional determination that the regulated subject matter demands uniform national supervision and that the power of the state authorities to act is withdrawn. However, the presence of a federal agency is not itself determinative for the question as to whether state action has been pre-empted[38]. Through statutory interpretation the courts should determine whether and to what extent the agencies indeed enjoy the power to regulate intrastate activities. For instance, in *Louisiana Public Service Commission v FCC*,[39] the Supreme Court rejected a FCC ruling that state regulation on the depreciation of telephone equipment was pre-empted. In the view of the Court, Congress had established a system that gave jurisdiction to the FCC to regulate depreciation of such equipment used in interstate communication, but left jurisdiction with the states, and in fact forbade the FCC to exercise jurisdiction over charges, classifications, and practices in connection with intrastate communication, and where in practice, a single piece of telephone equipment may be both used in inter- and intrastate communication.[40] On the other hand, in *AT&T Corp et al v IOWA Utilities*[41] the Court confirmed the power of the FCC to implement the local competition provisions of 1996 Telecommunications Act. The FCC had promulgated rules that determined the prices for interconnection and that provided that unbundled access to the local networks should be based on Total Element Long Run Incremental Cost. The state commissions insisted they had the authority to implement these pricing rules rather than the FCC. The Court did not agree with the view of the state commissions. In the view of the Court, by virtue of the 1934 Communications Act the FCC may prescribe such rules and regulations as may be necessary in the

[36] By virtue of the Commerce clause (US Constitution, Art I, s 8, cl. 3) Congress may only regulate intrastate activities in so far they substantially affect interstate trade and provided that the regulation of those activities complies with the Necessary and Proper clause (Art I s 8(18)). For an extensive analysis of the Commerce Clause see Tribe op cit 819.

[37] US Constitution, Art VI s 3, According to Tribe op cit 1176, the Supreme Court typically divides pre-emption analysis into three categories. The first category is express pre-emption where Congress has in so many words declared its intention to preclude state regulation of a described sort in a given area. The second category is implied pre-emption where Congress, through the structure or objectives of its enactments, has by implication precluded a certain kind of state regulation in the area. The third category is conflict pre-emption where Congress did not necessarily focus on pre-emption of state regulation at all, but where the particular state law conflicts directly with federal law, or otherwise stands as an obstacle to the accomplishment of federal statutory objectives.

[38] Tribe op cit 1214–17.

[39] 476 US 355 (1986).

[40] Tribe op cit 1216.

[41] 97 US 826 (1998).

public interest to carry out the provisions of the 1934 Act. Since Congress expressly directed that the 1996 Act, along with the local competition provisions, should be inserted in the Communications Act, the Court was of the opinion the Commission's rulemaking authority extended to the implementation of local competition provisions.

## III. CONSTITUTIONAL POSITION OF THE INDEPENDENT AGENCIES

### *A. Constitutional questions (questions 6, 7, and 8)*

Although the independent agencies are a reality in US government, their position and powers have raised and still raise fundamental questions. Under the influence of President Reagan's efforts to assert hierarchical control over the bureaucracy, the constitutional position of independent agencies was questioned. On the basis of the theory of the 'unitary executive', scholars asserted that the creation of independent agencies was constitutionally unfounded. The unitarian view was grounded in the Vesting Clause of Article II, which provides 'The Executive power shall be vested in a President'. This clause, together with the Take Care clause, that provides that the President has the duty to 'Take care that the Laws Be Faithfully Executed.'[42] would create a hierarchical, unified executive department under the direct control of the President. The President alone possesses all of the executive power and he therefore can direct, control and supervise agencies who seek to exercise discretionary executive power.[43] Other scholars oppose the theory of the unitary executive and advocate a more functional approach for the interpretation of the text of the Constitution. They

[42] US Constitution, Art II, s 3.

[43] SG Calabresi and KH Rhodes, 'The structural constitution: Unitary Executive, Plural Judiciary' (1992) 105 Harv L Rev 1153. According to Lessig and Sunstein, the modern unitarian view as amongst others proposed by Calabresi and Rhodes, does not comport with the intentions of the framers of the Constitution. Lessig and Sunstein argue that history suggests that the framers understood Congress to have broad power to structure government arrangements as they see fit. Nevertheless, Lessig and Sunstein are of the opinion that the belief in a strongly unitary executive has considerable appeal and fits well with important political and constitutional values, like political accountability and coordination of the law. Believing that these interests have constitutional status, they have founded the arguments for a strongly unitary executive not on the history of the Constitution, but on a method to interpret the Constitution faithfully over time and which takes into account changed circumstances. The argument comes down to this. At the founding period, the existence of a degree of independence in administration could not realistically have been thought to compromise fundamental constitutional commitments to political accountability and the avoidance of factionalism. Today, by contrast, a strong presumption of unitariness is necessary in order to promote the original constitutional commitments. The legislative creation of domestic officials operating independently of the President but exercising important discretionary policymaking power now stands inconsistent with founding commitments. Lessig and Sunstein art cit 1.

claim that the Necessary and Proper Clause,[44] that provides that Congress shall have the power ' to make all laws which shall be necessary and proper for carrying into execution the foregoing powers and all powers vested by this Constitution in the government of the United States', grants Congress the power to structure the executive department and insulate subordinate officers from unfettered removal power of the President.[45]

In addition to the questions on the constitutionality of independent agencies, questions arose as regards the constitutionality of the delegation of broad regulatory powers to both independent and executive agencies.[46] According to some scholars, the delegation of rulemaking powers to administrative agencies violated Article I, which provides that 'All legislative powers herein granted shall be vested in a Congress of the United States.'

Despite the fact that many scholars advocated a more formal approach to the Separation of Powers principle, which would amount to the abolition of independent agencies and the re-introduction of the non-delegation doctrine, the US Supreme Court, has not taken these dramatic steps. As will be discussed later on, the US Supreme Court has instead legitimised the constitutional status of independent agencies and their broad regulatory powers by adhering to a more functional approach to the Separation of Powers principle.

### *B. The constitutional status of independent agencies: Supreme Court case law*

#### *1.* Myers, Humprey's, *and* Weiner

The first case concerning the status of independent agencies is *Myers v United* States.[47] Myers was appointed postmaster for a 4-year term at Portland, under a statute providing that postmasters 'shall be appointed and may be removed by the President and with the advice and consent of the Senate'. President Wilson removed Myers from office, prior to the expiration of this term, without the consent of the Senate. The government claimed Myers's removal was lawful because it is unconstitutional to limit the President's power to remove an executive branch official by requiring the Senate's agreement. The Supreme Court agreed with the Government and reasoned:

> the power to remove subordinates is inherently part of the executive power, which article II, section one, vests in a President of the United States.

[44] US Constitution Art I, s 8, cl 18.

[45] Breger and Edles art cit 1157.

[46] D Schoenbrod, 'The delegation doctrine: Could the Court give it substance?' (1985) 83 Mich L Rev 1223.

[47] 272 US 52 (1926).

> Made responsible under the Constitution for the effective enforcement of the law, the President needs as an indispensable aid to meet it the disciplinary influence upon those who act under him of a reserve power of removal . . .
>
> . . . To require him to file charges and submit them to the consideration of the Senate, might make impossible that unity and co-ordination in executive administration essential to effective action.

The Court's considerations in *Myers* could be read in two different ways.[48] First *Myers* could be understood to mean Congress may not place any limits on the President's power to remove executive officers: or it could be read as embodying the proposition that, whatever the limits of presidential removal power, Congress could not cede to *itself* any role in removing government officials. The Court rejected the former reading in *Humprey's executor v United States*, where it drastically narrowed the application of the Myers rule.[49]

WE Humprey was a member of the FTC, who was nominated by President Hoover. On the basis of the Federal Trade Commission Act a FTC Commissioner could only be removed for cause, namely for 'inefficiency, neglect of duty or malfeasance in office'. President Roosevelt tried to remove Humprey on the ground that the aims and purposes of the administration with respect to the work of the Commission can be carried out most effectively with personnel of his own selection, but disclaiming any reflection upon the Commissioner personally or upon his services. Humprey never acquiesced in his action and filed a back pay suit. Relying on *Myers v United States* the Government argued that Humprey's removal was not unlawful, because the removal provision of the FTC Act constituted an unconstitutional interference with the executive power of the President. The Court did not agree with the government this time. It stated that in *Myers* it only decided the narrow point that the President had the power to remove a postmaster of the first class, without the advice and consent of the Senate as required by Act of Congress. In the view of the Court the office of postmaster is so essentially unlike the office at issue in Humprey that the decision in *Myers* cannot be accepted as controlling the decision in Humprey. Unlike Myers, who was a purely executive officer, a FTC Commissioner occupies no place in the executive department and exercises no part of the executive power vested by the Constitution in the President. In the opinion of the Court the character of the quasi-legislative and in part quasi-judicially powers of the FTC, justified the restrictions of the removal power of the President. Since the Court recognized and accepted that the independence of the agency was necessary for bringing into effect the legislative policies of the Act, it was willing to accept a more

[48] Tribe op cit 704. [49] 295 US 602 (1935).

functional approach to the Separation of Powers principle by focusing on the goals and the nature of the powers of the FTC. Although the Court in fact followed a more functional approach to the Separation of Powers Principle, its reasoning was not very strong, since it tried to reconcile the position of the FTC with the formal Separation of Powers principle by labelling the powers of the FTC as non-executive:

> The fundamental necessity of maintaining each of the three general departments of government entirely free from the control or coercive influence, direct or indirect, of either of the others, has often been stressed and is hardly open to serious question . . .
>
> The power of the removal here claimed for the President falls within this principle, since its coercive influence threatens the independence of a commission, which is not wholly disconnected from the executive department, but which, as already fully appears, was created by Congress as means of carrying into operation legislative and judicial powers, and as an agency of the legislative and the judicial departments . . .

The Supreme Court confirmed its ruling in *Humprey's Executor* in *Weiner v United States*,[50] a case which was comparable to *Humprey's Executor*. In *Weiner* the Supreme Court ruled that President Eisenhower's removal of a member of the War Claims Commission prior to the expiration of his term of appointment was invalid. In reaching this conclusion the Supreme Court, like in *Humprey's Executor*, endorsed its view that the nature of the function that Congress vested in the War Claims Commission, is the most reliable factor for drawing a conclusion regarding the President's power of removal.

### 2. INS v Chadha, Buckley v Valeo *and* Bowsher

The Supreme Court decided three cases that were of relevance for the position and powers of both independent and executive agencies in the seventies and eighties. These rulings were an important signal to Congress that it was illegal for Congress to retain supervisory powers over agency decision making after having delegated to those agencies discretionary powers. According to some commentators these rulings indicated that the Supreme Court had taken a more formal approach to the Separation of Powers principle and therefore posed a threat to the legality of independent agencies.

*Immigration & Naturalization Services v Chadha*[51] concerned the legality of the legislative veto. The basic goal of the legislative veto was to allow Congress an opportunity to control or veto agency decisions, especially if agencies acted under statutes that gave them broad discretion, amounting in practice to lawmaking.[52] Chadha, an East Indian born in Kenya,

[50] 357 US 349 (1958).
[51] 462 US 919 (1983).
[52] Breyer et al op cit 98.

remained in the United States after his visa expired. He was ordered to be deported. The Attorney General legally suspended his deportation, allowing him to remain in the United States, for reasons of hardship. The statute, however, provided, that either the Senate or the House of representatives could, by resolution, overrule the Attorney General's suspension of deportation. In this case the House of Representatives enacted a resolution overturning the Attorney General's decision. Accordingly the deportation proceedings were resumed and Chadha was ordered to be deported. The Supreme Court ruled that it was unconstitutional for Congress to reserve to itself the power to overrule an executive officer. According to the Court the veto was essentially legislative in purpose and effect. Therefore, Congress was obliged to comply with the constitutional provisions for the adoption of legislation, which require the affirmative vote of both Houses as well as the concurrence of the President. In the absence of the President's consent, legislation must pass each House by a two-thirds vote. The statutory provisions that empowered either House to overrule the Attorney General were an attempt to avoid these constitutional restrictions and were therefore invalid. It follows from this ruling that Congress is not allowed to block the administration of the law by executive officials, without having to follow the formal process of law making.

In *Buckley v Valeo*[53] what was at stake was whether Congress could create a Federal Election Commission that was composed of members that were appointed by the leadership of the Senate and the House and of two members that were appointed by the President. The Commission was structured in this way in order to enable the political leaders in Congress to control the Commission. Since the Commission was authorized to bring lawsuits to enforce restrictions on political fund raising, it was a very sensitive topic for the political parties. The Supreme Court declared that the appointments to the Commission were unconstitutional, since they did not conform with the requirements of the Appointments Clause.[54] So this was another unconstitutional attempt by Congress to supervise administration.

In *Bowsher v Synar*[55] the Court embraced the second reading of *Myers* that Congress cannot delegate any role in removing officers to itself. By virtue of the Balanced Budget and Emergency Deficit Control Act of 1985 (known as the 'Gramm–Rudman–Hollings Act'), Congress delegated to the Comptroller General the power to review estimates of likely budget deficits

[53] 424 US 1 (1976).

[54] By virtue of US Constitution, Art II, s 2, the President shall nominate, and by and with the advice and the consent of the Senate, shall appoint all other officers of the United States, whose appointments are not herein otherwise provided for, and which shall be established by law; but the Congress may by law vest the appointment of such Officers, as they think proper, in the President alone, in the Courts of Law or in the Heads of Departments.

[55] 478 US 714 (1986).

to determine whether the estimated deficit will exceed a specified amount, and, if so, to determine programme by programme, according to statutorily specified rules, how much appropriated money the President can spend. The relevant appointment statutes provided that the President appoint the Comptroller General from a list of individuals, which were recommended by the Speaker of the House and the Senate President. The Senate had to confirm the appointment. Congress could remove the Comptroller General for cause at any time by Joint Resolution (which requires a presidential signature or a two-thirds Congressional override of his veto).

According to the Court the removal clause was unconstitutional:

> We noted recently 'The Constitution sought to divide the delegated powers of the Federal Government into three defined categories, Legislative, Executive and Judicial. . . .
>
> That this system of division and separation of powers produces conflicts, confusion, and discordance at times is inherent, but it was deliberately so structured to assure full, vigorous and open debate on the great issues affecting the people and to provide avenues for the operation of checks on the exercise of government power.
>
> We conclude that Congress cannot reserve for itself the power of removal of an officer charged with the execution of laws except by impeachment. To permit the execution of laws to be vested in an officer answerable only to Congress would, in practical terms, reserve in Congress control over the execution of the laws. . . . The structure of the Constitution does not permit Congress to execute the laws . . .

To some critics the Court's ruling pointed to a revival of a formal Separation of Powers doctrine, meaning that a case against the constitutionality of independent agencies might also succeed. Although the Court did seem to follow a formal Separation of Powers approach in *Bowsher*, its ruling is not well grounded since it was not clear at all that Congress could actually control the administration. The Bowsher removal provision actually required presidential participation, for Congress's joint resolution of removal was subject to presidential veto. Moreover, the fact that Congress could remove the Comptroller General only 'for cause' pleaded against effective Congressional control. In fact, the Court had earlier argued a 'for cause' removal was precisely the element creating the independence from the President that justified delegation of judicial and legislative functions to an independent regulatory commission in *Humprey*. Thus, the proposition that the Comptroller General was in fact dependent upon Congress by virtue of the removal provision was hard to maintain.[56] Although the result of *Bowsher* was not wrong, the Court could have supported the ruling more convincingly by giving more attention to the impact of the Congressional

[56] Strauss 'Questions—A foolish inconsistency' (1987) Cornell Law Review 498.

arrangement on the President, Congress and the Judiciary, and the relationships between them.[57] As in *Myers, INS v Chadha* and *Buckley,* Congress had sought to aggrandize its powers at the expense of the President in *Bowsher.* In contrast, in *Humprey's* and *Weiner* Congress restricted the President's removal power through the 'for cause' limitation, but it did not involve a comparable expansion of the Congressional role.

With regard to the above it can be concluded that, none of the three cases of *Chadha*, *Buckley*, and *Bowsher* suggest that the executive powers of the sort that were delegated to the Comptroller or the Federal Election Commission may only be exercised by officers removable at will by the President.[58]

So unlike in *Humprey's* and *Weiner*, it can be stated that Congress tried to overreach and seize the powers of the other branches in *INS v Chadha, Buckley* and *Bowsher.* Although the latter three rulings do not cast doubt on the constitutionality of independent agencies as such, commentators are of the opinion that the results of the latter three rulings strengthen the constitutional scheme. The rulings create pressure on Congress to take responsibility for the political choices that are made. Members of Congress might wish that they could legislate generally and imprecisely, delegating policy decisions to agencies but retaining power to easily overrule the agencies when decisions particularly important to them were made. *Chadha, Buckley* and *Bowsher* deny them that option. Congress can delegate but then it has to live with that choice.

### 3. Morrison

Although the US Supreme Court has confirmed the constitutional status of independent agencies in *Humprey's* and *Weiner*, its approach was quite ambiguous since it did not become at all clear under what conditions the agencies tasks do not qualify as executive, but as quasi legislative or judicial.[59] Moreover, independent agencies frequently exercise functions similar to those performed by all three branches.[60] In *Morrison*[61] the Court finally acknowledged that *Humprey's* had introduced the problem whether the official functioned in an executive or in a 'quasi-legislative' or 'quasi-judicial' role. However, apparently recognizing the imperfection of its analysis in *Humprey's*, the Court accepted a more functional approach of the

[57] Ibid 517–21.

[58] Tribe op cit 709 and Verkuil, 'The Status of independent agencies after Bowsher v Synar' 792–3. It is interesting to note that in footnote 4 of the Bowsher Opinion, the Supreme Court explicitly endorses this view.

[59] Tribe op cit 706.

[60] Verkuil 'The Status of independent agencies after Bowsher v Synar' 784.

[61] 487 US 654 (1988).

Separation of Powers principle and insisted that the real question is whether the removal restrictions are of such nature that they impede the President's ability to perform his constitutional duty, and the functions of the officials in question must be analysed in that light.

With regard to the above, it might be concluded that the Court recognizes the constitutionality of independent agencies as long as Congress has not unacceptably encroached upon the powers of the President, no matter what the nature of the agency's activities are and no matter their position in Government.

### *C. Constitutional problems regarding the delegation of regulatory powers*

As previously mentioned, Congress delegates various powers to administrative agencies. Whereas the former paragraphs explained that Congress has limited authority in controlling agencies that are performing delegated powers, this paragraph explains to what extent Congress can actually delegate regulatory powers to administrative agencies.

Delegated powers may imply the operation of legislation upon an administrative agency official's determination of facts. Alternatively, Congress may grant authority to an agency to specify rules in an area where Congress itself has declared only general principles.[62] This means that agencies may formulate new rights and duties for the citizens. It is mainly the last category of delegations that are in tension with the Separation of Powers principle. The legitimacy of Congress's powers to intrude upon private autonomy is founded upon the supposed consent of the citizens that have elected members of Congress.[63] Therefore, it would be illegitimate for Congress to grant those powers to officials that are not directly accountable to the electorate. This does not mean that the executive branch lacks accountability, for the President is subject to the will of the people. However, the vesting of lawmaking power in Congress is designed to ensure the combination of deliberation and accountability that comes from saying that government power cannot be brought to bear on individuals unless diverse representatives, from various states of the union, have managed to agree on the details.[64] Despite these concerns of legitimacy, the US Supreme Court has consistently approved acts of Congress that have delegated broad regulatory powers to agencies. However, the Court has acknowledged the implicit constitutional requirements of consensual government under law by stipulating that a constitutional exercise of congressionally delegated powers requires Congress to 'lay down by legislative act an 'intelligible

[62] Tribe op cit 979.
[63] Ibid 984.
[64] C Sunstein, 'Is the Clean Air Act unconstitutional?' (1999) 98 Mich L Rev 336.

principle' to which the person or body authorized to act is directed to conform'.[65]

### D. *The non-delegation doctrine: Supreme Court case law*

The next sections discusses two cases that illustrate how the US Supreme Court deals with the delegation problem and how the court has reconciled this phenomenon with the Constitution. It is important to note that these cases are of relevance for the delegation of powers to both executive and independent agencies.

The first case *Whitman v American Trucking Associations,* Inc,[66] concerns the delegation of broad regulatory powers to the EPA by virtue of the Clean Air Act. The Clean Air Act requires the EPA to promulgate and periodically revise National Ambient Air Quality standards ('NAAQS') for each air pollutant identified by the agency as meeting certain statutory criteria. Section 109(b)(1) of the CAA instructs the EPA to set NAAQS the attainment and the maintenance of which, in the judgment of the Administrator, allowing an adequate margin of safety, are 'requisite to protect the public health'.

The EPA issued final rules revising the primary and secondary NAAQS for particulate matter ('PM') and ozone in July 1997. Numerous petitions for review have been filed for each rule. The EPA regarded ozone 'definitely', and PM 'likely', as non-threshold pollutants, that is ones that have some possibility of some adverse health impact (however slight) at any exposure level above zero. This means that the only concentration for ozone and PM that is utterly risk free, in the sense of direct health impacts, is zero. However, the EPA did not set the permitted concentration level at zero, instead it set the level at 0.08 ppm for ozone. The EPA explained that its choice is superior to retaining the existing level, 0.09 ppm, because more people are exposed to more serious effects at 0.09 than at 0.08. In defending the decision not to go down to 0.07 The EPA never rebutted the intuitive proposition, confirmed by data in its staff paper, that reducing the standard further than 0.08 would bring about comparable changes.

The Court of Appeals found that the EPA did not satisfactorily explain the level of residual risk admitted by picking any non-zero level.[67] The Court of Appeals was of the opinion that the EPA failed to provide any determinate criterion for drawing lines. It had failed to state intelligibly 'how much is too much'. Although, the Court of Appeals found the statutory language of the Clean Air Act involved a unconstitutional delegation of power, it was of the opinion that the EPA could remedy this constitu-

[65] Tribe op cit 984 and 488 US 361 (1989).
[66] 531 US 457 (2001).
[67] 175 F 3d 1027 (DC Cir 1999).

tional weakness by giving a determinate standard for the interpretation of the statute. So its response to the unconstitutional delegation of power would not be to strike down the statute, but to give the agency the opportunity to formulate clear standards that would restrict the exercise of its powers. Since the Court of Appeals found that the EPA did not provide any clear standards, it declared its rules unconstitutional. The US Supreme Court did not approve the Court of Appeal's reasoning that the EPA's interpretation (but not the statute itself) violated the non-delegation doctrine:

> In a delegation challenge, the constitutional question is whether the statute has delegated legislative power to the agency. Article I, paragraph I, of the Constitution vests 'all legislative Powers herein granted . . . in a Congress of the United States.' This text permits no delegation of those powers, and so we repeatedly have said that when Congress confers decision-making authority upon agencies Congress must 'lay down by legislative act an intelligible principle to which the person or body authorized to act is directed to conform'. We have never suggested that an agency can cure an unlawful delegation of legislative power by adopting in its discretion a limiting construction of the statute. . . .The idea that an agency can cure an unconstitutionally standardless delegation of power by declining to exercise some of that power seems to us internally contradictory. The very choice of which portion of the power to exercise-that is to say the prescription of the standard that Congress has omitted—would itself be an exercise of the forbidden legislative authority. Whether the statute delegated legislative power is a question for the courts, and an agency's voluntary self-denial has no bearing upon the answer.
>
> The scope of discretion the CAA allows is in fact well within the outer limits of our non-delegation precedents . . .
>
> (Congress) must provide substantial guidance on setting air standards that affect the entire economy. But even in sweeping regulatory schemes we have never demanded, as the Court of Appeals did there, that statutes provide a 'determinate criterion' for saying 'how much (of the regulated harm) is too much'.
>
> Section 109(b)(1) of the CAA, which to repeat we interpret as requiring the EPA to set NAAQS at the level that is 'requisite'—that is no lower or higher than is necessary- to protect the public health with an adequate margin of safety, fits comfortably within the scope of discretion permitted by our precedent.

Three important conclusions can be drawn from this opinion. First, the US Supreme Court rejected the interpretation of the non-delegation doctrine put forward by the Court of Appeals, according to which an agency could save a statute from unconstitutionality by limiting its own discretion through statutory interpretation. This interpretation interferes, indeed, with one of the fundamental points of the non-delegation doctrine, namely to ensure legislative rather than administrative judgments about the contents of federal law. The interpretation of the Court of Appeals would convert the non-delegation doctrine into something else, namely a general requirement of administrative transparency, a requirement with no obvious constitutional foundation and not in harmony with Article I.[68]

Secondly, the Supreme Court approved that Congress had delegated broad regulating powers to the EPA. By virtue of these powers the EPA may create new duties for a category of polluters. Moreover, the Court accepted that Congress had referred the making of important policy decisions as regards the permitted level of air pollution to the administrative agency. The substance of the CAA is meagre and merely requires the EPA to take the measures 'that are requisite to protect health'. However, for most pollutants, air quality at various levels is not 'either safe' or 'not safe' for there are diminishing degrees of risks associated with diminishing degrees of exposure. The EPA should determine on what basis a particular level of residual risk is appropriate and it should formulate the ingredients of any judgments that a certain risk is too high.[69] The EPA's decision will be based on a series of scientific, political, and economic judgments and compromises.

Thirdly, it seems that the Supreme Court has followed a formal approach to the Separation of Powers doctrine by designating the agency's powers as 'not legislative' but rather executive. The application of the Separation of Powers doctrine in *Whitman* looks artificial for the effect of the agency's rules will be comparable with the effect of acts of Congress. If the Court had applied a functional approach to the Separation of Powers principle, it would have achieved the same result. This is also acknowledged by Justice Stevens, with whom Justice Souter joins, concurring in part and concurring in the judgment. He states that it would be both wiser and more faithful to what we have actually done in delegation cases to admit that agency rulemaking authority is 'legislative power'. In the opinion of the concurring judge, it seems clear that an executive agency's exercise of rulemaking authority pursuant to a valid delegation from Congress is legislative. He notes, that as long as the delegation provides a sufficient intelligible principle, there is nothing inherently unconstitutional about it.

### *1. The delegation of accumulated powers*

The opinion of the Supreme Court in *Mistretta v United States*[70] indicates that it is legitimate for Congress to delegate to independent agencies accumulated powers that are originally vested in the President, Congress or the Judiciary.

In *Mistretta* the Court upheld the constitutionality of the independent United States Sentencing Commission, a body composed of seven members,

[68] Sunstein 'Is the Clean Air Act unconstitutional?' 351.
[69] Ibid 309.
[70] 488 US 361 (1989).

statutorily located in the judicial branch. The Commission had the legal power to write sentencing guidelines that are binding on federal judges who sentence criminal defendants. Congress wrote fairly detailed standards in the statute. The Court held the delegation of power did not violate the non-delegation doctrine and based the ruling on a functional Separation of Powers approach. The Court stated that in having adopted a flexible understanding of the Separation of Powers principle before, it has recognized the teaching of the framers of the Constitution that the greatest security against tyranny, does not lie in a hermetic division between the branches, but in a carefully crafted system of checked and balanced power within each branch. In the view of the Court, Congress' decision to create an independent rulemaking body to promulgate sentencing guidelines and to locate that body within the Judicial Branch, is not unconstitutional, unless Congress has vested in the Commission powers that are more appropriately performed by the other branches or that undermine the integrity of the Judiciary. The Court thinks it is consistent with the Separation of Powers principle that Congress may delegate to the Judicial Branch non-adjudicatory functions that do not tread upon the prerogatives of another branch and that are appropriate to the central mission of the judiciary.

The opinion makes clear that the Court accepts it to be legitimate that independent members of the Federal judiciary are involved in rulemaking. Therefore, this opinion confirms the power of Congress to delegate rule-making powers to independent agencies that are to some extent independent from the President. Moreover, in the light of Court's reasoning in *Mistretta*, there are good reasons to believe the Court has approved the accumulation of different functions within an administrative agency, on the condition that the prerogatives of each of the branches are respected and the combination of these functions is central to the mission of the agency.

### *E. A functional approach to the Separation of Powers doctrine: maintaining the checks and balances (question 7)*

It follows that the US Supreme Court is of the opinion that neither the text nor the history of the Constitution forbid Congress to create institutions (independent agencies) and legislative arrangements (delegation) that are not explicitly mentioned in the Constitution. The Court has realized that it should give Congress enough space to adapt governmental structure to changing circumstances and policies.

Although the US Supreme Court has followed a quite formal approach to the principle of the Separation of Powers in some cases, like *Bowsher* and *Whitman*, the opinion reached would have been the same in those cases had the Supreme Court had followed a more functional approach: An approach in which it would have examined whether the 'checks and balances' between Congress, the President and the Judiciary were maintained.

Professor Strauss is a leading advocate of the functional approach to the Separation of Powers principle, which is now well established in US legal doctrine and case law.[71] This functional approach recognizes that each of the three branches is the ultimate authority for a distinctive governmental authority type (legislative, executive or judicial). However, the functional approach does not require administrative government below the apex to be strictly divided into three parts. In assessing Congressional arrangements the important question should be whether the relationships between each of the three named actors of the Constitution to the exercise of their powers is such as to promise a continuation of their effective independence and interdependence. Every Congressional arrangement can be approved as long as adequate checks and balances between the three branches are maintained and they can effectively exercise their core functions in controlling agencies and the exercise of their powers.

A functional approach to the Separation of Powers principle makes the differences between the independent agencies and other agencies less important. Each such agency is to some extent independent of the three named branches and to some extent in relationship with each of them. The continued achievement of the intended balance and interaction among the three named actors at the top of government, with each continuing to have effective responsibility for its unique core function, depends on the existence of relationships between each of these actors and each agency within which that function can find a voice.[72] Both executive and independent agencies adopt rules, execute laws and adjudicate cases all pursuant to statutory authority. This conjoining of powers does not violate the Separation of Powers model since from a functional perspective the important fact is that an agency is neither Congress nor President nor Court, but an inferior part of government. Each agency is subject to control relationships with some or all of the three constitutionally-named branches, and those relationship give assurance—functionally similar to that provided by the Separation of Powers notion for the constitutionally named bodies—that they will not pass out of control.[73]

After having described that the US governmental structure as it exists today may well be reconciled with the Separation of Powers principle of the

[71] Strauss 'The Fourth Branch' 575–81, and Strauss 'Questions—A Foolish Inconsistency' 488–97. Tribe op cit 139, also adheres to a more functional Separation of Powers approach: 'The Court has repeatedly signalled it takes a pragmatic flexible view of differentiated governmental power-one that seeks not to 'implement a hermetic division between the Branches' but rather to avoid 'encroachment or aggrandizement by one branch against the others'.

[72] Strauss 'The Fourth Branch' 580.

[73] Ibid 579–80.

Constitution, the following paragraphs will analyse more deeply how the 'checks and balances' between the powers of the President, Congress and the Judiciary in controlling the actions of (independent) agencies are maintained in practice. In addition, they will look into how the participation of the public in administrative procedures forms a check upon the exercise of powers by the agencies.

## IV. ACCOUNTABILITY (QUESTIONS 2, 3, 9, 15, 18, AND 19)

### *A. Introduction (question 10)*

Although independent agencies are to some extent independent from politics, this paragraph explains that both Congress and the President have many instruments to control the agencies' actions. Agencies are accountable to Congress and the President, in that they should explain and account for their decisions to both institutions. Therefore, the citizens can control the agencies' actions through their representatives in Congress and through the President. Indirect political control by the electorate is not the only way to confer legitimacy upon the exercise of public powers. The following paragraphs will illustrate that in addition to representative democracy, participative democracy, meaning that interested parties have the right to participate in the agencies' administrative procedures, will contribute to the legitimisation of the agencies' actions.

### *B. Accountability: Congressional oversight (question 4)*

#### *1. Overview*

Congress has a variety of means at its disposal to control agency action. Indeed, the most direct way for Congress to control the substance of the rulemaking process is to specify the degree of the agency's authority. When agencies formulate rules Congress does not like, agency decisions can be overruled by passing legislation or they can be rendered of no relevance by the changing of the agency's jurisdiction.[74] However, it will be difficult for Congress to form an effective check on agencies activities through the formal legislative process, since this process is very heavy.

Congress can also influence agencies' actions by placing restrictions on the appropriated funds. Moreover, Congress has tried to change the powers of agencies through appropriations bills in the past. Of particular importance was an appropriations bill containing provisions to limit the power of

[74] Pierce et al op cit 42.

the EPA. Eventually, because of the threat of a presidential veto and controversies within Congress the proposals were not adopted.[75]

Congress can also shape administrative decisions indirectly by applying political pressure through the use of committee reports, through budgetary, oversight or investigatory hearings and hearings on the nominations of administrators and through direct communications with administrators.[76] The effectiveness of this last group of controls can be increased by requiring that agencies report to Congress before they act, by utilizing the General Accounting Office to investigate agency conduct and by employing the Congressional Budget Office to consider the economic effects of government programmes.

### 2. *How effective is congressional oversight?*

Although it is proved that political oversight techniques are able to influence the agency work,[77] the possibility of Congress threatening to use legislative sanctions, however, does not empower Congress to control the bureaucracy.[78]

Professor Kagan acknowledges the limits of Congress's ability to impose harsh sanctions. Statutory punishments require the action of full Congress, which is difficult and costly to accomplish. In order to impose sanctions, Congress has to go through the formal legislative process, meaning majority support is not enough: it must gain the approval of either the President or two-thirds of both houses. Moreover, Kagan is concerned about Congress influencing agency behaviour for two reasons. The first reason relates to the identity of the parties most engaged in Congress's oversight system. The fire-alarm system usually goes off in the committee and subcommittee rooms of Congress and not on the floors of the House or Senate. Usually these committees are comprised of legislators whose constituents have a special interest in its jurisdiction and these legislators tend to develop strong ties to these organized interest groups that sound the fire alarms. In the view of Kagan, the administrative policy set by these players will rarely reflect the preferences of Congress as a whole or the general public. The second aspect of concern of congressional control lies in its reactive nature. Mostly Congress will come into action in response to outside complaints. These complaints will usually arise from a change in

[75] Sunstein, Congress, 'Constitutional moments and the Cost-Benefit State' (1996) 48 Stan. L. Rev 247 282–4.

[76] Pierce et al art cit 42.

[77] See for an overview of the use and effectiveness of Congressional oversight techniques, CM Kerwin, 'How government Agencies write law and make policy' (1999) Congressional Quarterly 215.

[78] E Kagan ' Presidential Administration' (2001) Harvard Law Review 2258.

policy and not from the status quo. The result is that congressional oversight will tend to have a conservative quality. Moreover, these complaints will often be presented as an isolated problem, whereas they form part of broader regulatory issues. Therefore, Kagan concludes that complaint driven nature of congressional oversight, especially in combination with its reliance on committees, pushes toward the ad hoc rather than the systematic consideration of administrative policy.

Like Kagan, Sunstein is sceptical of Congress's ability to reform administrative policy. He argues that the election of the 104th Congress signalled the transformation of America into a genuinely post New Deal regulatory state.[79] The Acts that were adopted during the New Deal were criticized for not comprising any mechanisms to evaluate regulatory performance. There was consensus on the following problems in existing government regulation: bad priority setting; government should favour flexible, market-based incentives rather than rigid command; government should recognize and counteract harmful intended consequences of regulations; government needs more information and should create better incentives to compile and provide accurate information; government should respond to both expert and citizen judgments in regulating risks; government should concentrate on basic ends rather than the means and should use performance standards rather than design standards. Congress tried to reform the administrative state by proposing several bills that challenged the basic foundations of the New Deal acts. In the regulatory arena cost–benefit balancing dominated the debate.

On 22 March 1995 Congress enacted the Unfunded Mandates Reform Act.[80] This Act contains two provisions that are interesting from the perspective of regulatory reform. First, the Act requires that a statement containing a 'qualitative and quantitative assessment of the anticipated costs and benefits of the Federal mandate' accompany significant regulatory action. This provision is largely procedural and does not make much of a difference.[81] Presidential Executive Orders on Federal regulation impose nearly identical requirements. The second provision is more ambitious and requires that agencies 'identify and consider a reasonable number of regulatory alternatives and from those alternatives select the least costly, most cost-effective or least burdensome alternative that achieves the objectives of the rule'. The Act exempts agencies from these requirements if compliance would be inconsistent with the law or if the agency explains its reason for

[79] Sunstein Congress 'Constitutional Moments and the Cost–Benefit State' 247, 249.

[80] 2 USC ss 1501–171.

[81] This obligation is subject to limited judicial review. If an agency fails to prepare the written statement a court may compel the agency to prepare such a written statement. The inadequacy or failure to prepare such a statement shall not be used as a basis for staying, enjoining, invalidating or otherwise affecting agency rule.

not selecting the least burdensome alternative. Despite the fact that the Act does not apply if other statutes prohibit its being followed, it encourages agencies to choose cheaper ways of achieving regulatory goals. According to Sunstein, these two provisions of the Unfunded Mandates Reform Act offer cautious steps in the direction of general requirement of cost–benefit balancing[82].

In 1996 Congress enacted another Act strengthening Congress's role in reviewing agency rules. This Congressional Review Act requires agencies to submit all regulations to Congress and gives Congress an opportunity to 'veto' any rule through the formal process of lawmaking.[83] The effect of this procedure should not be overestimated. Before the adoption of the Act Congress already had the power to cancel a rule if it could get the President's concurrence (or override a presidential veto). Moreover, Congress is unlikely to get the presidential approval very often, since the President will defend agency rules most of the time.[84]

Sunstein concludes that Congress might be ill-equipped to attempt major reform, especially if it attempts to achieve a great deal at the micro level.[85] Legislators are generalists and not specialists, and they have many issues to address. According to Sunstein such a group of generalists is prone to sharp internal divisions that are not subject to reasonable mediation without a good deal of specialization in regulation. These claims about the institutional capacities are reinforced by the way Congress has been split between two different sets of interests: technocratic forces seeking to discipline agency decisions with better policy analysis and forces of reaction seeking to stop agency action even when it would improve social well-being. From this perspective, Sunstein argues that the executive branch has a major advantage as it can more easily use specialist experience.[86] For this reason it may be best for Congress to limit its efforts to providing broad signals about what is wrong and to allow the executive branch, within limits, to provide solutions. Although Sunstein thinks Congress should restrict itself to providing broad signals, he argues Congress can improve the quality of legislation by laying down clearer standards and giving more guidance to the agencies on which factors they should take into account in making rules. For instance, he argues that Congress should amend the Clean Air Act to identify the factors for the EPA to consider in making decisions as to appropriate national standards. Congress might offer substantive guidance by saying, for example, that the EPA must consider risk severity, size of affected population and likelihood of adverse effects at various exposure

82 Sunstein Congress 'Constitutional moments and the Cost–Benefit State' 273.
83 5 USCA ss 801–8
84 Pierce art cit 493.
85 Sunstein Congress 'Constitutional moments and the Cost–Benefit State' 286.
86 Ibid 251, 252, and 308.

levels. On the procedural side, it might require the EPA to identify, to the extent possible, the nature of the risks that it is reducing, and at the same time to quantify the relevant risk reductions.[87]

Indeed, Presidents have been more successful in reviewing agency rules on their compliance with cost–benefit and cost-effective principles. The following paragraph discusses and evaluates the techniques the President has at his disposal to influence the agencies' actions.

## V. ACCOUNTABILITY: PRESIDENTIAL OVERSIGHT (QUESTIONS 2,3)

### A. *Overview*

As discussed in Section II the President has several instruments at his disposal to manage government and to control the exercise of discretionary powers. An important instrument for the President to control the actions of the administrative agencies is the President's responsibility to present the budget. All but a few administrative agencies must have their budgets approved by the President's policy-coordinating agent, the Office of Management and Budget (OMB). The process of budget approval gives the President the opportunity to review agency performance and establish program priorities. Since the enforcement of statutory responsibilities is tied to funding, the budget process gives the OMB a chance to emphasize priorities of the President that may or may not be instinctively shared by the agencies.[88] The budget process has had an important impact on regulatory agencies since the Reagan administration.[89] The Reagan administration used its control over the budget of administrative agencies as part of an overall strategy to deregulate the economy and reduce the deficit. The Clinton administration utilized its control over the agencies' budget to eliminate the deficit. The OMB plays an important role in reviewing and influencing the substance of proposed agencies' rules. By virtue of the 'Take care duty' President Reagan was the first to institute, through two executive orders, a centralized mechanism for review of agency rulemaking.[90]

### B. *Era of presidential administration*

By virtue of Executive Order 12, 291[91] agencies were required to submit to the OMB's Office of Regulatory Affairs (OIRA) for prepublication review

[87] Sunstein 'Is the Clean Air constitutional' 376.

[88] Pierce art cit 86–7.

[89] Ibid 86.

[90] Professor Kagan has written in an interesting and enlightening article how these Orders have marked the beginning of an era of Presidential Administration, Kagan 'Presidential Administration' (2001) Harvard Law Review 2272–82.

[91] 46 Fed Reg 13193 (1980).

any proposed major rule, accompanied by a 'regulatory impact analysis' of the rule, including a cost–benefit comparison. The order also contained substantial requirements for the agency's rules. 'To the extent permitted by the law' an agency could regulate only if the benefits of regulating exceeded the costs and the choice among alternatives involved the 'least net cost to society'. Although the Order disclaimed any right on the OMB or the President himself to dictate or displace agency decisions, the Order gave the OMB a form of substantial control over rulemaking for under the Order the OMB had the authority to determine the adequacy of an impact analysis. Moreover, the OMB could prevent the publication of a proposed or final rule, even indefinitely, until completion of the review procedure.[92] Executive Order 12498[93] added a mandate that each agency submit for OMB Review an annual regulatory plan listing proposed actions for the year. Consequently the OMB got an earlier opportunity to influence agency rulemakings.

In the opinion of Kagan, the Orders had more of an impact than any prior review system and enabled President Reagan to substantially influence the agencies regulatory policies. Whereas during the Bush era the strengthened role of the Presidency in reviewing agencies rules was maintained, presidential control of the administration expanded significantly during the Clinton Presidency. It is important to note that President Clinton issued Order 12,866[94] to replace Orders 12,291 and 12,498. The new Order confirmed that cost–benefit analysis and cost-effectiveness, to the extent permitted by the relevant statute, continued to serve as the basic principles for the assessment of regulatory decisions. An important innovation of the new Order is that independent agencies are subjected to the regulatory planning process. This provision enabled the OMB to request 'further consideration' of proposed rules that appeared in conflict with other agency action, the Order's regulatory principles or the President's priorities.

In the view of Kagan, President's Clinton's principal innovation in the effort to influence administrative action lay in initiating a regular practice of issuing formal directives to executive branch officials regarding the exercise of their statutory discretion.[95] For instance, on 10 August 1995 President Clinton began a press conference announcing the publication of a proposed rule to reduce youth smoking. He stated he would restrict by executive authority the advertisement, promotion, distribution, and marketing of cigarettes to teenagers and he would authorize the Food and Drug Administration to initiate a broad series of steps all designed to stop the sales and marketing of cigarettes and smokeless tobacco to children. The final versions of the rules eventually adopted by the FDA reflected the heart of the proposals made by the President.

[92] Kagan 'Presidential Administration' 2278.
[93] 50 Fed Reg 1036 (1985).
[94] 58 Fed Reg 51735 (1993).
[95] Kagan 'Presidential Administration' 2281.

Kagan analyses the factors that contributed to Clinton's turn towards administration as a means of realizing his domestic policy ambitions.[96] Some of these factors have a more structural aspect, reflecting long-term trends that other Presidents are also likely to face. She points to the trend that the American public has high and rising expectations about what a President should be able to accomplish. The public demands of the achievements of the President are strengthened by modern press, which makes insatiable demands and places impossible pressures on the office of the President. For these reasons, the pressure on the President to demonstrate action, leadership and accomplishment has grown. Yet the possibility of any significant legislative accomplishment has grown dim in an era of divided government with high polarization between Congressional parties. According to Kagan, given these changes, it is not surprising that a President would turn to administration: a sphere in which he unilaterally can take decisive action. These factors also make it likely that other Presidents will continue Clinton's practices.

President Clinton's assertion of direct authority over administration raises, unlike the procedural oversight power exercised under OMB review,[97] constitutional questions. No Supreme Court case specifically addresses the question as to whether the President has the power to direct the executive agencies in exercising their discretionary powers. However, the conventional view is that by virtue of Separation of Powers arguments, implying that Congress must authorize presidential exercises of essentially lawmaking functions, the President does not have this power when Congress has only delegated discretionary powers to executive branch officials[98]. Conversely Kagan argues that the President, indeed, has the power to direct policy decisions of executive agencies (not of independent agencies).[99]

Whether or not Bill Clinton's directions were constitutional, Kagan's article illustrates very well the growing role of the President in managing the administrative state. The increasing role of the President is an inevitable consequence of the growth of the activities of administrative agencies making the coordination of their actions necessary. By virtue of a mandate from the electorate, the President can ensure that inconsistencies and redundancies in regulation are resolved. These developments do not have to threaten the balance of power between the three named branches. Indeed,

[96] Ibid 2309.

[97] See para 2.2.

[98] It is important to note here, that is generally accepted that the President does not have the power to direct the independent agencies to make certain decisions.

[99] Kagan art cit 2326–7. She argues that Congress usually has not stated its intent as regards the role of the Presidency when it has assigned discretionary authority to an executive official. At that moment an interpretative question arises and the choice of the correct interpretation would rest upon policy considerations, such as accountability and effectiveness.

Congress keeps the power to shape the delegated powers and might as a response to growing presidential administration even restrict the scope of delegated powers. However, this would not mean that Congress should stop delegating broad regulatory powers. Instead, as said before, Sunstein argues that Congress should improve the quality of legislation, for instance by giving more guidance to the agency on how to characterize the cost and benefit of regulatory action and on how to value those costs and benefits.[100] Furthermore, the courts continue to review the agency's actions, since presidential direction does not insulate the agency's actions from judicial review. However, increasing presidential involvement may stimulate courts to take a more deferential approach to policy choices being made by the agencies. Paragraph VII will discuss this topic. The following paragraph discusses how interest groups might influence the decisions of agencies.

## VI. ACCOUNTABILITY: PUBLIC PARTICIPATION (QUESTION 15)

### *A. Introduction*

Procedural safeguards are important in enhancing the political and public accountability of agencies. Procedural safeguards make the reasoning and the factual predictions of agency decisions transparent enabling Congress, the President and the Judiciary to review whether an agency has acted within its statutory limits and in a reasonable manner. Moreover, procedural safeguards give an opportunity to interested parties to state their views on the proposed rules enabling the agency to take account of their interests.

There are five potential sources of procedural requirements that agencies must follow; agency rules, the Constitution (Due Process Clause), statutes, Executive orders and the common law.[101] Since statutes are the dominant source of the procedures agencies must follow, this paragraph will only deal with the statutory procedural requirements. Two statutory sources are of relevance for the determination as to which procedures the agency must follow, namely the Administrative Procedure Act (APA)[102] and the organic legislation that authorizes the agency to take the action under consideration. The APA was enacted in response to criticism of the bad procedural safeguards in the organic acts. The stipulations of those acts were inadequate to protect the private parties affected by agency actions from deprivation of their rights and to ensure that the agencies' actions were in the public interest. Furthermore, the lack of uniformity in federal agency decision-making procedures, made it difficult for parties to participate effectively in agency

[100] Sunstein 'Constitutional moments and the Cost–Benefit State' 293.

[101] Pierce et al art cit 221.

[102] 5 USC 77 551–706.

proceedings because they often could not predict in advance the procedures an agency would use to make a particular decision.[103]

The APA comprises four procedures, that is two procedures that relate to the agencies adjudicatory powers and two procedures that relate to the agencies' rulemaking powers. The APA, however, does not direct the agency as to which procedure it should follow. The APA refers to the provisions of the agency's organic act as the basis for the determination as to which of the APA procedures the agency is required to use in taking a particular type of action. It is important to note that the APA applies to the activities of the executive as well to those of the independent agencies.

### *B. Distinction between adjudication and rulemaking*

Two old US Supreme Cases are important for analysing the distinction between adjudication and rulemaking. In these cases the Supreme Court had to determine whether The Due Process Clause was violated. By virtue of this clause 'No person shall . . . be deprived of life, liberty, or property, without due process of law' (XIV Amendment). The Due Process Clause only applies to the protected interests of individuals and does not protect the interests of a group of people. In *Londoner v Denver*[104] the US Supreme Court considered whether the City could assess and levy a special tax against individual property owners to cover the costs of paving a public street on which their property fronted, without affording the property owners any opportunity to be heard. The Court was of the opinion that the city had violated the Due Process clause. It put the following reasons forward:

> where the legislature of a State, instead of fixing the tax itself, commits to some subordinate the duty of determining whether, in what amount and upon whom it shall be levied, and of making its assessment and apportionment, due process of law requires that at some stage of the proceedings before the tax becomes irrevocably fixed, the taxpayer shall have an opportunity to be heard, of which he must have notice. . . .

In *Bi-Metallic Investment Co* the US Supreme Court[105] pointed out under what conditions acts of government do not come within the requirements of the Due Process Clause. Unlike *Londoner*, this case did not concern the levy of specific taxes on individuals, but an order of the City board increasing the valuation of all taxable property in Denver. In the opinion of the Court it would be impracticable that everyone should have a direct voice in the adoption of a rule that applies to more than a few people. The rights of the affected people are protected by their power, immediate or remote over

[103] Pierce et al art cit 104.
[104] 210 US 373 (1908).
[105] 239 US 441 (1915).

those who make the rule. The Court denied the constitutional right of an individual to be heard before the adoption of a general measure. It distinguished *Bi-Metallic* from *Londoner* by pointing out that in the latter case:

> A relatively small number of persons was concerned, who were exceptionally affected, in each case upon individual grounds . . .

According to Pierce, the distinction announced in *Londoner* and *Bi-metallic* lies at the core of administrative procedure. It is the basis for the modern relationship between agency rules and agency adjudication, and they remain crucial to legislative and judicial determinations of the types of procedural safeguards that should be required in various administrative decision-making contexts.[106] Pierce is of the opinion that the number of people affected or potentially affected is the dominant factor in determining whether the Due Process Clause applies at all to an agency action that affects protected interests.

With regard to the above, it can be concluded that adjudication, in general, concerns the determination of individual rights and duties in the application of a general rule, whereas rulemaking comprises the formulation of norms of general applicability and future effect. This distinction is also reflected in APA Section 551 (5)–(9) that defines adjudication and rulemaking for the purposes of the APA.[107] In general the APA imposes, in harmony with the Due Process Clause, stricter procedural requirements in the exercise of adjudicatory powers, than it does for rulemaking powers.

## *C. Adjudication*

### *1. Formal adjudication*

An agency is required to use the APA formal adjudication procedure when Congress has directed it to do so. By virtue of Section 554 APA the formal adjudication procedure is required when the organic statute stipulates that the adjudication should be determined 'on the record after opportunity for an agency hearing'. But even when statutes lack these words, the courts tend to interpret the statute as providing for a hearing on the record in cases where the agency is imposing a sanction or liability on a party. In this way, the Courts can ensure the statutes are interpreted in harmony with the Due Process Clause.[108]

[106] Pierce et al art cit 250.

[107] It should be noted that the APA definition of adjudication is not the same as the Due process definition, for the APA definition includes many management and administrative functions (eg agency decisions to spend or not to spend money) that would not be regarded as adjudication in the conventional sense, Breyer et al op cit 653.

[108] Ibid 654.

The formal adjudication procedure is regulated by Sections 554, 556, and 557 APA. Together these sections create a procedure that resembles a civil trial procedure. The persons entitled to a hearing shall be timely informed of the time, place and the nature of the hearings, the legal authority and jurisdiction under which the hearing is to be held and the matters of fact and law asserted. Interested or affected third parties may be entitled to intervene in the proceedings.[109] A party is entitled to present his case or defense by oral or documentary evidence, to submit rebuttal evidence, and to conduct such cross-examination as may be required for a full and true disclosure of the facts. The transcript of testimony and exhibits, together with all papers and requests filed in the proceeding, constitutes the exclusive record for decision.

It is interesting to note that these formal adjudication procedures are often presided over by an independent Administrative Law Judge (ALJ). This ALJ rules on admissible evidence and receives relevant evidence, regulates the course of the hearing and may make or recommend decisions. When the ALJ makes an initial decision that decision then becomes the decision of the agency without further proceedings, unless there is an appeal to the agency or the agency elects on its own motion to review the decision.

The Administrative Law Judges are almost entirely independent of the agencies at which they preside. The Office of Personnel Management of the President determines their pay, independently of any evaluations or recommendations made by the agency.[110] An agency can only take an action against an ALJ for good cause, to be established and determined by another agency on the record after opportunity for hearing.[111] Another important feature of the ALJ is that he cannot be subject to supervision or direction by an agency employee with investigative or prosecutorial functions.[112] Moreover, stipulations are included that guarantee that the AJL shall not have any ex parte communications on the merits of the proceedings with interested persons outside the agency.[113]

The idea of the drafters of the APA was to give the ALJs independence from where they worked, and to provide public evidence that factual determinations were being made by independent officials. But the agency, on review of the ALJ's decision, was free to apply its policy to the facts found by independent officials.[114]

[109] The right to intervene in adjudications is usually controlled by agency enabling acts and agency rules. In addition s 554 (b) APA serves as a basis for intervention. For the determination of which parties are entitled to intervene in the agency procedures, the case law on standing to obtain judicial review plays an important role.

[110] Pierce et al art cit 302 and s 5372 APA.

[111] Section 7521 APA.

[112] Section 554 (d) APA.

[113] Section 554 (d) APA and s 557 (d) APA.

[114] ALJ's decide on 'evidentiary facts', in that they decide what actually happened. Agencies, however, decide how policy impacts on those evidentiary facts. The term 'ultimate fact' is used to refer to a factual determination after it has been imbued with the agency's policy input. For

Since this ALJ operates rather independently from the agency, he or she plays an important role in ensuring procedural fairness and impartial decision-making. Moreover, the internal division between fact finding and policy-making, may remedy the negative effects of the conjoining of different powers in one agency.

### 2. *Informal adjudication*

About 90 per cent of all agency decisions are made through informal adjudication. Therefore, it is remarkable that the APA hardly deals with this category of procedures. In instances where a relevant statute does not require the adjudicatory decision to be made 'on the record after opportunity for agency hearing', the APA provides little procedural requirements. Section 555 APA only provides that:

- A person compelled to appear in person before an agency or representative is entitled to legal counsel;
- A party may obtain a copy of any data or evidence she provides;
- A party is entitled to a brief statement of the grounds for denying any written petition.

In addition Due Process can be the source of judicially imposed procedural safeguards if the agency's action adversely affects an individual's interest in life, liberty or property.[115] However, the procedural safeguards mandated by Due Process vary substantially depending on the specific circumstances of the case in issue.[116] Therefore, Pierce argues that the APA should be amended to include minimal procedural safeguards for informal adjudication. This would help the agencies in determining which procedures are appropriate for informal adjudication and would eliminate the need for agencies and the courts to attempt the difficult task of determining procedures appropriate for hundreds of types of adjudications through an ad hoc application of the Due Process Clause.

example, whether workers were distributing newspapers at street corners under the direction of the publisher would be an 'evidentiary fact', but whether those workers would be 'employees' within the scope of the National Labor Relations Act would be an 'ultimate fact', cf *National Labor Relations Board v Hearst Publications*, 322 US 111 (1944).

[115] Pierce et al art cit 343.

[116] The US Supreme Court has formulated a three-part balancing test for the determination of the procedural safeguards mandated under Due Process in *Matthews v Eldridge*, 424 US 319 (1979). Pierce describes that this balancing test may sometimes require the same procedural safeguards that are also provided for in formal adjudication. In other instances less strict requirements, like notice of the charges and informal opportunity to explain the facts, may be sufficient, Pierce et al 1999, 344.

## D. *Informal rulemaking*

### 1. *Informal or formal rulemaking*

When an agency chooses to take an action through rulemaking it has to make a choice as to whether it takes action through informal or formal rulemaking. Formal rulemaking is much like a trial type proceeding, which includes the taking of testimony and cross-examination and decision making on the basis of the evidence presented. Therefore, formal rulemaking is a very time-consuming procedure. The order of the *Supreme Court in United States v Florida East Coast Railway* was an enormous impulse for agencies to shift from adjudication to informal rulemaking to develop law and policy[117]. In this case the US Supreme Court, apparently aware of the delays and other dysfunctions attributed to formal rulemaking, confirmed that agencies were obliged to follow formal rulemaking procedures only when rules are required 'by statute to be made on the record after opportunity for an agency hearing'.[118]

### 2. *The notice and comment procedure*

As a consequence of *Florida East Coast* most of the rulemaking occurs through the 'notice and comment procedure'. The process of informal rulemaking is regulated by section 553 APA and consists of three steps. First, a general notice of the proposed rulemaking shall be published in the Federal Register. This general notice shall include a statement of the time, place and nature of the public rulemaking proceedings, a reference to the legal authority under which the rule is proposed and either the terms or substance of the proposed rule or a description of the subjects and the issues involved. Secondly, after the agency has given notice it shall give interested persons an opportunity to participate in the rulemaking through submission of written data, views, or arguments with or without the opportunity for oral presentation. Thirdly, after the agency has considered the relevant matter presented, the agency shall incorporate in the rules adopted a 'concise general statement of their basis and purpose'.

The basic notice and comment model of the APA seems rather simple and does not seem to impose too many procedural constraints on the agencies. However, the circuit courts have interpreted the provisions of the APA in a way that turned the informal procedures into new 'paper hearing' procedures.[119] The *Nova Scotia* case[120] decided by the 2d Cir Court illustrates very well the way federal appellate courts have transformed the notice and comment procedure into a more elaborate paper hearing process

[117] 410 US 224 (1973).
[118] Breyer et al op cit 657.
[119] Ibid 678.
[120] 568 F 2d 240 (2d Cir 1977).

that generates a documentary record and full agency opinion as the basis for judicial review.[121]

As regards the substance of the administrative record the Court ruled:

> If the failure to notify interested parties of the scientific research upon which the agency was relying actually prevented the presentation of relevant comment, the agency may be held not to have considered all 'the relevant factors'. To suppress meaningful comment by failure to disclose the basic data relied upon is akin to rejecting comment altogether.

As regards the obligation to formulate a 'concise general statement' the Court ruled:

> Appellants additionally attack the 'concise and general statement' required by section 553 APA as inadequate. We think in the circumstances, it was less than adequate. It is not in keeping with the rational process to leave vital questions, raised by comments which are of cogent materiality, completely unanswered. The agencies certainly have a good deal of discretion in expressing the basis of a rule, but the agencies do not have quite the prerogatives of obscurantism reserved to legislatures.

As a result of cases like *Nova Scotia*, an agency should publish in its public notice the factual and scientific basis of a proposed rule. It would indeed be impossible for the public to deliver high quality comments on a proposed rule when such data is not included in the notice. By imposing the requirement to include scientific and factual data the courts have prevented formal rulemaking procedures from becoming less effective. Another consequence of *Nova Scotia* is that the agencies should explain in the preambular statement accompanying a final rule their grounds for the decision, including their reasons for rejecting adverse outside comments on proposed regulations and the agency data and analysis disclosed in agency documents.[122]

The procedural requirements that were imposed by the courts have posed heavy burdens on the administrative process resulting in the so-called 'ossification' of the administrative process. The ossification of the administrative process became worse, because some courts went beyond the requirements of detailed explanation and a 'paper hearing' by requiring a limited trial-type hearing in notice and comments procedures. Excessive judicial review has slowed the pace of rulemaking at all agencies. Promulgation of a single major rule often requires 5 to 10 years and tens of thousands of agency staff hours, with only a 50 per cent probability of judicial affirmation of the resulting rule.[123] Consequently, instead of using the rulemaking process, the agencies issued interpretative rules or policy statements that are not subject to the notice and comment procedure.

121 Breyer et al op cit 689.

122 Ibid 690.

123 Pierce, 'Seven ways to deossify agency rulemaking' (1995) 47 *Admin L Rev* 65.

The Supreme Court seems to have recognized the adverse effect of excessively demanding judicial review on the rulemaking process. In this respect the opinion in *Vermont Yankee*[124] is of great importance, since it put a halt on the development of further judicial requirements going beyond 'paper hearing' rulemaking. In this opinion the Court states that agencies are free to grant additional procedural rights in the exercise of their discretion, but reviewing courts are not free to impose them if the agencies have not chosen to grant them. Although this opinion to some extent relieves the administrative burdens of some agencies, the remaining requirements of keeping an adequate administrative record and providing adequate justification still generate an enormous amount of work for the agencies. Therefore, various proposals have been made to improve administrative procedures. One suggestion is to relax the demand for extensive records and elaborate agency explanations and hard-look judicial review.[125] Other suggestions include the referral of major rules to Congress for adoption through 'fast-track legislation', bypassing judicial review in favour of direct political control, or greater reliance on executive oversight and control of rulemaking.

## VII. ACCOUNTABILITY: JUDICIAL REVIEW (QUESTIONS 9, 18, 19)

### *A. Introduction*

Affected parties have a constitutional right to judicial review if an agency action arguably infringes a constitutional right. However, the issue of whether a party has a constitutional right to judicial review of an agency action arises infrequently, because the legislature usually provides an explicit statutory right to judicial review.[126] Congress has usually provided that final agency actions are subject to judicial review in accordance with the provisions of the APA.

Section 702 refers to the standing requirements for judicial review, by providing that 'a person suffering legal wrong because of agency action, or adversely affected or aggrieved by agency action within the meaning of a relevant statute, is entitled to judicial review thereof'. The US Supreme Court applies a two-part test to analyse whether a party has standing.[127] At first, the question has to be answered as to whether the claimant alleges that the challenged action has caused him injury in fact, economic or otherwise. Secondly, the question has to be answered as to whether the interest sought to be protected is arguably within the zone of interests protected or regulated by the statute or constitutional guarantee in question. This first part

[124] 435 US 519 (1978).
[125] Breyer et al op cit 735.
[126] Pierce et al art cit 125.
[127] *Association of Data Processing Service Organizations vs Camp*, 397 US 150 (1970).

of the standing test is based on the requirements of Article III of the Constitution, that limits the powers of the Federal courts to the resolution of 'cases and controversies'. The second part of the standing test recognizes that, to the extent permitted by the Constitution, it is up to Congress to decide which parties have the power to obtain judicial review of an agency action. In theory the two part standing test may seem clear. However, both the US Supreme Court and the lower courts have applied it in different ways for many different purposes, producing seemingly inconsistent results.[128]

### *B. Scope of judicial review of the agencies' statements of reasons and facts*

Since the APA is usually determinant for the scope of judicial review, both the independent and the executive agencies' actions are reviewed under the same standards. Pursuant to section 706 APA the reviewing courts shall determine whether the agencies' findings of facts and reasons are 'arbitrary and capricious' and whether the action is not in accordance with the law. In case the agency decision is taken on the record after opportunity for hearing, the agencies statement of reasons and facts will be reviewed under the more strict 'substantial evidence test'. The original version of the 'arbitrary and capricious' test for the review of the agencies' findings of facts and reasons was quite deferential to the agencies' findings. However, since the courts have been imposing stricter procedural requirements on the agencies when acting through the notice and comment procedure, they have been scrutinizing the agencies' statement of facts and reasons more thoroughly. Therefore, it seems the 'arbitrary and capricious' standard and the 'substantial evidence' tests have converged.

While the Supreme Court in *Vermont Yankee* has put a halt on courts taking a hard look at the procedures that agencies should institute for taking their actions, it has not yet addressed in a definitive way to what extent the reviewing courts should engage in a detailed scrutiny of the substantive basis for agency actions that are based on scientific studies. This issue is heavily debated in the USA at this moment. The debate focuses on the question as to whether or not a substantive 'hard-look doctrine' should be accepted. Pursuant to this doctrine a court would be required to attempt to understand and to assess in detail the data and methodology an agency used to address a complicated scientific issue.[129]

Advocates of the hard-look doctrine point out that a hard-look approach would stimulate agencies to make good policy decisions. Political controls would not be adequate to assure agencies make wise policy decisions.[130]

[128] Pierce et al art cit 139.

[129] Ibid 388.

[130] Rodgers, 'A hard look review at Vermont Yankee: Environmental law under close scrunity' (1979) 67 Geo LJ 699.

Opponents of the hard-look approach point out that the courts should defer to the agencies' statement of reasons and facts since most of the agencies' decisions are policy decisions based on the interpretation and determination of uncertain scientific facts. A more detailed consideration of the facts and reasons would not eliminate the need to make policy judgements in favour of one or the other risk. Therefore hard-look review would merely result in delay.[131]

Indeed, one may agree with the opponents that it can be questioned whether the hard-look approach will generate better policy decisions. From the perspective of accountability and from the perspective of expertise, the agencies are in a better position than judges to assess complicated facts and scientific data. Therefore, it would be very inefficient were the judges to redo the agency's work and would require the agencies to take a new decision on the basis of their assessment of the facts. With regard to these factors, it would be better if the courts were to take a more deferential approach to the determinations of facts and reasons by the agencies and only intervene when agencies evidently have made errors in interpreting the facts and justifying their policy decisions.

For now, as will be discussed in the next paragraph, the opinion of the Supreme Court in *Motor Vehicle Manufacturers' Association v State Farm* provides the standard for the scope of review under the 'arbitrary and capricious' test.[132]

### 1. *Hard look review: Case law of the Supreme Court*

The National Highway Traffic Safety Administration (NHTSA) had issued a rule that rescinded the passive restraint requirement contained in the Modified Standard 208. This standard required that each car was either equipped with automatic seatbelts or with automatic airbags. The agency's changed view of the standard was related to the election of President Reagan and his deregulation policies. In the view of the Court the revocation of the rule had to be tested under the 'arbitrary and capricious' standard. It described the scope of review under this test as narrow and warned that a court is not to substitute its judgment for that of the agency. Nevertheless the Court found that the agency must articulate a satisfactory explanation for its action, including a rational connection between the facts found and the choices made. The Court then formulated under which circumstances an agency rule would be 'arbitrary and capricious':

[131] Breyer, Vermont Yankee and the courts' role in the Nuclear Energy Controversy (1978) 91 *Harv L Rev* 1804.

[132] 463 US 29 (1983).

if the agency has relied on factors which Congress has not intended it to consider, entirely failed to consider an important aspect of the problem, offered an explanation for its decision that runs counter to the evidence before it, or is so implausible that it could not be ascribed to a difference in view or the product of agency expertise.

In applying this standard of review the Court reversed the NHTSA's revocation of the rule on two different bases. The first reason for finding the rescission 'arbitrary and capricious' is that the NHTSA gave no consideration at all to the option of modifying the Standard to require that airbags would be installed. The agency had determined that detachable automatic belts would not attain anticipated safety benefits because so many people will detach the mechanism. However, given the effectiveness ascribed to airbag technology by the agency, the Court was of the opinion that the mandate of the Safety Act to achieve traffic safety would suggest that the logical response to the faults of detachable seatbelts would be to require the installation of airbags. Although the Court confirmed that it generally defers to the policy alternatives being made by the agency, the airbag option was more than a policy alternative to the passive restraint standard: it was a technological alternative within the ambit of the existing standard. Therefore, the agency should have addressed this alternative way of achieving the objectives of the Act and should have given adequate reasons for the abandonment of this alternative.

The second reason the Court found the revocation of the rule 'arbitrary and capricious' was that the agency was too quick to dismiss the safety benefits of automatic seatbelts. The NHTSA's critical finding was that, in the light of the industry's plans to install readily detachable belts, it could not reliably predict even a 5 per cent increase as the minimum level of used increase. The Court thought there was no direct evidence in support of the NHTSA's finding that detachable automatic belts cannot be predicted to yield a substantial increase in usage. The empirical evidence on the record reveals more than a doubling of the usage rate experiences with manual belts. Although the Court explicitly acknowledged that it should in general defer to an agency's finding with respect to uncertainty about the efficacy of certain measures, the agency had failed to explain how the findings of less than 5 per cent increase could be reconciled with the evidence of the increased use of manual belts.

It is interesting to note that the majority of the Court did not deal with the question as to whether the change of policy as a consequence of the election of a new President should have had implications for the scope of review under the 'arbitrary and capricious' standard. The majority confirmed that every change of policy should be based on a reasoned analysis, indicating that presidential involvement in the agency's rulemaking process would not lead to a different review standard. On the other hand, the dissenting judges were of the opinion that the change in administration brought about by the electorate casting their votes, is a perfectly reasonable basis for an executive agency's reappraisal of the costs and benefits of a regulatory programme. Therefore, they were of the opinion that the agency is entitled, within the bounds established by Congress, to change policy in the light of the philosophy of the administration, indicating that the Court should defer to those policy choices.

The reasoning of the Court in *State Farm* illustrates that the Court thinks the 'capricious and arbitrary' standard empowers the courts to review carefully whether the agency has considered all relevant scientific facts and whether its decision can be justified on the basis of the evidence of the record. However, since the Court makes some remarks on the deference to the agency's choice of policy alternatives and the agency's findings on uncertainty, the opinion of the Court does not indicate that courts should assess the agency's work in detail or should substitute the agency's assessments. Since the NHTSA left out a policy alternative it had previously deemed effective and since its record contained contradicting evidence, the Court's reversal of the decision can very well be reconciled with this deferring approach. So, therefore it might be argued the Court has not approved the hard-look approach.[133]

### C. *Interpretation of the law:* Chevron

Before the rise of the regulatory state, it was relatively clear that it was for the courts and not the executive to 'say what the law is'.[134] Consequently, the courts reviewed thoroughly whether the administration had respected the law. However, in the twentieth century, the role of the courts in determining the law was complicated, because Congress had frequently delegated discretionary, policy-making powers to administrative agencies. As a consequence of these developments courts sometimes said that agencies were entitled to interpret the statutes they had to administer and that courts would defer as long as the agencies' interpretations were reasonable.[135] This idea reflected the principles of administrative autonomy, limited judicial interference with the process of regulation and democratic accountability. At the same time, many courts continued to insist that the interpretation of statutes was first and foremost a judicial task.

It was not until 1984, when the Court decided the famous *Chevron*[136]

[133] This opinion is also advocated by HA Brooks, 'American Trucking Assocations v EPA: The DC Circuit's missed opportunity to unambiguously discard the hard look doctrine' 27 Harv Envtl L Rev 259 272.

[134] *Marbury v Madison*, 5 US (1 Cranch) 137, 2 L Ed 60 (1803).

[135] Sunstein analyses these developments in his 'Law and Administration after Chevron' (2001) 90 Colum L Rev 2072–82.

[136] 467 US 837 (1984).

case, that it became clear under what circumstances the courts should defer to the agencies' interpretations of the law. In *Chevron* the Supreme Court decided that the courts should defer to the agencies' interpretations of the law, if the law permits the agencies to make policy judgements and if the agencies' interpretations are reasonable.[137]

In *Chevron* the interpretation of the words 'stationary source' in the Clean Air Act were at issue. Under the influence of the Reagan administration, the EPA promulgated rules that allowed states to define an entire plant, containing many different kinds of pollution-emitting units, as if it were a single 'stationary source'. Thus, a firm could modify one unit within the plant and increase its emissions, or introduce a new unit, without complying with requirements of the Clean Air Act. It could do this as long as pollution from the plant, considered as a whole, did not increase, because it reduced equivalent emissions from other, existing units (bubble concept). The Court of Appeals held that the statute did not permit the EPA to allow a 'bubble-like' definition of 'stationary source', because it would undermine Congress' goal of speedy compliance with national air quality standards.

The Supreme Court did not approve the Court of Appeal's approach. The Supreme Court formulated two important questions that may arise when a court reviews an agency's construction of the statute it administers. First, always, is the question as to whether Congress has directly addressed the precise question at issue. If the intent of Congress is clear, that is the end of the matter, for the court as well as the agency must give effect to the unambiguously expressed intent of Congress. If, however, the court determines that Congress has not directly addressed the precise question at issue, the court does not simply impose its own construction of the statute. Rather if the statute is silent or ambiguous with respect to the specific issue, the question for the court is whether the agency's answer is based on a permissible construction of the statute.

In the light of these principles the Supreme Court thought that it was clear that the Court of Appeals misconceived the nature of its role in reviewing the regulations at issue. Based on the examination of the legislation and its history, the Supreme Court confirmed that Congress did not have a specific intention as to the applicability of the bubble concept. According to the Court, the EPA's use of the 'bubble concept' was a reasonable policy choice within the ambit of the Clean Air Act, which seeks to accommodate progress in reducing air pollution with economic growth. Therefore, it unanimously reversed the judgement of the Court of Appeals. The Court justified the deference to the agencies' policies decisions on the following grounds:

137 Sunstein, 'Law and Administration after Chevron' 2083–5, Pierce, 'Chevron and its aftermath: Judicial review of agency interpretations of statutory provisions' 41 VNLR 301.

Judges are not experts in the field, and are not part of either political branch of the government. Courts must, in some cases, reconcile competing political interests, but not on the basis of the judges' personal policy preferences. In contrast, an agency to which Congress has delegated policymaking responsibilities may, within the limits of that delegation, properly rely upon the incumbent administration's view of wise policy to inform its judgements. While agencies are not directly accountable to the people, the Chief Executive is, and it is entirely appropriate for this political branch of the government to make such policy choices-resolving the competing interests which Congress itself either inadvertently did not resolve, or intentionally left to be resolved by the agency charged with the administration of the statute in the light of everyday realities.

The relevance of *Chevron* is that it replaced a statute-by-statute evaluation of the agency's discretion with an across the board presumption that in case Congress has not expressed a clear intent, the agency was meant to enjoy discretion.[138] This discretion is based upon an implicit congressional intent of law-interpreting power, which can be justified on the ground that the resolution of ambiguities in statutes is sometimes a question of policy as much as it is one of law. As a consequence of their expertise and accountability to the President, agencies are in a better position than the courts to make policy choices within the ambit of the law.[139]

## VIII. CONCLUSION

The position of independent agencies with broad regulatory powers may well be reconciled with the Separation of Powers Principle of the US Constitution. It follows from the case law of the Supreme Court that it was never the intent of the Framers of the Constitution to make a hermetic division of government power into three branches. Congress may make any arrangement, not explicitly mentioned in the Constitution, as long as all of the three branches can effectively perform their core function and the checks and balances between the three powers are maintained.

The more functional checks and balances approach to the Separation of Powers principle has now been well established in US doctrine and case law. Where independent agencies are created each power should be able to check and balance the powers of the other powers in controlling the agencies' actions. The President, Congress and the Judiciary continuously check the actions of both the independent and executive agencies. In addition, a fourth power, not mentioned in the Constitution, plays an important role in maintaining the checks and balances between the three original powers.

[138] Scalia, 'Judicial Deference to agency Interpretations of the law (1989) Duke LJ 511.

[139] Sunstein 'Law and Administration after Chevron' 2087–8.

Indeed, the public forms an effective check on the agencies' actions through participation in administrative procedures. Judicially imposed procedural requirements, ensure fulfilment of the agencies' duty to adequately respond to comments being made by the public on proposed rules.

From the analysis, it follows that from a legal perspective the way the four actors control the activities of the independent agencies does not differ much from the way in which they control the activities of the executive agencies. Although the President will give more deference to the policy choices being made by independent agencies, it does not seem that the constitutional position of independent agencies is very different from the constitutional position of executive agencies. The analysis shows that each of the three branches and the public have their own role in controlling the agencies' actions.

The way in which the four actors perform their supervisory roles is a dynamic process and may adapt to changing circumstances. Indeed, due to the enormous growth of the activities of executive and independent agencies there was a growing need for a unitary force that would coordinate the agencies' activities. Due to a lack of institutional capacities, Congress has not been able to lay down a general philosophy for the administrative state, in order to ensure that the agencies actions are cost-effective, beneficial and that the agencies take account of the effects of their decisions on the policies that are formulated by other agencies. These circumstances explain why the Reagan era was the beginning of an era of presidential administration.

The growing importance of the presidential role does not have to upset the checks and balances between the different actors. To the present date, there does not seem to be a clear trend for courts to give more deference to agencies policies' that were directed by the President. As a matter of fact, the paper has illustrated that the courts have responded to the tremendous growth of administrative rulemaking by imposing strict procedural and substantive requirements on the agencies.

Finally, a lot of the criticism of the agencies' activities can be traced back to the quality of the organic acts. Often, Congress has failed to give substantial guidance to the agencies on which factors they should take into account in formulating rules and on how to evaluate the benefits and costs of their actions. Therefore, various proposals have been made on how Congress could improve the quality of legislation. For instance, it could improve the quality of legislation by laying down clear substantive principles and by trying to formulate legislation that is based on market-based incentives rather than on command-control.

If Congress succeeds in improving the quality of legislation, there may be less need for the delegation of broad regulatory powers, administrative rulemaking and for presidential administration.

# 2. INDEPENDENT ADMINISTRATIVE AUTHORITIES IN FRANCE

*Jeannette Bougrab**

How can administrative activities be managed differently? Independent administrative authorities or regulatory authorities are one of the answers to the crisis of the State, which is called upon to intervene in an ever-increasing number of spheres. Independent administrative authorities are more generally part of a broader movement specific to democratic countries which extends beyond the policy of decentralization and devolution, to a new method of distribution and exercise of State power in the delicate fields of the exercise of civil liberties and as the regulation of certain sectors or markets. This development leads one to call into question 'the unitary bureaucratic model, based on the concentration of decision-making power at the top',[1] a model whose features were systematized by Max Weber. In practice, two organic types of links guarantee this unity: hierarchy and supervision. These two links do not apply to independent administrative authorities.

The weakening of the traditional bureaucratic model has a variety of explanations. First and above all it results from a suspicion towards the traditional model of the State. The State's powers are challenged. Its impartiality and its efficiency are disputed. The undermining of the traditional bureaucratic model also implies an aspiration for new patterns of social regulation with a broader place granted to mediation or negotiated compromises. The targets set for public authorities can on occasion take priority over the formal respect of legal standards. Above and beyond this crisis of the bureaucratic model, it is in fact the conception of the organization, the conditions for the exercise of power that is called into in question.

Independent administrative authorities constitute an original and unprecedented category of structuring the State apparatus in France. Most of our administrative institutions originate in the *Ancien Régime* or the French revolution. One might take the examples of the prefects created by the Law of 28 pluviose year VIII or the *Conseil d'État* established by the Constitution of year VIII.

* Maître de conférences à l'université de Paris I, Panthéon-Sorbonne.

[1] Jacques Chevallier 'Réflexions sur l'institution des autorités administratives indépendantes' *JCP* (1986) I, no 3254.

The term of 'independent administrative authority' is one developed by the legislator and used for the first time in the law of 6 January 1978 to describe the new *Commission nationale de l'informatique et des libertés*. This expression did not appear by chance. A wide-ranging debate had taken place at the time concerning the guarantees to be given to the citizens in a context of information technology development. Everyone was aware of the need for State intervention in the field, and yet all feared that the public sector might use this intervention in order to extend their control over citizens, in particular through the misuse of data (social security, tax, police files). Thus the idea was born of creating 'within the State a largely independent authority which is to be in a way the organ of social conscience in relation to the use information technology.[2] The *Commission nationale informatique et liberté*, categorized as an independent administrative authority, meets those requirements since it is not subordinated to any hierarchical or supervisory power. Indeed, the expression 'independent administrative authority' matches the philosophy which underlies the creation of independent administrative authorities.

Over the past 25 years, the number of independent administrative authorities has soared, and there are more than thirty in France today. They intervene in a variety of sectors ranging from the audiovisual[3] to personal data protection contained in computer files[4] or the fight against the use of drugs in sport,[5] including markets regulation essential for the functioning of the economy.[6]

The creation of the independent administrative authorities in these very diverse areas has several justifications.

The *raison d'être* for the existence of the independent administrative authorities is to offer public opinion a guarantee of the impartiality of State intervention. This explanation is the most significant of all. It arose from the mistrust regarding both political and administrative powers. The State is considered partial or even unjust, while independent administrative authorities seem from their very birth to be provided with a 'veneer of

[2] *Rapport de la Commission informatique et liberté* La documentation française (1975) 89.

[3] *Conseil supérieur de l'audiovisuel* or CSA created as an independent administrative authority by Article 1 of the law no 89-25 from 17 January 1989 and which follows upon the *Haute autorité de la communication audiovisuelle* qualified as an independent administrative authority by the *Conseil constitutionnel* in its decision no 84-173 cd of 26 July 1984 and at the *Commission nationale de la communication et des libertés* qualified as an independent administrative authority by law no 86-1067 of 30 Sept 1986.

[4] CNIL created and qualified by Article 8 of the law no 78-17 of 6 January 1978 relating to information technology, files, and liberties.

[5] We know how this subject is linked to current affairs with the recent scandals surrounding the *Tour de France*, the *Conseil de prévention et de lutte contre le dopage CPCD* created and qualified by Article 14 of the law no 99-233 of 23 Mar 1999.

[6] The *Autorité des marchés financiers* or AMF created by the law no 2003-706 of 1 Aug 2003.

impartiality'. More surprising is the fact that the politicians themselves recognize this feature of independent administrative authorities, implicitly admitting that the traditional administration is under the influence of political power of which they are the origin. Thus Jean-Pierre Chevènement, the minister of the interior under the preceding government, during the first reading of the bill creating the *Conseil supérieur de déontologie de la sécurité* underlined that the objective for this institution was to fulfil its mission with 'impartiality, objectivity and independence'. The feature of impartiality is even more fundamental when one considers that the fields of intervention of independent administrative authorities are those concerning rights and liberties, which must be protected from the grasp of both interest groups and the political power. In this last point, one can see a certain distortion of the democratic principle, which postulates that State power should be exerted under the direct control of the elected officials of the Nation. One is therefore witnessing the emergence of a 'Republic of Wisemen' or, even worse of technocrats.

A second suggested justification for the creation of the independent administrative authorities is to allow to a wider participation of specialists in the creation of rules in technical areas. This is the expression of the notion participative democracy, or even continuing democracy, which signifies that 'the participation of all in forming the general will is not reduced to voting rights but continues between the elections, by citizens rights of legislative intervention and by their rights of glance and thus of control on the normative undertakings of the system.[7] The participation of professionals in fields as technical as the financial sphere, the stock exchange or banking guarantees a better information of the decision-making body on the issues and the consequences of measures to be taken, and guarantees the adaptation of these measures to the specific area, and reacting flexibly to any problem which might arise. The presence in these authorities, of the principal economic actors of the sectors to be regulated, provides a legitimacy in respect of the adopted rules and thus facilitates their application.

The third justification is based on the purportedly greater efficiency of the independent administrative authority model compared to the traditional modes of operation of administration, or the reaction of the judge which can seem to be too slow. Indeed in many respects, the autonomy conferred upon independent administrative authorities allows for theme to take decisions more quickly than the central administration. Independent administrative authorities are indeed exempted from a series of constraints that weigh on the traditional modes of administrative decision elaboration: there is no interdepartmental arbitration which could otherwise lengthen the deadlines, nor is any private office (of a Minister) exerting its influence on

[7] Dominique Rousseau 'La démocratie continue' *Déba,* (1997) no 86, 74

the decision. An independent administrative authority has the immense advantage of being able to take a decision as soon as it considers it is ready to take it, and not needing to take account of considerations external to the sector for which it is responsible.

Furthermore the simplified rules of operation make it possible to come to decision on disputes and to take disciplinary measures much faster than the ordinary criminal courts which are both overloaded with case-work and subject to numerous procedural constraints subject. The delays before the courts are too long, and France has been sanctioned for this on several occasions by the European Court of Human Rights.[8] The rapidity of reaction and response of the independent administrative authorities is important because the matters in which they are often changing rapidly. Immediate reactions are therefore required. This explains the reasons why ever-increasing powers, in particular of sanction, were entrusted to them within the framework defined by the *Conseil Constitutionnel*.

Independent administrative authorities have been established for more than 25 years in the French administrative landscape. Despite this establishment they remain at the centre of an age-old legal question, re-invoked due to the multiplying number of new independent administrative authorities, to such an extent that in less than 20 years the *Conseil d'État* has devoted two annual reports to it.[9] Both the concept as well as the legal status applicable to independent administrative authorities raise questions.

## I. THE CONCEPT OF INDEPENDENT ADMINISTRATIVE AUTHORITIES

The concept of independent administrative authority is a legislative creation in French law. As is often the case, the legislator omitted to define the concept of independent administrative authority or even to give the characteristic features of the independent administrative authorities. The three words of the expression 'Authority' (A), 'administrative' (B) and 'independent' (C) will be examined since each one allows us to identify the basic components of the concept of independent administrative authority.[10]

[8] CEDH 31 Mar 1992 X c/ France.

[9] F Gazier and Y Cannac *Études sur les autorités administratives indépendantes* EDCE (1983–4) no 35; Conseil d'État *Rapport public 2001, les autorités administratives indépendantes,* La documentation française (2001).

[10] A new thesis is substituted to the 'administrative' criterion: the power to adopt 'soft norm'. Independent administrative authorities can take norms which have to be followed by the administrations and the professionals of the concerned domain. Martin Collet *Le contrôle juridictionnel des actes des autorités administratives indépendantes* LGDJ, Bibliothèque de droit public, tome 233 (2003), 20.

### A. *Authority*

The word authority has a Latin origin (auctoritas): to dispose of a conferred power in order to exercise a function.

The concept of authority covers in reality two meanings. The first is the ability of a body to have a decisive influence, to be reference-point, without any legal constraints. The authorities do not manage the activities; they are not in charge of providing the services, but frame the development of a sector of social life, by attempting to ensure the respect of a certain balance. They are regulatory authorities. Thus they don't need substantial financial, human and material resources. They are equipped with light structures allowing them to escape from bureaucratic heaviness.

The notion of authority may go beyond this, signifying that the organs in question are not only limited to a purely consultative role, but instead possess a decision-making power which gives them the possibility of modifying the judicial order. Thus many independent administrative authorities such as AMF, CNIL, or the CSA can, in a certain number of spheres issue binding measures, which have the character of real regulations.[11] If the administrative authorities can enact general measures they can also take individual measures whether it be on a level of authorizations or on that of specific decisions aiming to resolve conflicts. By way of example, the *Conseil Supérieur de l'Audiovisuel*, appoints those who are accountable for public sector programmes, and the *AMF* delivers licences for financial services organizations.

If there is little doubt that the criterion of authority will be met in the case of the exercise of public power by an independent administrative authority, that is to say essentially where it holds a power of decision, the question is more controversial for bodies which only possess a power of influence (power of inquiry, of opinion, of proposition, of recommendation, of observation) and many authors deny to such organizations the qualification of independent administrative authorities. This is the opinion of Professor René Chapus for whom, 'the category of independent administrative authorities can only be accepted to have special features and the term of authority can only be justified if, contrary to certain opinions, it only consists of bodies holding for the accomplishment of their role a power of decision'.

Organizations have thus been excluded from the category of independent administrative authorities by some commentators based on the non-enforceable character of the powers granted to them such as the CADA, the administrative commission of access to administrative documents. Indeed,

[11] Some independent administrative authorities such as the *Autorité des marches financiers* must obtain the minister approval for general norm.

under Article 5 of law no 78–23 from 17 July 1978, the CADA possesses only a power of opinion (triggered by the claimant) and proposition to the competent authorities, even though the seizing of the CADA is an obligatory precondition of the decision to commence litigation.[12] The judge can refuse to follow the opinion of CADA.[13] This gives rise to the difficult problem of the superposition of regulation and judicial review.

Whilst academic commentators may be hesitant, the legislator is certainly not. It has thus qualified as independent administrative authorities institutions that do not possess a power of decision such as the *Comité national d'évaluation des établissement publics à caractère scientifique, culturel et professionnel*[14] created by law no 84–52 of 26 January 1984, an organ that limits its activity to evaluation, without legal consequences. The last report of the Court of Auditors criticizes the lack of power granted to this institution.

This last form of authority is well known by Common lawyers, it is described as 'sunshine regulation'. Public intervention obtains effective results by simply exposing practices which are contrary to the public interest. The opinions of the institution do not necessary have any legal consequences yet they will have a crucial influence. This is why one must agree with the following view of the *Conseil d'État*: 'it doesn't matter that independent administrative authorities do not all take executory decisions since their power of influence and persuasion or even imprecation conducts to the same result. It is the combination of their particular organization and their specific powers that makes them real authorities.'[15] This is confirmed by the thesis of Martin Collet: one of the criteria of independent administrative authorities is the power to take soft norms which have vocation to be followed.[16]

To utilize the metaphor of Mrs Catherine Teitgen Colly, there is a hard core of independent administrative authorities which have a decision-making power. On the other hand, there is a nebulous group of independent administrative authorities which do not have a decision-making power within the judicial meaning of the term.[17] Thus within this meaning independent administrative authorities are authorities but not any authorities, they are independent authorities.

[12] CE 19 Feb 1982 Dame Commaret *Recueil* 78.

[13] CE 2 Dec 1987 Pokorny *Recueil* 392.

[14] National Council for the Evaluation of Universities

[15] Conseil d'État *Rapport public 2001, Les autorités administratives indépendantes* (2001) La documentation française 290.

[16] Martin Collet *Le contrôle juridictionnel des actes des autorités administratives indépendantes,* LGDJ Bibliothèque de droit public, book 233 (2003) 20.

[17] Catherine Teitgen-Colly in Gérard Timsit (dir) *Les autorités administratives indépendantes* PUF Les voies du droit (1988).

### *B. Independence*

Independence is among the most essential justifications for the creation of the independent administrative authorities. It is in consequence the most important element of these bodies. One should note that the *Conseil Constitutionel* has never laid down independence as a constitutional requirement.

The notion of the 'independence' of administrative authorities is rather particular because it is contrary to the French administrative tradition. Indeed, according to Article 20 of the Constitution, the government 'disposes of' the administration. Yet the government has no authority over these institutions. The constitutionality of these organizations has been examined. The constitutional Council endorsed them.

In order to preserve the independence of independent administrative authorities, organic guarantees (1) and functional guarantees (2) have been created.

#### *1. Organic guarantees*

The independence of administrative authorities results above all from the rules governing the nomination of the members of the body. The first of these rules is their collegial structure. With the exception of the *Médiateur de la République* (Ombudsman), the *Médiateur du cinéma*, the *Défenseur des enfants* and the director of the *Institut national de la propriété intellectuelle*[18] named by the Council of Ministers (Cabinet), all independent administrative authorities are collegial organizations. The majority of independent administrative authorities have colleges whose membership varies from five to ten members such as the CADA although there are sometimes more numerous colleges like that of the CNIL (seventeen members) or of the competition authority (seventeen members).

The collegial structure is an important element of independence administrative authorities. It is indeed likely to meet a double requirement: to balance the influence of the various authorities which nominate the members of the board and to ensure a collective deliberation on significant subjects or complex questions, providing a guarantee of objectivity and responsibility.

The second rule ensuring the independence of these bodies is based on the composition of independent administrative authorities. The members of these authorities are often members of the senior judiciary (*Conseil d'État, Cour de cassation, Cour des comptes*), or from Universities, large administrative or technical bodies of the State or high-level civil servants. Its

[18] National Institute of Intellectual Property.

members thus have a personal stature that enables them to claim sufficient objectivity and independence. It is essentially the personal status of the members of the college that constitutes the keystone of independence of the authority.

Independence also results from the exercise of the mandate of a member of the authority. The members of the authorities are named for a fixed, and relatively long, term.[19] Their mandate is never renewable thus guaranteeing freedom and excluding any risk of sympathy toward those who named them. The irrevocability of the mandate is an additional guarantee of independence for independent administrative authorities. The *Conseil d'État* has asserted this rule (in the absence of any formal text) and moreover has held that the Government cannot legally put an end to the functions of a president of an independent administrative authority on the basis that he has attained the retirement age within his institution of origin.[20]

Other rules not related to the concept of independence but rather to the concept of impartiality are also retained as for instance the rules of incompatibility that contribute to the independence by preventing the risk of conflicts of interest. There are risks because of the presence of professionals in these bodies. Thus to prevent the risks of conflicts of interests for example, the Members of the *Commission de contrôle des assurances*[21] cannot receive remuneration from an insurance company during their mandate or during the 5 years which follow the end of the mandate.[22]

### 2. *Functional guarantees*

The organic guarantees are supplemented by functional guarantees. The independent administrative authorities exercise full autonomy in respect of administrative and financial management. They have their own administration, managed by their President, while retaining the possibility of calling where necessary upon the services of the State. They are also staffed by officers (civil servants placed at their disposal, *contractuals*) whom they recruit and manage with a good deal of flexibility, particularly given the fact that these bodies do not have to employ solely career civil servants. The president decides upon expenditure, and has a broad discretion in the way it is used, within the limits of the allocated budget. He only has a power of proposal on the budget to be allocated. The government could this use its budgetary capacity to put pressure on the policy of the independent administrative authority. However it has never done this.

[19] Five years for the CNIL, 6 years for the mediator.
[20] CE Ass 7 July 1989 Ordonneau *Recueil* 161.
[21] Commission of the Control of Insurances.
[22] Art 310-12 du code des assurances.

Above all independent administrative authorities are not subject to any hierarchy or supervision: placed outside the public sector hierarchy, they receive neither orders nor instructions from the government and they exert the functions which are entrusted to them with complete freedom. The decisions they take within the scope of their functions have binding force. The only limitations consist in the obligation to publish an annual report, as well as of course the control exerted by the administrative judge. Independent administrative authorities thus break with some of the fundamental principles of state organization, as Dean Hauriou stated 'they have changed our State'.[23]

Independence has an important limit: the legislator can suppress an independent administrative authority. Independence is 'subject to the law'.[24] For example, the legislator could suppress la *Haute autorité de la communication audiovisuelle*. The 'effet-cliquet' places a limit on this exception to the principle of independence. This technique allows the *Conseil constitutionnel* to declare unconstitutional a new legislative norm on the ground this new norm does not maintain the constitutional guaranties which existed in the previous text. The French *Conseil constitutionnel* did not sanction the legislator concerning the suppression of the *Haute autorité de la communication audiovisuelle*, as the legislator instituted a new mechanism to protect communication freedom: the *Commission nationale de la communication et des libertés*.[25]

### C. Administrative authority

'Law is the art of making good classifications.'[26] The role of a lawyer is to place in a given category all new bodies, and thus certain legal consequences will follow from this classifications. More precisely, for independent administrative authorities the question has arisen: which one of the three powers (according to Montesquieu's theory) do they belong; legislative, judiciary, or executive?

The categorization of independent administrative authorities has run up against great difficulties because independent administrative authorities did not match any of the traditional headings of the administrative organization of the State. 'The administrative character of independent administrative authorities is arrived at by a process of elimination.'

[23] Note Maurice Hauriou sous TC 9 Dec 1899 Association syndicale du Canal de Gignac, Sirey (1900) I, 49.

[24] Patrick Wachsmann *Libertés publiques* Dalloz Cours (4th edn 2002) 219.

[25] CC no 86-217 DC 18 Sept 1986, *Recueil* 142.

[26] Bernard Chenot 'L'existentialisme et le droit' *Revue françaisede science politique* (1953) 68.

Are independent administrative authorities part of the legislative power? Without a doubt, independent administrative authorities are not part of the legislative power. Although independent administrative authorities can enact impersonal and general measures, they do not have legislative value and they are not adopted by Parliament.

The independent administrative authorities are not judicial authorities. Confusion could arise because of the theoretical independence of the organizations and their role with regard to regulation, which can amount to punishment.

The case concerning the *Médiateur de la République* gave an opportunity to remove such ambiguity. The *Commissaire du gouvernement* held, after having analysed the characteristics of the *Médiateur,* that: '*Médiateur* cannot belong either to the judicial power or to the legislative power. Thus the *Médiateur* seems, by default, belong to what is called the executive power.'[27]

The *Conseil d'État* followed the conclusion of its *Commissaire du gouvernement* and decided that 'by reason in particular of his mode of nomination (a decree in the Council of Ministers) the mediator has the character of an administrative authority'.[28]

A few years later, the *Conseil constitutionnel* in its decision of 23 January 1987 dealt with this same question by specifying that these organizations were not judicial organs. However, even though they cannot be considered to be judicial organizations, they can nonetheless be regarded as courts within the meaning of Article 6 of the European Convention of Human Rights. The *Conseil d'État*, in its *Didier* decision of 3 December 1999, accepted in accordance with the interpretation of the European Court of the Human Rights to apply Article 6(1) to decisions not originating from a jurisdiction.[29] The Court reconsidered its case-law which had held that only a judicial organization should be recognized as court within the meaning of Article 6(1).[30]

In the *Didier* judgment, the issue was a sanction imposed by the *Conseil des marchés financiers*, an administrative organ holding disciplinary power. However the *Conseil d'État* laid down various conditions. On the one hand, the body in question must take a decision on the merits in respect of criminal matters or obligations as regards civil matters. On the other hand,

[27] CE Ass 10 July 1981 Retail *RDP* (1981) 1441, conclusions Franc.

[28] CE Ass 10 July 1981 Retail Lebon 303.

[29] Thee Conseil d'État, in its decission of 3 Dec 1999 Didier, rules: 'that although—and even though the Conseil des marchés financiers sitting in disciplinary formation is not a jurisdiction as regards national law—the means drawn from what it has ruled under conditions that would not respect the impartiality principle insisted upon under Art 6 s 1 mentioned above can, having regards to the nature, the composition and attributions of this organe becalled upon with basing oneself on an appeal with the the Council d'État against its decision'.

[30] Conseil d'État (avis) 31 Mar 1995 Sarl Auto-Industrie Méric *Recueil* 154.

the decision in question should not be subject to appeal before a court with is subject to procedures satisfying the requirements of Article 6(1).[31]

In view of the foregoing, a conclusion needs to be drawn: independent administrative authorities are administrative authorities. But what is an administrative authority? Unfortunately, there is no legal definition.

One first approach to determine whether we are in the presence of an independent administrative authority is possible: the procedural approach to the notion. An administrative authority is a body which enacts administrative acts. However, whilst it is true that independent administrative authorities take administrative acts, they can also take private law decision, for instance in the case of the *Conseil de la concurrence*. Such an approach is thus unsatisfactory.

One can then try to define this concept by a global solution. Administrative authorities would be defined as collective or individual bodies which act in the name of a public body. As regards independent administrative authorities, they are not equipped with legal personality and they act in the State's name and they engage the State's liability for their harmful acts. For this reason, the independent administrative authorities are indeed administrative authorities. The only qualification to this is the fact that administrative authorities are not attached to the hierarchical structures of central administration yet they are not external to the State. This conclusion should however be nuanced, as the Law no 2003–707 1 August 2003 which created an independent administrative authority equipped with the legal personality, the authority for financial markets which resulted of the fusion of the *Commission des operations boursières* (COB) and the *Conseil des marches financiers*[32] (CMF). This will lead to further interrogations as to the qualification of the authorities.

By way of conclusion of this first sub-section, one can say that the independent administrative authorities are full authorities of the State but independent ones and their administrative nature appears as an element 'in suspension' especially since the *Conseil constitutionnel* in its decision no 86–224 cd of 23 January 1987 relating to the *Conseil de la concurrence* put an end to the automatic link between the administrative nature of independent administrative authorities and the jurisdiction of the administrative courts.

[31] Conseil d'État 3 Dec 1999 Didier Chroniques M Guyomar and P Collin *AJDA* (2000) 126–36; conclusions Alain Seban *RFDA* (2000) 584–98.

[32] Fabrice Melleray 'Une nouvelle crise de la notion d'établissement public' *AJDA* (2003) no 14, 711–17.

## II. THE LEGAL REGIME OF THE INDEPENDENT ADMINISTRATIVE AUTHORITIES

To undertake their activities, independent administrative authorities have wide powers (A). In spite of the independence of these organizations, these wide powers must not be exercised in an arbitrary manner and that is why control mechanisms have been established (B).

### *A. Broad Powers*

Independent administrative authorities are vested with functions of sectoral regulation. Their role is to frame the development of a sector of social life, by ensuring the protection of civil liberties and arbitrating between the various involved interests. Thus by contrast with the judge, the independent administrative authority does not intervene only *ex post facto* to solve disputes but instead they are involved right form the start in order to fix the rules of the game and to define the desirable balance between conflicting interests. The regulatory function comprises of a global dimension and implies recourse to diversified means of intervention.

The independent administrative authority can thus make a recommendation that certain behaviour ought to be observed by private individuals. One should not be misled by this power of recommendation, which is sometimes the equivalent to a real decision-making power[33] that the *Conseil constitutionnel* endorsed in its decision of 18 September 1986. The independent administrative authorities can also make opinions or proposals to the administration, thus involving them in the rule-making procedure and the contributing to the increase of standards.

In addition to this they also have a power of investigation related to their control activity: transmission of information, hearings, investigations by means of documentary evidence and investigations *in situ*. The *Conseil constitutionnel* had the opportunity to come to a decision on this characteristic. The *Conseil* subjected the exercise of this power to Article 66 of the Constitution which institutes the judicial authority as a guardian of the personal freedom. Thus, the *Conseil constitutionnel* considered that the power given to an independent administrative authority to pursue visits in companies and to investigate once there, was in conformity with the Constitution, as long as this power is subject to the law with guarantees ensuring the effective control of the judge.[34]

[33] CE 20 May 1986 Labbé and Gaudin recommendation during elections period of the *Haute autorité de communication audiovisuelle* ; CE 24 Feb 2001 Tibéri recommendation of the *Conseil supérieur de l'audiovisuel* regarding the organization of a debate on TV during the municipal elections between M Delanöé and M Seguin.

[34] CC no 83-164 DC 29 Dec 1983, *Recueil* 67 ; Louis Favoreu and Loïc Philip *Les grandes décisions du Conseil constitutionnel* (Dalloz 2003) no 67.

The independent administrative authority, in order to ensure the respect of their measures, sometimes enjoys a power of injunction. This power of injunction consists in ordering an interested party to adopt such and such behaviour. The power is very important because for several years before the law of 8 February 1995, the administrative jurisdictions did not enjoy a power of injunction in respect of the administration. The independent administrative authorities were thus of real importance in remedial terms.

In the same way, the authorities can also exercise punitive powers. There are two main categories of sanctions: First, sanctions of a professional nature which will limit the perpetrators' capacity to act and the power which could even lead to cessation of their activity; the COB (now, AMF) can therefore prohibit on a permanent or temporary basis, the exercise of all or part of the provided services. Secondly, sanctions of a pecuniary nature, for instance the *Conseil de la concurrence*, can impose a fine of up to 5 per cent of the net turnover of a company.

The authorities can initiate legal proceedings. In some hypothesis, in fact they are *obliged* to do so in accordance with Article 40 of the code of penal procedure which obliges all independent administrative authorities to bring to the attention of an investigating judge all facts which could be punished on the ground of norms whose respect should be controlled by the authority.[35]

The independent administrative authorities also possess, as we have already seen, a decision-making power. It might concern individual decisions or true regulations. But as regards the decision-making power, the decision-making power of the independent administrative authorities has been strictly limited by the *Conseil constitutionnel*.

Indeed, the *Conseil constitutionnel* has been careful to re-assert the traditional rules related to the arrangement of the State powers provided by the Articles 13 and 21 of the Constitution, which set up a sharing of the regulatory powers between the president of the Republic and the Prime Minister. If it has accepted granting a regulatory power to the independent administrative authorities, it is on the condition of being applied within a specific domain and of being exercised within the frame set by the laws and regulations. Thus, the action of independent administrative authorities could not restrict the general decision-making power of the Prime Minister. Moreover, such actions may only concern measures of a limited range (with regard to their scope and content).

Over and above these normative powers, independent administrative authorities possess an essential power of influence and persuasion through the information and the advice they provide; ie through press conferences,

[35] About a refusal of the CNIL to apply the forty articles from the code de procedure pénale CE Sect. 27 Oct 1999, Solana *Recueil* 333.

public meetings, a use of the media and through the publication of measures which they enacted or suggest, and above all, through the annual report on their activity. The annual reports of these institutions are feared as they have an important media impact. The independent administrative authorities preserve a fundamental link with the public opinion and can benefit from the latter's support. This support of public opinion constitutes an essential means of strengthening the institution and is of such nature as to widen its legitimacy and independence *vis-à-vis* the public powers.

### *B. The controlled powers*

Even though the independent administrative authorities might escape from the hierarchical power, they certainly cannot escape from judicial control, namely the control mechanism that the rule of law implies. Some questions remain to be resolved. Which courts have jurisdiction? What is the nature of the exercised control?

#### *1. The control principle*

The very existence of a jurisdictional control in respect of independent administrative authorities has been criticized, with certain commentators considering that an authority can only be independent if it is granted immunity. The debate was covered in a judgment of the *Conseil d'État* (10 July 1981), which laid down that as a rule the administrative judge has jurisdiction to examine the legality of the decisions taken by the mediator. According to Professor Gaudemet:

> The independence granted to the mediator in respect of the exercise of his functions, must result in no judicial scrutiny, because due to the jurisdiction of the administrative judge on his acts, the authority action are subject to the control of the former ... The nature of the institution thus changes ... It would be a new and significant example of the assimilation power of an administrative system, upon which we attach a mechanism unknown to the system itself.[36]

Similarly, with regard to the control of the Mediator's acts by the administrative judge, Stéphane Rials writes that 'the venerable institution of the *Palais Royal* preserved an extraordinary appetite and has managed to assimilate some innovations which prima facie could seem not easily open to traditional analyses'. . . . [37]

Yet, such a thesis is difficult to reconcile with the rule of law. As with any public authority, independent administrative authorities are subject to judicial scrutiny. In addition to that, the *Conseil constitutionnel* has laid down

[36] Note Yves Gaudemet (Dalloz, IR 1981) 528.
[37] Note Stéphane Rials *RDP* (1981) 1441.

the principle of judicial control in two decisions. In the first, of 26–26 June 1986, the *Conseil constitutionnel* emphasized that the law could not exclude 'the other guarantees resulting from the principles and rules of constitutional value and in particular those related to the jurisdictional control and to the rights of defence'. Thus, judicial scrutiny is laid down as a constitutional principle. With its decision of 18 September 1986, the *Conseil constitutionnel* goes further as it specified with regard to the CNCL the legal nature of the independent administrative authorities while at the same time subjecting them to judicial control:

> in the exercise of its functions, the CNCL will, like any other administrative authority, be subject to the control of legality which can be initiated both by the government, which is responsible before the Parliament for the activities of the State's administrative bodies, and by any other person whose interests are at stake.

In the way, the *Conseil d'État*, in its report 1983–4, justifies the judicial scrutiny of the independent administrative authorities on the grounds that it does not impinge upon the principle of independence of the administrative authorities:

> if independent administrative authorities are strictly control by the administrative tribunals and the Conseil d'État, this can be explained by the fact that such a control does not undermine their independence but rather reinforces it.[38]

## 2. *The competent jurisdictions*

One encounters again the problem of the link between the nature of the independent administrative authority and the administrative judge. Jurisdiction is in principle granted to the administrative court over with the decisions of the independent administrative authorities, due to the administrative nature of these bodies. Yet, the legislator can decide the transfer of the dispute to the judicial judge, as is the case for the decisions of the *Conseil de la concurrence*. In their decision of 23 January 1987, the *Conseil constitutionnel* accepted the control of the judicial judge by setting the principles that must govern such an adjustment of jurisdiction. If the *Conseil* could do it, this is because the principle of the separation of the administrative and judicial authorities is not of constitutional value, but

> in conformity with the French conception of the separation of powers, one of the recognized fundamental principles recognized by the laws of the Republic, is that, with the exception of the matters expressly reserved for the (ordinary) judicial authority, the administrative judicial has final jurisdiction in respect of the annulment or the amendment of the decisions made in the exercise of the public powers by

[38] F Gazier and Y Cannac *Etudes sur les autorités administratives indépendantes*, ECDE (1983–4) no 35.

authorities exercising an executive power, their agents, the local authorities (*collectivités territoriales*) of the Republic or the public organizations which are under their control authority or their control.

Nevertheless,

in the realization of that principle, the application of a legislation or of a specific regulation could create diverse legal disputes which could be divided up, depending the customary rules of competence, to the administrative jurisdiction and the judicial jurisdiction, then the legislator is free, in the interest of the good administration of justice, to unify the rules of jurisdictional competence within the judicial order principally concerned.

Hence, the legislator can transfer to the judicial judge the dispute of the *Conseil de la concurrence*. The administrative judge is thus not the only competent person to decide on the legality of the acts of independent administrative authorities.

### 3. *The extent of the control*

The control carried out by the judge is of a variable extent. To begin with, certain acts of the independent administrative authorities cannot be challenged before a judge. Only the acts having the character of a decision can be the object of an appeal. So, mere opinions expressed by the independent administrative authorities are of no deciding character and in this way the opinions of the CADA are unsusceptible to appeal.[39]

Certain decisions are subject to normal review or even maximum review where the subject matter relates to civil liberties or matters of constitutional importance, such as pluralism in the media.[40]

Yet, sometimes the exercised control is a minimum control particularly where the body possesses a discretionary power.[41] The administrative judge will limit himself to verify that the independent administrative authority has not committed a manifest estimation fault.

No matter what the extent of the exercised control, the illegality of the acts of the independent administrative authorities is capable of rendering them liable in damages. The principle of the liability of independent administrative authorities was clearly asserted by the *Conseil constitutionnel* regarding the *Conseil supérieur de l'audiovisuel* in the 17 January 1989 decision.[42] It confirms that 'every decision of the *Conseil supérieur de*

[39] CE 27 Apr 1983 Epoux Deplace no 34, 773.

[40] CE 17 Jan 1990 Union nationale des associations des professions libérales, *Recueil* 9.

[41] CE 19 Jan 1990 Association 'La télé est à nous' *Recueil* 9.

[42] CC 17 Jan 1989 *Recueil*.18; Louis Favoreu *RFDA* (1989) 215 ; note Jean-Louis Autin *RDP* (1989) 490.

*l'audiovisuel* which is in violation of the legislative or regulatory dispositions is capable of giving rise to state liability'.

Independent administrative authorities have, by definition, no legal personality; only the State can be found liable for the wrongs committed and deficiencies discovered during the operation of the authorities. Hence, the harms caused by illegal decisions taken by the authorities can give the right to reparation, just like the wrongs for which they are blamed during the exercise of their supervisory role.

This characteristic of liability reveals the ambiguity on the State of independent administrative authorities: their decision-making and powers of control are exercised in circumstances that guarantee their independence and protect them against any kind of interference by authorities that represent the State, but their potential fault will not affect the directors or funds which the authorities possess. Can the State be found liable for acts which it did not take? Yes, because independent administrative authorities are part of the State.

Independent administrative authorities are hybrid institutions in our legal order, yet hybrid institutions that are well integrated into our administrative reality. As the *Conseil d'État* points out, the independent administrative Authorities have advantages as well as drawbacks; they do not constitute a magical formula and, on that ground.[43]

[43] Conseil d'État *Rapport public 2001, Les autorités administratives indépendantes* (La documentaton française) (2001) 385.

# 3. INDEPENDENT ADMINISTRATIVE AGENCIES IN GERMANY

*Anne van Aaken*

## I. INTRODUCTION

The concept of Independent Administrative Agencies (IAA) is not easy to capture. There are several types of IAAs in Germany which are more or less independent. Only the German Central Bank and the Federal Audit Court may be called genuine IAAs, since they are non-ministerial governmental bodies. Nevertheless, there are other semi-autonomous agencies, such as for example the Federal Cartel Office, which are deemed to be independent. At first sight, these are agencies which in principle fulfil primarily executive functions, but are not entirely subject to executive review. Furthermore, judicial review of their decisions and the position of their highest officials vary quite substantially.

The paper is aimed at giving an overview of IAAs in Germany taking into account their position in the German constitution, the Basic Law (Grundgesetz, GG). In the centre of the following article stands the question of how the constitutionally required principle of democracy may be reconciled with the need for delegation of powers to expert bodies which are independent from day-to-day politics. Pursuant to Article 20 (2) GG all state authority has to emanate from the people. Therefore, a continuous chain of legitimation between the sovereign people and state power must be shown generally for all powers.[1] Germany, as a representative democracy, thus focuses upon parliament as the central body from which all other powers have to derive their legitimacy. The democratic principle of the constitution might thus only be countervailed by other constitutional principles or provisions. Delegation of powers is therefore only legitimate within the borders of the constitution—and where those are situated is debated.[2] IAAs can be found in German legal history since the foundation

[1] Böckenförde 'Demokratie als Verfassungsprinzip' in Isensee and Kirchhof (ed) HdbStR, Bd I (1987) 887, 894, n 11.

[2] Eg, see Barbara Dutzler 'Der Status des ESZB aus demokratietheoretischer Sicht' in Der Staat 41 (2002) 495–522 for some general arguments against IAAs from a constitutional perspective. See also Böckenförde 'Demokratie als Verfassungsprinzip' in Isensee and Kirchhof (ed) op cit 887, 901, Rn 22 and 909.

of the German Reich.[3] Nevertheless, their number, scope of power, and intended tasks varied substantially over the years, becoming ever more important. Nevertheless, it is safe to say that in Germany, concerning the tension between the democratic principle and expert IAAs free from politics, the democratic principle still prevails, unless there are compelling reasons otherwise. IAAs remain an exception and need to be justified under the constitution. Therefore, in general, a legal form which requires dependency on government is chosen even if in practice the principle of non-intervention prevails. To balance the attenuated democratic principle concerning IAAs, the principle of the rule of law is invigorated to bind the IAAs at least to the law. Most IAAs are set up for economic reasons taken in a broader sense. There are nevertheless also IAAs which have as its concern fundamental rights protection, that is, for example, privacy protection or protection of the young by a Commission prohibiting books and media contents deemed dangerous for young people.[4]

## II. IAAS AND THE BASIC LAW

The GG names only the classic powers of government; those three being bound by basic rights as direct valid law.[5] The legislative power being granted to the Bundestag, and partially to the Bundesrat (Chamber of the states; Senate);[6] executive power granted to the Government[7] and judicial power granted to independent courts, which are only subject to the law.[8] IAAs are not mentioned independently from those three powers as a separate power. Administrative Agencies[9] are mentioned in the Constitution, but generally without stating their degree of independence. The only IAA explicitly dealt with in the Constitution is the Federal Audit Court insofar as judicial independence is granted for its members.[10] This is also the only institution for which it was debated in legal literature, if it is independent organ in the constitution and as such a fourth branch of power.[11] It is orga-

[3] An Audit Court, for example, can be found since 1875 in the German Reich; see Norbert Berthold Wagner '50 Jahre Bundesrechnungshof' in AöR 126 (2001) 93–133, 102. See also Stern 'Bundesrechnungshof und Finanzkontrolle aus verfassungsrechtlicher Sicht' DÖV (1990) 261–4.

[4] Bundesprüfstelle; Gesetz über die Verbreitung jugendgefährdender Schiften und Medieninhalte.

[5] Art 1 (III) GG.

[6] Art 76 ff GG.

[7] Art 62 ff GG.

[8] Art 92 and 97 (1) GG.

[9] Talking of administrative agencies, I mean IAAs as well as dependent administrative agencies. If an agency is considered independent, I talk of IAA.

[10] The independence of the organization as such has to be distinguished from the independence of its personnel.

[11] Joachim Wieland 'Rechnungshofkontrolle im demokratischen Rechtsstaat' in DVBl (1995) 894–904, 894. By now it is normally seen not as a constitutional organ, but as an

nized as a *supreme* federal agency ('oberste Bundesbehörde');[12] a status which—apart form the Central Bank—normally belongs only to the ministries and governmental offices. All other agencies which classify as independent have a legal status which as a rule allows for intervention by the government and are therefore part of the administration. In short: German administrative structure allows for two set-ups of high federal agencies: one type is completely independent: the supreme federal agencies and the other type—independent *higher* federal authorities—which are less independent legally and form—in their legal set-up—a subdivision of a ministry.

The Basic Law does not provide detailed information on how federal administration should be organized, but does provide information on how legislative power on the one hand and administrative power on the other have to be distributed between the federal and the state level. It also mentions the basic forms of organizational structures. Therefore, a short overview of the German administrative structure seems necessary.

On the legislative level, states (Länder) do have legislative powers, unless the GG states otherwise.[13] The same applies for the execution of federal laws: states do generally have the power to execute federal laws as well, as a matter of their own concern unless the Constitution provides otherwise, that is, the *federal* government only has the power to review the lawfulness of administrative decisions, but not the power of controlling for expediency or the power of giving instructions to the agencies.[14] Those provisions do, of course, not touch the rights of state governments to give instructions. This finely tuned distribution of power reflects the cooperative federal character of Germany.

Some federal functions may be executed by the states as agents of the federal government, but this set-up is limited to cases named in the constitution.[15] There, the federal government has the right of control for lawfulness (Rechtsaufsicht) and for appropriateness of execution (Fachaufsicht) including the right to give instructions to the highest state authorities. The government may, with the consent of the Senate (Bundesrat), issue general administrative rules; it may also regulate the uniform training of civil servants and other salaried public employees. The heads of authorities at the intermediate level are appointed in conformity with this agreement.[16]

administrative organ; Norbert Berthold Wagner '50 Jahre Bundesrechnungshof' in AöR 126 (2001) 93–133, 128.

12 Apart from the Audit Court and the Central Bank, there are only seventeen supreme Federal Authorities (Oberste Bundesbehörde): the Foreign Service, the Chancellery, the presidential Office, the federal ministries, the press office of the Chancellor, the Federal Commissioner of culture and media.

13 Art 70 GG, see the following articles for the distribution of legislative competencies.

14 Art 83, 84 GG.

15 Eg, nuclear energy statutes may be executed by the states acting as agents for the Federation, Art 87c GG. The same applies for aviation, Art 87d (2) GG.

16 Art 85 GG.

Nevertheless, there are also administrative agencies on federal level, the only ones being treated in this article due to space restrictions. The Basic Law enumerates the possibilities of direct federal administration[17] executing federal laws by federal corporate bodies or institutions under public law with their own administrative substructures. In those cases, the government issues, insofar as the statutes concerned contain no special provisions, pertinent general administrative rules. The government also provides for the establishment of the requisite authorities insofar as the statute concerned does not provide otherwise.[18] In addition, independent federal *higher* authorities ('selbständige Bundesoberbehörde') as well as new federal corporate bodies and institutions[19] under public law may be established by federal legislation for matters on which the Federation has the power to legislate. It is within the power of the legislation to choose the legal form of an agency. It was much debated, for example, whether the new Federal Financial Services Authority[20] should become a separate instrumentality under public law (Bundesanstalt; as it is now) or rather a part of the German Central bank, which is organized as a supreme federal authority also in the form of an independent instrumentality under public law. Those *higher* federal authorities (in contrast to the *supreme* federal authority) may be more or less independent, depending upon the law on which they are based. In general, they are a separate subdivision of a ministry with the right of the respective minister to give instructions, that is to say, they always remain accountable to a ministry. The same applies for the independent corporate bodies—they are also subject to the instructions of the ministry, but may be considered in some cases as IAAs. For the purpose here, only those agencies which are subject to control for lawfulness (Rechtsaufsicht), but not for appropriateness of execution (Fachaufsicht) are deemed independent, if, in addition some other variables, such as the appointment of the head the agency are not made by the ministry.

[17] Eg, the foreign service, the federal finance administration, the administration of federal waterways, and social insurance institutions; Art 87 (1), (2) GG.

[18] Art 86 GG.

[19] These may be foundations under public law (Stiftung öffentlichen Rechts), instrumentalities under public law (Anstalt öffentlichen Rechts) or association regulated by public law (Körperschaft öffentlichen Rechts).

[20] Federal Financial Supervisory Authority (Bundesanstalt für Finanzdienstleistungsaufsicht), established 1 May 2002 and combining the hitherto separated supervision of banking, insurance and securities. Pursuant to §2 Law on Integrated Financial Services Supervision (Gesetz über die integrierte Finanzaufsicht—FinDAG) the authority is subject to control for lawfulness (Rechtsaufsicht), and for appropriateness of execution, by the ministry of Finance. It is thus not deemed to be independent.

## III. NATIONAL DEFINITION OF IAA AND DIFFERENT TYPES

No explicit definition of IAAs exists in Germany. Nevertheless, it is possible to identify a consensus concerning some agencies viewed as independent. One may distinguish institutional, personnel, financial, and functional independence.[21] Institutional independence refers to the legal form taken by the agency including the right of the ministry to give instructions, personnel independence refers to the manner in which the highest members of the body are appointed; financial independence refers to the ability to manage one's own accounts, and functional independence embraces the question as to whether the agency is able to set and specify its own goals. The main criterion of calling an agency independent is the freedom from direct authority exercised by the executive branch, but the degree of independence varies substantially. As described above, administrative agencies have differing legal structures but the legal structure is only partially indicative of the independence of an agency. Rather, drawing a distinction between independent and non-independent administrative agencies is a multi-variable task, which only allows for a classification on a continuum, the most important variables being the possibility for governmental instructions, the position of the head of the AA, the scope of judicial review, the self-governance by by-laws and the precision of law by the legislature (with the goal of independence).

Generally speaking, one can place IAAs in a framework of powers, which is illustrated by the figure on the next page:

Following, I will discuss those variables which influence the degree of independence separately within the analysis of the different IAAs. All IAAs are bound within those depicted powers; just the extent to which they may be influenced varies substantially. Nevertheless, we can clearly distinguish the institutional setting found for the German Central Bank and for the Federal Audit Court on the one hand and other IAAs on the other. The former will be dealt with separately.

### *A. Supreme Federal Authorities*

The Central Bank and the Federal Audit Court are completely independent by law, from the government or the ministry respectively (so-called non-ministerial government). As mentioned above, the Federal Audit Court (FAC) is the only IAA, where the independence of its members is explicitly mentioned in the Constitution.[22]

[21] See for this distinction referring to central banks, Barbara Dutzler 'Der Status des ESZB aus demokratietheoretischer Sicht' in Der Staat (2002) 41 495–522, 496 with further references.

[22] Art 114 (2) for the Federal Audit court, which states that its members have judicial independence, not necessarily the organization as such.

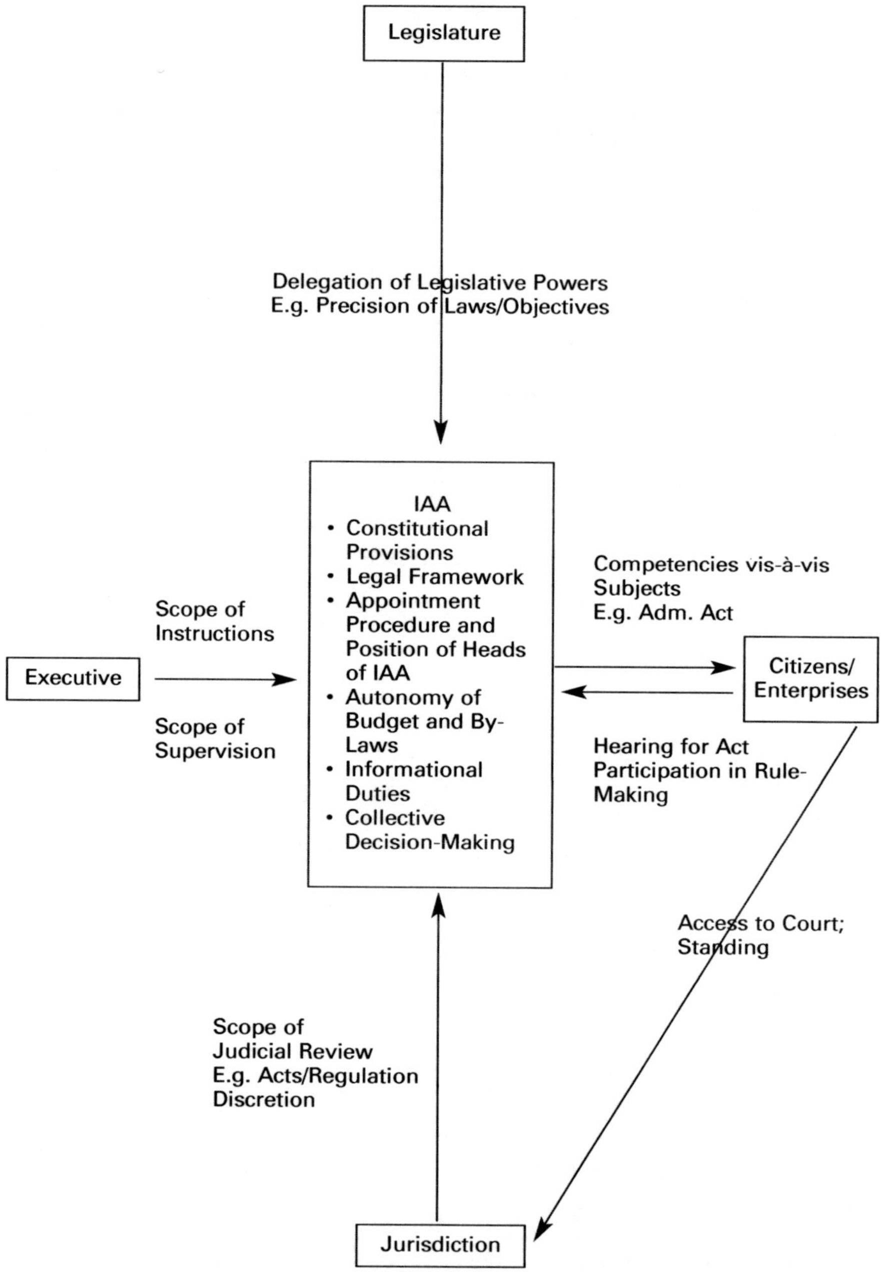


FIG 1: *Independent Administrative Agencies within the network of State powers*

Even though the German Central Bank (GCB) as an institution is mentioned in the constitution, its independence from instructions from the Federal Cabinet is only stated in the law.[23] Interestingly though, pursuant to the constitution, its power may only be conferred to a European Central Bank which is independent.[24] Both, the Central Bank and the Federal Audit Court have the status of supreme federal authorities (oberste Bundesbehörden).[25] They are thus subject to the law alone. Both have the power to give themselves their own by-laws[26] (ie to regulate their internal organization). Their tasks are stated in the laws which regulate them, but only in a general way (ie the goals and the means of carrying those out are stated). There are no provisions concerning the expediency of decisions—those considerations are left to the IAA.

We will first deal with the Federal Audit Court. Judicial independence is granted[27] for the members of the FAC, who are the President, the Vice-President, the heads of audit divisions, and audit units.[28] Thus, neither the executive nor the legislature may give instructions to the FAC.[29] The rest of the personnel does not enjoy judicial independence and they comprise the vast majority of staff working in the FAC.[30] They have to inform the members of the FAC and have to comply with their instructions. The President and the Vice-President are appointed as temporary civil servants for official terms of 12 years, just as Constitutional judges, and shall retire

[23] §12 BBankG. Nevertheless, as far as is possible without prejudice to its tasks as part of the European System of Central Banks, it shall support the general economic policy of the Federal Cabinet and cooperate with the Federal Cabinet, §13 BBankG. The GCB shall advise the Federal Cabinet on monetary policy issues of major importance, and shall furnish it with information on request. Members of the Federal Cabinet are entitled to attend the meetings of the Central Bank Council. They have no right to vote, but may propose motions.

[24] Art 88 s 2 GG. From this amendment of the Constitution in 1992, it is inferred that the GCB also has constitutionally guaranteed independence; see von Mangoldt, Klein, and 'Starck-Blanke' GG vol. 3 (4th edn 2001), Art 88 Rn 24 ff; Dreier-Pernice, GG vol 3 (2000) Art 88, Rn 18 f.

[25] §29 (1) BBankG and § 1 BRHG (Bundesrechnungshofgesetz; Federal Audit Court Act) 'The Bundesrechnungshof shall be a supreme federal authority and as an independent institution of financial control shall be subject only to the law. Within the context of its statutory functions, the Bundesrechnungshof shall provide assistance to the Federal Parliament and the Federal Government in reaching their decisions.'

[26] §34 BBankG: The by-laws of the GCB are adopted by the Central Bank Council. They are subject to the approval of the Federal Cabinet, and shall be published in the Federal Gazette. The Federal Audit Court only has the duty of notification but no need for the approval of the Federal Cabinet, the Bundestag and the Bundesrat, §20 BRHG.

[27] Art 114 (2), 97 GG and § 3 (4) BRHG. For a comparison between the independence of the members of the FAC and judges concerning collective decision-making procedures, allocation of duties and freedom of working time and place, see Hans Blasius 'Zur Unabhängigkeit der Mitglieder der Rechnungshöfe' in VR (1990) 124–9.

[28] §3 (1) BRHG.

[29] See von Arnim, DVBl (1983) 664, 670.

[30] In the year 1990 the members of the FAC granted judicial independence numbered only fifty-six. This small number is justified with the collective decision-making concerning the reports to the Bundestag and the government where the independent members are crucial.

after their tenure of office. They cannot be re-elected.[31] Upon the proposal of the Federal Government, the two Houses of Parliament elect the President and the Vice-President, respectively, without debate. The Bundestag elects its Members by majority vote in a secret ballot. The Federal President appoints those chosen.[32] The Federal President also appoints the other Members and any other officers of the FAC upon the proposal of its President, who shall consult the standing committee of the Senate of the FAC.[33] The President represents the authority. He is responsible for the general management of the FAC and has legal oversight, whereas the other Members shall assist the President in the performance of his functions. Such assistance must not prevent them from pursuing their original duties as Members of the FAC unless they otherwise agree, and their judicial independence must not be impaired.[34] Since 1994 other non-independent employees are appointed by the president of the FAC.[35]

In all other respects, the provisions of the Act on the Federal Civil Service concerning the civil servants appointed for life, are applied accordingly with the exception of the provisions on service careers and probationary periods.[36] The regulations governing independence and disciplinary action relating to judges of the federal supreme courts are applied accordingly.[37] Even though the president of the FAC has supreme authority, the internal decision procedures are taken collectively.[38] Collective deliberation and decision is meant to strengthen independence and autonomy.[39]

The FAC audits the account and examines the management of the budget and the conduct of business as to economy and correctness.[40] It is responsible for the examination of the entire financial management of the Federation, including its Separate Property Funds and undertakings. The

[31] §5 (1) BRHG.
[32] Ibid.
[33] §5 (2) BRHG.
[34] §6 BRHG.
[35] §20a BRHG. This change concerning employees who undertake the main research work (pre-auditing; Prüfungsämter) was brought, about because prior to this, they were part of the administration they were meant to control, thus leading to conflicts of interests. For a discussion, see Herbert Rischer *Zur Neuorganisation des Budnesrechnungshofes—Die Wahrnehmung von Prüfungsaufgaben durch Rechnungsprüfungsämter, Verwaltungsrundschau* (1999) 265–8.
[36] §3 (2) BRHG.
[37] §18 BRHG states that formal disciplinary proceedings against a Member of the FAC and inquiries are subject to the jurisdiction of the Federal Disciplinary Court. In respect of the President and the Vice-President of the FAC, the right of application vested in the supreme government departments under ss 63 Para (2) and 66, Para (3) of the Law on the German Judiciary shall be exercised by the President of the German Bundestag or the President of the Bundesrat.
[38] §8, 9 BRHG and §2 GO-BRH. Nevertheless, the president of the FAC has supreme power and distributes the work at the beginning of the year to the different departments.
[39] For a discussion of the development of collective decision-making in the Audit Courts in German history, see Hans Blasius 'Der Rechnungshof als körperschaftlich-kollegial verfaßte unabhängige Einrichtung' JZ (1990) 954–61.
[40] Art 114 (2) GG.

FAC is also entitled to audit bodies outside the federal administration if they implement parts of the federal budget or have expenses reimbursed by the Federation, administer federal funds or assets, receive grants from the Federation, or are bodies incorporated under private law, directly or indirectly majority-owned by the Federation and/or any of its separate property funds, are not exposed to competition, and if—pursuant to their specified objective—are engaged, entirely or for the most part, in the provision of public services or have been set up for that purpose, and receive for that purpose appropriated federal funds or guarantees from the Federation or one of its separate property funds.[41] It may also audit the management of private-law enterprises if the Federation has direct or indirect shareholdings in private-law enterprises and commercial or industrial cooperatives of which the Federation is a member.[42]

The FAC can determine the timing and nature of the audit and arranges for any necessary on-the-spot investigations to be carried out by its authorized officers. It can call on the assistance of experts.[43] The FAC has access to any information it requires and audited bodies have the duty to present all documents deemed necessary by the FAC.[44] Where, in the opinion of the FAC, a claim for damages should be pursued, it shall notify the agency concerned without delay.[45]

The FAC has a broad scope of audit and the power to examine receipts, payments, commitments to incur expenditure, assets and liabilities, measures with expenditure or revenue implications, provisional account entries for receipts and disbursements, the employment of funds allocated for independent administration (self-administered funds). It may restrict the audit scope and refrain from auditing specific accounts at its discretion.[46] The audit examines whether the regulations and principles of correct financial management have been observed, and in particular whether the Budget Act and the adopted estimates have been adhered to, receipts and payments have been properly substantiated and supported by vouchers, and whether both budget and capital accounts have been properly prepared, funds *are administered efficiently and economically*, functions might be performed with fewer human or material resources, or more effectively by other means.[47] The scope of control is thus very broad and is it debated, as to whether the scope is already political by nature.[48] Control for efficiency and effectiveness was only introduced in 1969 to ensure that not only an ex post control of already terminated administrative decisions takes place, but

[41] §91 BHO. [42] §92 BHO. [43] §94 BHO.
[44] §95 BHO. [45] §98 BHO. [46] §89 BHO.
[47] §90 BHO.
[48] For a discussion see Peter Jakobs-Woltering 'Erfolgskontolle der Rechnungshöfe als Eingriff in den politischen Bereich?' NVwZ (1995) 561–3.

also that current decisions are monitored.[49] The question as to whether the FAC may also check for inefficiencies is hotly debated, as this means that its task is not only classic auditing anymore but rather an all embracing control of the economic efficiency and effectiveness of public administration.[50] As the notion of efficiency is an indeterminate legal term, control of efficiency by the FAC may create tension with the democratic principle.[51] Furthermore, it is argued that the decision as to whether administrative goals may be achieved with extraordinary expenditures is a political question which needs to be decided democratically and not by an IAA.[52]

Another question hotly discussed is the problem of whether the FAC may only audit the administration or also the legislature. If, for example, a member of parliament prompts the administration to act inefficiently or if the financial parliamentary committee takes part in the execution of the budget, it is suggested that the legislature may also be monitored.[53]

By the Basic Law, the FAC is required to submit an annual report directly to the government as well as to the Bundestag and to the Bundesrat.[54] On the basis of its audit findings, the FAC may advise both Houses of the Federal Parliament, the Federal Government, and individual federal ministries. Where the FAC gives advice to Parliament, it will inform the Federal Government at the same time.[55] Apart form the annual reports, the FAC communicates audit findings to the appropriate agencies for comment within a period to be set by it. It may also communicate them to other agencies and to the Appropriations Committee (Haushaltsausschuss) of the Federal Parliament where it deems this to be necessary. The FAC informs the Federal Minister of Finance of any audit results of fundamental impor-

[49] Joachim Wieland 'Rechnungshofkontrolle im demokratischen Rechtsstaat' in DVBl (1995) 894–904, 896.

[50] See, eg, Joachim Wieland 'Rechnungshofkontrolle im demokratischen Rechtsstaat' in DVBl. (1995) 894–904, 896; Vogel and Kirchhof Art 114 in Bonner 'Kommentar'; Böning in Böning and von Mutius (ed) *Finanzkontrolle im repräsentativ-demokratischen System* (1990); von Arnim *Wirtschaftlichkeit als Rechtsprinzip* (1988) 21.

[51] Eg in 1993 the FAC criticized the Ministry of Finance on the ground that it did not sufficiently control lawfulness and expediency of the German Privatization Agency (Treuhandanstalt), referring to its constitutional task. The state Audit court of Hesse issued a press release in March 1995 criticizing the state legislature for not carrying out a financially responsible policy.

[52] Arguing that the control by the FAC is just a control for legality and not a political control is Peter Jakobs-Woltering 'Erfolgskontolle der Rechnungshöfe als Eingriff in den politischen Bereich?' NVwZ (1995) 561–3. It is argued that the supply of data concerning the impact and the costs of political decisions (and thus giving the parliament the data required for their decisions) is the geniune task of the FAC. The consideration of goals, for example, the question as to whether a school or an airport is to be built, is—in contrast—a political decision.

[53] Böning in Böning and von Mutius (ed) op cit 39, 42, 49.

[54] Art 114 (2) GG.

[55] §88 BHO (Bundeshaushaltsordnung; Federal Budget Code).

tance or of considerable financial significance.[56] The FAC may also at any time inform the two Houses of Parliament and the Federal Government of matters of particular importance. Where the FAC reports to Parliament, it shall at the same time inform the Federal Government.[57]

Concerning the control of the FAC itself, the accounts of the FAC are examined by both Houses of Parliament, who both grant discharge.[58] Its accounts are part of the federal budget, but in separate accounts.

The status of the FAC within the constitution was debated for a long time. Some voices considered the FAC to be a constitutional organ whereas others just gave it the status of an administrative agency, even if independent.[59] This debate may be considered concluded as, after a change of the BRHG in 1985, §1 BRHG still talks about a supreme federal authority and not—as in the Act on the Constitutional Court—of a constitutional organ. Nevertheless, in the literature it is called for standing for the FAC in those actions before the Constitutional Court where the formal or material compatibility of federal law or state law is in doubt (abstraktes Normenkontrollverfahren), normally reserved for constitutional organs. This would imply that the FAC could go to court to complain about, for example, the budgetary laws of the Federation. This is not the case at present, that is to say that only one-third of the Bundestag, the Government or a state has standing concerning this question.[60] As the individual citizen has no protection against dubious budgetary laws, since individual rights are not infringed upon, the discussion of control focuses instead on the FAC and, of course, on the sanctions by the European Union. Within the debate on the constitutional status of the FAC, it is also proposed to give it standing before the Constitutional Court in disputes between constitutional organs (Organstreitverfahren, Article 93 Nr 1 GG) concerning the extent of duties or rights of a higher federal body or of other parties concerned who have been vested with rights of their own by the Constitution.[61]

The FAC is considered to be apolitical and acting for the common good. Its press releases were in the last years better received by the public and they play an ever more important role in political debate. Whether the FAC has an active duty to inform the public is debated.[62] But not only is information going from the FAC to the public, the FAC also receives about 600 hints and petitions per year from citizens, mostly concerning issues of wasting tax-payers' money.

[56] §96 BHO. [57] §99 BHO. [58] §101 BHO.

[59] See, for an overview, Stern 'Bundesrechnungshof und Finanzkontrolle aus verfassungsrechtlicher Sicht' DöV (1990) 261–4.

[60] Art 94 Nr 2 GG.

[61] See Häußler 'Zur Antragsbefugnis der Rechnungshöfe im verfassungsrechtlichen Organstreit' DöV (1998) 544–50 and Stern 'Bundesrechnungshof und Finanzkontrolle aus verfassungsrechtlicher Sicht' 261–4, 264.

[62] In favour see von Arnim DVB (1983) 664 (675), and Wieland 902 against.

Judicial control of the FAC seldom occurs. Generally, the work of the FAC and its report do not concern citizens and their rights since they are internal matters of the executive or the parliament. In addition, the acts of the FAC are not legally binding and it does not have the authority to act with administrative coercion. It is thus a knight without sword. Furthermore, the benchmark of audit is not purely legal wherefore the scope of judicial review is substantially narrowed since the courts only review for lawfulness. Nevertheless, some few cases happened in which an action was brought against the FAC from citizens who felt that their rights had been infringed, for example, if they were mentioned in the reports (libel).[63] It is now common opinion that citizens have standing before an administrative court in such cases. Control of the FAC therefore might take place through administrative court review where private rights are infringed.[64]

Let us now turn to the German Central Bank. It is organized as a independent instrumentality under public law[65] which in exercising the powers conferred on it by the BBankG, is independent.[66] Since its independence is not stated in the Constitution, but only in the law, its independence is not viewed as constitutionally required.[67] Nevertheless it is also not seen as constitutionally forbidden. It is not viewed as a constitutional organ. It does not have a constitutionally granted legislative power.[68] Since 1st January 1999 its task has been converted into an advisory and executive function, as its monetary policy decision competence was assigned to the ECB-Council. The GCB is now part of the ECB, that is, that its power to issue notes is now assigned to the ECB. The GCB participates in the performance of the ECB's tasks with the primary objective of maintaining price stability,[69] and arranges for the execution of domestic and international

[63] OVG Münster 18 July 1975 DöV 1979, 682.

[64] See for this discussion Walter Krebs 'Die rechtliche Stellung der Rechnungshöfe und der Vorbehalt des §40 Abs 1 VwGO zugunsten der verfassungsrechtlichen Streitigkeit, VerwArch 71 (1980) 77–85.

[65] 'Bundesunmittelbare juristische Person des öffentlichen Rechts'; §2 BBankG (Gesetz über die Deutsche Bundesbank; Bundesbank Act). Its capital, amounting to 2,5 billion Euro, is held by the Federal Government.

[66] §12 BBankG.

[67] Stating that opinion BVerwGE 41, 334 (354 ff), Stern Staatsrecht II, arguing against that opinion Herdegen in Maunz/Dürig Art 88 GG Rn. 54 f.

[68] BVerwG 41, 334 (351).

[69] BVerfG 89, 155 (207 ff.)—'Maastricht': 'Diese Einschränkung der von den Wählern in den Mitgliedstaaten ausgehenden demokratischen Legitimation berührt das Demokratieprinzip, ist jedoch als eine in Art 88 Satz 2 vorgesehene Modifikation dieses Prinzips mit Art. 79 Abs. 2 GG vereinbar. . . . Diese Modfikation des Demokratieprinzips im Dienste der Sicherung des in eine Währung gesetzten Einlösungsvertrauens ist vertretbar, weil es der—in der deutschen Rechtsordnung erprobten und, auch aus wissenschaftlicher Sicht, bewährten—Besonderheit Rechnung trägt, dass eine unabhängige Zentralbank den Geldwert und damit die allgemeine ökonomische Grundlage für die staatliche Haushaltspoolitik und für private Rechnungen und Dispositionen bei der Warnehmung wirtschaftlicher Freiheitsrechte eher sichert als Hoheitsorgane, die ihrerseits in ihren Handlungsmöglichkeiten und

payments.[70] Interestingly, before 1999 the GCB was not bound by the principle of price stability.

The governing bodies of the GCB comprise the Central Bank Council (Zentralbankrat),[71] the Directorate (Direktorium) and the Executive Boards (Vorstände) of the Land Central Banks.[72] The Central Bank Council and the Directorate of the GCB have the status of supreme Federal authorities (oberste Bundesbehörden).[73] Again, as with the FAC, not all its employees are independent, but only the members (ie the Central Bank Council and the Directorate). The President of the GCB appoints the civil servants of the Bank; he is also the supreme institutional authority (oberste Dienstbehörde), and in this capacity he represents the Bank in and out of court. He disciplines civil servants, except in matters within the jurisdiction of the disciplinary courts, and is the authority instituting formal disciplinary proceedings.[74] The civil servants of the GCB are indirect Federal civil servants. On the whole, the regulations generally applicable to Federal civil servants apply to them.[75]

The *Central Bank Council* acts as the legislative body of the GCB and determines the Bank's business policy. It draws up general guidelines governing the conduct of business and administration, and defines the responsibilities of the Directorate and the Executive Boards of the Land Central Banks, in accordance with the provisions of the BBankG. In specific cases it may also issue instructions to the Directorate (the executive body) and the Executive Boards of the Land Central Banks.[76] The Central Bank Council deliberates under the chairmanship of the President or Vice-President of the GCB. It is also organized as a collective decision making body and takes its decisions by a simple majority of votes.[77]

The President, the Vice-President, and the other members of the *Directorate* are nominated by the Federal Cabinet and appointed by the President of the Federal Republic. Before making such nominations, the Federal Cabinet shall consult the Central Bank Council. Members of the Directorate are appointed for 8 years, or in exceptional cases for a shorter term of office, but not for less than 5 years. Appointments and retirements are published in the Federal Gazette (Bundesanzeiger).[78] Members of the Directorate hold office under public law. Their legal status relative to the

Handlungsmitteln wesentlich von Geldmenge und Geldwert abhängen und auf die kurzfristige Zustimmung politischer Käfte angewiesen sind.'

[70] §3 BBankG.

[71] The Central Bank Council is composed of the President and Vice-President of the GCB, the other members of the Directorate and the Presidents of the Land Central Banks, §6 (2) BBankG.

[72] §5 BBankG.

[73] §29 (1) BBankG.

[74] §35 of the Federal Disciplinary Code (Bundesdisziplinarordnung).

[75] §31 (2) and (3) BBankG.

[76] §6 (1) BBankG.

[77] §6 (3) BBankG.

[78] §7 (3) BBankG.

Bank, and particularly their salaries, retirement pensions and surviving dependants' pensions, are regulated by contracts with the Central Bank Council. These contracts are subject to the approval of the Federal Cabinet.[79]

Concerning the relations between the GCB and the government, the GCB is independent of instructions from the Federal Cabinet in exercising the powers conferred on it by the BBankG, Nevertheless, as far as is possible without prejudice to its tasks as part of the European System of Central Banks, it shall support the general economic policy of the Federal Cabinet.[80] Cooperation is supposed to take place between the government and the GCB in that the GCB advises the Federal Cabinet on monetary policy issues of major importance, and shall furnish it with information on request. Members of the Federal Cabinet are entitled to attend the meetings of the Central Bank Council. They have no right to vote, but may propose motions. The Federal Cabinet should invite the President of the GCB to attend its deliberations on important monetary policy issues.[81] There are thus—if no formal ways of influencing the GCB—certainly implicit ways of influencing its policy.

The accounts of the GCB are audited by one or more auditors appointed by the Central Bank Council in agreement with the FAC. The Central Bank Council then approves the annual accounts, which are thereupon to be published by the Directorate. The GCB is the most independent agency concerning its accounts, since its accounts are not part of the federal budget.[82] The report of the auditors serves as the basis for the audit which the Federal Court of Auditors carries out. The report of the auditors, together with the comments of the FAC are communicated to the Federal Ministry of Finance.[83]

The GCB publishes announcements intended for the general public particularly the calling-in of banknotes, the setting of interest rates, discount rates and minimum reserve ratios, and the ordering of statistics in the Federal Gazette.[84] The GCB may be dissolved only by an Act of Parliament.[85]

Once in a while there are quarrels between the ECB and the government—generally about how to use or evaluate the gold reserves of the bank. Recently it was suggested by government members to use the reserves for financing the East German communities which are highly indebted. A member of the directorate decisively criticized that plan.[86]

[79] §7 (4) BBAnkG. [80] §12 BBankG. [81] §13 BBankG.

[82] Hans Blasius 'Der Rechnungshof als körperschaftlich-kollegial verfaßte unabhängige Einrichtung' JZ 1990, 954–61, 958.

[83] §26 (3) and (4). [84] §33 BBankG. [85] §44 BBankG.

[86] See Handelsblatt 10 Apr 2003: 'Bundesbank gegen Stolpes Sonderfondspläne'. In May and June 1997 there was a serious discussion between the government and the GCB over the

There is no judicial control of GCB policy by citizens as their rights are not infringed by its policies. Also the government is not able to control ECB decisions. Judicial control of the GCB's decisions thus does not take place.

### *B. Higher Federal Authorities*

Sixty-eight higher federal authorities exist as legal organizations, starting with the Department for Alternative Civilian Service, the Fiscal Department, the Department for Traffic of Goods, the Environmental Department, the Department for Radiation Protection, and not ending with the Federal Office for the Protection of the Constitution.[87] Some of them protect individual rights,[88] others have general federal tasks and again others deal with regulating economic affairs. There are several which are deemed independent or semi-autonomous. Here, a sample of those agencies which are deemed independent and which cover all kind of functions, that is, not only economic regulation but also the protection of individual rights, will be analysed. That way an overview of the diversity of IAAs in Germany is provided. This article will deal with the Federal Cartel Office, the Regulatory Authority for Telecommunications and Posts, the Federal Data Protection Commissioner, and the Constituency Commission. These agencies come in different legal forms. The Federal Financial Services Authority—an equivalent to the US-American SEC, is not considered to be an IAA, as it is subject to a control of the appropriateness of its decisions by the ministry.

One agency generally viewed as an IAA is the federal German competition authority, the Bundeskartellamt (Federal Cartel Office; FCO).[89] The FCO is an independent higher Federal authority which is responsible to the Federal Ministry of Economics.[90] The FCO is responsible for the enforcement of the German competition law, the GWB.[91] It has jurisdiction in all

government's plans to revalue the country's gold reserves in order to classify for the EMU. Faced with a budget short-fall and strong political opposition, Germany's then Minister of Finance, Waigel, attempted to introduce a change in the GCB's bookkeeping procedures in order to bring them in line with the standard practices of other European Central Banks. The GCB resisted, arguing that the changes would infringe upon its closely guarded independence.

[87] For an overview of such higher federal authorities, see <http:// www.bund. de/ Verwaltung-in-Deutschland/Bund/Institutionen-des-Bundes/Bundesoberbehoerden-.4393.htm>.

[88] Eg, Bundesamt fuer ausländische Flüchtinge, which as a higher federal authority is part of the Ministry of Interior.

[89] §51 (1) Act against Constraints of Competition (Gesetz gegen Wettbewerbsbeschränkungen; hereinafter GWB) mentions the Federal Cartel Office as an independent higher federal authority (selbständige Bundesoberbehörde).

[90] §51 (1) GWB.

[91] Other agencies responsible for competition matters are the Ministry of Economy and the state competition authorities, §48 GWB.

cases that have effect beyond one of the federal states (Länder). While the FCO is technically subordinate to the Federal Minister for Economics (FME), in practice, policy decisions are usually made by the FCO.[92] Such decisions are given to the FME only when they have some overt political significance.[93] Furthermore, the FCO exercises direct cartel authority except in three specific situations,[94] in which direct political responsibility for a decision is considered desirable and the cartel authority is exercised by the FME. Otherwise, the FME only indirectly exerts influence over the FCO through its ministerial duties.[95] The FCO does thus not have the final authority over German mergers and acquisitions. That authority is reserved for the political level, the Ministry for Economics,[96] which on more than one occasion has overruled the FCO.[97] Nevertheless, the Minister until now has not given specific instructions for decisions of the FCO.[98] In practice, thus, the FCO is deemed quite independent.[99] The FCO is deemed to take a legalistic approach to competition issues, while the FME, as a political

[92] In between those two there is also the Commission of Monopolies (Monopolkommission) which has as its task to supervise the economic concentration in Germany and to notify the Government and the public about this. It is also consulted for legislative projects. To this end, the Commission delivers advisory opinions as to legislative power. The Commission is independent and has five members experienced in economics, competition law, technology, and business administration. They are nominated by the Government and appointed by the Federal President for 4 years and may be re-elected. They shall not be members of the legislature, the government, or the public service (except professors or staff members of scientific institutions) and shall not represent a trade union or an employer's organization, and should not have done so up to one year before taking office, §§44 GWB.

[93] See James Maxeiner, *Policy and Methods in German and American Antitrust Law 1* (1986) 92.

[94] These three situations are: (1) when a cartel agreement which is prohibited by s 1 of the GWB does not fall within one of the exceptions in ss 2–7 and the FME finds that 'the restraint of competition is necessary for overriding reasons concerning the general economy and the common welfare' (2) when an export cartel is an agreement or resolution which 'serves to protect and promote exports, provided that they are limited to the regulation of competition in markets outside the territory in which this Act applies'; and (3) when ministerial authorization is allowed because 'the restraint of competition is compensated by the overall economic advantages'.

[95] The FME can exert ministerial authority in several ways: (1) by issuing directives to the FCO office, (2) by making appointments to the decision divisions, (3) by attaching its opinions to the FCO's biannual report, and (4) by resolving conflicts between the FCO and other governmental authorities responsible for regulated industries.

[96] See Alissa A Meade 'Modelling a European Competition Authority' (1996) 46 Duke LJ 153, 172 f.

[97] See, eg, the most famous recent case of the takeover of Ruhrgas by EON. The FCO forbade the takeover, but the Minister of Economic Affairs allowed it. Owing to an action by nine competitors, the OLG Düsseldorf forbade the takeover in a provisional hearing. The ministerial permission was then reformulated more strictly and the court further upheld its own decision. Just before the hearings in January 2003, EON reached a settlement with the competitor-claimants and so the takeover could proceed.

[98] Wilhelm Eschweiler 'Die Regulierungsbehörde im Spannungsfeld zwischen Unabhängigkeit und Weisungsunterworfenenheit' K&R (2001) 238–42, 241.

[99] It is even said that it amounts to customary law that the minister does not issue specific instructions, see Möschel ORDO vol 48 (1997) 241, 245.

government cabinet, does not.[100] This may create tension because the FME pursues national economic policies that sometimes do not promote free competition. Accordingly, the FCO's decisions do not always coincide with the FME's interests. The German system was established with these countervailing powers because it was envisaged that the authority with the most direct effect on competition should not be one subjected to excessive political lobbying or to public opinion, but rather one which applies the laws and policies in a highly legalistic manner.[101]

Because the FCO's staff and management are not elected but appointed by the government (for the president of the FCO: on nomination of the Minister of Economics) as lifelong civil servants,[102] the institution is generally considered to be apolitical. They may also not own or manage any undertakings, nor may they be members of a management board of an undertaking or a professional organization.[103] The FCO is thus generally viewed upon as independent from the business community.

Decisions of the FCO are made by decision divisions established in accordance with instructions by the Federal Ministry of Economics. Since decisions within the division units are made by a chairperson and two other members ('tres faciunt collegium'),[104] there is a collective decision-making procedure and the decision units are deemed to act quite independently. For other matters, the President determines the allocation and handling of duties in the FCO by rules of procedure requiring confirmation of the Ministry.[105] Any general instruction given by the Ministry of Economics with regard to the issuance or non-issuance of decisions pursuant to the GWB is published in the Federal Gazette.[106] Due to this provision, the instructions are made transparent and prevent undue influence by the Ministry. This enables the public to criticize decisions taken and the influence by the ministry.[107]

Every 2 years the FCO publishes a report on its activities and on the situation and development in its field of responsibilities. The report includes the instructions given by the Ministry. The Government submits the report to the Bundestag together with its comments.[108] It also has to regularly publish its administrative principles,[109] and several individual decisions or ministerial authorizations enumerated by the law in the Federal Gazette.[110]

100 This is most evident in the FME's use of its ministerial authority to approve mergers which the FCO had prohibited when the FME believes that the public interest outweighs the restraint on competition that results from the merger. See GWB 24(3).

101 See Meade op cit 153, 172 f.

102 §51 (4) GWB.

103 §51 (5) GWB.

104 Digesten 50, 16, 85.

105 §51 (2) GWB.

106 §52 GWB.

107 Nevertheless a violation of the publishing requirement does not render the instruction or the decisions based on it illegal, see Eschweiler op cit 238–42, 240.

108 §53 (2) GWB.

109 §53 (1) GWB.

110 §43 GWB and §62 GWB.

The FCO has the power to institute administrative proceedings ex officio or upon application. It may also do so for the protection of a complainant. Parties in those proceedings are the complainants, persons or associations whose interests are substantially affected or those against who the proceedings are directed.[111] It has normal administrative powers and may issue administrative acts, that is to say, it may prohibit certain activities or it may impose administrative fines.[112] It is supposed to give the parties involved an opportunity to comment and, on request, summons them to a hearing. Furthermore, it may give representatives of business circles affected by the proceedings an opportunity to comment. This is in accordance with the general administrative rules concerning hearings of the parties concerned,[113] but stated separately in the GWB. In a proceeding concerning abuse of dominant market position (§19 GWB), the FCO shall decide on the basis of a public hearing, if no important reasons indicate otherwise.[114] Also, in accordance with the general administrative rules, it is necessary for the FCO to include a statement of reasons and advise as to available legal remedies in their decisions.[115]

The FCO may also conduct any investigations and collect any evidence required on its own. It may request all information needed to conduct its task from the persons and undertakings under investigation. This includes information on their economic situation as well as the surrender of documents. It may inspect and examine business documents during normal business hours. The constitutional right of inviolability of home and office (Article 13 GG) is thus restricted. Searches may only be conducted with the consent of a local judge, unless there is danger in delay; then the persons entrusted with the task by the FCO may act alone—here the same rules apply as for criminal proceedings.[116] It may also seize objects which may be of importance as evidence in the investigation.[117] In this case, the FCO has to seek confirmation by the local Court within three days.[118] The person affected by the seizure has to be informed without undue delay about the seizure and his rights and may request judicial review of the seizure at any time.[119]

The FCO may issue preliminary injunctions in cases specified in the law to regulate matters on a temporary basis. Decisions of the FCO may be appealed and may be based on new facts and evidence. All parties who may have an interest in the proceedings may also appeal, ie competitors also have standing before the court. An appeal may also be made if the FCO

[111] §54 GWB.

[112] It just imposed a record fine of about 660 million Euro to a cartel of cement in Germany, involving all big producers of cement, see *Financial Times Deutschland* 14 Apr 2003.

[113] §28 VwVfG.

[114] §56 (3) GWB.

[115] §61 (1) GWB.

[116] §58 GWB.

[117] §57 GWB.

[118] §58 (2) GWB.

[119] §58 (3) GWB. The respective norms of the code of Criminal Procedure apply.

fails to make a decision in an application.[120] An appeal has in general a suspensory effect unless the GWB states otherwise or the FCO orders immediate enforcement if it is required by public interest or by the prevailing interest of a party.[121] The suspensory effect is a general principle in German administrative law and is deemed a manifestation of the constitutional principle of the rule of law (Rechtsstaatlichkeit).[122] Exceptions to it are more and more prevalent for public interest reasons, so the GWB is not an exception allowing for the immediate effect of decisions.

An appeal has to be made exclusively by the Court of Appeal (Private Law Court) of the district in which the FCO has its seat, which is the Court of Appeals in Düsseldorf.[123] There is thus an exclusive jurisdiction of one court guaranteeing uniformity in court decisions and excluding forum-shopping. The court examines the facts ex officio and informs the parties also ex officio[124]—a deviation from the Code of Civil Procedures and a rapprochement to the administrative procedures. The court may reverse the decision of the FCO, or, if it has become moot, declares its non-admissibility. It may find the decision by the FCO inadmissible only if the FCO has improperly exercised its discretionary powers, in particular if it has exceeded the statutory limits of its discretionary powers or if it has exercised its discretion in a manner violating the purpose and intent of the GWB.[125] The scope of judicial review is thus limited to lawfulness and to the interpretation of indeterminate legal terms in the GWB. The decisions of the Court of Appeals may be appealed only on grounds of law.

We will now turn to the Regulatory Authority for Telecommunications and Posts (RegTP).[126] This agency is especially interesting due to the existence of an independent agency which is supposed to regulate the market impartially and independent from the fact that its regulation mainly affects the former state monopoly in which the State still holds stakes, which is much debated. The reason for setting it up was not only European Directives,[127] but the insight that the former monopoly operators in the postal and telecommunications markets, Deutsche Post AG and Deutsche Telekom AG, will be able to maintain their dominant positions long after

[120] §63 (1)-(3) GWB. [121] §§64 f. GWB. [122] §80 VwGO.

[123] §63 (4) GWB. [124] §70 (1) and (2) GWB.

[125] §71 (5) GWB.

[126] For a comparison with the US FCC, see Winfried Ulmen and Thomas Gump *Die neue Regulierungsbehörde für Telekommunikation und Post CR* (1997), 396–402.

[127] Commission Directive 90/388/EEC of 28 June 1990 on open competition in the markets for telecommunications services states that 'Member States must ensure that from 1 July 1991 the granting of operating licences, the control of type approval and mandatory specifications, the allocations of frequencies and surveillance of usage conditions are carried out by a body independent of the telecommunications organizations.' The Directive 97/51/EG also asks explicitly for independence. The WTO also commands an IAA in Nr 5 of the fourth protocol of the General Agreement on services of Apr 1997.

market liberalization.[128] The general competition law was thus deemed not enough to regulate the market. The core task of state regulation is to keep a check on each dominant provider's position in the market and to create a level playing field to protect the new entrants. The tasks associated with such regulation are deemed too specialized to be fulfilled under general competition law. Hence the need for sector-specific regulation, at least until effective competition is established in the postal and telecommunications markets. The federal government's regulatory approach hence goes beyond merely policing anti-competitive behavior ex post but regulates the market ex ante.

Article 87f (2) section 2 GG requires that telecommunications and postal service is regulated by federal administration itself. This implies, as in Art. 86 GG, that the agency has to be submitted to ministerial supervision. It was thus not set up as a supreme federal authority.[129] The Regulatory Authority is tasked with promoting the development of the postal and telecommunications markets through liberalization and deregulation,[130] but the plurality of goals stated in the law give the agency considerable freedom when weighing those goals.[131] The agency is supposed to be a framer, as its sets rules for the market, a controller, and an arbitrator.[132]

The RegTP is a higher federal authority within the scope of business of the Federal Ministry of Economics and Labour, and has its headquarters in Bonn.[133] In derogation of the provisions of the Restraints of Competition Act, there is no scope for ministerial decisions.

[128] Independence is partially guaranteed by the fact that RegTP is part of the Minstry of Economics, whereas the shareholders interests of the Federation are administered by the Ministry of Finance. The Federation holds directly or indirectly 43 per cent of the shares and thus is the biggest shareholder of Telekom.

[129] Gunnar Bender 'Regulierungsbehörde quo vadis?' K&R (2001) 506–15, 508.

[130] BT-Drucksache 13 3609, S 51.

[131] See §1 and 2 of the Telecommunications Act (Telekommunikationsgesetz; hereinafter TKG) for regulatory purposes and aims. The RegTP's main functions under the Telecommunications Act ('TKG') and the Postal Act ('PostG') are, through liberalization and deregulation, to safeguard the interests of telecommunications, postal and radiocommunications users and maintain telecommunication and postal secrecy, ensure fair and effective competition, in rural as well as urban areas, in the markets, ensure provision throughout Germany of basic telecommunications and postal services (universal services) at affordable prices, promote telecommunications services in public institutions, ensure efficient, interference-free use of frequencies while accommodating broadcasting requirements, protect public safety interests. Also part of the RegTP's remit, aside from regulation of the telecommunications and postal markets, are, for instance licence awards, provision of input for standardization solutions, frequency management and number administration, tracing and eliminating radio frequency interference, market watch, and consumer advice, especially on new regulations and their implications.

[132] Bender op cit 506–15.

[133] This is criticized by Telekom competitors as Telekom also has its headquarters there and cooperation is feared due to personal linkages.

The President and two Vice-Presidents are appointed by the Government upon the proposal of the advisory Council of the RegTP and nominated by the President of the Federation. If the government does not approve the proposal, the council has the right to make other propositions.[134] The President of the RegTP, who represents the authority in and out of court, determines the distribution and course of business by rules of procedure, which require confirmation by the Minister.[135] Where the Minister gives general instructions governing the issue or non-issue of decisions under the TKG to the RegTP, they have to be published in the Federal Gazette—this provisions stems from competition law.[136] Those instructions concern not a specific case but some guidelines concerning the application of the law, for example an interpretation of indeterminate legal terms. Until now the Minster did not issue any general instruction.[137] The question as to whether the Minister may issue specific guidelines to the RegTP is hotly debated. Even though the law provides only for general instructions, an analogy is drawn to the FCO and a constitutional argument is made that there is only exceptionally non-ministerial government. As the general principle of administration is hierarchy (Article 65 GG), no special law is considered necessary to allow for specific instructions. It is argued, that if the legislature would have wanted a non-ministerial agency, it would have needed to set up the RegTP as a supreme federal authority. On the other hand it is argued that if the law states only general instruction, specific ones must be excluded. Furthermore, the similarity of the Chambers' decision-making to judicial decision-making bodies militates for independence as the instruction chain to the minister is broken by this.[138]

Section 67(1) and (2) TKG provide for the constitution of an Advisory Council at the RegTP.[139] The Council consists of nine members of the German Bundestag and nine from the German Bundesrat. The members and their deputies are appointed by the federal government upon the

[134] §66 (3) and (4) TKG. [135] §66 (2) TKG. [136] §66 (5) TKG.

[137] This applies for the telecommunication area; for the postal area there was one; see Eschweiler op cit 238–42, 240.

[138] See for this discussion ibid 238–42, 240 f.

[139] The Advisory Council, which is required to meet at least once a quarter, has the following functions under s 69 of the Act: 1. It makes proposals to the federal government on appointment of the President and Vice-Presidents of the RegTP. 2. It participates in the decisions made under s 73(3) of the Act. This means that determinations on award proceedings for licences, as set out in s 11 and on the imposition of universal service obligations as set out in s 19, are made in consultation with the Advisory Council. 3. It is entitled to request measures with which to implement regulatory aims and ensure universal service. The RegTP must decide on its response within a period of 6 weeks. 4. It is entitled to obtain information and comments from the RegTP which has a duty to provide all such information. 5. It advises the RegTP in the preparation of the report on its activities which the RegTP is required under s 81(1) of the Telecommunications Act and s 47(1) of the Postal Act to submit every 2 years to the legislative bodies of the Federal Republic. It must be consulted during the preparation of the frequency usage plan as specified in s 46 of the Telecommunications Act.

proposal of the Bundestag and the Bundesrat. The members belonging to the Bundestag are appointed for the duration of the legislative period (ie 4 years). Reappointment is possible. Members of the Bundesrat are also appointed for 4 years but may be removed at will if another person is proposed.[140] The Council decides by collective decision-making with simple majority in non-public meetings.[141] It is autonomous in giving its own by-laws but needs the confirmation of the Minister,[142] which again limits the independence of the RegTP.

Every 2 years the RegTP submits a report on its activities and the development of the telecommunications sector to the legislative bodies. It also publishes at regular intervals in its official Gazette the principles of its administration, in particular those relating to licensing conditions. It also submits a biannual report to the Monopoly Commission concerning the question as to whether regulation pursuant to the TKG continues to be necessary.[143]

The Regulatory Authority's determinations are made by its Ruling Chambers. The Chambers rule generally in the composition of a chairman and two assessors[144]—this collective decision-making again is in analogy to competition law. The members of the Chamber are lifelong civil servants appointed by the minister.[145] This fact gives the minister considerable influence. Their decisions are taken by means of an administrative act which allows for direct control by Administrative Courts as no preliminary proceedings within the authority are permitted.[146] This is contrary to the general administrative principle of §68 VwGO. The determinations can thus not be quashed by the supervisory authority (the Economics and Labour Ministry) in the event of legal action. By this means it is guaranteed that the minister cannot influence the decisions of the RegTP, and these are solely controlled by the court. Thus, greater independence is achieved. Legal action against the RegTP does not have an automatic suspensory effect—in contrary to the general principle.[147] This aims at prohibiting the regulated entities to obstruct the regulation and render it ineffective by going to court. Nevertheless, it is possible through general administrative law to appeal to court to reinstate the suspensory effect in a preliminary decision.[148] Apart from those specific norms, proceedings and standing are the same as in competition law.[149] The companies directly concerned take part in the Ruling Chamber proceedings. Representatives of business circles affected may be summoned to attend proceedings. In particular, the RegTP

140 §67 (2) TKG.
141 See for desicion procedures of the Council §68 TKG.
142 §68 (1) TKG.
143 §81 TKG.
144 §73 TKG.
145 §73 (1) TKG.
146 §80 (1) TKG
147 As a rule, appeals against administrative decisions have a suspensory effect; §80 (1) VwGO.
148 §80, 80a, 123 VwGO.
149 See §§74 ff TKG.

is equipped with the same effective procedures and instruments with which to enforce the regulatory aims as the FCO concerning inspection, auditing, requesting information and searches.[150] These include information and investigative rights as well as a set of sanctions, similar to those of the FCO.

One problem highly discussed in the literature and pending in the courts is the question of right of disclosure by competitors concerning the information the RegTP has. In general administrative law, the right of access to the respective files is granted if there is a justified interest. In economic issues concerning competitors, the agency has to weigh the interests of the parties concerned. It was decided by the OVG Münster[151] that competitors may not have the right to access to the files; a decision now pending with the BVerwG and much criticized as it makes it almost impossible for the competitors to bring a substantiated claim against the RegTP.[152]

As a general rule, judicial review is encompassing, especially concerning indeterminate legal terms, with the exception of prognostic considerations concerning the market and the usual discretion.[153] There is thus only small room for non-controllable decisions by the RegTP.

One IAA will be treated here which has as its task the protection of individual right. The Federal Data Protection Act 1990 grants the individual data subject a variety of possibilities aiming at the respect of his individual data protection rights, a constitutional right developed by the Constitutional Court. There are in the first place the means of self-protection of the individual. Public and private-sector organizations must on request provide the citizen with details of the data they hold on him.[154] An independent Federal Data Protection Commissioner was nevertheless deemed necessary to effectively implement and enforce those rights. The Federal Data Protection Commissioner is responsible for the audits/controls of all federal agencies, all telecommunication services and all postal services.

The Federal Parliament elects, on a proposal from the Government, the Federal Data Protection Commissioner with over half of the statutory number of its members, that is to say not the usual simple majority of those members of parliament present. The candidate must be at least 35 years old at the time of his election. The person elected is appointed by the Federal

[150] §72 TKG.

[151] OVG Münster, K&R 1999, 41 = MMR 1999, 553 ff. Nevertheless it is argued that the RegTP is not favouring the Telekom, as the Telekom appeals against almost all the decisions of the RegTP. As the court proceedings up to the highest court take a lot of time, legal security is for the moment almost non-existent.

[152] See for details Bender op cit 506–15, 513.

[153] See for details Robert Heine and Robert Neun 'Konkurrentenklagen im Telekommunikationsrecht, Die gerichtliche Kontrolle von Entscheidungen der RegTP' MMR 6 (2002) 352–60, 357 ff.

[154] §19 and 34 of the Federal Data Protection Act—Bundesdatenschutzgesetz (BDSG).

President.[155] The term of office of the Commissioner is 5 years; it may be renewed once.[156] The Federal Commissioner is established with the Federal Ministry of the Interior. The incumbent has a public-law official status with respect to the Federation.[157] He is provided with the personnel and material resources necessary for the performance of his duties. These resources are shown in a separate chapter of the budget of the Federal Ministry of the Interior. The posts of his office are filled by the Minister in agreement with the Federal Commissioner. If they do not agree to the envisaged measure, staff members may be transferred, delegated or relocated only in agreement with the Federal Commissioner.[158] He is independent in the performance of his duties[159] and subject to the law alone.[160] He is subject to legal supervision (Dienstaufsicht) by the Federal Ministry of the Interior.[161] The Commissioner may only be removed against his will by the Federal President on the proposal of the Government when there are grounds which, in the case of an established judge, justify dismissal from service.[162] The Commissioner may not hold any other paid office,[163] such as an office in a supervisory board or management or obligations to secure his independence.[164]

The Commissioner monitors compliance by public bodies of the Federation with the provisions of the Federal Data Protection Act and other data protection provisions.[165] Where personal data in records are processed or used, the Federal Commissioner monitors their collection, processing or use if the data subject adequately indicates that an individual's rights have been infringed or if the Commissioner has in his possession adequate indications of such infringement.[166] Public bodies of the Federation are obliged to support the Commissioner and his assistants in the performance of their duties.[167] In particular they are granted information in reply to their questions as well as the opportunity to inspect all documents and records, espe-

155 §22 (1)–(5), (23) BDSG.

156 §22 (3) BDSG.

157 §22 (4) BDSG.

158 §22 (5) s 1, ss. 3–5 and (6) BDSG.

159 Eg, §23 (4) BDSG rules that the Commissioner is entitled to refuse to give testimony as a witness against persons who have entrusted information to him in his capacity as Federal Commissioner and on such information itself. This also applies to the staff of the Federal Commissioner, on condition that he decides on the exercise of this right. Within the scope of the Commissioner's right to refuse to give testimony as a witness, he may not be required to submit or surrender records or other documents.

160 See also Directive 95/46/EC s 28 (1), where it is required that the Commissioner acts with complete independence in exercising the functions entrusted in him.

161 §22 (5) s 2 BDSG.

162 §23 (1) BDSG.

163 The Commissioner receives the remuneration of a grade B 9 federal official which means that his salary—and thus by implication his rank—is that of head of department in a federal ministry, §23 (7) BDSG.

164 §23 (3) BDSG.

165 §24 (1) BDSG.

166 Federal courts are subject to monitoring by the Commissioner only where they deal with administrative matters. §24 (3) BDSG.

167 §24 (4) BDSG.

cially stored data, data processing programmes, and access to all official premises at any time. The Commissioner informs the respective public body of the results of his monitoring. If he discovers infringements of the Federal Data Protection Act or of other data protection provisions or other irregularities in the processing or use of personal data, the Commissioner will submit a complaint to the competent authority. In the case of the federal administration he does so with the supreme federal authority and he requests a statement by a date which he determines.[168] The Commissioner may dispense with a complaint or with a statement from the body concerned especially if the irregularities involved are insignificant or have meanwhile been rectified.[169] He may combine a complaint with proposals for improving data protection, especially for rectifying irregularities discovered in the processing or use of personal data.[170]

The office of the Commissioner prepares an annual plan for its activities regarding supervision, investigation and auditing. It is free to set its own priorities and to create its own agenda which is enabling it to be more responsive to current affairs. The several units of the Commissioner's office carry out investigations into various types of information systems, based upon citizens' complaints or a suspicion that a particular area requires detailed examination. Systematic audits are planned over a several-year period, thus increasing the scope and range of data protection activities. Every 2 years the Federal Commissioner submits an activity report to the Federal Parliament. Such a report should also contain a description of the main developments concerning data protection in the private sector. The federal report is delivered to the President of the Federal Parliament and then published as an official document of the legislature.[171] The Commissioner will also, when so requested by Parliament or the Government, draw up opinions and reports. He also investigates data protection matters and occurrences at public bodies of the Federation, when so requested by the Federal Parliament, the Petitions Committee, the Internal Affairs Committee or the Federal Government. It is the Federal Commissioner's right to consult Parliament in a direct manner at any time.[172] The Commissioner may make recommendations on the improvement of data protection to the Federal Government and to certain bodies of the Federation and may advise them in matters regarding data protection.[173] In a practical manner this means that the Commissioner assists in the development of new laws on data protection, the modification of existing laws and the establishment of new guidelines. The Commissioner

[168] §25 (1) BDSG. [169] §25 (2) BDSG. [170] §24 (5) BDSG.

[171] §26 (1) BDSG. Afterwards the report is printed in brochure form and contained in a CD-ROM version both of which are available free of charge at the Commissioner's office.

[172] §26 (2) BDSG. [173] §26 (3) BDSG.

advises federal ministries and individual committees of the Parliament on the implications of a great many different legislative proposals.

Concerning the rights of the individual citizen, there are plenty of provisions in the Act.[174] If personal data are stored for the first time, generally the data subject has to be notified of this storage.[175] It is an important tool in answering the question as to who is processing what data about an individual. Furthermore there are the data subject's rights to correction, erasure and blocking of data[176] and the possibility to exercise the right of objection vis-à-vis the controller of the data file to the use or communication of data for purposes of advertising or of market or opinion research.[177] Anyone may appeal to the Commissioner if he believes that his rights have been infringed through the collection, processing or use of his personal data by public bodies of the Federation.[178]

Another Commission which may be deemed independent is the Constituency Commission whose role is to deliver constituencies.[179] The appointment of an independent commission aims to avoid gerrymandering by political parties. The permanent Constituency Commission is appointed by the Federal President. It consists of the President of the Federal Statistical Office, a judge from the Federal Administrative Court, and five other members. The Commission has the task of reporting changes in the population figures in the electoral area and to show whether and which changes in the division of the electoral area into constituencies it considers necessary. In its report, it may also propose changes for other reasons. The report is submitted to the Federal Ministry of the Interior within 15 months of the beginning of the legislative term of the Bundestag. The Federal Ministry of the Interior forwards it to the Bundestag immediately and publishes it in the Federal Gazette. On request of the Federal Ministry of the Interior, the Commission must submit a supplementary report. Again, we find the principle of the rule of law as a countervailing force to the independence of the Commission: when it is making proposals concerning the division of the electoral area into constituencies, it has to observe certain principles specified in the law.[180] If there is a change proposed in the constituencies—as after the federal election in 1998—the Bundestag then decides on a modifi-

174 See §§33 ff BDSG.

175 §33 (1) BDSG.

176 §20 and §35 BDSG.

177 §28 (4) BDSG.

178 §21 BDSG. This applies to the collection, processing or use of personal data by courts of the Federation only in so far as they deal with administrative matters.

179 §3 Federal Electoral Law (Bundeswahlgesetz; BWahlG).

180 §3 (1) BWahlG states as follows: '1. The Länder boundaries shall be respected. 2. The number of constituencies in the individual Länder shall correspond to the population proportion as far as possible. 3. The population of a constituency should not deviate from the average population of the constituencies by more than 15 per cent in either direction; where the deviation is greater than 25 per cent, the boundaries shall be redrawn. 4. Each constituency should form a coherent area. 5. Where possible, the boundaries of the communes, districts and urban districts should be respected.'

cation to the Federal Election Act. It generally follows the proposals of the Commission.

## IV. CONCLUSION

Germany is very cautious of setting up IAAs due to the constitutional principle of democracy. Even if independence from the political day-to-day life is required or deemed important, Germany is reluctant to set-up strictly non-ministerial government. Thus, only the agencies mentioned in the constitution are set up as supreme federal Authorities, which act in complete independence. Also These are generally not subject to judicial review, since individuals are not directly affected by their decisions.

All other agencies are set up as independent higher federal authorities, even if independence is required in EC law or WTO law. Thus, ministerial instructions are possible, but those have to be published. In practice, the respective Ministry responsible, abstains from issuing specific instructions. If the agencies are concerned with economic regulation or with the protection of individual rights, the affected parties have standing in court and thus judicial review is permitted. This judicial review is—in accordance with the development of general administrative law—quite all embracing; with the exception of discretionary decisions, in general, the interpretation of the law by the agency is fully controlled by the courts. As a countervailing measure to their general dependency, decisions within the agencies are made by chambers, thus permitting collective decision-making. The Heads of the agencies are appointed by the whole government and generally may not be removed at the will of a Minister.

In short: even if most of the IAAs are legally dependent, influence by the executive branch is minimized as far as possible through various means.

# 4. INDEPENDENT ADMINISTRATIVE AUTHORITIES IN ITALIAN LAW

*Roberto Caranta**

## I. ON TERMINOLOGY (QUESTION 1)

*Autorità amministrative indipendenti* was a term of art in Italian law well before it was applied in any legislative act. Italian scholars versed in comparative law were quick to point out that Italy was walking the path taken almost a century before by the United States of America and—from a later date—by France.[1] In actual fact, the term was a direct translation from the French *Autorités administratives indépendantes*.[2]

The term *autorità amministrative indipendenti* has now passed into the legislation. No specific authority however is expressly characterized as such. Rather, the legislator has made a generic reference to these authorities while dealing with other subject matters. A case in point is Article 23 *bis* of l. 6 dicembre 1971, n 1034, as introduced by Article 4 of l. 21 luglio 2000, n 205. The latter statute has introduced a fast track judicial review procedure in given instances. Among them, judicial review of decisions taken by *autorità amministrative indipendenti* (Article 23 *bis* (1) lett. *d*). Other pieces of legislation differ on terminology. Concerning for instance access to administrative documents, Article 23 of l. 7 agosto 1990, n. 241, as modified by Article 4 (2) of l. 3 agosto 1999, n. 265, talks of *Autorità di garanzia e di vigilanza*. It is however broadly agreed that what the legislator had in mind was administrative independent authorities.[3]

The meaning to be conveyed concerns authorities which, albeit being charged with regulatory and adjudicatory functions, are not part of the traditional ministerial framework. Generally speaking, neither the government nor any minister has the power to give orders to independent administrative authorities to issue guidelines as to how they must discharge their duties, to take a decision in their stead, or to quash decisions taken by them.

* Writing this paper was made possible by MIUR grants.

[1] The US experience is considered with reference to the Italian developments by N Longobardi 'Les autorités administratives indépendantes, laboratoires d'un nouveau droit administratif' in *Petites affiches* (1999) n° 171, 4 ff.

[2] See M D'Alberti *Diritto amministrativo comparato* (Bologna il Mulino 1992) 144 ff.

[3] M Balestrieri 'La nuova formulazione dell'art. 23 della l.n. 241 del 1990. La posizione del legislatore sull'accessibilità degli atti di diritto privato dell'amministrazione' in *Giust civ* (2000) II, 307.

The core idea is that these authorities must have a significant, albeit variable, degree of insulation from politics.[4] In a sectarian polity like Italy, this is to ensure they act in an unbiased manner: they are also considered to be authorities possessing impartiality to a high degree (*autorità ad alto livello di imparzialità*).[5]

The insulation from politics, and more importantly from the Government and the majority in Parliament, is the one feature setting administrative independent authorities apart from other bodies having some degree of autonomy, concerning for instance their budget or internal management, such as the *Autorità per l'informatica nella pubblica amministrazione* (charged with helping the introduction of new technologies into the public sector); the *Agenzia per la rappresentanza negoziale delle pubbliche amministrazioni* (representing public authorities in wage and other negotiations with trade unions); the *Commissione per l'accesso agli atti amministrativi* (overseeing the respect of the rules on access to documents, which is part of the of the organisation of the Prime minister's offices and most of its members are appointed on the proposal of the Government), and many others.[6]

The *Consiglio di Stato* and the *Corte dei conti* are normally dealt with separately from independent administrative authorities. They are charged with advice and audit functions respectively; if administrative in their character, these functions come with judicial competences which are today considered to be prevalent; this so much so that their members have a status which is broadly comparable with that of magistrates. Also normally excluded are the many *ombudsman* such as institutions which lack regulation and adjudication powers.

This does not mean all administrative independent authorities in Italy conform to the same invariable pattern. Quite the contrary, significant differences exist, mainly as to the ways in which their independence is granted and as to the powers which are bestowed upon them.

The 1990s were the heyday of independent administrative authorities in Italy. Many new authorities were created and some pre-existing ones were granted such prerogatives and powers as to be considered independent.[7]

[4] F Merusi and M Passaro *Le autorità indipendenti* (Bologna il Mulino 2003) 7, go as far as writing that independent administrative authorities were set up out of spite for politics and politicians; TAR Lazio Sez. I, 10 aprile 2002, n 3070, *TAR* 2002, I, 844; *TAR* 2002, II, 411, note MP Santoro 'Il sindacato del giudice amministrativo sull'operato della CONSOB', held that independent administrative authorities were set up to dispel the suspicion that decisions taken in given matters were politically motivated (point 9.4).

[5] Again D'Alberti op cit 144.

[6] Merusi and Passaro *Le autorità indipendenti*, at 54 ff.

[7] C Franchini 'Le autorità indipendenti come figure organizzative nuove' in S Cassese and C Franchini (eds) *I garanti delle regole* (Bologna il Mulino) 1996 69 ff, makes the case that independent administrative authorities are a new form among others in a deeply changing institutional architecture.

Today, the setting up of such new administrative independent authorities is no longer contemplated. Those already existing perform their functions among continuing talk about some general reform aimed at streamlining their operations if not at getting rid of most of them. It is however doubtful whether such talks will lead anywhere.

## II. ADMINISTRATIVE INDEPENDENT AUTHORITIES, THE PRESIDENT, THE PARLIAMENT AND THE GOVERNMENT (QUESTIONS 2–5)

Italian institutional arrangements conform to the traditional pattern of parliamentary government. The President of the Republic is elected by the Parliament, with an enlarged composition, not by the people directly, opposed to the situation in France. He or she (so far, he) is often characterized as the supreme notary of the Republic, meaning that he is a referee rather than a player in Italian politics. He chooses the Prime minister and the ministers, who must have and must retain the confidence of the majority in both houses of Parliament.

Parliamentary responsibility is the rule laid down in Art. 95(2) of the Constitution concerning ministerial activities. Ministers are answerable to the Parliament, ie to the majority therein, for all actions taken or not taken by their respective ministries. A similar pattern applies to regional and local government.

Administrative action is dealt with specifically in Articles 97 and 98 of the Constitution. Article 97(1) lays down the principle of impartiality which can be read as a rule against (mainly political) bias. Administrative action should not be driven by partisan considerations.

There is a certain strain if not open contradiction between the rules laid down in Article 95(2) and those in Article 97(1). Traditionally, politics has tended to take the upper hand in Italy, shredding impartiality. Ministers and other elected officials acting at a regional and local level have been known to meddle with everyday administrative activities, bending it to partisan ends. Ministerial responsibility has been to very little or no avail; the majority is far too ready to condone any biased activity advancing its own partisan interests.

Independent administrative authorities were introduced as a way to break the link between the politicians and the administrative decision makers.[8]

The standard formula employed in the legislation starting form 1990 provides that the authority operates in full autonomy and with independence from judgement and evaluation.[9]

[8] Another way has been to differentiate the tasks of elected officials and public servants, limiting the say of the former in everyday administrative activities: R Caranta 'Point de vue sur les reformes récentes en matière de fonction publique en Italie' in *Perspectives pour la fonction publique. Conseil d'État—Rapport public 2003* (Paris La documentation française 2003) 399.

[9] Eg Art 10 (2) l. 10 ottobre 1990, n 287, concerning the Antitrust Authority: '*L'Autorità opera in piena autonomia e con indipendenza di giudizio e di valutazione.*'

Independent administrative authorities are in no way linked to the traditional ministerial structure. The Government does not have the power to give directives to the authorities. Consequently, ministerial responsibility does not play any role with reference to the activities of independent administrative authorities.[10]

At times independent administrative authorities are charged with supervisory powers which extend to certain aspects of the Government's activities. This is the case, for instance, with the authority charged with overseeing public works procurement.

Independent administrative authorities have closer links with Parliament. They are set up by statutes, that is by act of Parliament. The act outlines their jurisdiction. It also lays down the rules that the authorities will have to apply in their activities. Parliament usually plays an important role in the appointment of members of the authorities. Normally the authorities report to Parliament on a regular basis; in many cases they may also give advice on bills proposed to the Houses of Parliament.[11]

Independent administrative authorities have nationwide jurisdiction. There are no specific rules concerning their relationships with regional and local governments, some of whose activities can fall under the jurisdiction of this of that authority. The recent constitutional reform, which has made Italy's institutional structure closer to the federal model, has not addressed the position of independent administrative authorities. The question is likely to surface again in the near future in the framework of the progressive federalisation of the Italian State.

## III. INDEPENDENT ADMINISTRATIVE AUTHORITIES AND THE CONSTITUTION (QUESTIONS 6–8)

The present Italian Constitution does not deal with independent administrative authorities. This fact can be easily explained, as the Constitution dates from the late 1940s.[12]

Some authors have pointed out the difficulties in grafting independent administrative authorities onto the Constitution. The Constitution stuck very much to tradition when it laid down the rules concerning the public administration; its approach to the administration is still deeply rooted in the nineteenth century. The rule-making powers granted to some authorities as well as the breaking up of the link between the decision maker and political actors have been strongly criticized. The introduction of the new

[10] But see Cons St, Comm Spec, 29 maggio 1998, n 988/97, in *Foro amm* 1999 414, referred to below, text corresponding to footnote 17.

[11] Eg Art 22 l. 10 ottobre 1990, n 287, concerning the Antitrust Authority.

[12] Merusi and Passaro *Le autorità indipendenti* at 67 f.

authorities has been perceived by some as a drift towards a technocratic government devoid of popular legitimacy.[13]

The debate has remained almost exclusively academic. No rule made or decision taken by an Italian independent administrative authority has ever been challenged and brought to the attention of the Constitutional court on the ground that the very existence of such an authority was in breach of the Constitution.

At one point, the *Garante per la radiodiffusione e l'editoria* (the then media regulator) even tried to pose as an institution whose powers were grounded in the Constitution;[14] the Constitutional court, while rebuffing the attempt, in no way put in doubt the consistency of the arrangements regarding the *Garante* with the balance of powers embedded in the Constitution.[15]

The only case in which the Constitutional court has had to deal with the compatibility of a statute setting up an independent administrative authority, with the fundamental law, was brought up by some regional governments complaining that the new authority charged with overseeing public works procurement was to act in sectors pertaining to their jurisdiction. The challenge was roundly rebutted by the Court; it held that the supervisory powers allotted to the new authority did not encroach on any existing competence. The Court also held that supervisory tasks concerning public works procedures were best left to an authority characterized by the technical expertise of its members.[16] The ruling concerned an authority whose actual powers are fairly limited. It is therefore doubtful whether its doctrine can be generalized.

[13] The most articulate criticisms were voiced by M Manetti *Poteri neutrali e Costituzione* (Milano Giuffré 1994); also by G De Minico *Antitrust e Consob. Obiettivi e funzioni* (Padova CEDAM 1997) 249 ff.

[14] See G Grasso 'La Corte costituzionale si pronuncia solo parzialmente sulla natura giuridica e sulla collocazione costituzionale delle Autorità amministrative indipendenti' in *Quad reg* (1995) 237.

[15] Corte cost, 7 aprile 1995, n 118, *Giur cost* (1995) 942, e Corte cost, 2 giugno 1995, n 226, *Giur cost* (1995) 1658, note G Gemma 'Garante per la radiodiffusione e l'editoria e conflitti di attribuzione tra poteri dello Stato'; S Niccolai 'Quando nasce un potere', and Passaro 'Il Garante per la radiodiffusione e l'editoria come potere dello Stato'; see also Grasso 'La Corte costituzionale si pronuncia solo parzialmente sulla natura giuridica e sulla collocazione costituzionale delle Autorità amministrative indipendenti. Considerazioni sparse sulle decisioni n 57, n 118 e n 226 del 1995' in *Quad reg* (1995) 237; more recently Corte cost, 23 luglio 2002, n 378, *Giur cost* (2002) 2818, note Manetti 'Regioni e autorità indipendenti in conflitto'.

[16] Corte costituzionale 7 novembre 1995, n 482, in *Regioni* (1996) 373, note Morbidelli 'Esiste ancora la materia "lavori pubblici di interesse regionale"?'; in *Giur cost* (1995) 3806, note Ciolli 'L'Autorità per la vigilanza sui lavori pubblici: il primo passo della Corte verso l'accettazione dei poteri neutri?' in *Riv trim appalti* (1995) 75, note L Anelli 'L'art 1, secondo comma, della legge 11 febbraio 1994, n 109 alla luce della sentenza della Corte costituzionale n 482 del 7 novembre 1995', Nicodemo 'I lavori pubblici tra legislazione statale e regionale', and D Senzani 'La programmazione dei lavori pubblici dopo la sentenza della Corte costituzionale n 482 del 1995'.

In a case concerning the Antitrust authority, the *Consiglio di Stato* acting in its capacity as a legal adviser to the government has somewhat qualified the reading by the Constitutional court. It held that the general principle of impartiality provided for in Art. 97 (1) of the Constitution is developed to the highest level possible with independent administrative authorities. However, the *Consiglio di Stato* maintained that there is a link between the Authority and the Government; the latter is to issue guidelines on the Authority's use of the power to exempt agreements from the application of competition rules; thus the Government is politically responsible for the choices made by the Authority in conformity with Article 95 of the Constitution.[17]

It is doubtful whether the simple issuing of guidelines, not coupled with powers to enforce the application of the same guidelines against the Authority is enough to establish the liability of the Government under the Constitution.

The attitude prevailing today among Italian scholars is that Articles 95 and 97 refer to two alternative, if not mutually exclusive models of administrative authority. Independent administrative authorities conform to the latter model and are to be preferred whenever regulation does not entail the making of policy decisions as between possibly conflicting interests.[18]

A minority view has it that authorities which are really independent, having broken any link with the Government, are no longer administrative in their nature but rather quasi-judicial or judicial.[19] That position, however, raises even more difficult problems of consistency with the Italian Constitution: Article 102 (2) thereof expressly forbids the setting up of new jurisdictions.[20]

[17] Cons St, Comm Spec, 29 maggio 1998, n 988/97, in *Foro amm* (1999) 414.

[18] This idea has been championed by V Cerulli Irelli 'Premesse problematiche allo studio delle "amministrazioni indipendenti"' in Bassi and Merusi *Mercati e amministrazioni indipendenti* (Milano Giuffré 1993) 23 ff.; see also Amato 'Autorità semi-indipendenti e autorità di garanzia' in *Riv trim dir pubbl* (1997) 960 f; Falcon 'Il "primo", il "secondo" ed il "terzo" garante nei settori dell'editoria e della radiodiffusione' in Bassi and Merusi *Mercati e amministrazioni indipendenti* at 96, and Caringella 'Le amministrazioni indipendenti tra neutralità e paragiurisdizionalità: il problema della copertura costituzionale' in F Caringella and R Gaforoli (curr) *Le autorità indipendenti* at 64 ff.

[19] Notably M Clarich 'Per uno studio sui poteri dell'Autorità garante della concorrenza e del mercato' in Bassi and Merusi *Mercati e amministrazioni indipendenti* at 136 ff; D'Alberti 'Autorità indipendenti (dir amm)' in *Encicl Giurid Treccani* (1996) 5 f; Longobardi 'Les autorités administratives indépendantes, laboratoires d'un nouveau droit administratif' in *Petites affiches* (1999) n° 171 6 f.; S Cassese 'Le autorità indipendenti: origini storiche e problemi odierni' in S Cassese and C Franchini (eds) *I garanti delle regole* at 222.

[20] Cass, 20 maggio 2002, n 7341 in *Giur it* (2003) 856, note V Vanacore 'Le Autorità indipendenti tra natura amministrativa e dovere di imparzialità'; Cons St, Comm Spec, 29 maggio 1998, n 988/97, in *Foro amm* (1999) 414; see also Grasso 'Spunti per uno studio sulle autorità amministrative indipendenti: il problema del fondamento costituzionale (Italia Francia Stati Uniti d'America)' in *Quad reg* (1993) 1332 f.

A few years ago, in the framework of a wider attempt at constitutional reform, specific amendment proposals concerning independent administrative authorities were put on the table.[21] The final draft of the proposal, passed on 4 November 1997, intended to allow the Parliament to set up specific authorities charged with the task of protecting and overseeing the exercise of Constitutional rights and freedoms. Members of the authorities had to be elected by the upper house of Parliament (the Senate). A majority of three-fifths of the members was required for the election to be successful. The duration of the term in office, the requirements needed for election, and the rules buttressing the independence of the members were to be laid down by a statute (by the most logical inference, the same that set up the authority). Authorities were required to refer to both houses of Parliament on their activities (Article 109 of the proposal).[22]

The proposed provision did not speak clearly of independent administrative authorities, but there was no doubt that was their object. Specific provisions were to deal with the Bank of Italy (Article 110)[23] and the *ombudsman* (Article 111).[24]

Had those amendments passed into the law books, the difficulties in harmonizing the existence of independent administrative authorities with the constitutional framework would have been overcome once and for all. This was not to be the case. The more general reform project was aborted before giving life to any change in the Constitution.[25]

Present talks about the future of independent administrative authorities do not envisage constitutional reform, but that could be necessary to address the question of the role, if any, of regional governments.

[21] For a general discussion see the contributions in SP Panunzio *I costituzionalisti e le riforme* (Milano Giuffré) 1998 341 ff; more specifically on independent administrative authorities S Baroncelli La costituzionalizzazione delle autorità amministrative indipendenti: una scelta di stabilità' in P Caretti (cur) *La riforma della Costituzione nel progetto della Bicamerale* (Padova CEDAM, 1998) 265 ff.

[22] 'Per l'esercizio delle funzioni di garanzia o di vigilanza in materia di diritti e libertà garantiti dalla Costituzione la legge può istituire apposite autorità. Il Senato della Repubblica elegge a maggioranza dei tre quinti dei suoi componenti i titolari delle Autorità di garanzia e di vigilanza. La legge ne stabilisce la durata del mandato, i requisiti di eleggibilità e le condizioni di indipendenza. Le Autorità riferiscono alle Camere sui risultati dell'attività svolta'.

[23] 'La Banca d'Italia svolge le sue funzioni in materia monetaria e di vigilanza su sistema creditizio in condizioni di autonomia e indipendenza.'

[24] 'La legge può istituire l'ufficio del difensore civico quale organo di garanzia nei rapporti tra il cittadino e la pubblica amministrazione'.

[25] Further proposals are in the pipeline: for some documents see Cerulli Irelli *Costituzione e amministrazione. Documenti di un itinerario riformatore (1996–2002)* (Torino Giappichelli 2002) 355 ff.

## IV. THE QUEST FOR LEGITIMACY (QUESTIONS 9–11)

The question of the legitimacy of independent administrative authorities is strictly interwoven with the problem concerning their compatibility with the overall design of the Constitution. However it has certain specific features.

To avoid excessive generalization, the legitimacy issue should be raised with reference to each specific authority. It was rightly remarked that some authorities are independent from the Government, but strictly linked to the Parliament.[26] The question also involves some general aspects; only they can be dealt with here.

First, independent administrative authorities are set up and ruled by legislative provisions. These provisions can be changed any time Parliament thinks fit. Parliament has not forfeited once and for all ministerial powers to the benefit of independent administrative authorities. Even sharing the position according to which given competencies can only be assigned to independent authorities, it does not follow that the legislator has no power to terminate the operation of any authority just by changing the rules on the way it works and/or the way it is staffed. This is far from being a purely theoretical possibility. The Italian Parliament has changed the authority charged with overseeing the media a number of times, by shutting down the existing one and setting up a new one.

In a way, the legitimacy of independent administrative authorities can be induced by default from the fact that—and as long as—the Parliament, and thus the chosen representatives of the people, do not think it is necessary to interfere with their activities.

Secondly, representative democracy is not the only way to confer legitimacy upon the exercise of public powers. Judges do not usually—and they certainly do not in Italy—derive their legitimacy from the democratic process.[27]

Independent administrative authorities are not usually charged with policy decisions (ie weighting conflicting public and private interests). Normally, they have to pursue one prevailing interest in what they perceive to be the most technically efficient way.[28] A clear case in point is the mandate of the Bank of Italy following the coming into effect of the

[26] Amato 'Autorità semi-indipendenti e autorità di garanzia' at 660; he was pointing to the case of the Authority for telecommunications.

[27] Cassese 'Le autorità indipendenti: origini storiche e problemi odierni' at 220 f.

[28] C Malinconico 'Le funzioni amministrative delle autorità indipendenti' in Cassese and Franchini (eds) *I garanti delle regole*, at 45 f.; P Lazzara *Autorità indipendenti e discrezionalità* (Padova CEDAM 2001); A Romano Tassone 'Situazioni giuridiche soggettive e decisioni delle autorità indipendenti' *Dir amm* (2002) 471 s, rightly maintains that the end of ideologies and globalization have much reduced the scope for decisions taken on (possibly conflicting) political grounds.

European System of Central Banks: price stability is now the paramount aim of the Bank.[29]

The fact that independent administrative authorities do not normally take policy-laden decisions was recognised by a decision by the *Corte di cassazione* while dealing with a case concerning the *Commissione di garanzia per l'attuazione della l. 12 giugno 1990, n. 146, in materia di sciopero nei servizi pubblici essenziali* (the Commission regulating strikes in sectors providing essential services to the public).[30] Independent administrative authorities are simply given regulatory and adjudicatory powers under a sufficiently precise legislative framework; expertise is enough to meet the needs of legitimacy.[31]

Representative democracy does not have much to do with the application of technical rules.[32] Democratic legitimacy as a whole would be much reinforced were the necessary attention paid to setting up procedures which effectively protect the rights of all parties concerned, including representatives from the civil society and public interest groups.[33] Participative democracy is less familiar to the Continental legal system but by no means less relevant than representative democracy. In Italy it has strong support in Articles 2 and 3 of the Constitution.[34]

There are some significant exceptions to the principle of not allowing independent administrative authorities to choose between conflicting interests;[35] one such exception is the power conferred to the Antitrust

[29] Merusi and Passaro *Le autorità indipendenti* at 16.

[30] Cass, 6 novembre 1997, n 10889 in *Giust civ* (1998) I, 1693, note C Corsinovi 'Sui requisiti di legittimità procedurale dell'ordinanza di precettazione nel contesto dell'art 8, legge n 146 del 1990'; the Court remarked that the Commission was not given the power to order workers not to abstain from work or to resume work in order to avoid it stepping into the political arena: 'accolta l'idea, accentuatamente innovatrice, di istituire un'Autorità amministrativa indipendente, quale la Commissione di garanzia, espressamente finalizzata a valutare l'idoneità delle misure volte ad assicurare il contemperamento dell'esercizio del diritto di sciopero con il godimento dei diritti della persona costituzionalmente tutelati, il legislatore non ha spinto il disegno riformatore fino all'estrema conseguenza di assegnare alla Commissione stessa il potere di precettazione, risultando all'evidenza che l'esercizio di questo potere implica un impatto sociale che può essere anche molto incisivo, soprattutto nei conflitti di livello nazionale, e che può anche dilatarsi fino ad attingere il livello di opposizione all'indirizzo politico dell'esecutivo, sicché l'imputazione del provvedimento direttamente all'Autorità di garanzia avrebbe rischiato di comportare una sovraesposizione di quest'ultima, incompatibile con la sua posizione di terzietà.'

[31] Cassese 'Le autorità indipendenti: origini storiche e problemi odierni' at 220 f.

[32] D Sorace 'La desiderabile indipendenza della regolazione dei servizi di interesse economico generale' in *Mercato concorrenza regole* (2003) 343.

[33] Also Longobardi 'Les autorités administratives indépendantes, laboratoires d'un nouveau droit administratif' in *Petites affiches* (1999) n° 173, 11.

[34] This position is not yet widely shared in Italy: see A Barbera 'Commento all'art 2' in G Branca (ed) *Commentario alla Costituzione. Principi fondamentali* (Bologna–Roma Zanichelli 1975) 102 ss; for a reference to the importance of Art 3 see MA Sandulli 'Partecipazione e autonomie locali' in *Dir amm* (2002) 555.

[35] The point is underlined by Longobardi 'Les autorités administratives indépendantes, laboratoires d'un nouveau droit administratif' in *Petites affiches* (1999) n° 173, 13.

authority to allow anti-competitive agreements beneficial to consumers; conflicting competitors' and consumers' interests are balanced against one another;[36] at times, even conflicting constitutional rights are at stake.[37]

This can be addressed by other—and admittedly more open to debate—considerations.

Thirdly, representative legitimacy finds important constraints in the present constitutional framework. The parliamentary majority can no longer do whatever it pleases. Its powers are curtailed by the Constitution. Law making power—as any other power in Italy—must abide by the Constitution.

Representative legitimacy is of little relevance when the majority is denied the power to change the legal rules applicable to a given field.[38] This is so any time that the Constitution itself, or any other higher law, has already made the relevant policy choices, leaving room for implementation only.[39] This is also the case when delicate balancing acts between possibly conflicting rights all having their place embedded in the founding charter, such as the right to strike and other rights protected by the Constitution.[40]

Here again, expertise is a potentially better legitimacy—and a better guarantee of adequate regulation and adjudication—than representative democracy.

In many cases the Constitution itself has directly and expressly chosen to forgo any governmental—democratically legitimized—decision making power, charging the courts with the implementation of constitutional provisions. These cases go under the label of *riserve di giurisdizione*, the first and most important instance being in connection with personal freedom (Article 13 of the Constitution).[41]

More than half a century has passed since the Constitution came into force. In the meantime, due to the progress in economic integration, both at a regional and global level, traditional economic rights have seen a great increase in their importance. At best the provisions of the Italian

[36] Merusi and Passaro *Le autorità indipendenti*, at 30; M Clarich 'Per uno studio sui poteri dell'Autorità garante della concorrenza e del mercato' at 134; according to Cons St, Comm Spec, 29 maggio 1998, n 988/97, in *Foro amm* (1999) 414, however, the Authority's decision making power is curtailed by the Governmental power to issue guidelines.

[37] It was remarked that the authority does not have the power to stop industrial action from taking place, that power is given to the Government: Cass, 6 novembre 1997, n 10889 in *Giust civ* (1998) I, 1693, note C Corsinovi 'Sui requisiti di legittimità procedurale dell'ordinanza di precettazione nel contesto dell'art 8, legge n 146 del 1990'.

[38] Similar remarks by Sorace 'La desiderabile indipendenza' at 342 f.

[39] This line of thought was developed in R Caranta 'Politica e amministrazione nella Costituzione' in *Studi in onore di Umberto Pototschnig* (Milano Giuffré 2002) 307 ff.

[40] A D'Atena 'Costituzione ed autorità indipendenti: il caso della Commissione di garanzia dell'attuazione della legge sullo sciopero nei servizi pubblici essenziali' in A Predieri (cur) *Le autorità indipendenti nei sistemi istituzionali ed economici* (Firenze le Monnier 1997) 262 ff.

[41] V Angiolini *Riserva di giurisdizione e libertà costituzionali* (Padova CEDAM 1992).

Constitution concerning economics were an uneasy compromise between the main socialist and social-catholic parties favouring considerable public intervention in the economy on the one hand and, on the other hand, a minority of liberals. At worst, they were a mish-mash of conflicting options. In fact, for the best part of the second half of the past century the Italian economy was largely in public hands and widely subsidised. Economic freedoms were not held very highly. Then came market liberalization. Markets are to be regulated according to principles which are utterly inconsistent with the short-term vision, inherent in pressured decision-making by politicians who are under pressure to win the next elections; which are always 'coming up soon', be it at local, regional or national level. Leaving the Government with too much control would have conflicted with the drive toward free market. In the end, market liberalization brought traditional economic rights back to the forefront of values having constitutional standing.[42]

In the past two decades new rights have emerged which need to be protected first and foremost against the Government. Privacy and consumers' rights are very strong cases in point. Independent administrative authorities address new concerns which the Government is not in a good position to deal with.

Moreover, European integration has given constitutional standing to many of these brand new or new-old rights. Alongside with the Constitution, the European Treaties are now considered to be the highest law of the land.[43]

In one instance the Treaties themselves provide for the independence of national administrative institutions. Article 108 (formerly Article 107) of the EC Treaty makes it clear that national central banks and members of their governing bodies must be protected from pressures coming from Community institutions and Member State Governments and from other organs.

Other Treaty provisions can be and have been referred to with reference to Italian independent administrative authorities. This has notably been the case with regard to the Antitrust Authority and to the authorities given powers concerning newly privatised markets and enterprises, such as for instance telecommunications, electricity and gas.[44]

[42] Generally Cassese *La nuova Costituzione economica* (Roma-Bari Laterza 1995); G Della Cananea and G Napolitano (curr) *Per una nuova costituzione economica* (Bologna il Mulino 1998); also Caranta 'Intervento pubblico nell'economia' in *Digesto IV, Disc pub, Appendice* (Torino UTET 2000).

[43] M Cartabia and JHH Weiler *L'Italia in Europa* (Bologna il Mulino 2000) 163 ff.

[44] Concerning telecommunications, a measure of independence of national regulatory authorities is required by Art 1 of Directive 97/51/EC: see FM Salerno 'Telecomunicazioni e autorità indipendenti: appunti sullo sviluppo dei rapporti tra diritto comunitario e organizzazione amministrativa interna' in *Riv it dir pubbl comunitario* (2003) 679.

Only one Italian independent administrative authority, the *Commissione di garanzia in materia di sciopero nei servizi pubblici essenziali* (the Commission regulating strikes in sectors providing essential services to the public) cannot be brought one way or the other under the broad protective wings of Community law.[45]

Usually, Community law is thought to be relevant in that it lays down rules whose application does not entail the making of (major) policy choices. This is the same no politics argument we have already discussed.

It is also possible to claim that many (mainly economic) rights which have their ultimate source in European law benefit from a higher law rank. The (national) majority cannot dispose of them. The independent administrative authorities take charge.

European law is of further relevance in that some independent administrative authorities take decisions directly affecting non-national and also non-resident firms and individuals. This is the case with the Antitrust Authority. The EC Commission is not alone in applying Community competition law to anti-competitive behaviours with cross border effects and super-national relevance. In the future, even more relevant tasks are to be transferred to national Antitrust Authorities.[46]

Regulation and supervision of insurance companies are an even better case to highlight that national boundaries are no longer a limit to administrative decision-making powers. Under EC Directive 92/96, licences to insurance firms are issued by the national regulatory authority of the country where they have their head office. Licences allow the firms to operate all over Europe. Concerning supervision, Directive 92/96/EEC has adopted the home country control system. This means that the national authority, having issued the licence, is competent to oversee the cross-boundary activities of insurance firms, albeit in close cooperation with other national authorities. In the context of the freedom of movement of capital, decisions taken by administrative authorities charged with regulatory powers over financial markets and their operators also have effects beyond national borders.

Regulation and adjudication with cross-border effects have not yet been the object of deep analysis at Community level,[47] but when the issue is

[45] Merusi and Passaro *Le autorità indipendenti* at 52.

[46] COM (2000) 582 del 27 settembre 2000. See S Kingston 'A "new division of responsibilities" in the proposed regulation to modernise the rules implementing Articles 81 and 82 EC? A warning call' in Eur Comp L Rev (2001) 340; T Jones 'Regulation 17: The Impact of the Current Application of Articles 81 and 82 by National Competition Authorities in the European Commission's Proposals for Reform' in Eur Comp L Rev (2001) 405.

[47] German scholars have recently started to tackle the issue of administrative decisions having effects in multiple jurisdictions: M Ruffert 'Der transnationale Verwaltungsakt' Die Verwaltung (2001) 453; J Becker 'Der transnationale Verwaltungsakt' Deut Verw Blatt (2001) 855.

considered, the problem of the legitimacy of independent administrative authorities shines in a different light.

Legitimacy through representative democracy (and more specifically through the Parliamentary processes) is the ground upon which Article 95 of the Italian Constitution was built. It is but a facet of the constitutional and institutional arrangement of the Nation State. In the nineteenth century the whole system made a lot of sense. Legitimacy for legislation and administration came from those primarily affected by legislative acts and administrative decisions. Once the link is broken, the legitimacy problem can no longer be sensibly discussed at national level.

This can be yet another reason to lament the so-called democratic deficit of the European institutions. Given that independent administrative authorities were often set up to address the shortcoming of representative democracy, it would seem more judicious to insist on working participative democracy rather than just pretending to exactly replicate the old legitimacy-through-election pattern.

## V. WHICH BODIES CAN BE CONSIDERED TO BE INDEPENDENT ADMINISTRATIVE AUTHORITIES AND WHAT ARE THEIR MAIN TASKS? (QUESTIONS 12–14 AND 16)

There is much discussion in Italy as to which authorities can really be considered to be independent administrative authorities. This is due both to the absence of general provisions dealing with these institutions and to the fact that the authorities have been created at different times and according to different rules. The uncertainties as to the exact scope of the notion have led to many different scholarly arrangements of the subject matter.

A (mostly) chronological type of narrative is preferred here. It highlights some interesting points in the evolution of the legislation on the matter.

The main distinction is between purpose built independent administrative authorities and authorities which, while established according to more traditional models, later metamorphosed into administrative independent authorities.

The first body to be created as an independent administrative authority was the *Commissione di garanzia in materia di sciopero nei servizi pubblici essenziali* (the Commission regulating strikes in sectors providing essential services to the public). It was introduced by Article 12 of l. 12 giugno 1990, n 146.[48] The members of the *Commissione* are appointed by the President of the Republic following the indications of the Presidents of the two Houses of Parliament. According to a praxis still used in those days, one of

[48] <http://www.commissionegaranziasciopero.it>.

the two presidents was chosen among MPs of the minority parties in Parliament. A fairly satisfactory degree of bipartisanship was thus assured by having the choice of the Authority's members made jointly by the Presidents of the two Houses. There are nine members in the *Commissione*, making it a fairly large body when compared with the other authorities which are usually slimmer. The number is probably due to the desire to have many different ideological positions represented; this explanation sits uncomfortably alongside the rather high requirements for appointment, possibly the strictest for any authority. The authority has the power to decide on its internal organization and on how to spend its budget; it is financed from the national budget.

The *Commissione* is charged with reconciling conflicting rights which are all protected under the Constitution: on the one hand, the right to strike and take other forms of industrial action; on the other hand, various rights, ranging from life and health to education, to the freedom of movement across the country, which can be adversely affected by industrial actions. According to Article 13 of l. 12 giugno 1990, n 146, which was amended by Article 10 of l. 11 aprile 2000, n 83, the main tasks given to the *Commissione* include the power to approve agreements between social actors aimed at laying down the minimal services which have to be provided to the public even in the case of industrial action; to adopt substitutive provisions in case the agreements fail to materialize; to invite the Government or decentralised public authorities to take actions designed to limit the exercise of the right to strike so that minimal services are not denied; to fine individuals and trade unions acting in breach of protected rights of the public.

What is really the purest model of an Italian independent administrative authority was also introduced in 1990. The *Autorità garante per la concorrenza ed il mercato* (the Antitrust authority) set up by Articles 10 of l. 10 ottobre 1990, n 287.[49] Its members are named by the Presidents of the two Houses of Parliament acting jointly. The rules on proceedings before the Authority are laid down in a statutory instrument adopted following deliberation by the government. The authority has the power to decide on its internal organization and on how to spend its budget; it is financed from the national budget.[50]

The Authority was originally charged with the application of Italian antitrust law; Italian antitrust law is quite in line with Articles 81 and 82 (formerly Articles 85 and 86) of the EC Treaty; Article 1: (4) l. 10 ottobre 1990, n 287, which states that Italian antitrust law has to be construed in conformity with Community law. In preparation for the decentralised

49 <http://www.agcm.it>.

50 M Ramajoli *Attività amministrativa e disciplina antitrust* (Milano Giuffré 1998).

application of EC antitrust law, Article 54, 5° comma, della l. 6 febbraio 1996, n 52, made the Authority competent also with reference to EC law. Later d.lgs. 1992, n. 74, gave the Authority powers concerning misleading commercial advertisements.

The creation of the *Autorità per la vigilanza sui lavori pubblici* (Vigilance or Supervisory authority over public works) was foreseen by Articles 4 and 5 of l. 11 febbraio 1994, n. 109; the application of those provisions was however almost immediately set aside, and it was not until l. 18 novembre 1998, n 415 finally entered into force that the authority was finally set up.[51] The members of the Authorities are named by the Presidents of the two Houses of Parliament acting jointly. The authority has the power to decide how to spend its budget; it is financed from the national budget.

The Authority is charged with overseeing the public procurement for works passed by procuring entities. It should ensure that procurements are passed in a legal, transparent, and convenient way, but it has no power to interfere with specific award procedures.[52] All it can do is to submit reports and proposals to the Parliament, to the Government and to public prosecutors.[53] The very limited powers the Authority enjoys have induced some scholars not to include it among the independent administrative authorities.[54]

In the framework of the liberalization of utility markets, Article 2 of l. 14 novembre 1995, n 481, prepared the ground for the creation of different authorities for different market sector.[55] Article 3 thereof expressly established the *Autorità per l'energia elettrica e il gas* (Electricity and Gas Authority).[56] The procedure leading to the choice of its president and of its two other members is quite cumbersome. They are appointed by the President of the Republic acting on the proposal of the Government; this proposal, however, can only be met if the candidates have been accepted by the committees of the two Houses of Parliament acting according to a two thirds majority of their members. The real power to choose the members lies with the Parliament rather than with the Government or the President;

[51] <http://www.autoritalavoripubblici.it>.

[52] A first instance decision held the Authority does not even have the power to invite a municipality found guilty of having broken the law to redress the breach: see TAR Piemonte, Sez I, 21 dicembre 2001, n 1427, *Riv giur edil* (2001) I, 94, note V Parisio 'L'Autorità per la vigilanza sui lavori pubblici alla ricerca di identità: cenni'; *Urbanista e appalti* (2001), 425 note R Damonte 'I limiti dei poteri dell'Autorità per la vigilanza sui lavori pubblici'.

[53] See generally E Cannada Bartoli 'Commento all'art. 4' and S Mirate 'Commento all'art 5' both in A Angeletti (dir) *La riforma dei lavori pubblici* (Torino UTET 1999), 89 ff.; Caranta 'Commento agli artt 4 e 5' in Caringella (cur) *La nuova legge quadro sui lavori pubblici* (Milano IPSOA 1999) 167 ff.

[54] Merusi and Passaro *Le autorità indipendenti* at 59.

[55] See generally L De Lucia *La regolazione amministrativa dei servizi di pubblica utilità* (Torino Giappichelli 2002).

[56] <http://www.autorita.energia.it>.

because of the high majority required, the opposition must agree with the choice. The authority has the power to decide on its own internal organization and on how to spend its budget; it is indirectly financed from a contribution imposed by the law on firms providing the services; the Treasury Minister (today the Minister of Economics) can change the measure of the contribution to make it adequately meet the costs of the regulation Authority. Article 2 (14) says that the Authority is bound by the choices made by the government on matters of general policy. This has led some scholars to doubt of the possibility of considering the Electricity and Gas Authority a truly independent authority.[57]

The Authority oversees the production and distribution of electricity and gas; it approves the tariffs firms charge to their customers, making sure they are in line with the costs the firms themselves shoulder. Since under Article 3 tariffs for comparable customer categories must be the same all over Italy, the Authority is charged with putting in place and managing a 'set off mechanism', compensating the different production costs firms shoulder in different parts of the country. The electricity market is regulated to a fairly considerable extent in Italy. The Authority has been transferred most of the functions concerning this market which were once the preserve of the (now) Ministry for Industry and Trade.

L. 31 dicembre 1996, n 675, laid down a general framework aimed at protecting personal data. Article 30 thereof created the *Garante per la protezione dei dati personali* (Privacy Authority).[58] It has four members, two elected by each House of Parliament; each MP can only cast one vote, so that usually the majority in the Houses cannot command more than half of the members of the Authority. The authority has the power to decide on its internal organization and on how to spend its budget; it is financed from the national budget.

The functions of the Authority have been somewhat altered by Article 11 of d.lgs. 28 dicembre 2001, n 467. It is charged with watching over all public and private institutions, firms, and organizations collecting personal data; under the system set up by l. 31 dicembre 1996, n 675, the Authority must be notified of all data banks; it has general policing powers, including the approval of codes of conduct; it can forbid ways of treating personal data which it holds as inconsistent with the law; it can fine all persons or institutions found to be in breach of the law. The Authority lays down the rules concerning the organization of its offices. The national budget provides for its funding.

The model laid down in Article 2 of l. 14 novembre 1995, n 481 could

[57] Eg Longobardi 'Les autorités administratives indépendantes, laboratoires d'un nouveau droit administratif' in *Petites affiches* (1999) n° 172, 6.

[58] <http://www.garanteprivacy.it>.

have been applied to telecommunications too. However, Parliament preferred to pass specific rules. Article 1 of l. 31 luglio 1997, n 249, thus introduced the *Autorità per la garanzia nelle comunicazioni* (Communications Authority).[59] It is the last of a series of administrative independent authorities from time to time charged with dealing with the rather delicate matter of media regulation in Italy.[60] Its structure is quite complicated in that for most of its functions it is divided into two sub-committees: one for infrastructures and networks, the other for services and products. The Authority's president is appointed according to the rules laid down in Article 2 of l. 14 novembre 1995, n 481; the four members of each sub-committee are elected by the two Houses of Parliament, each electing two members; each MP can vote for just one member of each sub-committee; this is to make sure that minority MPs have a say in the choice of the Authority's members.

The functions allotted to the Authority are quite complex. Among them, it regulates the relationships between network owners and service providers making sure the principle of equality of treatment is respected. It is the antitrust authority in the communications field. It acts in strict cooperation with the Government on planning and licensing. It is the executive arm of the Parliament concerning the enforcement of the rules laid down by the specific Parliamentary committee overseeing television and radio broadcasting; in this respect it is instrumental to the protection of such Constitutional rights as the freedom of expression and the freedom of information. It is charged with functions concerning the protection of human health (again a fundamental right) against emissions from communication installations.[61] At times, the division of roles between the Authority and other institutions is not entirely logical nor really clear cut.

With l. 31 dicembre 1996, n 675, and l. 31 luglio 1997, n 249, the creative era of independent administrative authorities drew to a close in Italy. Amendments to previous statutes were introduced in many cases, and some of them have been mentioned here.

In the meantime, the metamorphic processes leading to the transformation into administrative independent authorities of three relevant bodies were also completed. These transformations have often been accompanied with an important increase in their responsibilities.

The most important body which had its status improved to that of independent authority is the Bank of Italy.[62] It was set up by l. 10 agosto 1893,

59 <http://www.agcom.it>.

60 As to the predecessors see Passaro *Le Amministrazioni indipendenti* cit161 ss; Falcon 'Il "primo", il "secondo" ed il "terzo" garante nei settori dell'editoria e della radiodiffusione' at 69 ff.

61 The dual nature of the *Autorità* as both a sectoral market regulator and a guardian for some fundamental rights is highlighted by Merusi and Passaro *Le autorità indipendenti* at 44.

62 <http://www.bancaditalia.it>.

n 449, which merged together some pre-existing financial institutions. It was not until 1926 that the Bank was given exclusive power to issue paper money. In form, it is still a public limited company even if at a given point in history it was given the status of a governmental agency. Its shares can be owned by certain banks and social security institutions. The governing body is elected by the shareholders while the chief executive officer (the *Governatore*) is nominated by the President of the Republic acting on the proposal of the Prime Minister following an indication from the governing body of the Bank itself acting on a two-thirds majority. The growing independence of the Bank is much more a matter of fact than a matter of law: in the past decade or so, most of the shareholding banks were privatized; as such they are no longer under the direct influence at the Government. The tenure of the *Governatore* is not fixed and he can be removed from his office only following the same procedure as that of appointment. The Bank is not financed from the State budget, taking its resources directly from its operations.[63]

Traditionally, most of its powers were exercised in strict cooperation with the government, more specifically with the Treasury Ministry. From the early 1990s the Bank was granted autonomous decision-making power. This was the case for instance with l. 7 febbraio 1992, n 82; it gave the Bank the power to set interest rates; d.lgs. 1° settembre 1993, n. 385 did away with the practice of having the Bank financing the State budget by the compulsory buying of State bonds which went on the market unsold; the same piece of legislation further but not fully emancipated the Bank's supervisory functions over the banking system from governmental guidance.[64]

The *Commissione nazionale per la società e per la borsa* (the Financial Markets and Stock Exchange Commission), usually known under the acronym of *CONSOB*, was first set up under d.l. 8 aprile 1974, n 95 and l. 7 giugno 1974, n 95.[65] Its quite old origins are the reason for the central role played by the Government in the choice of the Commission's members, who are named by the President of the Republic acting on the proposal of the Prime Minister; the role of Parliament is quite limited, since all it can do is to audition proposed members.[66] It also has full financial autonomy, being financed through its operations.[67]

[63] V Mezzacapo 'L'indipendenza della Banca d'Italia' in Bassi and Merusi *Mercati e amministrazioni indipendenti* at 31.

[64] Passaro *Le Amministrazioni indipendenti* at 104 and 109.

[65] <http://www.consob.it>.

[66] Passaro *Le Amministrazioni indipendenti*, at ss 139 maintains that this does not really bite on the independence of the authority, since the choice has to be made among people having specific knowledge, experience, and of known moral standing and independence; this however is quite a usual and fairly generic formula applied to many other independent administrative authorities, which by itself does not seem to be enough of a remedy against partial behaviour.

[67] G De Minico *Antitrust e Consob. Obiettivi e funzioni* cit; see also E Cardi and P Valentino *L'istituzione CONSOB* (Milano Giuffré 1993); Cassese 'La Commissione Nazionale

In the beginning the *CONSOB* was but one specialized organ within the structure of the Treasury Ministry; its tasks were limited to supervision of companies listed on the Italian Stock Exchange. Today the *CONSOB* oversees all kinds of financial operations. Apart from policing the listing on the Stock Exchange and on other lesser exchanges, the *CONSOB* oversees the operation of every financial intermediary; it determines which information is to be disclosed to actual and prospective investors. L. 4 giugno 1985, n 281, severed the *CONSOB* from the ministerial structure, setting it up as a separate legal entity acting in full autonomy.[68]

The *Istituto per la vigilanza sulle assicurazioni private e di interesse collettivo* (the insurance sector regulator), going under the acronym of *ISVAP*, was originally created by l. 12 agosto 1982, n 576.[69] As is the case with the *CONSOB*, the President of the *ISVAP* is named by the President of the Republic acting on the proposal of the Government; the other members are directly chosen by the Government itself.[70] The *ISVAP* has full financial autonomy, being financed from contributions the law imposes on insurance firms.[71]

Originally the *ISVAP* was grafted onto the organization of the Ministry of Industry and its powers were in the main confined to giving advice to the Minister. Most functions concerning the insurance market have been transferred to *ISVAP*; they include the issue and withdrawal of licences to insurance firms, the supervisory powers over the insurance market, and regulatory powers aimed at policing insurance contract conditions to inform and protect customers. The transfer has been gradual, with a long and almost exasperating list of pieces of legislation, the last of them being l. 5 marzo 2001, n 57.[72]

*CONSOB* and *ISVAP* are administrative independent authorities much more for what they do (having taken out of ministerial hands the power of overseeing a specific market sector), rather than by the way their insulation from political pressure has been strengthened (which has been done to a very limited extent).

## VI. WHAT ARE THE PROCEDURAL RULES APPLICABLE TO IAA (QUESTION 15)

In spite of occasional references to a supposed quasi-jurisdictional character

per le Società e la Borsa—Consob e i poteri indipendenti' in *Riv soc* (1994) I, 412; N Marzona 'Il regolamento sull'organizzazione e sul funzionamento della CONSOB' in *Giorn. dir amm* (1995) 522.

68 Passaro *Le Amministrazioni indipendenti* at 135.

69 <http://www.isvap.it>.

70 Here again Passaro *Le Amministrazioni indipendenti*, at 139 ss maintains that independence in not in danger due to the specific requirements nominees must have.

71 As Passaro *Le Amministrazioni indipendenti* at 153, remembers, contrary to other administrative independent authorities, the ISVAP is not exempted from audit by the *Corte dei conti* (the Italian Court of audits).

72 See Merusi and Passaro *Le autorità indipendenti* at 25 f.; less recent developments were analysed by Caranta 'La nuova ISVAP' in *Resp civ prev* (1998) 17 ff.

of this or that independent authority, the prevailing opinion is more that these authorities are administrative in their nature.[73] No one has ever proposed to apply the same rules applicable to court proceedings to IAA proceedings.[74]

The problem is to what extent rules on administrative proceedings also apply to independent administrative authorities.

The specific statutes setting up the different authorities are normally silent on the point. Article 33 (1-*sexies*) of *l. 31 dicembre 1996*, n 675, which was added by Article 2 d.lgs. 26 febbraio 1999, n 51, concerning the Privacy Authority expressly refers to l. 7 agosto 1990, n 241, as regards the principles concerning the person responsible for the proceedings; this does not mean that the principles concerning other aspects, such as participation, do not apply. A specific by-law applies to the Antitrust Authority; it also grant the right to take part in the proceedings to both competitors and public interest groups.[75]

Until fairly recently there was no statute in Italy dealing with the general principles of administrative procedure; each proceeding was ruled under specific statutes and by-laws even if the case law had developed some more general principles.[76] In 1983 the Government set up a Commission, chaired by a leading scholar, the late Prof. Mario Nigro,[77] to work on a draft statute on administrative procedure.[78] The outcome of this work led to a lively debate among experts.[79]

[73] Eg Falcon 'Il "primo", il "secondo" ed il "terzo" garante nei settori dell'editoria e della radiodiffusione' at 97; Longobardi 'Les autorités administratives indépendantes, laboratoires d'un nouveau droit administratif' in *Petites affiches* (1999) n° 173, 13.

[74] TAR Lazio Sez. I, 10 aprile 2002, n 3070 *TAR* (2002) I, 844; *TAR* (2002) II, 411, note MP Santoro 'Il sindacato del giudice amministrativo sull'operato della CONSOB', remarked that different rules apply to judicial procedures and to proceedings in front of independent administrative authorities (point 9.4).

[75] DPR 30 aprile 1998, n 2171; the procedure followed by the Antitrust Authority has probably been the most thoroughly examined by scholars: Lazzara *Autorità indipendenti e discrezionalità*, at 371 ff; M Ramajoli *Attività amministrativa e disciplina antitrust*, cit; A Zito *Attività amministrativa e rilevanza dell'interesse del consumatore nella disciplina antitrust* (Torino Giappichelli 1998).

[76] Caranta 'Procedural Errors and Substantive Legality in Italian Administrative Law' in K-H Ladeur (ed) *The Europeanisation of Administrative Law* (Aldershot Ashgate 2002) 23; R Caranta and M Protto 'Italy' in *Comparative Analysis of Administrative Law, European Public Law Series—Bibliothèque de droit public européen* vol XXIV (London Esperia Publications; Bruxelles Bruylant 2002) 203.

[77] See his contribution to the discussion entitled 'Procedimento amministrativo e tutela giurisdizionale contro la pubblica amministrazione (il problema di una legge generale sul procedimento amministrativo)' published in *Riv dir proc* (1980) 267.

[78] See M Nigro, 'Commissione per la revisione della disciplina dei procedimenti amministrativi. Appunto amministrativo (dic 1983)' *Riv trim sc amm* (1984); see also G Pastori 'Commento all'art 1'; A Travi (ed) *Commentario della legge 7 agosto 1990* n 241, *Nuove leggi civ. commentate* (1995) at 5 ff.

[79] For a broad overview see *La disciplina del procedimento amministrativo. Contributi alle iniziative legislative in corso, Atti del XXXII° Convegno di scienza della amministrazione* (Milano 1989).

Though considerably watered down as to its most innovative aspects in the Governmental bill and by the following Parliamentary readings, the draft put together by the Commisione Nigro finally made its way into the Administrative Procedure Act 1990.[80]

The statute deals with administrative procedure and gives a comprehensive discipline of access to administrative documents, whether connected to administrative procedure or not.[81] Concerning administrative procedure, it is to be remarked that the subject matter of the Italian act is somewhat narrower than the Spanish *Lei de régimen jurídico de las administraciones públicas y procedimiento administrativo común* of 1992 and the German *Verwaltungsverfahrensgesetz* of 1976. The Italian statute does not deal with the general discipline of administrative decisions; in particular, nothing is said about what a valid decision is and what is not. Proceedings leading to the adoption of general rules and planning decisions are excluded from the application of the 1990 Act.[82]

The most important rules on administrative procedure are those on the office and the person responsible for the proceeding (*responsabile del procedimento*) and those on participation of all parties concerned, including public interest groups.[83] The due process principle was traditionally foreign to Italian administrative law; participation was limited to cases where the law expressly provided for it. The 1990 Act has turned this situation on its head. Participation is now the rule for proceedings leading to individual decisions.[84]

Articles 22 and following of the 1990 Act give a fairly generous right of access to administrative documents and files to anyone showing an interest in the information contained therein.[85]

Participation and access have been seen as a way to compensate for the somewhat feeble (representative) democratic legitimacy of independent

[80] G Corso 'El procedimiento administrativo en Italia' in J Barnez Vasquez (ed) *El procedimiento administrativo en el derecho comparado* (Madrid Civitas, 1993) 473 ff.

[81] Generally IF Caramazza 'Dal principio di segretezza al principio di trasparenza. Profili generali di una riforma' in *Scritti in memoria di A. Piras* (Milano Giuffré 1996) 77.

[82] For references to the case law see R Caranta and L Ferraris *La partecipazione al procedimento amministrativo* (Milano Giuffré 2000) at 27 ff.

[83] See also G Virga *La partecipazione al procedimento amministrativo* (Milano Giuffré 1998).

[84] Under Art 7 of the 1990 Act, 'If there is no special urgency, both those who might be directly affected by the final decision and those who are called to take part to the procedure by the law are informed of the opening of the file following the rules laid down in Art 8. In the same way, when the final decision might affect adversely people, other than the addressee of the final decision, whose identity is either known or might be easily known, the authority is under a duty to inform them, following the same procedure, of the opening of the file'; Art 9 provides for the participation of public interest groups; Caranta and Ferraris *La partecipazione al procedimento amministrativo* at 120 ff.

[85] F Caringella, R Garofoli, and MT Sempreviva *L'accesso ai documenti amministrativi. Profili sostanziali e processuali* (Milano Giuffré 1999).

administrative authorities. Increased participative democracy has thus been advocated.[86]

The issue has been raised as to the applicability of the Administrative Procedure Act 1990 to proceedings by independent administrative authorities. Today the principle of participation in administrative proceedings, as specified by the rules laid down by the 1990 Act, is recognized as a general principle of administrative law.[87] On one occasion at least, the courts seemed to be ready to apply the principle of participation even in cases where the specific legislation applicable could have been read as implicitly excluding participation.[88]

Most problems have centred on the right of access. Specific rules enacted with reference to certain administrative authorities tend to be somewhat restrictive when compared to the general provisions to be found in the 1990 Act.

Recently Article 4 of l. 3 agosto 1999, n. 265, amended Art. 23 of the 1990 Act; Art. 23's last phrase now reads: 'The right of access to information held by regulatory authorities is ruled according to their specific statutes and by-laws according to provisions of Art. 24.'Article 24 lays down limits to the right of access. The provision of Article 23 is somewhat ambiguous, since it refers to the general rules on access while at the same time opening up the road to specific enactment.[89]

Unsurprisingly, a lot of litigation has ensued.

Administrative courts have generally upheld specific legal rules declaring secret all documents and information held by the Bank of Italy in connection with its functions as bank supervisory authority.[90]

Specific and restrictive rules concerning *CONSOB* have instead been

[86] Merusi and Passaro *Le autorità indipendenti* at 94; Longobardi 'Les autorités administratives indépendantes, laboratoires d'un nouveau droit administratif' in *Petites affiches* (1999) n° 173, 11; the same position is shared by this chapter.

[87] Cons St, Ad plen, 15 settembre 1999, n 14, *Giur it* 2000, 412, note S Verzaro 'Il principio del "giusto procedimento" nelle procedure di esproprio'; *Giorn dir amm* 2000, 162, note Caranta 'Giusto procedimento ed espropriazione'.

[88] Cons St, Sez VI, 1° ottobre 2002, n 5105, note S Rodriquez 'Il rapporto tra l 7 agosto 1990, n 241, come legge di principi generali e le forme di partecipazione previste da disposizioni speciali'.

[89] The terms of the problem have not been much changed by the new law; the earlier literature is therefore still of much interest: see Garofoli 'Procedimento, accesso e autorità indipendenti' *Foro amm* (1998) 3335; A Scognamiglio 'Autorità indipendenti: principio di collaborazione tra autorità e segreto d'ufficio nella vigilanza sugli intermediari finanziari (art 30 d lgs 415/96)' *Dir amm* (1997) 505; F Castiello 'La partecipazione ai procedimenti amministrativi di controllo del credito nella prospettiva della l n 241 del 7 agosto 1990' in *Scritti in onore di P Virga*, vol I (Milano 1994) 515.

[90] Cons St, Sez VI, 17 giugno 1998, n 990, *Foro amm* (1998) 1790; Cons St, Sez VI, 5 giugno 1998, n 936, *Foro amm* (1998) 1771; TAR Veneto, Sez. I, 5 marzo 1997, n 818, *Banca borsa tit. cred.* (1998) II, 467, note C Barbagallo 'Ispezioni di vigilanza presso banche e diritto d'accesso'.

brought to the attention of the Constitutional court.[91] In an earlier decision the Court held that on their true construction the specific rules did not prevent access in that particular case, which concerned an access request from a firm having being fined by the CONSOB;[92] the administrative court allowed access.[93] The *Consiglio di Stato* was not convinced by the 'case by case' approach taken by the Constitutional court; a new and possibly harder case, concerning access from a third party rather then from a fined firm, was referred to the Constitutional court a few months ago.[94]

Even under Art. 24 of the 1990 Act, access can be ruled out for the sake of privacy and industrial secrets. In this framework, it was held that the Antitrust Authority was right in refusing access to documents pertaining to industrial secrets in cases where the documents sought had had no material relevance to the decisions taken by the Authority.[95]

## VII. WHAT ARE THE REMEDIES AGAINST DECISIONS TAKEN BY IAAS? (QUESTIONS 17–20)

In Italy, both civil courts and administrative courts have jurisdiction to hear actions brought against public bodies. Article 2 of l. 20 March 1865, n 2248, All ER, is still the rule of general application, even if challenged by a growing number of exceptions. According to Article 2, civil courts have jurisdiction when civil and political rights are at stake. Administrative courts, on the contrary, have jurisdiction with reference to *interessi legittimi*. To simplify a matter which has been the subject for hot dispute for well over a century, two broad rules can be given. First, the person asking for a decision from an administrative authority has no right, just an *interesse legittimo*. For instance, those asking for a licence to open a shop, for building permission, a school grant or any other benefit, or submitting a bid in a public procurement procedure, are all said to be entitled to an *interesse*

[91] Cons St, Sez VI, 22 aprile 1999, n 523 (ord), *Giust. civ* (1999) I, 3543, note L Gili 'Procedimento sanzionatorio CONSOB: diritto d'accesso e segreto d'ufficio'.

[92] Corte cost, 3 novembre 2000, n 460, *Giur it* (2001); the cases were referred to the Court by Cons St, Sez VI, 22 aprile 1999, n 523 (ord), *Giust civ* (1999) I, 3543, note L Gili 'Procedimento sanzionatorio CONSOB: diritto d'accesso e segreto d'ufficio'; Cons St, Sez VI, 12 aprile 2000, n 2190 (ord), *Foro amm* (2000) 1367.

[93] Lazio, Sez I, 25 marzo 2000, n 2281, *Foro amm* (2000) 3706.

[94] Cons St, Sez VI, 5 luglio 2002, n 3700 (ord), *Giur it* (2002); *Giust civ* (2003) I, 243, note G Fares 'Diritto di difesa e segreto d'ufficio: nuove problematiche in tema di accesso agli atti della CONSOB'; the case is still pending.

[95] Cons St, Sez VI, 20 marzo 2001, n 1671, *Foro amm* (2001) 625; Cons St, Sez VI, 12 febbraio 2001, n 652, *Foro amm* (2001) 556; Cons St, Sez. VI, 22 gennaio 2001, n 191, *Giust civ* (2001) I, 1413, note M Bonini 'I limiti al diritto di accesso fra trasparenza dell'attività amministrativa ed efficienza dell'economia di mercato'; *ivi*, 2553, note G Cassano 'Diritto d'accesso ai documenti amministrativi o richiesta surrettizia?'.

*legittimo*. Since most economic activities in Italy are, or at least were till fairly recently, made conditional upon the delivery of a licence or permission, *interessi legittimi* are widespread. Secondly, even a *diritto soggettivo* turns into an *interesse legittimo* when confronted with an administrative decision, quite independently from the question of whether the decision is legal or not.[96]

The overall consequence of the system just sketched is that administrative courts usually have jurisdiction when administrative decisions have been adopted or when a public body has failed to address a request.

The question as to the competent jurisdiction has been somewhat simplified concerning the decisions taken by many independent administrative authorities.[97] In many cases Parliament has expressly named one or the other jurisdiction.[98]

Somewhat tentative and rather complex rules were first enacted with reference to the Antitrust Authority.[99]

Article 33 (1) of l. 10 ottobre 1990, n. 287, provides that decisions taken by the Authority are to be challenged in front of the first instance administrative court in Rome having exclusive jurisdiction (ie independently from the nature—*diritto soggettivo* or *interesse legittimo*— of the infringed legal right). Article 33 (2) provides that actions to nullify agreements in breach of antitrust law, to seek damages flowing from anti-competitive behaviour, and to ask for interim relief must all be brought before appeal courts (civil jurisdiction).

The dual jurisdiction arrangement is necessary since Italian and Community antitrust law are both applied by antitrust authorities (including the EC Commission) and by civil courts (civil courts having jurisdiction in Italy to hear competition cases). Parallel proceedings bring the risks of

[96] This last judge-made rule has been subject to strong scholarly criticism but still stands: E Cannada Bartoli 'Affievolimento' in *Enciclopedia del Diritto* vol I (Milano Giuffré 1958) 670, and id 'Interesse (diritto amministrativo)' in *Enciclopedia del Diritto* vol. XXII (Milano Giuffré 1972) 13; A Angeletti, *Aspetti problematici della discriminazione delle giurisdizioni e Stato amministrativo* (Milano Giuffré 1980).

[97] The different interests protected by independent administrative authorities have been analysed by A Romano Tassone 'Situazioni giuridiche soggettive e decisioni delle autorità indipendenti' at 459 ss; L Torchia 'Gli interessi affidati alla cura delle autorità indipendenti' in S Cassese and C Franchini (eds) *I garanti delle regole* at 55 ff.

[98] F Caringella 'La tutela giurisdizionale amministrativa nei confronti delle autorità amministrative indipendenti ieri, oggi e domani' in *Conso. St* (2000) II, 1535; ME Schinaia 'Prime notazioni sulle modifiche apportate al processo amministrativo con la legge n 205 del 2000 concernenti le autorità amministrative indipendenti' in *Cons St* (2000) II, 1785; a less fully up-to-date report can be read in R Caranta 'La tutela giurisdizionale nei confronti degli atti delle autorità amministrative indipendenti' in Caringella and Gaforoli (curr) *Le autorità indipendenti*, at 143 ff; an earlier version was ead 'Il giudice delle decisioni delle autorità indipendenti' in Cassese and Franchini (eds) *I garanti delle regole* at 165 ff.

[99] A Frignani and G Rossi 'EU and Italian Antitrust Rules: Concordances and Discordances' in *Dir Comm Internaz* (2001) fasc 4.

conflicting decisions; so far this has not been the case in Italy, possibly because competitors generally prefer to go to the Antitrust authority rather than bring their case to civil courts; civil appeal court actions are the remedy of choice only when interim relief is sought.[100]

The Italian Antitrust Authority has no power to adopt interim measure in cases concerning anti-competitive behaviour; the Authority has to go all the way through its investigation and proceeding; at the same time, administrative courts can be asked to intervene only after the Authority has taken a decision,[101] or (in theory at least since no case has been already brought), if the Authority fails to act in due time; it is at present uncertain whether civil courts can anticipate by way of interim relief decision in the competence of the Antitrust Authority.[102]

Another question focuses on locus standing. Some cases held that competitors have no standing to challenge Antitrust Authority decisions to clear mergers or finding other agreements not to be in conflict with antitrust law.[103] Such case-law is inconsistent with the rather generous standing criteria usually applied by administrative courts.[104]

Uncertainties also characterize the judicial application of Article 31 of l. 10 ottobre 1990, n 287. The provision states that l. 24 novembre 1981, n 689, applies to fines inflicted by the Antitrust Authority. The 1981 Act provides both substantive and procedural rules concerning administrative (ie not criminal) fines. It gives jurisdiction to civil courts to hear cases when fines are challenged. The *Corte di cassazione*, which is responsible for allotting jurisdiction, quite reasonably held that firms fined by the Antitrust Authority must be challenged in administrative courts, more specifically the first instance court in Rome. The administrative court will apply substantive

[100] See also Lazzara *Autorità indipendenti e discrezionalità* at 452 ff.

[101] Lazio, Sez I, 5 maggio 1994, n 652, in *TAR* (1994) I, 1709; Lazio, Sez I, 2 novembre 1993 n 1549 in *Foro it* (1994) I, 146; Lazio, Sez I, 2 novembre 1993 n 412 in *Riv it dir pub comunitario* (1993) 1257, note M Antonioli 'La legge antitrust dinanzi al giudice amministrativo: gli atti impugnabili, le azioni esperibili e la tutela della concorrenza e del mercato fra diritto interno e diritto comunitario'.

[102] This option has been ruled down by App Roma, 14 gennaio 1993 in *Foro it* (1993) I, 3377, con nota di PF Valdina 'Prime osservazioni sulla tutela cautelare antitrust'; App Milano, 15 luglio 1992, in *Foro it* (1992) I, 3393, note A Mastrorilli 'Rifiuto di contrarre, monopolio legale, abuso di posizione dominante'; other decisions allow interim relief in respect of liability actions App Milano, 8 ottobre 1994, in *Foro it* (1995) I, 1325, note A Barone 'Abuso di posizione dominante: competenza concorrente della corte d'appello?', and App Milano, 5 febbraio 1992, *Giur comm* (1992) II, 437, note S Vezzoso 'Questioni in tema di monopoli legali fra il diritto antitrust e il diritto di autore'.

[103] Lazio, Sez I, 26 settembre 2001, n 7797, and Lazio, Sez I, ?? luglio 2001, n 7286, *Giur it* (2002) 625, note Caranta 'Una lacuna nel sistema della tutela giurisdizionale dei singoli: provvedimenti dell'*Antitrust* e (carenza) di legittimazione ad agire di fronte al giudice amministrativo'.

[104] See ibid.

and remedial rules laid down in l. 24 novembre 1981, n. 689, including the power to annul the fine or to reduce its amount.[105]

The exclusive jurisdiction of administrative courts has been the choice by most of the successive statutes setting up independent administrative authorities. This is the case with Article 2 (25) of l. 14 novembre 1995, n 481, concerning utility regulation authorities and more notably the electricity and gas regulator (the first instance administrative court in Milan, where the *Autorità* has its seat, has jurisdiction); with Article 1 (26) of l. 31 luglio 1997, n. 247, concerning the communications regulator (the first instance administrative court in Rome was chosen even if the authority has its seat in Naples), and with Article 4 (7) of l. 11 febbraio 1994, n 109, as amended by l. 18 novembre 1998, n 415 (no specific first instance administrative court indicated here; somewhat clumsy drafting of the provision could end in its failing to bring all possible cases within administrative courts jurisdiction).

Article 33 of d.lgs. 31 marzo 1998, n 80, as validated by Article 7 l. 21 luglio 2000, n 205, has introduced the exclusive administrative courts jurisdiction with reference to older administrative authorities later turned independent, such as the Bank of Italy and the insurance market and stock market regulators (*ISVAP* and *CONSOB*).

As recalled above, Article 23 *bis* (1) lett. *d*) of l. 6 dicembre 1971, n 1034, as introduced by Article 4 of l. 21 luglio 2000, n 205, has introduced a fast track judicial review procedure of decisions taken by *autorità amministrative indipendenti.*

The arrangement concerning decisions taken by the Privacy Authority is an exception to the preferential option for administrative courts jurisdiction. Dual proceedings options are present with reference to privacy rights too. A person believing his or her privacy has been infringed can either bring an action in front of a civil court or lodge a complaint with the Authority; the complaint cannot be lodged with the Authority if courts have already been seized; this way, parallel proceedings, with the involved risk of conflicting decisions, are ruled out. According to Article 29 of l. 31 dicembre 1996, n 675, if the person having brought the complaint is dissatisfied with the decision taken by the Authority, he or she can challenge it in a civil courts. Given the civil law nature of cases relating to privacy, the concentration of all judicial claims in front of civil courts is not only sensible, but in the end could lead to a more consistent approach and stable case law.

The *Consiglio di Stato* has also held that, apart from true judicial remedies, decisions taken by independent administrative authorities can be chal-

[105] Cass, Sez un, 5 gennaio 1994, n 52, *Nuova giur civ commentata* (1995) I, 276, note EM Cangianelli 'Sui rimedi giurisdizionali contro i provvedimenti di irrogazione di sanzione pecuniaria adottati dall'Autorità garante della concorrenza e del mercato'; *Foro it* (1994) I, 713, note A Barone 'Sanzioni pecuniarie antitrust e questione di giurisdizione'.

lenged by way of *ricorso straordinario al Capo dello Stato*; that is having them reviewed by the President of the Republic acting on the proposal of the Government, in turn following the advice of the *Consiglio di Stato* itself.[106]

Since the advice by the *Consiglio di Stato*, if not strictly binding, can be departed from only by giving reasons, the *ricorso straordinario* was held not to be inconsistent with the very nature of independent administrative authorities.

An important question is the depth of judicial review. Italian courts, both civil and administrative, are not supposed to go into the merits of administrative decisions. Review is somewhat peripheral. Italian courts do not give administrative decisions the same hard look German and, to a lesser extent, French courts are used to give. Apart from incompetence and breaches of legal rules, including procedural rules,[107] administrative decisions can be reviewed under the heading of *eccesso di potere*. *Eccesso di potere* manifestly derives from the French *excès de pouvoir*, but the Italian idea diverges from the original model.[108] At the beginning, *eccesso di potere* performed the role played in France by *détournement de* pouvoir.[109] It then tended to crystallise around a number of hypothesis recurring in the case law: among them, the failure to give reasons; insufficient or inconsistent reason given; discriminatory treatment of similar situations; manifest factual mistake.[110]

These hypotheses seems to coalesce around a rather vague general principle of reasonableness; still, courts refrain from substituting their judgment to that of the competent administrative authority.

Generally speaking, decisions taken by independent administrative authorities are scrutinized the same way as decisions taken by any other administrative bodies.

Most of the case-law has developed concerning decisions taken by the Antitrust Authority.[111] The *Consiglio di Stato* has constantly held that it is

[106] Cons St, Comm Spec, 29 maggio 1998, n 988/97, in *Foro amm* (1999) 414; L Mazzarolli 'Ricorso straordinario e amministrazioni indipendenti' *Dir amm* (2002) 393.

[107] One case was Lazio, Sez I, 10 aprile 2002, n 3070, *cit*, where a decision taken by the CONSOB was quashed because procedural rules concerning the collegiality of the decision-making process had been breached.

[108] See D'Alberti, *Diritto amministrativo comparato* (Bologna Il Mulino 1992) 133 ff.; D'Alberti, 'Mutamenti e destini del "recours pour excès de pouvoir"' in *Scritti in onore di MS Giannini*, vol III (Milano Giuffré 1988) 300 ff.

[109] For a comparison of the Community and Italian notions of *détournement de pouvoir* see L Musselli 'Evoluzione del détournement de pouvoir in ambito comunitario ed ipotesi di raffronto con l'ordinamento amministrativo interno' *Riv dir pub comunitario* (1996) 119.

[110] In Lazio, Sez I, 10 aprile 2002, n. 3070, *cit*, another reason to quash a decision taken by the CONSOB was that the authority had departed from its previous assessment of some relevant facts without giving any reason.

[111] The *leading case* is Cons St, Sez VI, 23 aprile 2002, n 2199, *Giur comm* (2003) II, 170, note Caranta *I limiti del sindacato del giudice amministrativo sui provvedimenti dell'Autorità garante della concorrenza e del mercato*.

not going to substitute the Authority's view with its own on such issues as the choice of rules to be applied to decide which market is relevant when assessing whether a proposed merger has anti-competitive effects. Such a choice will be struck out only if it is manifestly unreasonable, that is so unreasonable even people with no specific knowledge as to the matter would find it tenable. Courts sometimes refer to the German idea of *Unbestimmterechtsbegriffe*; in Italy however the concept is used to call off judicial intervention rather then as a way to make it possible.[112]

Once the Authority has made its choice as to the technical rules applicable to a given case, courts will review whether their application has been correct or not. Since the entry into force of l. 21 luglio 2000, n 205,[113] courts can have recourse to expert witnesses; so far, they have refrained to do so.[114]

Under Article 31 of l. 10 ottobre 1990, n 287, which refers to l. 24 novembre 1981, n 689, a stricter form of review is applicable to fines; administrative courts can change the amount of the fine if they think it is not appropriate to the gravity and other relevant elements of the breach committed by the firms concerned; the Authority's assessment as to the facts leading to the fining decision is reviewed in the usually less than 'invasive' way.[115]

This leads to the remedies available. As a rule civil courts cannot annul administrative decisions (Articles 4 and 5 l. 20 marzo 1865, n 2248, all. *E*). Article 29 (7) of l. 31 dicembre 1996, n. 675, dispenses from this prohibition civil courts dealing with decisions taken by the Privacy Authority.

Conversely, Administrative courts had the power to annul administrative decision but used to have no jurisdiction to award damages; the position has been turned upon its head by Article 35 of d.lgs. 31 marzo 1998, n. 80, as validated and widened in its scope of application by Article 7 l. 21 luglio 2000, n. 205.

So far no liability case against independent administrative authorities have been brought in front of administrative courts. Some cases were heard before of civil courts which used to have a wider jurisdiction before l. 21

112 See S Mirate 'Giudici amministrativi e valutazioni tecniche tra nuove conquiste e antiche resistenze' *Giur it* (2002) 1088.

113 The possibility to have recourse to expert witnesses had been discussed even before the statute was passed: eg Cons St, Sez IV, 10 febbraio 2000, n 715, *Urbanistica e appalti* (2000) 1334, note Caranta 'I sassi e lo stagno (il difficile accesso al fatto del giudice amministrativo)'; *Giur it* (2000) 2401, note Mirate 'La consulenza tecnica nel giudizio di legittimità: verso nuovi confini del sindacato del giudice amministrativo sulla discrezionalità tecnica della pubblica amministrazione'.

114 Cons St, Sez VI, 23 aprile 2002, n 2199, *cit*; this a more general pattern: see also Cons St, Sez V, 5 marzo 2001, n 1247, *Giur it* (2002) 1084, note Mirate 'Giudici amministrativi e valutazioni tecniche tra nuove conquiste e antiche resistenze'; *Urbanistica e appalti* (2001) 866, note M Protto 'La discrezionalità tecnica sotto la lente del GA'.

115 Again Cons St, Sez VI, 23 aprile 2002, n 2199, *cit*.

luglio 2000, n 205 was passed. Those cases were brought against the bank and financial market regulators.[116]

One case predates the time regulatory functions were transferred to independent administrative authorities. A liability action was brought personally against a former Minister for Industry, commerce and crafts, Mr Altissimo. That is in itself a rare occurrence; under Article 28 of the Italian Constitution all public servants are individually and personally responsible for breaches of individual rights; civil actions are however usually brought against public bodies whose solvency is not in doubt.[117] The minister was then the authority responsible for supervision of financial institutions other than banks. A number of claimants claimed that he had revoked the authorization to one such institution due to serious mismanagement, but he had allowed it to transfer its activities to another company which was part of the same financial group. The latter company later collapsed leading to financial losses for the claimants. Mr. Altissimo defended himself claiming that as a supervisory authority he enjoyed wide discretionary powers; even if he had been mistaken in the use he had made of his powers, the depositors could only claim a breach of *interessi legittimi* not sounding in damages. The *Corte di cassazione* departed from its earlier case law and adopted an approach usually concerning liability cases linked to the performance of operational tasks. It held that the public authority has to abide to the *neminem laedere* principle even when it exercises discretionary powers. More pointedly, and with a shift from the above-mentioned principle we need not to be concerned with here, the *Corte di cassazione* held that depositors could claim a *diritto soggettivo* had been breached if they could show that the Minister had acted or failed to act in ways falling outside the limits of his discretionary powers.[118] The case was then referred back to a lower court for a new trial and the same approach was followed in subsequent cases.[119]

Another important case issued from the Cultrera bankruptcy. A company controlled by Cultrera asked the public for money to finance the development of some tourist facilities on prime seafront estates. Under the relevant legislation in force at the time, to do so it had to have a brochure

[116] R D'Ambrosio and F Rossi 'The Italian Legal System' (paper presented to the conference on *Accountability of National and Supranational Regulators* held at the BIICL on 21 March 2003.

[117] M Clarich, 'The Liability of Public Authorities in Italian Law' in J Bell and AW Bradley *Governmental liability: a comparative study* (London UKNCCL 1991) 207, 233 ff.

[118] Cass, Sez un, 2 giugno 1992, n 6667 in *Resp civ prev* (1993) 576.

[119] Cass, Sez un, 27 ottobre 1994, n 8836, in *Giust civ* (1995) I, 1295; in *Banca, Borsa e Tit. cred* (1995) II, 525, by C Scognamiglio 'Responsabilità dell'organo di vigilanza bancaria e danno meramente patrimoniale'; Cass, 27 July 1998, n 7339, in *Foro it* (1999), I, 2001, note A Palmieri 'Il comunicato mistificatorio costa caro all'amministrazione (ma incombe la responsabilità per omessa o cattiva vigilanza).'

detailing the conditions of the operation approved by the *CONSOB*, the Italian financial market watchdog. The brochure was submitted to and approved by the Authority and the company was thus allowed to ask the public for money. The brochure was riddled with false statements, most prominent among them was one claiming that the real estate was already the property of another company of the same group. In due time the entire scheme collapsed and the angry depositors turned against the *CONSOB*. The first time the case reached the *Corte di cassazione*, the Court held that the action for liability should fail because investors could only claim *interessi legittimi* as to the way the *CONSOB* used its powers; the case was sent back to a lower court to be dismissed.[120] The lower court considered the powers delegated to the *CONSOB* by the legislature to be limited to a rather formal control to ensure that the brochure was filled with all the information required by the law and did not include any power to verify the correctness of the same; it then dismissed the case claiming that it could not be shown that the Authority had acted outside its powers. The case came back to the *Corte di cassazione*—a usual occurrence in Italy— and this time the Court reversed its previous approach (this is less usual). It claimed that the *CONSOB* had the power to check the reliability of the information given in the brochure and that, in any case, the liability of supervisory authorities was not limited to cases where they acted outside the limits of their discretion. Quite on the contrary, they could also be liable for failing to perform the tasks assigned to them in the public interest.[121]

The case has been sent back once more to the trial judge which will have to assess what damages were inflicted upon the investors due to the CONSOB failure to notice that the brochure contained false statements (which was apparent from the documents which the supervisory authority had received) and also its failure to take any action whatsoever after the false statements were reported in the national press.

What is worth noticing is that civil courts have dealt with liability cases using the usual yardstick applied to cases brought against private individuals; they have held that public law concepts play no role in deciding liability actions.

[120] Cass, Sez un, 14 gennaio 1992, n 367, *Giur it* (1993) I, 1, 1795, note F Satta 'La lesione di interessi legittimi: variazioni giurisprudenziali sull'inammissibilità del risarcimento e principi comunitari'; *Resp civ prev* (1993) 332, note Caranta 'Problemi di responsabilità degli organi di vigilanza sui mercati mobiliari'; in *Giust civ* (1992) I, 2727, note C Santoriello 'Nuovi orientamenti in tema di ripartizione della giurisdizione fra giudice ordinario e giudice amministrativo'; in *Banca, Borsa e Tit Cred* (1992) II, 393, note N Marzona 'Le posizioni soggettive del risparmiatore secondo il giudice della giurisdizione: una difficile tutela'.

[121] Cass, 3 marzo 2001, n 3132, *Resp civ prev* (2001) 562, note Caranta 'Responsabilità della CONSOB per mancata vigilanza e futuri problemi di giurisdizione'; *Giust civ* (2001) I, 907, note G Giacalone 'Prospetto non veritiero e responsabilità della Consob'.

It is doubtful whether administrative courts, which now have jurisdiction concerning liability cases brought against the majority of independent administrative authorities, will be ready to go to the same length in deciding liability cases. Possibly, they will refrain from challenging what are perceived as discretionary decisions taken by the authorities.

## VIII. CONCLUSIONS

Administrative independent authorities are today a significant feature of the Italian institutional framework. They answer deeply felt needs of the legal system, foremost among them the unbiased implementation of rules whose ultimate end is the protection of some important, at times fundamental, citizen's right. They are probably here to stay.

They challenge some basic assumptions underpinning national administrative law. The answer cannot be denial or fuzzy legal thinking. Those assumptions must be thought over again and adapted to the law in question. An Italian scholar has quite rightly emphasized '*le besoin urgent de réviser en profondeur la théorie traditionnelle du droit public [. . .]. En fait, pour faire face à la nouveauté, on prêterait encore à la théorie traditionnelle une intégrité qu'elle a (si elle l'avait jamais possédée) définitivement perdue. Elle devient ainsi un simple fétiche*'.[122]

Top in the agenda is the introduction of effective means of participative democracy. The participation of all stakeholders has to be properly organised by the law to make sure that anyone concerned is able to make his or her voice heard and his or her opinion is duly considered by the decision maker. The participation of all stakeholders can provide the legitimacy required by independent administrative authorities.

[122] Longobardi 'Les autorités administratives indépendantes, laboratoires d'un nouveau droit administratif' in *Petites affiches* (1999) n° 173, 13.

# 5. INDEPENDENT ADMINISTRATIVE AUTHORITIES IN THE NETHERLANDS

*Alex FM Brenninkmeijer*[1] *and Saskia Lavrijssen*[2]

## I. INTRODUCTION

A central feature of Dutch constitutional law is its strong tendency towards a pragmatic approach to constitutional questions.[3] The role of our constitution (de Grondwet) itself[4] is illustrative. Our written constitution is in more respects only of little importance for the legal practice. Constitutional changes seldom derive from amendments to the Constitution. The Dutch constitution is seen as a rigid one, and is extremely hard to change. This rigidity of the constitution implies that it has not become a 'living document' in our constitutional law. Changes in constitutional law are reflected in the written constitution only after a time had elapsed.

Although the constitution has a higher rank in the hierarchy of norms than statute laws, there is no constitutional review before a constitutional or any other court and statute laws enacted by government and parliament together are inviolable in relation to the constitution. Article 120 of the constitution stipulates that acts of parliament and treaties shall not be reviewed by courts. However, acts of parliament are not inviolable in relation to self executing provisions of treaties.[5] Without case law on constitutional questions, Dutch constitutional law is only developing slowly. Recently the introduction of some kind of constitutional review has come under discussion, on the impetus of minority parties in the parliament.

1 Professor of Constitutional and Administrative Law of the University of Leiden.

2 Lecturer of European Public Law, Tilburg University.

3 CAJM Kortmann and PPT Bovend'Eert *The Kingdom of the Netherlands. An introduction to Dutch Constitutional Law* (Deventer/Boston Kluwer Law and Taxation 1993); EA Alkema 'Constitutional Law', in J Chorus, E Hondius, P-H Gerver, and A Koekoek, *Introduction to Dutch Law for Foreign Lawyers* (Deventer/Boston Kluwer 1997) 1–40; M Pompeo ' A comparison between the Dutch and Italian constitutional system' in Z Penders et al Tilburg *Foreign Law Review* (1996), vol 5, no 4, 349–55; L Prakke, JL de Reede, and GJM van Wissen *Handboek van het Nederlandse staatsrecht Van der Pot-Donner* (14e druk Deventer WEJ Tjeenk Willink 2001).

4 See for the English version of the Dutch Constitution: <http://www.minbzk.nl/contents/pages/00012485/grondwet_UK_6-02.pdf>.

5 Arts 93 and 94 of the Constitution.

Government and parliament are the most important interpreters of the constitution. And they are only to a certain extent limited by the text of the constitution, because the constitution attributes broad powers to the legislator itself.

Essential elements of our constitutional monarchy are not regulated in our constitution, like the competence of parliament to send away a minister (*de vertrouwensregel*). The *trias politica* is not laid down in the constitution as a constitutional dogma.[6] The *trias politica* is to some extent reflected in our state organization, but this matter is dealt with in a pragmatic way as well. We are loyal to the theory of the *trias politica* in as much as the constitution contains elements of it and government and parliament pay attention to it. The independence of the judge is one of the main elements of the Dutch implementation of the *trias politica*. However, the democratic principle has no special position in our constitution. Indeed, the parliament plays a role in the lawmaking process, and ministers are accountable to the parliament. But there are no points of reference for the test whether a certain legal construction is in accordance with the democratic principle as such.

Our constitution has an open character and therefore leaves ample competence to the legislator, which is of importance for the phenomenon of Independent Administrative Authorities (IAA). On the central level of government the legislator (the government and parliament together) has the power to introduce IAAs and to regulate their tasks and organization and the constitution does not directly limit this power.[7] Consequently, there has been an uncontrolled growth of IAAs in the Netherlands. Even the adjective 'administrative' in the expression Independent Administrative Authorities is not free of Dutch pragmatism, for under Dutch administrative law even private law entities can exercise administrative authority.

There are hundreds of IAAs (Zelfstandige bestuursorganen) in the Netherlands. There is an ongoing political and academic debate on IAAs and especially the lack of ministerial accountability for most of them. Is democracy leaking away because of the existence of such a large number of IAAs? Legislation has been drafted for the regulation of IAAs, but has not yet been adopted by parliament. This Framework Act on Independent Agencies has been the subject of passionate parliamentary debate, because it is questionable whether this Act provides an effective instrument to cope with the disadvantages of IAAs. The General Chamber of Audit (Algemene Rekenkamer) has published a critical report on the spectacular growth of IAAs. It appeared that IAAs spend a considerable budget: 200 billion

[6] M Oosterhagen 'Separation of powers as a form of control and the Dutch Constitution' in CM Zoethout, G van der Tang, and PWC Akkermans *Control in Constitutional Law* (Dordrecht/Boston 1990) 71–85.

[7] Art 81 Constitution.

guilders in 2000 (about 900 billion Euros). There are almost 4,000 legal entities with legal tasks and which are entirely or in part financed from the proceeds of charges imposed pursuant to law,[8] and which are for that reason relevant for the control of the General Chamber of Audit. About 475 of those legal entities have private legal personality. This large number of IAAs is the result of a long period in which the legislator opted for a more or less independent organization for various not especially coherent reasons.

Politicians and political parties have limited influence on the administration in the Netherlands. First, there is an unwritten code that influence should not be affected by party policy. The government is based upon a coalition and the main policy guidelines are set out by the council of ministers. So, the minister may never follow his own party policy, if this is not in accordance with the policy of the coalition. Special provisions in the constitution protect the unity of government policy.[9] Ministers have in principle no party-related staff, or cabinet. Although this separation between party policy and daily governmental life is subject to certain tension, it is still upheld. For that reason, IAAs are primarily not established to get rid of direct party-political influence in the Netherlands. As we will see below, there are however various other reasons for the establishment of IAAs.

We start with a closer look at the constitutional and legal background of independent agencies in Section II. For that purpose we will make a distinction between independent authorities with a separate constitutional status (decentralized entities such as provinces and municipalities, waterboards and 'public bodies' which have special tasks for the professions and trades, the Council of State, the General Chamber of Audit and the Ombudsman) and other independent bodies. The latter bodies are established by Act of Parliament and they have no special status. It is the latter type of agencies that are referred to as IAAs (zelfstandige bestuursorganen) under Dutch law and that especially raise questions as to their democratic accountability and legitimacy. In sections three and four we deal with a soft law instrument and the draft Act on IAAs that provide rules on the legal position and the establishment of IAAs. Section V discusses the legal position, tasks, activities, and powers of different IAAs. We discuss IAAs that have the task of promoting the respect for human rights and IAAs that regulate or supervise markets to illustrate that the concept of independence has not been well defined in the Netherlands and to make clear that the nature of the IAA's tasks and powers are not uniform. Section VI discusses how interested parties can obtain legal review of the IAA's decisions. Section VII provides

[8] H Kummeling and T Duijkersloot 'Agencies in the Netherlands' in L Verhey and T Zwart (eds) *Agencies in European and Comparative Perspective* (Intersentia 2003) 79–107.

[9] Art 45 Grondwet.

some conclusions. It may be concluded that there are many different IAAs and that the degree of independence can vary to a great extent. Moreover, there are no truly independent administrative agencies in the Netherlands. The IAAs are checked and balanced by the minister, the courts and the public in various ways. Therefore, the idea that the position of IAAs is in tension with the democratic principle should not be exaggerated.

## II. INDEPENDENT AUTHORITIES WITH A CONSTITUTIONAL BASE

The Netherlands is—apart from the links with the former colonies (Het Koninkrijk)[10]—a decentralized unitarian state. On the level of the regions (provincies)[11] and the municipalities (gemeenten) and for the performance of special tasks like water care (waterschappen)[12] there are democratic public legal entities with autonomous powers, including regulatory powers. Those entities can establish IAAs. This paper will only deal with independent agencies at the level of central government.

The constitution does not include a general stipulation on the power of the legislator or government to found IAAs. However, the constitution does contain some stipulations on specific independent authorities which have a special position within the decentralised organization of the Dutch State. Article 134 of the Constitution introduces 'public bodies' which have special tasks concerning the professions and trades and other public bodies which may be established and dissolved by or pursuant to an Act of Parliament (The Social Economic Council (De Sociaal Economische Raad) and industry and commodity boards).[13] The Dutch Bar Association is one of them. Those public bodies have certain autonomy as well. They can have regulatory powers and they fulfil these powers independently. The competent minister has some limited supervisory instruments which are laid down in special legislation. Article 134 of the Constitution is mainly based upon the tradition of the organization of social economic life in the Netherlands and simply mentions those bodies without stipulating special requirements. To a certain extent Article 134 provides an elementary framework for those administrative bodies, that is that they should be installed by or pursuant to Act of Parliament; Article 134 stipulates that:

> The duties and organization of such bodies, the composition and powers of their administrative organs and public access to their meetings shall be regulated by Act

[10] On the basis of the Statuut voor het Koninkrijk der Nederlanden, the Netherlands are part of a more or less federal construct with the Netherlands Antilles and other former colonies.

[11] Arts 123–32 Grondwet.

[12] Art 133 Grondwet.

[13] See <http://www.ser.nl/default.asp?desc=en_index>.

of Parliament. Legislative powers may be granted to their administrative organs by or pursuant to Act of Parliament. Supervision of the administrative organs shall be regulated by Act of Parliament. Decisions by the administrative organs may be quashed only if they are in conflict with the law or the public interest.

More recently installed IAA are not based upon Article 134 but on Act of Parliament.

Moreover, the constitution comprises special stipulations on the following organizations: the Council of State[14] (Raad van State) and the General Chamber of Audit (Algemene Rekenkamer).[15] This special position is primarily based upon their constitutional role as outlined in the organic law, which applies to them.

The members of the Council of State[16] and of the General Chamber of Audit[17] are appointed by the government for life with special precautions for involuntary dismissal, which are comparable to the restrictions that apply to the dismissal of judges. This may be seen as an indication of their independence under Dutch constitutional law. The Comptabiliteitswet—on financial accountability—gives these two organs a special independent financial position. They are known as High Councils of State (*Hoge Colleges van Staat*).

The judiciary has, as one of the three powers of the *trias politica*, no special position.[18] The members are appointed for life and their legal position is ruled by law. A large part of the judiciary is organized in the recently founded Council for the Judiciary (Raad voor de Rechtspraak, 2002).[19] However, the Council of State and the Supreme Court (Hoge Raad) are excluded from this organizational umbrella. One of the reasons for the Hoge Raad's exclusion is related to the fact that the Hoge Raad has special powers in relation to the removal of ministers for reasons of bad conduct. The Council of State has been excluded, because it has a mixed political and judicial role as a consequence of its French origin. The minister of justice has quite a lot of controlling and supervisory powers *vis-à-vis* the board of the Council for the Judiciary: appointment, suspension, dismissal, control over the budget, the obligation for the Council for the Judiciary to give information to the minister and the power to give general directions (not

[14] Art 73–5 Grondwet.

[15] Art 76–8 Grondwet.

[16] See <http://www.raadvanstate.nl/>.

[17] See <http://www.rekenkamer.nl/9282200/v/index.htm>.

[18] T Barkhuysen, A Brenninkmeijer, and M van Emmerik, 'Access to justice as a fundamental right in the Dutch legal order' in EH Hondius, *Netherlands Reports to the Fifteenth International Congress of Comparative Law* 395–420. AFM Brenninkmeijer 'The judicial organization' in J Chorus, E Hondius, P-H Gerver, and A Koekoek, *Introduction to Dutch Law for Foreign Lawyers* (Deventer/Boston Kluwer 1997).

[19] The district courts (rechtbanken), the courts of appeal (gerechtshoven) and two specialized administrative courts. The Supreme Court and the Council of State are excluded from the Council of the Judiciary.

concerning the adjudication of cases). We mention this position of the Council for the Judiciary, because it illustrates a more general feature of the approach to 'independence' in the Netherlands. If we search for a suitable concept of Independent Administrative Authorities, we have to take into account that even the Council for the Judiciary is subject to a vast regime of ministerial control. This is partly a consequence of the fact that this council was only recently set up. The minister of justice wants to have a strong grip on the first steps of the Council. But, on the other hand, it illustrates a tendency in Dutch law: most Independent Agencies in the Netherlands are not as independent as one would expect. We will elaborate on this point later in the following sections.

The Council of State plays a central role in government. The Queen herself is the President of the Council of State, although this function is primarily ceremonial. The Council consists of a mixture of politicians (for instance, former ministers), high administrators (former secretary generals of ministries, former mayors of big cities), judges from other courts and academics. The Council of State plays a double role: first, it is an administrative court (of appeal) and secondly the Council has an important advisory role in the lawmaking process. The Council of State is seen as an independent part of our State organization.

The General Chamber of Audit is seen as an independent part of our State organization as well. The General Chamber of Audit plays an important role in relation to IAAs because it exercises financial control over the spending of all government budgets. Party policy plays a—mitigated—role in the appointment of the three members, because they are supposed to reflect the political composition of parliament. This practice is based on an unwritten code. The General Chamber of Audit should, and apparently does, fulfil a strictly independent role in our State organization.

The Ombudsman[20] is the third independent body which is a Hoog College van Staat as mentioned before. However, the Ombudsman is not mentioned in the constitution. This fact illustrates that the rigid constitution does not reflect the actual situation. The creation of the Dutch Ombudsman dates back to 1981. The Ombudsman has a competence directly based upon the National Ombudsman Act (*Wet Nationale Ombudsman*). He is appointed for six years with the possibility of reappointment, according to a special procedure: by the Lower House of Parliament taking into account a recommendation of at least three persons, made, after joint consultations, by the vice-president of the Council of State, the president of the Supreme Court and the president of the Netherlands Court of Audit. He should, and actually does, fulfil a strictly independent role in our state organization.

[20] See <http://www.ombudsman.nl/brochureframe_uk.html>.

With regard to the above it may be concluded that the Council of State, the Netherlands Court of Audit and the Ombudsman may behave legally and factually very independently from the government. Therefore these authorities can be deemed independent authorities. However, it should be noted that these organizations are not seen as IAAs under Dutch law. The main reason for this is that these bodies are not administrative authorities within the sense of the General Administrative Law Act (GALA). Indeed, as will be discussed below, independent agencies are deemed IAAs if they are administrative authorities that have the power to exercise public authority within the meaning of the General Administrative Law Act. The establishment of the latter type of agencies is not regulated by the constitution. The Netherlands Court of Audit and the Ombudsman merely have advisory tasks; the Council of State has a mixed advisory and adjudicatory role.

## III. DIRECTIVES FOR DRAFTING LEGISLATION

Besides the independent authorities with a special constitutional position, the legislator can establish IAAs. As we have seen before the legislator has considerable freedom with regard to the organization and attribution of powers to IAAs. Moreover, in the Netherlands the concept of 'the thirteen law families' is used as a well-known description of the influence of the thirteen different departments in The Hague. Every department has its own style of legislation and has its own way of organizing IAAs.

The lack of constitutional guidelines has led to the adoption of a soft law instrument. The council of ministers (ministerraad) has issued Directives for drafting legislation (the Directives hereafter). These Directives are intended to give some self-binding rules for the ministerial departments when they draft laws and by-laws. The Council of State controls the application of these Directives when it advises on draft legislation prior to its submission to the parliament. A special paragraph in the Directives is dedicated to Independent Agencies, with approximately twenty items.

It is of particular importance that the Directives provide a definition of IAAs. The Directives define an IAA as an administrative authority on the level of central government that is not hierarchically subordinate to a minister and which is not an advisory college as referred to in the Framework Act on Advisory Bodies (Kaderwet adviescolleges), whose main role is advisory.

This definition is fairly broad. The most important element of the definition seems to be non-subordination to a minister, in that the minister is not allowed to give the IAA specific directions. Nevertheless, from the directives on the establishment of IAAs it may be concluded that the influence of the minister on the IAAs' performance may still be considerable.

Another important element of the definition is the concept of administrative authority, which is defined by the GALA. An administrative authority is according to Article 1:1 of the GALA an organ of a legal entity which has been established under public law[21] or another entity or body vested with any form of public authority.

According to this definition some acts of private law entities can have a public law character, namely if the law attributes the private law entity the power to exercise public authority (for instance the grant of subsidies or the exercise of supervisory powers). The Directives express a preference for a public law character of IAAs, but the Explanatory Memorandum to a statute can make clear why a private law body is preferable. Since the application of the GALA is based on the definition of the concept of administrative authority by the GALA, the public or private law character of an IAA is of no importance for the application of the GALA. For the administration of social security law and scholarships Dutch law has established IAAs. The legislator opts for a private or public law character of IAAs dependent on the actual political state of mind. Privatization and public control are important notions in public and parliamentary debates on these subjects.

The Directives stipulate under what circumstances IAAs may be established. The reasons for establishing Independent Authorities are the following:

(1) if there is a need for independent judgment based upon specific knowledge or;
(2) if a task concerns the strict application of binding rules or;
(3) if the participation of stakeholders is relevant for the administrative task at stake.

Moreover, it should be examined as to whether the advantages of less ministerial control will be compensated by the disadvantages of fewer possibilities for parliament to control the IAA through the minister's powers as regards the IAA.

In addition to the definition of the concept of IAA and the reasons for the establishment of IAAs the Directives provide several rules concerning the establishment, structure and powers of IAAs. Most rules in the Directives are of a procedural kind, in that the legislator should provide rules for a certain subject, without prescribing what rules should be given in specific cases. The Directives deal with the following subjects:

[21] It should be noted that the General Administrative Law Act excludes the following organs from the definition of administrative authority: 'the legislator, the parliament, the independent courts, Council for the Judiciary, Council of State, General Chamber of Audit and the Ombudsman.'

- the organization of the IAA as a public law body and by exception as a private law body;
- the obligations to state the reasons for the establishment of an IAA in the explanatory note of the legislation;
- the obligation to establish IAAs by statutory law, with a possibility to establish them in exceptional cases by by-law;
- the attribution of regulatory powers to IAAs is only allowed in exceptional cases, namely if it concerns organizational or technical subjects, and in other cases only if the rules are subject to formal consent of the minister;
- the obligation to give an accurate description of the IAA's tasks;
- the appointment, suspension, dismissal of members of the IAA's board (by the minister or the government) and the prohibition to appoint subordinates of the minister on the board;
- the obligation to regulate the relation with the minister. The minister might be attributed the power to give the IAA general directions or to annul its decisions.
- the obligation of the legislator to provide supervisory powers to the minister in case of mismanagement by the IAA;
- the obligation to give rules on the IAA's budget;
- the obligation for the IAA to draw up a yearly budget and report;
- the openness of meetings of the IAA's board;
- the obligation to report to the minister and give him any necessary information if requested for, and
- the legal position of the staff.

With regard to the above it may be concluded that IAAs are independent in that the minister is not allowed to give the IAA specific directions. However, statutory laws that establish IAAs usually contain several control and accountability mechanism that enable the minister to control the general performance of the IAA and to take action in case an IAA acts contrary to the law or the policy wishes of the minister. Indeed, IAAs are not as independent as their definition might imply, which indicates that the debates on their lack of democratic accountability should not be exaggerated.

The Directives form to a certain extent a blueprint for the proposed Framework Act on IAAs, which will be dealt with in the following section.

## IV. FRAMEWORK ACT ON IAAS

As a consequence of the parliament's desire for a more consistent approach to the regulation of IAAs, which was stimulated by the General Chamber of Audit's critical reports, the Ministry of the Interior and Kingdom

Relations has filed a proposal for a Framework Act on Independent Administrative Agencies (Kaderwet zelfstandige bestuursorganen).[22] The Framework Act has four goals. At first, the act aims to harmonize the organizational and institutional aspects of IAAs. Secondly, the act aims to provide a clear regulation of the ministerial accountability for IAAs. Thirdly, the act contains some harmonised rules on the financial control of IAAs and finally, the act aims to promote the transparency of the existence and the activities of IAAs.

The Framework Act is a general act, which should be respected by both the legislature and the independent agencies themselves. Although the Framework Act is a general act, it has no special status, meaning that specific laws may derogate from the Act. The Framework Act will only apply to independent agencies that are at the level of central government, that are not subordinate to the minister and that have the power to exercise public authority by virtue of the law. This means that agencies at the level of the municipalities or provinces, agencies with purely advisory tasks or without any public authority do not come within the scope of the Framework Act.

The Framework Act regulates many subjects that are already covered by the Directives, such as the reasons for establishing an independent agency and the organization of IAAs as public law bodies instead of private law bodies. However, whereas the rules of Directives are of more of a procedural nature, the Framework Act provides more substantive rules on some elements.

For instance, Article 9 stipulates that a member of an IAA cannot also be a civil servant who is subordinate to the minister. According to Article 12 the responsible minister appoints, suspends and discusses the members of an IAA. Article 12 provides that the members of an IAA can only be removed at their own request or 'for cause', namely because for incompetence, unsuitability, or any other weighty personal reasons. Pursuant to Article 13, a member of an IAA is not allowed to fulfil any additional jobs that may threaten an adequate or independent performance of the function. The member of an IAA should notify the minister of every intention to accept additional jobs. The additional jobs of an IAA member will be made public.

Furthermore, the Framework Act contains a minimum list of control powers that the responsible minister may exercise as regards the IAA's activities:

- if an IAA has the power to fix tariffs, these need to be approved by the minister. The minister can withhold approval in case the tariffs violate the law or the general interest (Article 17);

[22] Voorstel voor regels betreffende zelfstandige bestuursorganen (Kaderwet zelfstandige bestuursorganen), *Kamerstukken I*, 2001–2002, 27426, nr 276.

- the IAA has an obligation to publish an annual report, which deals with its activities, policies and quality performance. The annual report should be sent to the minister and both houses of the Staten Generaal (Article 18);
- the IAA is obliged to provide the minister with all the necessary information for the execution of his role, at the minister's request. The obligation to provide the minister with all necessary information may cover business information to the extent that the minister needs this information for the proper execution of his role (Article 20, paragraph 1). If necessary, the IAA should notify the minister of the confidentiality of the information provided (Article 20, paragraph 2);
- the minister has the power to formulate policy rules (general directions) on the IAA's tasks. The policy rules should be published in the Official Gazette (*Staatscourant*) (Article 21);
- the minister may annul the decision of an IAA (Article 22). The decision to annul will be published in the Official Gazette;
- if the minister is of the opinion that an IAA has seriously neglected its tasks, the minister can take the necessary measures (Article 23). The minister will not take the measures, except for urgent cases, before the IAA has had the opportunity to adequately execute its tasks itself within the period set by the minister. The minister will inform both houses of the Staten Generaal immediately after he has taken the measures;
- the minister will send a report to both chambers of the Staten Generaal on the efficiency and effectiveness of the IAA's performance every 5 years (Article 39).

Moreover, the Framework Act contains quite detailed rules on the financial control of IAAs. Different rules apply to different categories of IAAs that can be divided according to their separate legal personality or public law or private law character (Articles 24–38). In particular, the rules that apply to IAAs with separate legal personality (non-State bodies) are detailed and include rules on ministerial approval of the budget, annual accounts and private law transactions. When a private law IAA exclusively performs the administrative tasks and immediately related activities are allocated to it by the law, it is governed by the same stipulations as are applicable to the non-state public IAAs. Except for an obligation to submit the draft budget to the minister, no further rules apply to public IAAs without legal personality (state bodies), since the latter type of IAAs are governed by the exhaustive regulations of the Government Accounts Act.

Kummeling and Duijkersloot have criticized the Framework Act for its minimal character.[23] In their opinion the Act should have contained more

[23] H Kummeling and T Duijkersloot 'Agencies in the Netherlands' in L Verhey and T Zwart

organizational stipulations, for example on the organization of the executive board, the public aspects of meetings and the role of Supervisory Councils within the IAAs. Furthermore, the Framework Act, unlike the Directives, does not contain any limiting stipulations regarding the allocation of legislative powers.

Generally it can be concluded, that notwithstanding the fact that the Framework Act does contain some general minimum rules, it does not result in an overall harmonization of the legal position, organization, tasks and powers of IAAs. Therefore, to get a clear picture of the position, tasks and powers of an IAA, it will always be necessary to consult in addition to the Framework Act the specific organic act by virtue of which the IAA has been founded. The specific organic acts may and in actual fact will deviate from the Framework Act by providing new and more detailed rules on the position of the IAAs or by explicitly declaring some stipulations of the Framework Act non-applicable.

## V. A DEEPER ANALYSIS OF THE POSITION AND POWERS OF IAAS

Although independent agencies have some common characteristics, the agencies that are deemed independent under Dutch law may vary according to their structure, powers and legal position in various ways. In the literature it has been pointed out that the independence of agencies can be analysed more structurally by examining four different elements of independence, namely: institutional independence, financial independence, personal independence and functional independence.[24] Institutional independence refers to the relation between the IAA and other governmental organizations. Functional independence refers to the degree of autonomy in taking (legally binding) decisions. Financial independence relates to the degree of autonomy in disposing of financial means. Personal independence concerns the degree in which the civil servants working at the IAAs are protected from external pressures.

The next paragraphs analyse more deeply the differences between various independent agencies to illustrate that independence is not a well-defined concept and that some agencies may be more independent than others. The analysis illustrates that the IAA's activities may cover various subjects like the regulation of markets and the protection of human rights.

(ed) *Agencies in European and Comparative Perspective* (Intersentia 2003) 79–107; CAJM Kortman 'Het voorstel voor een Kaderwet zelfstandige bestuursorganen: weinig kader voor veel diversiteit' in *Gemeentestem*, nr 16, Feb 2001, 65–8

[24] See for instance BMJ van der Meulen 'Marktautoriteiten, aanzet tot een interne rechtsvergelijking' in BMJ van der Meulen and AT Ottow (ed) *Toezicht op markten* (Den Haag, Boom Juridische Uitgevers 2003) 52–62.

After having briefly described the legal position and powers of IAAs that protect human rights, the paper will mainly deal with independent agencies that have the power to supervise and regulate markets. The latter type of agencies is interesting from a European and national perspective. First, European law or policy has meant that these agencies are positioned to some extent independently from politics. Secondly, these agencies cooperate in a formal or in an informal way with their counterparts in other EU Member States in exercising their tasks. For instance, European competition authorities have to cooperate in a more formal way within a network of European competition authorities which has been established by the European Commission to ensure a closer cooperation in the application of Community competition rules by virtue of Regulation 1/2003.[25] Moreover, recently the Commission established the European Regulators Group for electronic communications networks and services, in which the national telecommunications authorities will cooperate to ensure the consistent application in all Member States of the regulatory framework for electronic communications networks and services.[26] From a national perspective the position of market authorities is interesting, since their independence is subject to debate in the Netherlands. This debate stems from the fact that market authorities should apply legal norms that have not yet been crystallized, which means that market authorities in some instances have to make policy choices. Moreover an effective performance of their tasks, actually requires the market authorities to dispose of powers that are flexible enough to adapt to new market circumstances.[27] With regard to these developments some academics and politicians argue there is a democratic deficit, if the minister is not fully accountable for the market authorities' activities, in that he is not able to give the market authorities both specific and general directions.[28] These arguments are based on the democratic principle, which has, as discussed before, no

[25] Council Regulation (EC) no 1/2003 of 16 Dec 2002 on the implementation of the rules on competition laid down in Arts 81 and 82 of the Treaty, OJ 2003 L 1/1. See the also the Commission's draft notice on the cooperation within a network of competition authorities, OJ 2003 C 243/11.

[26] Commission decision of 29 July 2002, OJ 2002 L 200/38.

[27] AT Ottow, 'Het verschil tussen duivenhokken en telecommunicatie, de bestuurs(process)rechtelijke obstakels bij het toezicht op de telecommunicatiemarkt' in BMJ.van der Meulen and AT Ottow (ed) *Toezicht op markten* (Den Haag, Boom Juridische Uitgevers 2003) 131 t/m 231.

[28] See for instance HRBM Kummeling 'De betekenis van de Kaderwet zbo's voor de omvorming van de NMa (zoals gewijzigd door het wetsvoorstel voor de zbo-statuut van de NMa)' in JW van de Gronden and RJGM Widdershoven *Mededingingsautoriteiten als zelfstandig bestuursorgaan: Onafhankelijk toezicht?* (Deventer Kluwer 2002) 4. See also, SE Zijlstra *Zelfstandige bestuursorganen in een democratische rechtsstaat: Een onderzoek naar democratisch-rechtstatelijke en positiefrechtelijke aspecten van het gebruik van zbo's, meer in het bijzonder op gemeentelijk niveau* (Den Haag VUGA 1997) 99 and HJ de Ru 'Toezicht moet geen nieuwe staatsmacht worden' (2003) Markt en Mededinging nr 5, 178.

special place in our constitution. Nevertheless, these arguments stimulated the legislator to formulate the market authorities' powers as narrowly as possible, preventing an effective performance of the market authorities' tasks. Moreover, these arguments have also delayed the adoption of the amendments of the Competition Act which will give the Netherlands Competition Authority a more independent status.

With regard to the developments mentioned above it is of particular interest to illustrate how independent the Dutch market authorities actually are and whether the democracy principle is violated because those authorities are or will be attributed wide discretionary powers.

But before we come to that subject we will focus our attention on independent authorities in the field of human rights.

### *A. The protection of human rights*

Two bodies are of special interest for the protection of human rights. First, the Equal Treatment Commission, that has been established by the General Equal Treatment Act. Secondly the Data Protection Commission, that was established by the Personal Data Protection Act 2000.

The Equal Treatment Commission (ETC) is functionally independent.[29] It derives its competence from the law. Article 1 of the constitution prohibits discrimination. The 1994 Dutch Equal Treatment Act (AWGB) specifies this norm. The AWGB prohibits discrimination in specific fields (employment, education and the provision of goods and services) on a limited number of grounds (religion, belief, political orientation, race, sex, nationality, sexual preference, marital status, working hours, or temporary contract). The Equal Treatment Commission promotes and monitors compliance with this Act as well compliance with other specific non-discrimination and equal treatment legislation in the Netherlands. The ETC actively investigates a case, after is has received a report of a complaint. The ETC can also initiate an investigation by virtue of its office. Recently the ETC gave a judgment on the power of a school board to prohibit headscarves in the classroom. The headscarf was also relevant in a case concerning law clerks. An important field of interest for the ETC is labour and civil servant law.[30]

The ETC consists of a panel of nine members, including the president and two vice-presidents. The members should be qualified as judges. They are appointed by the minister of justice (in agreement with four other ministers) for a period of 6 years, with a possibility of reappointment. Some

[29] <http://www.cgb.nl/english/asp/awgb.asp>.

[30] Arts 7:646 and 7:648 of the Civil Code (Burgerlijk wetboek) and Art 125g of the Civil Servants Law (Ambtenarenwet).

provisions governing the legal position of judges equally apply to the ETC's members, for instance those concerning suspension and dismissal. The members may be considered as independent. However, the staff of the ETC is subordinate to the minister of justice. The remuneration of the members is ruled by a by-law enacted by the minister of justice. The court rules of the ETC are laid down in a by-law as well. The ETC should send an annual report to the minister and provide him on request with any information which may be of interest.

The Data Protection Commission (DPC) is the successor of a commission with limited powers (de Registratiekamer)[31] and is functionally independent.[32] It derives its powers directly from the Personal Data Protection Act 2000, which makes reference to Article 10 of the Constitution, on the right to privacy, and European law.[33] The task of the DPC is to concentrate on any operation or any set of operations concerning personal data, including in any event the collection, recording, organization, storage, updating or modification, retrieval, consultation, use, dissemination by means of transmission, distribution or making available in any other form, merging, linking, as well as blocking, erasure or destruction of data. All processing of data should be notified to the DPC. The DPC has a supervisory task concerning the processing of personal data in accordance with the provisions laid down by the Data Processing Act 2000. The Commission shall also oversee the processing of personal data in the Netherlands, if the processing takes place in accordance with the laws of another country of the European Union.

The DPC consists of three members. The president should be qualified as a judge. The members are appointed by the Crown (government) for 4 years. The president is appointed for 6 years. The rules concerning the suspension and dismissal of judges apply to the members and their remuneration is governed by a by-law enacted by the minister of justice. The DPC draws up the statute of the commission, which requires the approval of the minister of the interior. Consequently they should report to the minister every year and should provide him with any information which may be of interest.

### *B. Market Authorities*

The Dutch Central Bank (De Nederlandsche Bank NV; DNB) was founded in 1814 and is the oldest IAA in the Netherlands. Partially, as a consequence of European developments there has been a tremendous growth of

[31] See <http://www.cbpweb.nl/en/index.htm>.

[32] Art 52 Data Protection Act 2000.

[33] Directive 95/46/EC of the European Parliament and of the Council of the European Union of 23 Nov 1995 on the protection of individuals with regard to the processing of personal data and on the free movement of that data (OJ 1995 L 28/1).

independent agencies that have the power to supervise and to regulate markets since the end of the eighties. Van der Meulen recently gave a non-exhaustive enumeration of important IAAs with the task of supervising or regulating markets.[34]

Dutch Media Authority, 1988 (Commissariaat voor de Media; CvdM);

Railned, 1994;

Independent Postal and Telecommunications Regulator, 1997 (Onafhankelijke Post en Telecommunicatie Autoriteit: OPTA);

Netherlands Competition Authority, 1998 (Nederlandse Mededingingsautoriteit: NMa);

Office for Energy Regulation, 1999 (Dienst Uitvoering en Toezicht Energie: DTe);

Office for Health Service Regulation, 2000 (College Tarieven Gezondheidszorg (CTG): preceded by the Centraal Orgaan Tarieven Gezondheidszorg from 1982 which preceded the Stichting Centraal Orgaan Ziekenhuistarieven from 1962);

Pensions and Insurance Supervisory Authority of the Netherlands, 2001 (Pensioen- & Verzekeringskamer, preceded by the Verzekeringskamer);

Office for the Supervision of Health Insurers, 2001 (College Toezicht Zorgverzekeraars (CTZ): preceded by the Commissie toezicht uitvoeringsorganisatie (CTU);

Netherlands Transport Regulatory Authority (Vervoerskamer, which is a special unit within the NMa and has been active since 2002);

Netherlands Authority for the Financial Markets, 2002 (Autoriteit Financiële markten (AFM): preceded by the Security Exchanges Authority);

the Dutch Food and Non Food Authority, 2002 (Voedsel en Warenautoriteit: VWA).

Some of these authorities will be analysed more deeply in the following paragraph.

### *1. Dutch Central Bank (DNB)*[35]

*Structure, organization, and tasks*

The DNB may be deemed as one of the most independent authorities in the Netherlands. The DBN is a limited liability company (NV). This means that the DNB is a private legal entity, which is an independent bearer of rights and obligations.

By virtue of the Bank Act 1998 the DNB has tasks within the framework

[34] BMJ van der Meulen 'Marktautoriteiten, aanzet tot een interne rechtsvergelijking' in BMJ van der Meulen and AT Ottow *Toezicht op markten* (Den Haag Boom Juridische Uitgevers 2003) 19–20.

[35] See, for an excellent analysis of the legal position of the DNB under the Bank Act 1998, JB Jansen, *De positie van de Nederlandsche Bank N.V. onder de Bankwet 1998* (Amsterdam NIBE-SVVV 2001).

of the European System of Central Banks (ESCB) and non-ESCB tasks.[36] Within the framework of the ESCB, the Bank shall contribute to the definition and implementation of monetary policy within the European Community (EC). The ESCB tasks are entirely regulated by the Maastricht Treaty. Decisions in these areas are taken at the European level by the ECB governing council, on which the president of the Nederlandsche Bank has a seat. The non-ESCB tasks among other things relate to the supervision of banks, investment institutions, and exchange offices.[37]

The Bank Act 1998 and specific acts, like the Act on the Supervision of the Credit system 1992 and the Act on the Supervision of Investment Institutions,[38] attribute specific powers to the DNB to execute the tasks mentioned above.

The DNB consists of several organs. The Bank is governed by the governing board of the DNB.[39] The governing board consists of a president and of at least three and at the most five directors. The governing board should take all necessary measures to execute the tasks that are allocated to the DNB by virtue of the Bank Act 1998. The decisions of the governing board are taken according to the principle of collegiality. The supervisory board supervises the management of the Bank's affairs and adopts the annual accounts.[40] The supervisory board consists of at least nine and at the most twelve, members. One member of the supervisory board is appointed by the government. This member is also a member of the bank council, an advisory body of the DNB. The president of the bank reports to the bank council on the general economic and financial situation and discusses the policy conducted by the DNB, of course, within the boundaries set by the EC Treaty.

*Institutional independence*

The DNB has a high degree of institutional independence. First, this is a result of the fact that the DNB is a separate legal entity that is not part of the State. Although the Dutch State is the only shareholder of the DNB, this does not threaten the Bank's institutional independence, since the Bank Act 1998 restricts the shareholder's powers. Furthermore, in accordance with EU law, the DNB cannot receive any instructions from the minister of

36 Arts 3 and 4 Bank Act 1998.

37 See, for a useful and clear description of the DNB's tasks, the DNB's website for a clear description of its role and tasks <http://www.dnb.nl>.

38 It should be noted that the Act on the Supervision of the Investment Institutions actually attributes the powers to the Minister of Finance. However, by virtue of the Act the Minister of Finance is empowered to attribute part of these powers to other legal entities. The Minister has attributed some of his powers to the DNB and some of them to the FAM.

39 Art 12 Bank Act 1998.

40 Art 13 Bank Act 1998.

finance, or any other person or institution, as regards the performance of the ESCB tasks.[41]

Although European law permits the DNB to receive instructions from other institutions as regards the execution of non-ESCB tasks, specific acts, like the Act on the Supervision of the Credit System and the Act on the Supervision of Investment institutions, do not attribute to the minister the power to give general directions to the DNB.

Although the DNB can function quite independently from politicians and any other persons and institutions, the Bank Act 1998 and the specific acts include accountability instruments.

Within the boundaries set by EC law, the president of the bank can be asked to appear in one of the houses of the *Staten Generaal* for a hearing on the performance of ESCB tasks.[42] This provision was included in the Bank Act 1998 at the request of the parliament and resulted from the fact that the minister of finance is no longer accountable to the parliament as regards the ESCB tasks. Since the minister himself is no longer accountable, it would make sense that the president of the DNB himself instead of the minister, within the strict boundaries of EC law, informs parliament on monetary policy issues.[43]

The minister also has the power to request the DNB to provide information on the ESCB activities that the minister deems necessary for the formulation of the financial-economic policy of the government. The DNB should provide the information requested, on the condition that it respects the strict boundaries of EC law.[44] The exchange of information between the minister and the DNB as regards non-ESCB activities is regulated in the specific acts on the Supervision of the Credit System and on the Supervision of the Investment Institutions.

The governmental supervisor is another channel through which the minister of finance can obtain information on the DNB's activities. Within the boundaries set by EC law, the governmental supervisor may ask the governing board inquiries about the way the DNB performs its tasks and report to the minister of finance his findings that are based on the information provided.[45] The supervisory board is obliged to provide the supervisor with the information requested, with the exception of information that is confidential by virtue of EC law. The governmental supervisor is a '*trait d'union*' between the government and the DNB. The information exchange between the governmental supervisor and the minister enables the government to be well informed about the DNB's performance.[46]

[41] Art 3, para 3, Bank Act 1998.
[42] Art 19 Bank Act 1998.
[43] Jansen op cit 53.
[44] Art 19 Bank Act.
[45] Art 14 Bank Act.
[46] Jansen op cit 55.

*Personal independence*

The independence of the members of the governing board is strengthened by the fact that they are appointed for a fixed term. The members are appointed by the government for a relatively long period, namely for 7 years, and they may be reappointed after the expiry of this term.[47] Since the Bank Act does not impose special requirements on the persons to be appointed, it looks as if the government has the possibility to influence the Bank's policies through the appointment process. However, the Bank Act contains special procedural requirements for the appointment of the board's members. The members are appointed by the government on the basis of a non-binding nomination of three persons that is made by a joint conference of the governing board and the supervisory board. Notwithstanding the fact that the appointment is based on a non-binding nomination, the special procedural requirements complicate the appointment of the board members and therefore strengthen their independence.[48] Moreover, the independent position of the board's members is strengthened by the fact that they can only be removed 'for cause', in that they no longer possess the necessary capabilities or that they have seriously failed in the exercise of their duties.[49]

The government seems to have quite a lot of possibilities to influence the DNB's policies through the appointment of the governmental supervisor to the supervisory board by the minister of finance. The governmental supervisor will be appointed for a period of 4 years and can be reappointed.[50] The Bank Act does not impose special requirements on the person to be appointed nor any other procedural requirements, such as a nomination procedure. However, it should be noted that the governmental supervisor merely has an informing and notifying function and in any event may not function as an instrument of close governmental supervision of the bank's activities. Moreover, the governmental supervisor does not have special voting rights.[51]

The other members of the supervisory board are appointed for a renewable period of 4 years and are appointed by the bank's shareholder, the Dutch State as represented by the minister of finance.[52] Although the Bank Act does not impose any special requirements on the persons to be appointed, the appointment should be based on a binding recommendation of the supervisory board which nominates three persons for every vacancy. Since the Bank Act 1998 does not provide any special requirements on the removal of each of the members of the supervisory board, the minister of finance in principle is unrestricted in suspending and removing the members of the supervisory board. However, in practice the minister of finance will

[47] Art 12 Bank Act.

[48] Jansen op cit 49.

[49] Art 12, para 3, Bank Act 1998.

[50] Art 13, para 2, Bank Act 1998.

[51] Jansen op cit 65.

[52] Art 13, para 3, Bank Act 1998.

not remove or suspend any member of the supervisory board except for compelling reasons.[53]

With regard to the above it can be concluded that the government may formally influence the DNB's policies through the appointments process. However, special nomination procedures, removal requirements and good practice ensure that in actual fact the government has very little possibility to influence the DNB's policies through the appointments process.

*Functional independence*

The DNB disposes of broad discretionary powers to execute both ESCB and non-ESCB functions by virtue of the Bank Act 1998 and the other specific acts.[54] It should be noted, that the DNB does not perform the ESCB tasks on an independent basis, because these tasks have been allocated to the ESCB, which the DNB is part of. The DNB does not possess any regulatory powers for the execution of the ESCB tasks, since these have been attributed to the ECB. The Bank does, however, have the power to formulate rules for the execution of non-ESCB tasks by virtue of the specific acts.[55] Therefore, it can be concluded that the DNB disposes of considerable functional independence.

*Financial independence*

Due its private law structure, the DBN enjoys a great deal of financial autonomy. The approval of the budget is mainly an internal matter. The DNB is only obliged to submit the budget for information to the ministry of finance by virtue of the Act on the Supervision of Investment Institutions. The DNB's financial autonomy is enforced by the limited powers of the General Chamber of Audit to investigate the legal and efficient use of financial means by the DNB.[56]

With regard to the above it can be concluded that the DNB can behave independently from politics to a great extent. It should be noted that the

[53] Jansen op cit 65.

[54] Art 5 Bank Act 1998. Pursuant to this Article the DNB is empowered to perform those activities that are necessary for its tasks.

[55] See, for instance Arts 22 and 24 of the Act on the Supervision of the Credit System. See for a useful analysis of the DNB's tasks and powers pursuant to the specific acts, APW Duijkersloot and FCMA Michiels 'Taken en bevoegdheden van onafhankelijke toezichthouders: mogelijkheden en beperkingen' in HJ de Ru and JAF Peters (eds) *Toezicht en Regulering van nieuwe markten* (SDU 2000) 21.

[56] See Jansen op cit 57–61. With the entry into force of the third phase of the EMU the Minister of Finance is not accountable for the ESCB-tasks anymore. Consequently, the General Chamber of Audit does not seem to have the power to investigate the use of means for the performance of ESCB-tasks anymore. In any event, an investigation into the efficiency of the performance of the DNB's ESCB-tasks would threaten the independence of the DNB and therefore violate European law. Therefore, the General Chamber of Audit's investigative powers seem to be restricted to the use of financial means for the execution of non-ESCB tasks. The General Chamber of Audit should exercise these powers in a reserved way.

DNB's independence is the strongest as regards the performance of the ESCB tasks. Although the DNB is one of the most independent Dutch institutions from a functional, institutional, financial and personal perspective, it is not completely independent. Indeed, the DNB should respect the law, the members of its organs are appointed by the government and both the Bank Act and the specific acts contain some accountability instruments, which ensure that the parliament and the minister are informed of the execution of its tasks.

## *2. OPTA*

### *Structure, organization, and tasks*

OPTA is also deemed as an independent administrative agency, though in some respects OPTA is less independent than the DNB.[57] OPTA was founded by virtue of the OPTA Act 1997.[58] OPTA is a public law IAA with separate legal personality (a non state body).[59]

Since the Dutch State is an important shareholder in dominant companies that operate in the postal and telecommunications market, OPTA was placed at a distance from the Ministry of public transport, public works, and water management in order to prevent conflicts of interest. Moreover, European directives on the liberalization of the telecommunications and postal market require the national regulatory authorities to be structurally and functionally separated from the market parties.[60]

OPTA's tasks are enumerated in the OPTA Act, the Telecommunications Act[61] 1998 and the Postal Act.[62] By virtue of these acts OPTA has the

[57] See for more information on the OPTA <http://www.opta.nl>.

[58] Wet houdende regels inzake de instelling van een college voor de post- en telecommunicatiemarkt' Staatsblad 1997 nr 320.

[59] Art 2 Wet OPTA.

[60] According to Art 12 of the Postal directive, each Member State shall designate one or more national regulatory authorities for the postal sector that are legally separate from and operationally independent of the postal operators (OJ 1997 L 15/14). According to Art 3 of the Framework directive, Member States shall guarantee the independence of national regulatory authorities by ensuring that they are legally distinct from and functionally independent of all organizations providing electronic communications networks, equipment or services. Member States that retain ownership or control of undertakings providing electronic communications networks and/or services shall ensure structural separation of the regulatory function from activities associated with ownership or control (OJ 2002 L 108/83).

[61] Wet van 18 oktober 1998, houdende regels inzake de telecommunicatie (Telecommunicatiewet) Staatsblad 1998 nr 610. As a consequence of the entry of force of new European Directives on electronic communications, the Telecommunications Act 1998 will soon be amended, Gewijzigd voorstel van wet tot wijziging van de Telecommunicatiewet en enkele andere wetten in verband met de implementatie van een nieuw Europees geharmoniseerd regelgevingskader voor elektronische communicatienetwerken en—diensten en de nieuwe dienstenrichtlijn van de Commissie van de Europese Gemeenschappen, Kamerstukken I, 2003–2004, 28851.

[62] Wijziging van de Postwet en enige andere wetten in verband met richtlijn 97/67/EG van

power to supervise telecommunications operators, the operator of the postal monopoly and other postal companies. Moreover, OPTA has various executive and regulatory tasks, like the registration of telecommunications operators, the administration of telephone numbers, the settlement of disputes between telecommunications operators and the regulation of operators that have been designated as Significant Market Powers Operators (SMP-operators). The governing board of OPTA, which consists of at least three and at most of five members, is the competent decision making body. Collegial decision making ensures the independence of the decision making process.

*Institutional independence*

Since OPTA has a separate legal personality and the minister of public transport, public works and water management cannot give any specific directions to OPTA as regards the exercise of its powers in a specific case, OPTA has considerable institutional independence. However, the minister has several instruments at his disposal to control and guide OPTA, making OPTA less independent than the DNB. It should be noted that the responsibility for the functioning of OPTA was recently transferred from the minister of public transport, public works and water management to the minister of economic affairs. Therefore, it is now the minister of economic affairs that in fact exercises all powers as regards the way OPTA performs its tasks.

First, OPTA should, upon request, provide the minister with all the relevant information for the execution of his role. The minister has the power to formulate procedural and substantive rules on the exchange of information between the minister and OPTA.[63]

Secondly, the minister has the power, after consultation of OPTA, to formulate policy rules (general directions) as regards the exercise of OPTA's powers.[64] The ministerial power to establish policy rules is rather a large curtailment of OPTA's independence. Nevertheless, during the parliamentary debate on the OPTA Act the minister acknowledged the excessive nature of his power and promised to make use of it in a reserved way. The obligation for the minister to publish the policy rules in the Official Gazette, reinforces this promise.

Thirdly, if in the opinion of the minister OPTA seriously neglects its tasks the minister may determine by governmental order (AMVB) that the

het Europees Parlement en de Raad van de Europese Unie van 15 december 1997 betreffende gemeenschappelijke regels voor de ontwikkeling van de interne markt voor postdiensten in de Gemeenschap en de verbetering van de kwaliteit van de dienst (PbEG 1998 L 15) (Staatsblad 2000) nr 201.

[63] Art 18 OPTA Act.

[64] Art 19 OPTA Act.

powers that are related to those tasks no longer belong to OPTA. In that case OPTA's tasks and powers will be taken over by the minister.[65]

Fourthly, OPTA is obliged to establish an internal administrative regulation, which should be approved by the minister.[66]

Fifthly, every year OPTA should draw up an annual report that should be sent to the minister. The report deals with OPTA's policies and the efficiency and the effectiveness of the activities it has performed during the last year.[67] Another important control and accountability instrument is the fact that the minister should evaluate the effectiveness and the efficiency of OPTA's performance every four years.[68] OPTA is obliged to cooperate with the minister for the performance of the evaluation. The minister should send a report on the evaluation of OPTA to the *Staten-Generaal*. This report includes findings on the desirability of the continuation of OPTA (sunset clause). This sunset clause indicates that OPTA is not seen as a permanent institution, but merely as an instrument to achieve the liberalization of the postal and telecommunications market.

*Personal independence*

The minister appoints, suspends and fires the permanent members of the governing board of OPTA.[69] One of the permanent members will be appointed as the president, who will represent the governing board. The permanent members will be appointed for a fixed period of 4 years and can be reappointed. Because of three reasons it might seem that that the minister has strong possibilities to influence the board's decision making process. First, the minister's power to appoint the board's members is not regulated, which implies that the minister is free in deciding who to appoint to the board. Secondly, after the expiry of the 4-year term the board's members may be reappointed, making them susceptible to political influences. Thirdly, the minister has the power to determine the legal position of the board's members. Nevertheless, the OPTA Act contains additional guarantees to ensure that the board's members operate independently. First, it is explicitly stipulated that the members serve on the governing board through personal title and that they exercise their tasks without receiving instructions.[70] The board's members can only be removed for compelling reasons, which include in any event unfitness and incompatibility of functions or interests, or at their own request.[71] The OPTA Act explicitly states which functions or interests are incompatible with the membership of the governing board, such as working for a ministry, being a parliamentarian or

[65] Art 23 OPTA Act.
[66] Art 8 OPTA Act.
[67] Art 17 OPTA Act.
[68] Art 25 OPTA Act.
[69] Art 3 OPTA Act.
[70] Art 3, para 6, OPTA Act.
[71] Art 3, para 7, OPTA Act.

having financial or other interests with market parties which may influence the impartiality of the member.[72]

The governing board has the power to appoint associated members to the governing board who have special expertise on one of the governing board's tasks. The associate members have a purely advisory role and do not have voting rights.[73]

Despite the fact that the minister has quite a wide discretion in appointing the governing board's members, there are sufficient legal provisions that in fact have guaranteed that OPTA's governing board has so far performed its functions very independently from politics.

*Functional independence*

Like the DNB OPTA has independent decision-making power. Since the OPTA has to apply rather vague legal concepts, like 'reasonable' and 'cost oriented', it has discretionary powers. However, its discretion is more limited than the DNB's discretion. It was the original intention of the legislator to formulate OPTA's powers as strictly as possible. This meant OPTA would not be given the power to formulate legislative rules, nor would OPTA be given broad discretionary powers. The old regulatory framework (Telecommunications Act 1998) was based on the assumption that the minister would be responsible for the formulation of telecommunications policy, whereas OPTA's role would be restricted to the implementation of the Telecommunications Act 1998. In practice, the assumption on which the regulatory framework for the telecommunications sector was based, namely a strict separation between the formulation of policy and the implementation of policy, did not prove to be workable. OPTA must apply technical and economic concepts in performing its task. It cannot apply those concepts without an appropriate margin of appreciation of the relevant facts.

As a consequence of its narrow legal mandate and restricted powers, OPTA had not been able to respond adequately to developments in the market under the regime of the Telecommunications Act 1998.[74] In response, OPTA had been searching for ways to (illegally) extend its powers. The competent Court of Appeals (Court of Appeals in Rotterdam) has consistently annulled OPTA's decisions that were based on an over-extensive interpretation of the law.[75] An amended Telecommunications Act

[72] Art 4 OPTA Act.

[73] Art 7 OPTA Act.

[74] AT Ottow 'Over toezicht en rechtsbescherming: de omissies in de Telecommunicatiewet' Mediaforum (2002–4) 108–13.

[75] See, for instance, Voorzieningenrechter, Rechtbank Rotterdam, 29 Nov 2002, VTELEC 02/2675 RIP, *Dutchtone ea v OPTA*, Rechtbank Rotterdam, 25 Apr 2003, Regnr Telec 02/2156 GERR, O2 and *KPN Mobile v OPTA* and Rechtbank Rotterdam, 26 Feb 2003, TELEC 99/2658 RIP, *Kabeltelevisie Amsterdam v OPTA*. See for a review of the case law concerning OPTA's decisions: AT Ottow 'Het verschil tussen duivenhokken en telecommunicatie, de bestuurs(process)rechtelijke obstakels bij het toezicht op de telecommunicatiemarkt'

entered into force recently. Stimulated by new European directives on the communications sector, the new act will extend OPTA's discretionary powers. Nevertheless, OPTA will not be granted any power to formulate legislative rules.

*Financial independence*

Since OPTA has separate legal personality, it has some financial autonomy. This means OPTA may make its own decisions on the hiring of personnel and may be held liable for contract breaches or for unlawful decision-making. During the parliamentary debate on the OPTA Act, separate legal personality was seen as an additional guarantee of the independent functioning of the OPTA. Nevertheless, the OPTA Act gives several powers to the Minister to control the financial administration of OPTA. The minister has the power to approve the budget and certain important private law transactions.[76] Moreover, OPTA has to publish a financial year report which has to be certified by an accountant.[77] The minister may formulate rules on how OPTA draws up the budget and the financial year report.[78] Moreover, the General Chamber of Audit may investigate whether OPTA has made an efficient and lawful use of its financial means.

With regard to the above it may be concluded that OPTA is less independent than the DNB in some important elements. Although, in theory the minister has some heavy instruments at his disposal, such as a fairly unlimited power to give general policy directions, to influence OPTA's decision-making process, OPTA has exercised its functions rather independently so far.

### *3. NMa*

*Structure, organization, tasks*

Although the NMa generally is seen as an independent agency, it formally was not an independent agency. The NMa was subordinate to the minister of economic affairs until recently.[79] During the parliamentary debate on the adoption of the Competition Act in 1997, it was recognized by both the minister of economic affairs and the parliament that impartial decision-making plays an important role in the enforcement of the Competition Act.[80] Nevertheless, the government preferred to keep the NMa under full ministerial accountability during the first period of its existence, so that the

in BMJ van der Meulen and AT Ottow (ed) *Toezicht op markten* (Den Haag, Boom Juridische Uitgevers 2003) 131–231.

76 Art 10 and Art 22 OPTA Act.

77 Art 20 OPTA Act.

78 Art 21 OPTA Act.

79 See <http://www.nmanet.nl>.

80 Wet van 22 mei 1997, houdende regels omtrent de economische mededinging' Staatsblad 1997 nr 242.

minister could intervene were the NMa to have to make politically sensitive decisions or were there to be problems with the execution of the Competition Act during the starting period. However, the minister of economic affairs promised that he would make use of the power to give specific directions in a reserved manner and that after a period of 3 years he would examine whether the NMa could be made a 'true independent agency'. Consequently, notwithstanding the fact that the NMa fell under full responsibility of the minister of economic affairs, it has exercised its powers quite independently so far. The NMa has its own decision-making powers and in exercising these powers the minister of economic affairs has not given any directions to the NMa. Recently the Dutch parliament adopted a proposal to amend the Competition Act.[81] As a consequence of the amendments the NMa will not be subordinate to the minister of economic affairs anymore, in that the minister will lose the power to give the NMa specific directions in specific cases. In drafting the new Act, the legislature has been guided by the stipulations of the new Framework Act on Independent Administrative Agencies, though the new act deviates from the Framework Act by not including some of the Framework Act's provisions or by giving more detailed rules.[82]

The NMa enforces the Competition Act, which includes a prohibition on the abuse of a dominant position, a prohibition on cartels and a merger control regime. The powers to enforce the Act are attributed to the director-general of the NMa. When the new Act will enter into force, the director-general will be replaced by a governing board consisting of three members. This new structure will enforce independent decision-making.

*Institutional independence*

Since the NMa is part of the ministry of economic affairs, it is has no separate legal personality, meaning that it is less independent than the OPTA. This status of the NMa will not change after the entry into force of the new Act.

The Competition Act attributes several instruments to the minister, which enable the minister to control and guide the NMa. The minister has the power to give general directions to the NMa as regards the exercise of the powers that are allocated to the latter by virtue of the Competition

[81] Wijziging van de Mededingingswet in verband met het omvormen van het bestuursorgaan van de Nederlandse Mededingingsautoriteit tot zelfstandig bestuursorgaan, Kamerstukken I (2001–2) 27 639, nr 228.

[82] HRBM Kummeling 'De betekenis van de Kaderwet zbo's voor de omvorming van de NMa (zoals gewijzigd door het wetsvoorstel voor de zbo-statuut van de NMa)' in JW van de Gronden and RJGM *Widdershoven Mededingingsautoriteiten als zelfstandig bestuursorgaan: Onafhankelijk toezicht?* (Deventer Kluwer 2002) 1–18.

Act[83]. These general directions should be published in the Official Gazette.[84] The NMa should publish an annual report every year. The minister of economic affairs will send this report, including his findings and an explanation of his interference with specific cases, to both houses of the Staten Generaal.[85] With regard to the above it can be stated that the minister's power to give the NMa directions seems unlimited. However, transparency requirements guarantee that the minister will make use of his power to give directions only in a reserved way.

After the entry into force of the new Act the minister will lose the power to give special directions to the NMa. However, new instruments will compensate the loss of ministerial accountability for decision-making in specific cases. These instruments are comparable to the kind of instruments that the minister may exercise as regards OPTA. Unlike the Framework Act on IAAs, the minister of economic affairs will not have the power to annul the NMa's decisions.

*Personal independence*

After the entry into force of the new Act, the government will appoint the members of the governing board upon the nomination of the minister of economic affairs. It is of particular interest, that, unlike the members of OPTA's governing board, the members will be appointed on the basis of their expertise in the area of the NMa's jurisdiction. Because of these additional requirements the independence of the board's members will be strengthened.

The president of the governing board will be appointed for a maximum period of 6 years, the other members for a maximum period of 4 years. All the members can be reappointed for a maximum period of 4 years. In harmony with the Framework Act on IAAs, the board's members can only be removed 'for cause' or at their own request.

After the entry into force of the new Act, the NMa will not have separate legal personality, meaning that the NMa will be dependent on the minister of economic affairs for the hiring of new personnel. The minister will put personnel at the disposal of the NMa for the performance of its tasks. Although this element reduces the NMa's independence the personnel will be solely supervised by the NMa and will only have to account for their performance to the NMa.

*Functional independence*

The Competition Act is the basis for the NMa's powers. The NMa may exercise its powers independently. Like the Telecommunications Act of

[83] Art 4, para 1, Competition Act.
[84] Art 4, para 4, Competition Act.
[85] Art 5, Competition Act.

1998 the Competition Act was based on the false assumption that the legislator and the government would formulate competition policy and that the NMa would merely execute the law. Nevertheless, like OPTA, the NMa needs some discretion in applying the provisions of the Competition Act.[86] However, since the provisions of the Telecommunications Act are less clear, OPTA enjoys more discretion than the NMa. The NMa enjoys the highest degree of discretion in assessing whether agreements that restrict competition 'contribute to improving the production or distribution or to promoting technical or economic progress'. Within these conditions the NMa may weigh economic and non economic interests, which has caused a lot of debate on the question of whether it is actually legitimate from a democratic point of view to give the NMa a truly independent status.[87]

*Financial independence*

Since the NMa is part of the ministry of economic affairs it enjoys no separate legal personality and therefore no financial autonomy. After the entry into force of the new Act this situation will not change, so the NMa will be entirely dependent on the minister for the use of its financial means. The General Chamber of Audit may give its opinion on the use of financial means by the NMa through the budget of the ministry of economic affairs.

With regard to the above it might be concluded that from a formal point of view, the NMa is in some important elements less independent than OPTA. However, in practice the NMa has so far functioned quite independently. After the entry into force of the new Act, the position of the NMa will be more comparable to that of OPTA, with the exception of its financial autonomy.

### 4. *DTe*[88]

Finally a few remarks should be made on the legal position of the DTe. Although the DTe is sometimes referred to as an independent agency, from a legal point of view it was not independent, since it was subordinate to the minister of economic affairs. This means that the minister of economic affairs had the power to give the DTe, like the NMa, specific directions.

The DTe has the task to supervise and regulate the energy sector by

[86] The NMa has published many policy rules in order to clarify the way it exercises its discretionary powers. See M Harmsen and MA Heldeweg 'Richtsnoeren voor mededingingstoezicht, Een juridische analyse van enkele richtsnoeren van de NMa' Markt en Mededinging (2003) nr 5, 163–70.

[87] See, for instance, the advice of the Council of State as regards the proposed amendments of the Competition Act, Kamerstukken II (2001/2002) 27639, B.

[88] <http://www.dte.nl>.

virtue of the Electricity Act 1998[89] and the Gas Act.[90] Originally, the director of the DTe was the decision-making body of the DTe. The legal position of the director of the DTe was quite complicated, because the DTe is organized as an organizational unit (*kamer*) within the NMa. In order to ensure a uniform competition policy, the DTe was subordinate to the NMa in exercising its regulatory tasks by virtue of the Electricity Act 1998 and the Gas Act.[91] In order to ensure that the DTe did not receive conflicting instructions from the NMa and the minister, the minister consulted with the NMa before giving the DTe any directions.

Since the DTe is an organizational unit within the NMa a lot of things that are mentioned as regards the independence of the NMa also apply to the DTe. However, since the minister of economic affairs has actually given specific and general directions to the DTe, from an institutional perspective the DTe could be deemed less independent than the NMa.[92] From a functional perspective, the DTe could perform some of its tasks quite independently, such as the regulation of the conditions of access to the electricity and the gas networks, in that the Electricity Act and the Gas Act explicitly attributed these broad discretionary powers to the director of the DTe.[93] However, since the Electricity Act contained many unclear provisions and did not contain a stipulation that could be used by the DTe to take all necessary measures to implement its powers and the intentions of the legislator in case there was a gap in the legislation, the DTe has had trouble finding an adequate legal basis to implement the intentions of the legislator as regards economic regulation. Consequently, the Court of Appeals for Trade and Industry has annulled important decisions concerning access regulation, despite the fact that at the same time amending legislation was pending at the Parliament that would clarify the stipulations of the Electricity Act.[94]

The DTe also performs various tasks by virtue of a mandate from the ministry of economic affairs, like the regulation of the energy supply to households. By virtue of the latter construction the DTe is totally dependent on the minister of economic affairs, who can even decide to exercise the powers himself.

After the entry into force of the amendments of the Competition Act, the powers of the director of the DTe will be attributed to the governing board

[89] Elektriciteitswet 1998, Staatsblad 2004, nr. 443.

[90] Gaswet, Staatsblad 2004, nr. 444.

[91] Art 5 and 8 Electricity Act 1998.

[92] See, for instance, M de Rijke 'De DTe onthoofd?' in van de Gronden and Widdershoven (eds) op cit 61–70.

[93] See Arts 36 and 41 of the Electricity Act 1998 and Art 13 Gas Act.

[94] CBb, 13 Nov 2002, AWB 01/841, 01/847 t/m 853, 01/955, 01/956, Netbeheerders v. DTe.

of the NMa. The governing board will mandate those powers to the director of the DTe, who formally will not have public authority anymore, but will nonetheless remain a separate unit within the NMa.

## VI. REMEDIES

The General Administrative Law Act (GALA) was introduced in 1994. The GALA will gradually be built up through the addition of new parts, called 'tranches'.[95] The fourth tranche entered into force in 2003. The first tranches concerned rules for the preparation of administrative decisions, the codification of some general principles of good governance, and a set of remedies. The GALA provides a uniform and effective system of remedies against acts of all administrative authorities including IAAs. The exercise of public power, especially the making of orders (administrative decisions, plans, etc.) is subject to general rules for their preparation, mainly based upon general principles of good governance: for instance, the right to be heard, the openness of documents with the option of secrecy for specific reasons, the duty of care and the right of the interested party to a written decision within a certain time limit, which states the reasons for the decision.[96] Furthermore the GALA provides general rules for making an objection[97] and lodging appeal at an independent court.[98] However, not every administrative act is subject to remedies under the GALA, because orders containing generally binding rules (by-laws) or policy rules are excluded.[99] For those administrative acts one can start (civil-law) proceedings at the normal courts on the grounds that the act implies an unlawful act. These proceedings do not occur frequently, because mostly general binding rules or policy rules can be tested in an indirect way when one lodges appeal against the order based upon them.

As we have already seen, the exercise of public power is subject to the GALA. The fact that some administrative powers are exercised by private law entities is of no importance for the application of this act.[100] Public law entities as well as private law entities that exercise public authority are subject to a system of objection and appeal at an independent court.

The right to make an objection is laid down in a uniform procedure with specific safeguards for good governance: for instance the right to be heard,

[95] LJA Damen et al Bestuursrecht, Deel 1, Systeem, Bevoegdheid, Besluitvorming en Handhaving, Boom Juridische uitgevers, Den Haag 2003, and ibid deel 2, Rechtsbescherning tegen de overheid, Bestuursprocesrecht, Den Haag 2002.

[96] Art 3:2–4:15 GALA.

[97] Art 7:1 GALA.

[98] Art 8:1 GALA.

[99] Art 8:2 GALA.

[100] Art 1:1 GALA.

the openness of documents, etc. and the right to a written decision within a certain term which states the reasons for the decision. The objection should be made with the public body itself and is aimed at a second evaluation of the decision on reasons of law and policy.[101] No fee required for these procedures. They have an informal character and some administrative authorities aim to settle the case during the procedure of making an objection. Mediation is becoming more important, mainly because the courts can refer the case to a mediator as well. The courts use the short term procedure to settle the cases that are suitable for it.

In the short term the GALA will be amended with the introduction of an option for the parties to a dispute to skip the obligation to make an objection. In particular, when the preparation of the order was preceded by intensive consultation of the interested parties, the procedure of making an objection appeared to be a repetition of the primary decision-making process. This amendment expresses the tendency to speed up administrative proceedings. For the same reason the courts of first instance have drawn up court rules that should guarantee that cases are decided within a year. The courts of appeal have followed this good example.

In first instance, the administrative branch of the ordinary court is usually competent.[102] These courts are spread regionally over the country and there are nineteen of them. In some special cases one court of first instance is competent for the whole territory of the Netherlands. For instance, the court of Rotterdam is uniquely competent in competition law cases. In most cases there is a right to appeal at a higher administrative court. The general court of appeal is the Council of State. There are two other specialized administrative courts of appeal: the Centrale Raad van Beroep (CRvB, social security law, civil servant law) and the College van Beroep voor het Bedrijfsleven (CBB, social-economic law). This last court is by way of exception to the general system the court in first and last instance in many cases. The decisions of these three administrative courts are in principle not subject to a system of cassation at the Supreme Court (Hoge Raad). The way to safeguard the uniform application of administrative law is a subject of debate. In this debate there are two mainstreams. One is based upon the idea that all cases (criminal, civil, and administrative) should be brought before the ordinary courts, with the Hoge Raad at the top. This idea has already been implemented in the courts of first instance, because the ordinary courts have criminal, civil and administrative law divisions. The other mainstream is in favour of the continuation of the judicial role of the Council of State and the other specialized administrative courts (CRvB and CBB). In that case there should be a system for the coordination of the uniform application of administrative law and especially the GALA.

[101] Ch 7 GALA. [102] Ch 8 GALA.

From the moment an administrative decision is taken, an interested party is entitled to start a short-term procedure before a single judge from the court of first instance. A condition for this procedure is that a party has made an objection or has initiated proceedings before a court. The short-term procedure should always be connected to the normal procedure. Suspension or another appropriate measure can be asked for, if there are serious doubts on the legality of the decision of the administrative authority involved. The short term procedure applies to the phase of making an objection as well. Judgments that are decided in the short-term procedures are not subject to appeal. The court of appeal is competent to suspend the decision by way of interim measure in appeal.

The decision of the administrative body taken in the procedure for making an objection can be appealed in the administrative proceedings before the courts. The proceedings are in principle aimed at the annulment of this decision. After annulment the administrative authority is obliged to take a new decision taking into account the judgment of the court. In exceptional cases the court is competent to take the decision which the administrative authority should have taken.

The courts decide cases on the basis of legality and respect for the general principles of good governance, which are partially codified in the GALA. The separation of powers is of special interest for the demarcation of the limits of judicial control. The court may not infringe upon the power of administrative authorities to make their own policy judgements and to weigh all relevant factors concerning a certain case. The GALA has codified the case-law of the Hoge Raad on this subject. According to this case law, which was largely followed by administrative courts, the relevant question was whether an authority could not reasonably have come to this decision. This question has a strictly limited ambit. The courts are eager to protect the discretion of administrative authorities. In cases concerning sanctions this criteria is transformed into proportionality, which implies that judicial control is much more intensive. The reason for this can be found in the case law of the ECHR on article 6 of the European Convention on Human Rights.

The procedural law as laid down in the GALA provides rules for the compensation of damage caused by the unlawful act of an administrative authority. The liability of the State and other public legal persons was developed in the case law of the ordinary courts during the twentieth century. This State liability was based on civil law. The introduction of the GALA did not change this situation. The basis of State liability is still civil law, but under the GALA the administrative courts apply the concept of state liability as well. The courts are competent to sentence the administrative authority to pay the damages of the interested party. The judgment that the decision of the administrative authority was contrary to a (written or unwritten) law proves the unlawfulness of the administrative authority's act. New case law on the basis of the GALA implies the competence of administrative courts in cases concerning decisions of administrative authorities relating to State liability. This case law is not very clear and has lead to many disputes. The Hoge Raad has decided that the ordinary courts are still competent in these cases. So, interested parties can chose whether they address the administrative or the ordinary courts. This double competence is not satisfying. Administrative proceedings are in general less formalized and less complicated than civil law cases. There is a limited court fee and there is no risk of having to pay the legal costs of the other party, unless there is abuse of (procedural) rights.

## VII. CONCLUSION

With regard to the above it can be concluded that under Dutch law independence is not a well-defined concept, in that there are many authorities of many different forms, which are more or less independent. The tremendous and inconsistent growth of IAAs is partly due to a pragmatic approach to constitutional questions in the Netherlands. Although the constitution does contain some elements of the Trias Politica, it does not contain a clear separation of powers nor a formulation of the democratic principle. Therefore, the constitution does not provide any indications as to when and how the legislator or the government may establish IAAs. The constitution does provide some provisions on special independent agencies, the so-called Hoge Colleges van Staat, namely the Council of State and the General Chamber of Accounts. The Ombudsman is not yet integrated in the Constitution. The latter type of agencies (the Hoge Colleges van Staat) are the most independent agencies in the Netherlands, because the legal position of its members is comparable to that of judges and they have an independent financial position. However, these authorities are usually not the subject of political and academic debate, as these agencies fulfil internal advisory or judicial roles, and they do not take administrative decisions that create rights and obligations for the citizens.

The type of independent agencies that are subject to debate in the Netherlands are the independent administrative agencies, which are agencies at the central level of government that are not subordinate to a minister and which may exercise public authority within the meaning of the GALA (zelfstandige bestuursorganen). The legal position of IAAs is not governed by the constitution, but merely by their organic laws and a soft law instrument (the Directives on IAAs).

Although the latter type of agencies have some common characteristics, their mean feature is that the responsible minister cannot give them specific directions. As follows from the analysis of the position of four market authorities and of two human rights bodies, the legal position of the IAAs can differ substantially and it is not likely that the proposed Framework Act on IAAs will harmonize the legal position of the IAAs to a great extent. The differences between the IAAs cannot be explained on the basis of a coherent theory, but is due to historical and political reasons and to the fact that they emerge from different departments in The Hague. Furthermore, some IAAs, like the DTe and the NMa, had to apply a new legal regime comprising legal norms that have not yet been crystallized. This had made the responsible minister decide not to give these agencies a formal independent position right away. This would enable him to keep full control of the development of the legal norms in the starting period, although he had sincere intentions to treat these organizations rather independently.

Although IAAs can behave independently from politics to some extent, the analysis shows that IAAs are not completely independent from politics. The responsible minister has various instruments at his disposal to check and balance the general performance of the IAAs and the regulatory framework by virtue of which the latter operate. Moreover, the agencies' actions are not only checked and balanced by the responsible minister but also by the judiciary and the public which may participate in administrative procedures by virtue of the GALA. Therefore, the statement that the position of IAAs is in tension with the democratic principle or the statement that they should never be attributed any broad discretionary or any regulatory powers seems to be exaggerated. Moreover, it is an illusion to think that the responsible minister is in any case capable of controlling every individual decision that has to be taken by an IAA.

Instead of merely focusing on the power of the minister to decide on how an IAA should decide in a specific case and on a narrow formulation of the independent agency's powers, it would be more fruitful to examine how to ensure that an authority can perform its task in an adequate way. Indeed, as illustrated by the difficulties OPTA has faced in carrying out its legal mandate, this approach may imply that market authorities like OPTA, the NMa and the DTe need flexible powers to adapt the legal regime to quickly changing circumstances. Provided that the legislator clearly formulates the goals and principles which should guide the IAAs' powers and provided that the minister, the judiciary and the public can fulfil their respective roles in checking and balancing the IAAs in an efficient and effective way, this pragmatic approach to the position of IAAs may well be fitted within our pragmatic constitutional tradition.

# 6. INDEPENDENT ADMINISTRATIVE AUTHORITIES IN SPAIN

*María Salvador Martínez**

## I. INTRODUCTION

In Spain, the independent administrative authorities (IAAs) appeared relatively recently. The first bodies of this kind were created a mere 20 years ago although it is true that some specialized bodies had already existed as part of the administration with a degree of autonomy to perform functions of supervision and appraisal. These bodies have been regarded as the immediate antecedents of today's IAAs.[1]

The influence of certain foreign models has been a key factor in the creation and development of Spain's IAAs, in particular the *independent agencies* of the United States and the *autorités administratives indépendantes* in France, even though the latter only predate Spain's IAAs by a few years. It should also be stressed that, from the 1980s on, the creation of IAAs in Spain has coincided with, and to a considerable extent been a response to, the process of European integration and the phenomena of internationalisation and so-called economic globalisation. As is well known, in the last three decades of the twentieth century the free movement of capital and the internationalization of markets set in train major changes, not only of an economic order, but also ideological, political, and organizational; among these changes may be counted the IAAs.

1980 saw the creation of the Spanish *Consejo de Seguridad Nuclear* (CSN) and the reform of the status of the public broadcasting corporation (*Radiotelevisión Española*) and the Bank of Spain (*Banco de España*), the aim being to confer on the latter two bodies a high degree of autonomy. The first body to be regarded as an independent authority was the CSN since it had been created along the lines of the *independent agencies* in the United States. In the late 1980s and throughout the 1990s, new bodies were set up with 'qualified autonomy', as a result of which (and not including the public universities) Spain today has about eight IAAs at the national level,

* Senior lecturer in Constitutional Law, University of Alcalá.

[1] The *Reales Academias*, whose members are elected by co-option and with no government interference, the *Conferencias Hidrográficas*, consortiums that regulate economic sectors in semi-independence of the government, the *jurados provinciales de expropiación*, and the *Tribunales económico-administrativos* are some examples.

to which should be added those created at the regional level of the *Comunidades Autónomas* (the different territories into which the Spanish state is organized politically). After some years when the creation of bodies of this sort was proposed as a solution to any legal-political problem, the only IAA at the national level for whose creation a need is felt today would be entrusted with the job of overseeing the audio-visual sector.

## II. WHAT ARE THE IAAS? (QUESTIONS 1, 5, AND 12)

### A. *The meaning of 'independent administrative authorities' in the Spanish legal order*

It is by no means easy to define and identify the IAAs. No legal definition exists, nor any jurisprudential construction which would permit them to be identified with certainty. Only once has the legislator used the expression 'independent authority',[2] and although judges and the Constitutional Court have had occasion to make pronouncements on some particular aspect or other of these bodies, the only conceptual delimitation of the IAAs is to be found in the work of academics. The first article on the subject was published in 1984,[3] but it was not until the 1990s that the doctrinal debate really got under way and that the expressions '*autoridades administrativas independientes*' or '*administraciones independientes*' were coined (under the influence of the French expression *autorités administratives indépendantes*).

Although this doctrinal debate has been in progress for some years now,[4] there is still no definition of the IAAs which satisfies all doctrinal positions. The truth is that there has been no genuine debate on the matter; rather the definition is somehow taken for granted. Where there is agreement, it is on

[2] *Ley 2/2000, de 4 de mayo, del Consejo del Audiovisual de Cataluña*, defines this council as 'a public body of an institutional nature which, as an *independent authority* with its own legal identity and full powers to act, operates independently of the state administration in the discharge of its functions' (Art 1.1).

[3] JM Sala Arquer 'El Estado neutral. Contribución al estudio de las administraciones independientes', REDA nº 42 (1984) 410 ff.

[4] The principle studies of IAAs are: TR Fernández Rodríguez 'Reflexiones sobre las llamadas autoridades administrativas independientes' in A Pérez (coord), *Administración instrumental. Libro homenaje a Manuel Francisco Clavero Arévalo* vol 1 (1994) 427 ff; A Betancor Rodríguez *Las administraciones independientes* (1994); E García Llovet 'Autoridades administrativas independientes y Estado de derecho' RAP, nº 131 (1993) 61 ff; LA Pomed Sánchez 'Fundamento y naturaleza jurídica de las administraciones independientes' RAP nº 132 (1993) 117 ff.; R Parada, *Derecho administrativo II. Organización y Empleo público* (14th edn 2000); M Magide Herrero *Límites constitucionales de las administraciones independientes* (2000); A Rallo Lombarte *La constitucionalidad de las administraciones independientes* (2002); M Salvador Martínez *Autoridades independientes* (2002).

the question of the IAAs' organization, for their chief characteristic is the degree of autonomy they have been given and that autonomy's qualitative superiority with respect to the autonomy given to other institutions and bodies that form part of the administration. For that reason, the IAAs are, according to some, on the limit of the administration's purlieu, characterized for its subjection to the government, while for others they are beyond its purlieu strictly speaking.

It is taken as read that the 'independence' of these 'authorities' answers to the need to ensure that particular functions are discharged from a position of 'political neutrality', in other words, from a position beyond the reach of any direct influence from political parties. As we shall see, the functions assigned to this kind of body are not always the same. In most cases their function is to regulate some key sector or other of the economy or society, but in others it is to offer particular public services.

For this 'qualified autonomy' to be guaranteed, it is considered that government participation in the appointment and dismissal of IAA members should be restricted and that the actions of 'authorities' should be untouched by government orders or instructions and by the administration's usual control mechanisms. It is just these features which define the 'qualified autonomy' of the 'independent authorities' and which distinguish them from the entities and bodies that form part of the traditional administration, especially the *entes instrumentales* (the entities which have emerged as a result of the administration's functional decentralization).[5] Nonetheless, these requirements are not met by every single one of the bodies which Spanish legal opinion regards as an IAA. Furthermore, there are some important differences between them in terms of their functions and the specific way in which they are organized, which is why a more precise definition of an 'independent authority' cannot be given.

### *B. The Spanish IAAs*

The *Ley de Organización y Funcionamiento de la Administración General del Estado* (LOFAGE), which deals with the organization and working of

[5] In Spain the administration is subject to government control, although not all administrative bodies and institutions stand in the same relationship to it. The centralized administration, which depends directly on the government, is essentially a pyramidal, hierarchical organization, in which the upper bodies exercise competences over the lower bodies in matters of organization, coordination, and control. Meanwhile, the functionally decentralized bodies (*entes instrumentales*) have their own legal identity separate from the central administration, with respect to which they maintain a relationship of 'instrumentality', basically taking the form of the appointment and revocation of the body's office-holders at the discretion of the relevant minister, issuing ministerial directives, for the development of which the instrumental body enjoys executive or operational autonomy, and governmental mechanisms for prior control and for the later control of efficacy or results.

the administration, includes a list of bodies to which the law does not apply, being subject only to their own specific regulation.[6] Not all the bodies listed are IAAs, but most bodies which have to date been considered as such are included in the list. The list itself is not a definitive catalogue, a *numerus clausus*; rather its purpose is simply to indicate which bodies fall outside the scope of the law.

Despite the list of bodies in the LOFAGE and the work done by some scholars on the delimitation of the IAAs as distinct from other similar bodies,[7] there is no unanimity when it comes to deciding exactly which are the IAAs that exist in Spain because, as stated above, there is no concept of sufficient precision on which to base such a decision. But there is general agreement that the following institutions may be regarded as IAAs:[8]

1. The *Consejo de Seguridad Nuclear* (CSN), set up in 1980 in line with the organizational model of the *independent agencies* in the United States, more specifically, the model of the *Nuclear Regulatory Commission*. The CSN was accordingly the first body to attract the attention of scholars on account of its uniqueness and the first to be given the label 'independent authority' by those scholars. The function of the CSN consists in overseeing private activities related to nuclear security and radiological protection.[9]
2. The *Banco de España*. In the wake of the Constitution of 1978, the Bank's status was modified in 1980 with a view to granting it autonomy in the execution of the economic and monetary policy as determined by the government. In 1994, as a response to the demands arising from the European process of economic and monetary union, the Bank was also given autonomy to formulate economic and monetary policy; however this competence was passed over to the European Central Bank in 1998.[10]

[6] Ley 6/1997, de 14 de abril, de Organización y Funcionamiento de la Administración General del Estado (Disps Adds 6–11).

[7] See, for all bodies, Martínez op. cit 255–8.

[8] Regarding RTVE, the CNE and the universities, there is no unanimity for the following reasons: first, some authors express, or introduce implicitly into their definitions, the requisite of performing a particular task—the regulatory or supervisory function—and therefore do not regard as IAAs those bodies, such as the universities and RTVE, that carry out other sorts of functions; secondly, some authors believe that the functional measures related to staff that have been implemented for some bodies are not sufficient to guarantee their 'independence', even if they are similar to those established for the other IAAs, as is the case with RTVE and the CNE.

[9] Ley 15/1980, de 22 de abril, del Consejo de Seguridad Nuclear (LCSN) and RD 1157/1982, de 30 de abril, por el que se aprueba el Estatuto del Consejo de Seguridad Nuclear (ECSN). Further information at <http://www.csn.es>. For the CSN, F López Ramón 'El Consejo de Seguridad Nuclear, un ejemplo de Administración independiente' RAP nº 126 (1991),189 ff.

[10] Ley 13/1994, de 1 de junio, de autonomía del Banco de España (LABE) and Reglamento Interno publicado por Resolución de 28 de marzo de 2000 (RIBE). Further information at <http://www.bde.es>. For the Banco de España see LA Pomed Sánchez El Régimen jurídico del Banco de España (1996).

3. The public broadcasting corporation, *Radiotelevisión Española* (RTVE), is the outcome of the successive modifications made to the former *Dirección General de Radiodifusión y Televisión*, set up in 1962. In 1980 the status of public radio and television was modified in order to adapt its organization to the Constitution, to the new democratic system established thereby, and to the rights and freedoms recognized therein. To that end, the act stated that measures were to be adopted that would guarantee a high level of independence among the members of public radio and television. Since then, its status has undergone no significant further modifications.[11]
4. The universities. In 1983 was passed the *Ley Orgánica de Reforma Universitaria* (replaced in 2001 with the new *Ley de Universidades*), in development of Article 27.10 of the Constitution, where the autonomy of the universities is recognized.[12]
5. The *Comisión Nacional del Mercado de Valores* (CNMV), set up in 1988, on the occasion of the reform of the securities market which had been undertaken with a view to achieving the European Community goal of capital market deregulation. Its function consists in overseeing the activity of the different financial markets and watching over their correct functioning. The influence of IAAs from other countries is discernible in the creation of the CNMV, more precisely the US independent agency, the *Securities and Exchange Commission*, which also served as a model for other similar bodies set up elsewhere in Europe such as France's *Commission des opérations de bourse* and the United Kingdom's *Financial Services Authority*.[13]
6. The *Agencia de Protección de Datos* (APD), set up in 1992, although its current regulation dates from 1999. Its function consists in guaranteeing the right of the citizens to protection for their personal data. In its creation may be detected the influence of European Community law and of IAAs from other countries, above all France's *Commission nationale de l'informatique et des libertés*.[14]

[11] Ley 4/1980, de 10 de enero, por la que se aprueba el Estatuto de la Radio y la Televisión (ERTV). For RTVE, J Juan González Encinar 'La televisión pública en España' in González Encinar La televisión pública en Europa (1995) 187 ff.; E García Llovet El régimen jurídico de la radiodifusión (1991) 277–80.

[12] LO 6/2001, de 21 de diciembre, de Universidades (LOU).

[13] Ley 24/1988, de 28 de julio, del mercado de valores (LMV). Further information at <http://www.cnmv.es>. For the CNMV see M Fuertes López La Comisión Nacional del Mercado de Valores (1994) 373 ff.; E Malaret i García 'La Comisión Nacional del Mercado de Valores (una aproximación a su configuración institucional)' REDA, nº 76 (1992) 557 ff.

[14] LO 15/1999, de 13 de diciembre, de protección de datos de carácter personal (LOPD), and RD 428/1993, de 26 de marzo, por el que se aprueba el Estatuto de la Agencia de Protección de Datos (EAPD). Further information at <http://www.agenciaprotecciondatos.org>. For the APD see, among others, X Muro i Bas 'La Agencia de Protección de Datos' RAP nº 147 (1998) 381 ff.

7. The Comisión del mercado de las telecomunicaciones (CMT) was set up in 1996 after the model of the United Kingdom's Office of Telecommunications and, ultimately, the United States' *Federal Communications Commission*. The CMT appeared in response to the needs arising from the European process of deregulation in the telecommunications sector. It was created as an independent body that would safeguard compliance with the principles of free competition, transparency and equal treatment in the telecommunications market, and to arbitrate in conflicts between operators in the sector.[15]
8. The *Comisión Nacional de Energía* (CNE) was set up in 1994, although its current status dates from 1998. Its brief is to oversee the electricity sector and to watch over the correct functioning of the hydrocarbons (both gas and liquid) sector. This body, like the CMT, was created in response to needs arising from the European process of deregulation in the electricity and hydrocarbons sectors; in its design the influence of the United States' *Federal Energy Regulatory Commission* has been detected.[16]
9. The *Tribunal de Defensa de la Competencia* (TDC) was set up in 1963, although its current regulation in the field of the defence of competition dates from 1989. The status of the TDC was given a thorough overhaul in 2001 in order to give it greater autonomy. Once more, European influence has been decisive in the final design of this body, as has the influence of US independent agencies, particularly the *Interstate Commerce Commission and the Federal Trade Commission.*[17]

### C. *IAAs and Spain's territorial organization*

All the IAAs mentioned above have been created at the level of the central state, but the *Comunidades Autónomas* (the sub-state territorial entities, or regions) have also set up 'authorities' of the same kind which pose up the same kind of problems. In some *Comunidades Autónomas* IAAs have been

[15] Ley 12/1997, de 24 de abril, de Liberalización de las telecomunicaciones (LLT), RD 1994/1996, de 6 de septiembre, por el que se aprueba el Reglamento de la CMT (RCMT), and Orden de 9 de abril de 1997 por la que se aprueba el Reglamento de Régimen Interior de la CMT (RRICMT). Further information at <http://www.cmt.es>. For the CMT see JM Sala Arquer La Comisión del Mercado de las Telecomunicaciones (2000).

[16] Ley 34/1998, de 7 de octubre, reguladora del sector de hidrocarburos (LSH); RD 1339/1999, de 31 de julio, por el que se aprueba el Reglamento de la Comisión Nacional de Energía (RCNE). Further information at <http://www.cne.es>. For the CNE see V López-Ibor Mayor 'La liberalización del sector eléctrico: perspectiva jurídica' REDA nº 98 (1998) 205.

[17] *Ley 16/1989, de 17 de julio, de Defensa de la Competencia* (LDC). Further information at <http://www.tdcompetencia.org>. For the TDC see LL Cases Pallares *Derecho Administrativo de la Defensa de la Competencia* (1995); JE Soriano García *Derecho público de la competencia* (1998); and S Hierro Anibarro 'EC Law and the Spanish Competition Court' EBOR vol 3 (2002) 833 ff.

set up after the model of those that exist at the central, national level, such as the regional data protection agencies or broadcasting corporations, which have taken as their models the APD and the RTVE respectively. However, in some *Comunidades Autonomas* 'independent audio-visual authorities' have also been set up. These are especially odd since there is no equivalent 'independent authority' at national level. The *Consejo Audiovisual de Cataluña* was the first 'independent audio-visual authority' to be set up, and it has served as a model for those which have been created subsequently in other *Comunidades Autónomas*.[18] These audio-visual boards enjoy the 'qualified autonomy' proper to the IAAs, while their function is to oversee activity in their *Comunidad Autónoma*'s audio-visual sector.[19]

Lastly, in connection with the IAAs and territorial organization, it should be pointed out that the chief problems they raise concern the distribution of competences between the central bodies of the State and the *Comunidades Autónomas*. At times, the latter have felt that the IAAs created by the central State have invaded the competences that belonged to them, as a result of which they have appealed before the Constitutional Court.[20] There have been such cases involving the universities, the APD, the CNMV and the TDC.[21]

## III. JUSTIFICATION FOR THE IAAS (QUESTIONS 3 AND 6)

The argument used in Spain to justify the setting up of IAAs is that of 'political neutrality', 'depoliticization' or 'political impartiality'. These are just some of the words or expressions employed to explain how the creation of IAAs is a response to the need for certain functions to be discharged at a safe distance from the political battleground. In other words, there is a need to seal off particular activities and decisions from the sphere of influence of

18 The *Consejo Audiovisual de Cataluña* was set up in 1996 but its current regulation is to be found in *Ley 2/2000, de 4 de mayo, del Consejo del Audiovisual de Cataluña* (further information at <http://www.audiovisualcat.net>). Similar features are shared by the *Consejo Audiovisual de Navarra*, set up by *Ley 18/2001, de 5 de julio, por la que se regula la actividad audiovisual en Navarra y se crea el Consejo Audiovisual de Navarra* (further information at <http://www.consejoaudiovisualdenavarra.es>).

19 For these authorities see J Tornos Mas *Las autoridades de regulación de lo audiovisual* (1999).

20 S Muñoz Machado 'Las modulaciones de las competencias de las Comunidades Autónomas por las regulaciones del mercado y las nuevas tecnologías' RAP nº 153 (2000) 195 ff; A Embid Irujo 'La autonomía universitaria y la autonomía de las CCAA' RAP nº 146 (1998) 7 ff; Muro i Bas 'La Agencia de Protección de Datos' op cit 385–6; M Fuertes 'Mercado único de valores y Comunidades Autónomas' RAP nº 145 (1998) 147 ff.; P Biglino 'Principio de competencia, inconstitucionalidad y nulidad a la luz de la STC 208/1999' in REDC nº 59 (2000) 303–30.

21 SSTC 290/2000; 133/1997; and 208/1999 respectively.

political parties and, more precisely, from the State institutions where the political conflict is played out. The goal is stated to be that of ensuring a certain 'neutrality' or 'impartiality' in the discharge of a given function, which is why that function has to be assigned to a body which is 'distant' from ('independent' from) the State's political institutions. Political neutrality in the discharge of a function is, then, the objective to be guaranteed, and the means to achieve it is the 'independence' of the body charged with the performance of that function. At times this argument is given an airing as a reaction to actual cases of political corruption, while at other times it is put forward in a pre-emptive bid to prevent cases of political corruption from happening.[22]

If political neutrality is accepted as necessary, it is logical that the next question should be, which activities or functions ought to be separated or hived away from the cut and thrust of party politics? The IAAs that exist today have basically been set up to discharge two kinds of functions: those whose end is to guarantee the effective exercise of a fundamental right, and those of an economic or technical nature which are related to the regulation and supervision of activities in a particular private sector.

With respect to the functions whose end is to guarantee a fundamental right, legal opinion did not take long to declare that neutrality and independence are *de rigueur*, indeed constitutionally so. Spain's Constitution only gives express recognition to the autonomy of universities,[23] but it is evident that the need to set up other IAAs may be deduced from a reading of the text of the Constitution, especially of the norms dealing with fundamental rights. Of course, the Constitution should not be understood as requiring the creation of an IAA for the exercise of all functions related to a fundamental right because in the last analysis every public function is related somehow or another with the guarantee of some or other right. It is therefore necessary to analyse each particular case in turn and to decide whether the norm regarding the fundamental right permits the deduction of a constitutional requirement that an authority of this kind should be created.

Thus, along with the universities, whose autonomy is expressly directly required by the Constitution, the 'independence' of the APD and RTVE has also been interpreted as answering to a constitutional requirement. The APD was created to guarantee the fundamental right to have protection for personal data, a right recognized by the Constitutional Court.[24] The

[22] Sala Arquer 'El Estado neutral' op cit 410 ff.; LA Pomed Sánchez 'Fundamento y naturaleza jurídica de las administraciones independientes' op cit 121; Betancor Rodríguez op cit 25; M Salvador Martínez *Autoridades independientes* op cit 264 ff.

[23] Art 27.10 *Constitución Española*. In the Constitutional Court's jurisprudence, STC 26/1987, FJ 4a; 55/1989 FJ 2; 106/1990 FJ 6; 130/1991 FJ 3; 235/1991 FJ 1.

[24] STC 254/1993, FJ 6°; 143/1994, JF 7°; 11/1998, JF 4°; 94/1998, JF 6°; 202/1999 JF 2°; 290/2000, FJ 7°; 292/2000, FJ 5°.

requirement that it should exist stems from, on the one hand, the need for a rapid, technically specialized and pre-emptive response given that, in the face of the wide range of real and potential developments in information technology, the process of law is insufficient and ill-equipped to protect personal data;[25] on the other hand it stems from the need to set up a watch-dog body independent of the government, since the public data bases are owned by the administration, which is one of the subjects under its control.[26] As for RVTE, it should provide an objective and impartial public radio and television service, on which depend the guarantee of the rights and freedoms associated with communication, the guarantee of an open and free process of individual and public opinion-forming, and, in short, the proper working of the democratic state.[27]

As is evident, from the constitutional perspective an important distinction is thus established between those IAAs whose 'independence' is required constitutionally and whose creation is enforced by the legislator, and those others which have been created as the result of a free decision taken by the legislative body. In this regard, it should be added that in Spain there has been no proposal or discussion of any constitutional reform aimed at justifying the creation of a particular IAA or, more generally, of the existence of IAAs

In addition to the IAAs which have been set up to guarantee the effective exercise of particular fundamental rights, there is another type of IAA, namely those that have been set up on the decision of the legislator in order to discharge certain economic or technical functions. In these cases there is no constitutional requirement despite the occasional attempts of legal opinion to demonstrate the contrary by appealing either to the protection of one of the fundamental rights or to another constitutional norm.[28] Generally these IAAs are said to have been created in order to intervene in particular sectors, while the features peculiar to those sectors—dynamism, a significant technical slant, national and international transcendence, the activity's economic and social impact—are said to account for the need for a politically neutral body to take charge of the regulation or supervision of activity in those sectors, instead of the traditional administration.

Each case has its own arguments. With respect to the CSN, the accident at Harrisburg (USA) and episodes such as the Cuban missile crisis saw trust

[25] STC 290/2000, FJ 9º.

[26] JM Sala Arquer op cit 426; E Pérez Luño *Constitución, derechos humanos, Estado de Derecho* (1991) 391; JM Castells Arteche 'La libertad informática', in *Estudios Homenaje a E. García de Enterría* (1991) 925.

[27] For all of these, Juan González Encinar op cit 244; id 'El derecho de la televisión' op cit 19 ff.

[28] In the case of the CMT, appeal is made to the rights of communication; in the case of the *Banco de España* it has been claimed that economic stability is a value of constitutional import; and in the case of the CSN, recourse has been had to the right to a fit environment.

in politicians plummet while fervour for technical competence soared. This fuelled the belief that only independent bodies could guarantee the peaceful and safe use of nuclear energy. As for the *Banco de España* and the CNMV, the argument runs that the function to be discharged is an economic function of particular transcendence and calls for a stability and impartiality which the state's political bodies are apparently unable to deliver. In fact, as far as the Bank is concerned, this was the argument used by the European Community when insisting that all Member States should confer autonomy on their central banks as a prerequisite of integration in the European System of Central Banks.[29] As for the CMT and the CNE, charged with overseeing deregulated markets, the community institutions require as a general rule of organization that the regulatory function, discharged in traditional public services by the administration that owns the service, be separated from the actual running of the service and allotted to functionally independent bodies.[30] Similarly, the TDC is a response to the European Community requirement that the control of company mergers and ensures the defence of free competition should be the responsibility of a body quite independent from the government. It is then clear that all IAAs that discharge an economic function have been set up in response to European Community requirements for, generally speaking, their appearance in Europe in the last two or three decades of the twentieth century coincided with deregulation of the markets, the European Union enforced end of State monopolies, and privatization.

Now that the 'political neutrality' argument has been explained, it should be pointed out that in Spain this argument has come in for criticism on the grounds of democratic principles, in so far as it might seem to be the expression of a feeling of mistrust towards politics and political parties, and, indirectly, of lack of confidence in the democratic system. However, while no one is unaware of the problems deriving from the nature and workings of the political parties, the solution should perhaps be found in strengthening the mechanisms of democratic control, not in removing all those activities that should be carried out with impartiality from the ambit in which those controls function and decisions are taken democratically. Moreover, it is doubtful that IAAs may actually act with neutrality: the danger of 'capture by the regulated sector' is well known and political

[29] Art 108 Treaty establishing the European Community.

[30] The *Libro Verde de las Telecomunicaciones* (1987) had already alluded to the need to separate both activities—sector regulation and exploitation. This need was subsequently covered by, for example, Directive 90/388, regarding competition in the telecommunications markets, and Directive 92/44, regarding the application of the open network supply to rented lines. See S Muñoz Machado *Servicio público y mercado. Los fundamentos* vol I (1998) 254 ff.; Tornos Mas *Las autoridades de regulación de lo audiovisual* op cit 169.

parties may also be considered perfectly capable of finding ways to 'capture' IAAs.[31]

## IV. FUNCTIONS AND POWERS OF IAAS (QUESTIONS 14, 16, AND 17)

The functions attributed to IAAs take the form of either providing a public service or regulating and overseeing a particular sector of the economy.

In Spain two IAAs are entrusted with the provision of a public service: the universities and RTVE. In both cases the provision of that service (radio and television and higher education respectively) enables a fundamental right to be guaranteed, and in both cases it is that fundamental right that justifies each IAA's existence. No particular problem has arisen in relation to the competences attributed to RTVE and the universities since they are administrative powers of the kind that traditionally correspond to bodies that carry out a service-providing activity. Nonetheless, worth pointing out are the rule-making powers attributed to both RTVE and the universities which enable them to formulate internal and external rules. RTVE can only issue rules regarding the broadcasting of advertising; in contrast the universities have wide-ranging rule-making powers in so far as they pass their own statutes and exercise their rule-making power without being subject to the limits imposed on most IAAs.[32]

The regulatory function has been attributed to most IAAs. This is a new type of function, which is essentially the consequence of the processes of deregulation imposed by the European Union. Its aim is to safeguard free competition and the proper functioning of the deregulated sectors. The indisputable benchmark is the United States' regulation function, which consists in regulating in a broad sense, namely, in organizing all the activity of a private sector and guaranteeing that sector's proper functioning, not only by passing general rules (regulation in the strict sense of the word), but also through one-off actions, such as the granting of authorizations or the resolution of conflicts. To this end, the regulatory body enjoys all the necessary competences—essentially competences to regulate and control. However, in Spain the remit of the regulatory authorities is more limited than that of the *independent agencies* in the United States, consisting above

[31] JM Bilbao Ubillos 'Las agencias independientes: un análisis desde la perspectiva jurídico-constitucional' in *Anuario de la Facultad de Derecho de la Universidad Autónoma de Madrid* nº 3 (1999) 180–1; Rallo Lombarte *La constitucionalidad de las administraciones independientes* op. cit 7; and Pomed op cit 167.

[32] For RTVE's rule-making power see Art 8.1.j) ERTV. For the universities' rule-making powers, STC 55/1989, FJ 4º, and the detailed analysis of JM Baño León 'Las potestades normativas de las Universidades' in *Revista Aragonesa de Administración Pública* nº 11 (1997) 39 ff.

all in overseeing the working of a sector rather than in organizing its activity—or at least Spain's regulatory authorities do not organize to the same extent as their United States counterparts. Sector organization is a task which Spain's 'independent regulatory authorities' share with other public authorities, chiefly with the government.[33] That is why some prefer to use the word 'supervision' instead of 'regulation' when referring to the work done by these IAAs.[34]

Among the regulatory IAAs, special attention should be given to the APD, whose job is to watch over compliance of data protection legislation and to control its application. The APD differs from the other 'regulatory authorities,' first because, as the Constitutional Court has recognized, the end it pursues is the guarantee of a fundamental right,[35] and secondly, because it controls not only private personal data files but also public ones. Unlike the APD, the other 'regulatory authorities' have not been set up in order to guarantee the exercise of a fundamental right and their supervisory activity extends exclusively to the activity of one particular private sector.[36]

The regulatory or supervisory function takes the form of a group of different modes of intervention in the private sector, as a consequence of which legislation has attributed to the 'regulatory authorities' a varied group of competences, including rule-making competences, competences to control, sanction and advise, and others of an executive nature. It should however be pointed out that not all 'regulatory authorities' have the same competences. Indeed it may be the case that despite discharging the same function, one body, for instance the CMT, has considerable regulatory capacity, while the competences attributed to others are so scant that in practice the 'independent authority' acts almost solely as an advisory body or as a collaborator of the government, as is the case of the CNE; this is because the real regulatory competences still lie in the hands of the Ministry of Industry.[37]

The competences attributed to the regulatory IAAs are as follows:

[33] For the regulatory function see Salvador Martínez *Autoridades independientes* op cit 350 ff.

[34] The term 'supervisión' is used by, among others, A Betancor op cit 247–8 and Magide op cit 324.

[35] STC 290/2000, FJ 8° and 13°.

[36] The CSN is charged with overseeing activities related to nuclear energy in order to guarantee compliance with measures concerning nuclear security and radiological protection. The CNE is regulator of the electricity market and the liquid and gas hydrocarbons markets. The CMT has been attributed the function of safeguarding effective competition in the telecommunications market. The CNMV is charged with the supervision and inspection of the securities markets and of those who participate in the trade of those markets; it keeps an eye on transparency, correct pricing and investor protection. The TDC has been attributed the function of preserving the competitive operation of the markets and of guaranteeing the existence of effective competition in them. The *Banco de España* must watch over price stability, execute the monetary policy as defined by the European Central Bank, and oversee the sector.

[37] Among others see Sala Arquer *La Comisión del Mercado de las Telecomunicaciones* op cit 17–18, 23, and 27.

(a) Most of the 'independent regulatory authorities' have been attributed powers to formulate internal and external rules, although most of the latter require express endorsement in the form of government rule. The Constitutional Court has recognized the constitutionality of these powers, although express legal attribution is required, and, according to the greater part of legal opinion, the rules formulated by the IAAs are also subject to government rules.[38]
(b) All IAAs have powers to inspect and to gather information since they are basically designed as supervisory bodies.
(c) Most 'regulatory authorities' have also been attributed the power to sanction although all share the exercise of this power with the government, with the exception of the APD and the TDC.
(d) The regulatory IAAs grant authorisation or licences to carry on activity in the sector and authorise particular operations, but only the CMT can fix tariffs or prices (to be more precise, the maximum prices for interconnections between operators in the telecommunications sector).
(e) Some 'regulatory authorities', specifically, the CMT, the CNE, and the TDC, can act as arbitrators in conflicts between sector operators. However, proceedings of this sort have never yet been undertaken and, given their voluntary nature, it is unlikely that they would be effective.
(f) Finally, as experts in a particular area, the regulatory IAAs also advise the government and inform the citizens.

## V. ORGANIZATION OF IAAS (QUESTIONS 13 AND 15)

The autonomy of the IAAs which have been analysed to this point is guaranteed through a series of organizational measures. Above all, these measures aim to guarantee the functional and personal autonomy of the 'authorities' by prohibiting the government to give orders and instructions, by laying down standard causes for dismissal (thus avoiding arbitrary dismissals), and, albeit to a lesser extent, by restricting government intervention in the appointment of IAA members.[39] Occasionally, the autonomy of these 'authorities' also takes the form of particular measures to guarantee

[38] SSTC 135/1992; 87/1993 and 204/1993, all regarding the *Banco de España*. For opinion see L Parejo Alfonso 'La potestad normativa de las llamadas administraciones independientes: apunte para un estudio del fenómeno' in A Perez, *Administración instrumental. Libro homenaje a Manuel Francisco Clavero Arevalo* (1994) 635 ff.; Gallego Anabitarte and Menéndez Rexach 'Art. 97. Funciones del Gobierno' in O Alzaga Villaamil (coord. *Comentarios a la Constitución* tomo VIII (1998) 41 ff.

[39] Among others see Sala Arquer op cit 411; López Ramón op cit 206; García Llovet op cit 100 and 106; Parada *Derecho administrativo* op cit 286; Betancor Rodríguez op cit 186.

them a degree of organic and financial autonomy. Nevertheless, it should be stressed that there is no single organizational model to which all IAAs conform, for the same form of organization is not adopted by each and every one of them.

### A. Creation and legal status

Both their creation and dissolution by law (by a decision of the parliament) have been regarded as defining features of the legal status of IAAs.[40] All have been created by an act of the parliament. From the point of view of the Constitution, it should be emphasized that the acts by which IAAs have been set up are ordinary acts (*leyes ordinarias*, laws passed by simple majority in parliament) and in this regard there has been some debate over whether the acts that create those IAAs which guarantee a fundamental right should be *leyes orgánicas* (laws passed by absolute majority in parliament), given that Article 81.1 of the Constitution requires that the development of fundamental rights should be performed through such laws.

The second feature of the IAAs is that they are all legal entities in their own right.[41] Although nothing of any great consequence, it is the first indication of autonomy and serves as a yardstick to distinguish IAAs from other administration bodies which are also autonomous but are not independent legal entities. Also worth mentioning is the fact that all Spain's IAAs have been given the public law status of *instituciones de derecho público*.

Despite being independent legal entities, most IAAs are attached to a ministry,[42] albeit that attachment is merely formal, since the 'independence' of these bodies obviously excludes them from any real integration in another entity of the administration.

### B. Relevant law

The IAAs are governed by their own particular rules, their own statutes, and—but only complementarily—by the general rules that determine the organization and functioning of the State administration. To be more precise, in the exercise of public powers they are governed by the stipulations of their specific rules, that is to say, by a special public law, even if generally, and as a complementary measure, they are subject to the application of the *Ley de Régimen Jurídico de la Administración Pública*, which

[40] García Llovet op cit 95; Pomed Sánchez op cit 162.

[41] Art 5.2 ERTV; Art 35.1 LOPD; Art 2.1 LOU; Art 1.1 LCSN; Art 14 LMV; Art 1.1 LABE; Disp Adic 11ª, primero. 2 de la LSH; Art 1. uno LLT; and Art 20.1 LDC.

[42] RTVE is attached to the Ministry of the Presidency, the CNMV, the CNE, and the TDC to the Ministry of the Economy, and the CMT to the Ministry of Public Works.

is the law that establishes the rules for the operation and procedures of the public administration. In regard of their external relations, asset purchases and engagement of personnel, the IAAs are subject to private law.[43]

At this point mention should be made of the fact that the IAAs have come in for criticism on the grounds that their legal status is tantamount to a 'flight from administrative law'. Legal opinion had already criticized the so-called 'flight from administrative law' on the part of the *entes instrumentales* (those organizations born of the administration's functionally decentralization) which in certain matters are subject to private law and thus manage to dodge some of the controls to which the activity of the public administrations is submitted.[44] But the IAAs not only 'flee' from public law to private law; like the *entes instrumentales*; they also slip the grasp of general administrative law in favour of a public law devised specially for them which makes available a combination of greater prerogatives and fewer controls.[45]

The legal regime of the IAAs is laid down in the legislation whereby they are set up and topped up with their own internal rules or statutes. Apart from the universities and the *Banco de España*, the IAAs have no powers to pass their own internal regulations; instead it is the government which passes them.[46] As for the CMT and the TDC, in addition to their government-approved internal regulations they also possess, or may possess, an internal regulatory code passed by themselves.[47] Meanwhile, as and when necessary the RTVE may formulate dispositions, instructions and circulars regarding internal operation and organization.[48]

### *C. Functional autonomy*

Although legal opinion considers independence from orders and instructions to be one of the hallmarks of the IAAs, only in two of the acts whereby these 'authorities' have been created do we find any prohibition of

[43] Art 5.2 del ERTV; Art 35.2 LOPD; Art 6 LOU; Art 1.1 LCSN; Art 14 LMV; Art 1 LABE; Disp Adic 11ª. primero. 2 LSH; Art 1. uno LLT; Arts 20.6 and 50 LDC. In this regard, the LOFAGE establishes that: 'those public bodies whose *functional independence or special autonomy* from the general state administration are, on the coming into force of this act, given express recognition will be regulated by their specific regulation in regard of those aspects that are necessary for that independence or autonomy to become fully effective. On all other counts and, in any case, in matters associated with personnel, assets, contracts and budgeting, they will adapt their regulation to those of this act's precepts concerning public bodies which may apply in each case, bearing in mind the characteriztics of each body' (Disp Adic 10ª 2).

[44] See, among others, JM Sala Arquer 'Huida al Derecho privado y huida del Derecho' REDA nº 75 (1992) 399 ff.; I Borrajo Iniesta 'El intento de huir del Derecho Administrativo' in REDA nº 78 (1993) 233 ff.

[45] Betancor op cit 274.

[46] Art 6.2 LOU and Art 21.1 (f) LABE.

[47] Art 2.3 RCNE, Art 1.cuatro LLT and Art 24.3 LDC.

[48] Art 11 (c) ERTV.

the government's—or any other body's—issuing orders and instructions to these bodies: the APD's act stipulates that it is not to receive instructions from any authority,[49] and both the *Banco de España's* act and the European Community Treaty lay down that the bank cannot receive instructions from the government or from any other national or European Community entity, although guidance and directions may be accepted from the European Central Bank.[50] As for those IAAs whose acts make no express prohibition of orders and instructions, the weight of legal opinion agrees that these 'authorities' should also be understood as not admitting of any subjection to government orders or instructions.[51]

As for the IAAs functional autonomy, the fact that competence over a particular matter is attributed exclusively to the relevant 'independent authority' is considered to be a guarantee of autonomy, but in Spain, only the act setting up the CSN establishes the board's exclusive competence in its field of activity,[52] and even then, the government retains considerable powers, such as the grant of licences.

From the outset, legal scholars have defended the view that IAA decisions should not be appealed at a higher level of administrative organization, for that would be to contradict the very functional autonomy which they are intended to enjoy. Rather, legal scholars are of the view that IAA decisions should be appealed directly before the judges or the courts by means of contentious administrative proceedings.[53] But this does not happen in all cases. On the one hand there is a group of IAAs, composed of RTVE, the APD, the Universities, the CSN, the CMT and the TDC, whose decisions are appealed directly before the contentious administrative court;[54] on the other hand, there is a second group, formed by the CNMV, the *Banco de España* and the CNE, whose decisions are contested, depending on their content, either before the hierarchically superior administrative institution (the Ministry with competence in the matter) or directly before the courts by means of contentious administrative proceedings.[55]

[49] Art 36.2 LOPD and Art 16 EAPD.

[50] Art 108 TCE and Arts 1.3 and 7.4 LABE.

[51] See, among others, LA Pomed Sánchez op cit 159; Jiménez Blanco *Derecho público del mercado de valores* op cit 98; Magide Herrero op cit 86.

[52] Art 1.1 of the LCSN gives shape to the CSN as 'the only body with competence in matters of nuclear safety and radiological protection'.

[53] See, among others, Pomed Sánchez op cit 160; García Llovet op cit 98; Magide Herrero op cit 89.

[54] Art 16.2 ERTV; Art 2.4 EAPD and Art 48.2 LOPD; Art 6.4 LOU; Art 49 LDC; Art 1. ocho LLT and Art 3 RCMT; Arts 33.15 and 70 ECSN; generally, *Ley 29/1998, de 13 de julio, reguladora de la Jurisdicción Contencioso Administrativa* (LJCA), Disp Adic 4ª 5.

[55] The CNMV's decisions in the matters of sanctions and of the intervention and substitution of administrators are liable to appeal before the Ministry of Economy; all other decisions must be appealed before the contentious administrative judge (Arts 16 and 107, LMV). In the

IAA decisions are binding, except for reports or proposals, which are not. The one exception is the CSN whose reports, prescriptive in nature, are binding both if they are negative or refuse a concession and, in respect of the conditions they establish, if they are positive.[56]

Finally, functional autonomy also finds expression in the ability of IAAs to appeal decisions of the state administration, an ability which they may put to use in order to defend their exercise of the functions attributed to them.[57]

### D. *Personal autonomy*

Personal autonomy is chiefly determined by the provisions relating to the appointment and dismissal of IAA members and, complementarily, by the requirement of requisites for eligibility on the one hand and the existence of grounds for incompatibility and of special rules concerning length of mandate on the other.

(a) *The system for electing members.* There is a generalized feeling that the way to limit government influence on IAA members is to let other bodies and institutions take part in the election of members. The legislator has also devised different systems or procedures for the election of board or council members for each IAA, even though in most cases the government still enjoys a decisive influence. The different systems that have been established are as follows:[58]

- Single-member executive body chosen directly by the government, while the collegiate body that accompanies it is elected by a qualified majority of parliament (RTVE);
- Single-member executive body chosen by the government, while the collegiate body is chosen by various public and private institutions (APD);
- Collegiate executive body chosen by the government (CNMV and TDC);

case of the *Banco de España*, decisions regarding monetary policy and the issue of banknotes, as well as regarding the sanctions which, where appropriate, it imposes as a consequence of the former, must be appealed before the contentious administrative judge; in contrast, the decisions taken in the discharge of other functions, and the sanctions imposed, may be appealed before the Minister of Economy and the Exchequer (Art 2 LABE). As for the CNE, in general the Commission's decisions may be appealed before the Ministry of Economy, except for those resolutions which are passed in order to solve conflicts regarding the economic and technical management of the electricity system and transport, and of the circulars relating to information, which must be appealed before the contentious-administrative judge (Disp Adic 11ª, tercero. 5 LSH).

56 Art 2(b) LCSN and Art 6 ECSN.

57 Arts 19.1 (f) and 20 (c) LJCA.

58 Arts 8.1, 7.1, and 10.1 ERTV; Arts 38 and 36.1 LOPD; Art 5.2 LCSN; Art 17 LMV; Arts 20 and 24 LABE; Disp Adic 11ª, primero. 4 LSH; Art 1. tres 1 and 2 LLT; Art 33 RCMT; Art 21.1 and 4 LDC; and Arts 13 ff. LOU.

- Collegiate executive body chosen by the government which must appear in Congress to report appointments (*Banco de España*, CMT and CNE);
- Collegiate executive body chosen by the government after communicating its decision to Congress, which, through the competent Committee and with the agreement of three-fifths of its members, will declare its acceptance or veto together with reasons in the space of one month (CSN); this is undoubtedly the most unusual system;
- the case of the universities is different for, unlike the others, their governing bodies are elected by the different sectors of the university community.

It should be said that although in most cases the government is responsible for appointments, in practice a sort of 'quota system' has been instituted whereby the appointments are shared out among the different political groups in proportion to the number of seats they hold in parliament. Of course, this sort of sharing out is no guarantee of the body's political neutrality; rather it transfers to the IAAs the same balance of political persuasion as exists in parliament, with the result that inter-party conflict also makes itself felt in the IAAs.[59]

Now that the different systems of election have been described, some remarks are in order regarding participation by parliament. There is a widespread feeling in legal opinion that there are better guarantees of 'independence' if parliament instead of the government is responsible for appointments. In this regard, it should be stated that parliamentary participation is no guarantee of neutrality either, for parliament is just as 'political' an institution as the government; what is more, in a parliamentary system such as Spain's, it is the parliamentary majority which forms the government. What appointments made by parliament do guarantee—especially if reinforced majorities are required—is debate and compromise between the different political parties, thus avoiding appointments of an arrantly partisan nature.[60] But it should not be forgotten that reinforced majorities may also lead to deadlock or, at the very least, harmful delays, as has happened in Spain with the recent process to renew members of the Constitutional Court.

Finally, it has to be said that in reality those who are appointed to IAAs are normally people who not only satisfy the eligibility requirements but are also in the confidence of the party that selects them. This means that the election systems undeniably endow the political parties with the power to influence the activity of IAAs, which is why any genuine autonomy they

[59] Salvador Martínez op cit 301.
[60] Magide Herrero op cit 100.

may have ultimately depends on periodic bouts of muscle-flexing and, to a large extent, on the character and temperament of the combatants.[61]

(b) The aim behind the inclusion of *eligibility clauses of requisites* is to ensure that members are duly qualified and to de-politicise the appointment process. Most of the acts setting up IAAs demand that their members be renowned for their competence, know-how or prestige in the relevant area, and some acts include other requisites.[62]

(c) By determining a series of *incompatibility clauses* it is hoped to guarantee the 'independence' of the members of these 'authorities' from any type of influence, interference or pressure, whether public or private, and thus to avoid outside interests taking priority over those which it is the job of the 'independent authority' to satisfy. It is a matter of shielding the board or council members not only from the influence of the government or other public authorities, but also from the pressures that may be exerted on them by private groups. Thus IAA members are subject to a system of incompatibilities which is the same as, or similar to, that which applies to senior officials of the state civil service,[63] with in some cases the addition of other measures, such as, for example, the stipulation that on leaving the post and during the subsequent two years, board or council members may not carry on any professional activity related to the sector.

(d) *Length of mandate and removal from office.* In order to safeguard the stability and independence of authority members, it is clearly important for the authorities to have in place measures concerning length of mandate, possibility of renewal and, above all, the removal of members. As a general rule, the mandate of IAA members does not coincide exactly with the legislative period; rather renewals are stepped and the mandate can only be renewed a limited number of times. The existence of standard grounds for removal is one of the guarantees of 'independence' which characterizes the IAAs as distinct from other administrative bodies. In most cases, these standard grounds coincide from one IAA to another. Removal may be on the grounds of renunciation of office, end of mandate, or reaching the age of retirement; but in addition, the government may remove board or council members in any of the following circumstances: supervening incompatibility, conviction for fraud, grave dereliction of duties, or supervening incapacity.[64] According to the standard procedure, after scrutiny of the case the government will agree the removal from office by issuing a decision with

61 Salvador Martínez op cit 323–4.

62 Art 7.1 ERTV; Art 5.1 LCSN; Art 17 LMV; Art 24 LABE; Disp Adic 11ª, primero 4 LSH; Art 1. tres 2 LLT; Art 33 RCMT; Art 21.1 LDC.

63 The rules concerning incompatibilities are set out in Arts 2–6 of the *Ley 12/1995, de 11 de mayo, de Incompatibilidades de los miembros del Gobierno y de los Altos Cargos de la Administración.*

64 Art 12 ERTV; Art 36.3 LOPD; Art 20 LMV; Art 7.1 LCSN; Art 25.4 LABE; Art 1 tres 5 LLT, and Art 35 RCMT.

statement of reasons.[65] Only in the case of the removal of board members of the CSN is a different procedure contemplated, in so far as the same process is followed as for appointments, namely a government decision is ratified by Congress by a three-fifths majority. This is also the only case where parliament intervenes in the process of removing members of an 'independent authority'.[66]

Only in the cases of the TDC and the universities does the government take no part in the removal of members. TDC members may only be removed for grave dereliction of duties on the proposal of three-quarters of the TDC members,[67] while in the universities the representatives of the university community may only be removed by those they represent.[68]

### E. *Internal organization*

With the exception of RTVE and the APD, Spain's IAAs are organized around a collegiate body responsible for the main decisions taken inside the institution. IAAs are supposed to be organized as follows: a collegiate body holds the chief competences and takes decisions by majority, while a monocratic body subordinate to it is responsible for executing the collegiate body's decisions.[69] Depending on the kind of 'independent authority', the existence of a central collegiate body makes it possible either for representatives of the various interests at stake to participate or for a group of experts in the matter to meet together, the result being in both cases that in the bosom of the collegiate body there is scope for the necessary debate and exchange of opinions.[70] The collegiate principle is also believed to constitute a guarantee of independence since a college is always less prone to be influenced than a single-person body and since the collegiate body, with its internal rules, reinforces the elements of guarantee, above all those that have to do with procedure.[71]

[65] Art 7.2 LCSN; Art 20 LMV; Art 1 tres 5 LLT; Art 36.3 LOPD; Art 25.4 LABE.

[66] Art 7.1 (e) LCSN.

[67] The members of the TDC cease in office '(a) on their renunciation; (b) on expiry of the term of their mandate; (c) for supervening incompatibility; (d) on conviction for fraud; (e) on the grounds of permanent incapacity; (f) on their removal, determined on the grounds of grave dereliction of the duties pertaining to their office at the proposal of three-quarters of the collegiate body' (Art. 23 LDC).

[68] Art 2.2 (b) LOU.

[69] FJ Jiménez de Cisneros Cid *Los organizmos autónomos en el ordenamiento jurídico español* (1987) 313; Magide Herrero op cit 110; García Llovet op cit 100 ff.

[70] García Llovet op cit 101–2.

[71] JA Santamaría Pastor 'La teoría del órgano en el Derecho Administrativo' in REDA nº 40–1 (1984) 80.

### *F. The system of finance*

With respect to financial autonomy, the first point to be made is that, surprisingly, the burden of legal opinion regards it as a guarantee of a lower order. The second point is that financial dependence does not condition the activity of an 'independent authority' charged with regulating or overseeing a private sector and advising the government in the same way that it conditions the activity of an 'authority' charged with the provision of a public service such as education or radio and television, for in the latter case the provision of the service depends directly on the economic resources available to the body.

In relation to those IAAs charged with the provision of a public service, it should be pointed out that the universities and, to an extent, RTVE have been granted a financing guarantee. The *Ley Orgánica de Universidades* lays down that the universities 'must dispose of sufficient resources for the discharge of their functions';[72] meanwhile, the Protocol on the system of public broadcasting in the Member States, annexed to the Treaty establishing the European Community, provides that 'the Member States will have powers to finance the public broadcasting service (. . . ) which carries out the function of a public service'. Nevertheless, both these IAAs are currently facing considerable financial difficulties.[73]

As for the financing system, the acts setting up the IAAs coincide in their establishment of two types of income: on the one hand there are the public monies that proceed from the relevant section of the national budget, and on the other hand there are the IAAs' own incomes derived from the profits of their activity and from their funds.[74] Of these two sources, public finance generally constitutes the main source of income, as a result of which the government or parliament is equipped with a potentially significant means of influencing the IAAs.[75] The CSN, the CNMV, the CMT, the CNE, the TDC, and the *Banco de España* also receive the income generated by the various tariffs charged on the services they provide, which sometimes constitutes a major source of alternative finance.

[72] Art 79.1 LOU.

[73] M Martínez Sospedra 'La reforma de la LRU. Algunas cuestiones políticamente poco correctas' in *Cuadernos Constitucionales de la Cátedra Fadrique Furió Ceriol*, nº 22/23 (1998) 150 ff. (156–9). The situation of RTVE is even more complicated than that of the universities since its income from advertising and from the public purse is insufficient, and it has been running at a loss for some years now; see Juan González Encinar 'La televisión pública en España' op cit 216–19.

[74] Art 32 ERTV; Art 35.4 LOPD and Art 32 EAPD; Art 9 LCSN; Art 24 LMV; Art 4 LABE; Disp Adic 11ª. primero. 7 LSH and Art 43 RCNE; Art 1. siete. 2 LLT; Art 81.3 LOU; Art 20.4 LDC.

[75] For RTVE see Juan González Encinar 'La televisión pública en España' op cit 216–19; for the universities see Martínez Sospedra 'La reforma de la LRU. Algunas cuestiones políticamente poco correctas' op cit 156.

As for the preparation of budgets, experts in the field believe that the IAAs should have autonomy to pass their own budgets and are critical of the fact that, with the exception of the universities and the *Banco de España*, no other 'independent authority' has the power to do so.[76]

As for the IAAs' financial autonomy, there has also been criticism of the fact that most are subject to control by the *Intervention General de la Administration del Estado* (the governmental office responsible for inspecting the financial management of the administration), that is to say, by the same system to which the public administration is subject, even if in some cases the level of control differs. Not only that, but the IAAs are also subject to control by the *Tribunal de Cuentas* (parliament's ancillary body for the inspection of the financial management of public bodies) and, thereby, to parliamentary control.[77]

## VI. IAAS: BETWEEN THE GOVERNMENT AND THE PARLIAMENT (QUESTIONS 2 AND 4)

As mentioned above, the argument used in Spain to justify the creation of IAAs is that of 'political neutrality'. According to this argument, if 'neutrality' is to be guaranteed in the discharge of particular functions, IAAs need to be set up to act outside the political arena and at a distance from the state's political institutions. In this regard, the point should be made that in Spain's system of parliamentary government to be at a distance from the political arena is tantamount to being at a distance from the party in power, that is to say, from the party which enjoys a parliamentary majority and has formed the government. However, it has often been thought that 'independence' may be safeguarded by distancing the 'authorities' from government but bringing them closer to parliament. In fact, the IAAs may be characterized by the very fact that they have been distanced from government control and brought closer to parliament.

In any case, the 'independence' of the IAAs is relative. True enough, limits have been put on the government's powers to direct and control 'authorities' of this kind, but both the government and parliament still exercise considerable competences in their regard.

## VII. IAAS AND THE GOVERNMENT

The government exerts considerable influence over the activity of most

[76] Betancor Rodríguez *Las administraciones independientes* op cit 188.

[77] See Art 30 ERTV; Art 33.1 EAPD; Art 14 LMV; Art 14 LABE; and Disp Adic 11ª, primero. 2, of the LSH; Art 45.1 RCNE; Art 81.5 LOU; and Art 20.5 LDC.

IAAs. It appoints most of the board or council members and holders of directorial offices, it intervenes in the exercise of certain competences, it may review some IAA decisions, it approves the draft budgets of most IAAs, and, on occasion, it has at its disposal instruments of political control over the IAAs.

With respect to the political control exerted over the IAAs by the government, it should be noted that in general terms, and notwithstanding the exceptions referred to below, the legislation does not attribute to government functions of political control over the IAAs. But this does not of course mean that the government does not have at its disposal the wherewithal to influence the activities of these 'authorities'.

The government is generally considered to have competence to control IAAs (except for the universities and the TDC) in so far as the respective legislation permits the government to remove their members for grave dereliction of duties. That is to say, the government is not attributed competences to control the ordinary or day-to-day working of these 'authorities' and, accordingly, is not accountable for it; but the government is competent to control the exceedingly deleterious effects on an IAA's working that would be entailed by grave dereliction of the legally stipulated duties, and in such cases it may dismiss the IAA's members responsible for that dereliction. Thus it is that the government is accountable for an IAA's exceedingly deleterious working.[78]

As for particular IAAs, legislation does attribute the government some specific control mechanisms. Thus, in the case of RTVE, the government may determine on a periodical basis the duties deriving from its nature as a public broadcasting service, duties which it may enforce;[79] meanwhile, the Ministry of Public Works oversees and controls RTVE's compliance with the act that transposes the EC directive 'Television *sans frontiers*'.[80] As for the *Banco de España*, the law establishes that the Bank should report regularly to government and parliament regarding the goals and execution of its monetary policy.[81] With respect to the CNE and the TDC, the competent minister undertakes efficiency controls;[82] also, with respect to the CNE, the Minister may have a say, though no vote, on the management board whenever he/she deems it necessary in view of the items on the agenda; for this

[78] Betancor Rodríguez *Las administraciones independientes* op cit 191.

[79] Art 21 ERTV.

[80] Art 19 de la *Ley 25/1994, de 12 de julio, de transposición de la Directiva 'Televisión sin fronteras'*.

[81] Art 10 LABE.

[82] Disp Adic 11ª, primero. 2 of the LSH, and Art 45.2 RCNE; Art 20.6 LDC. The purpose of this control is to check both the degree to which the objectives are met and the proper use of assigned resources; this is the control to which, in accordance with the LOFAGE (Art 51), the functionally decentralized bodies (*entes instrumentales*) are to be subject.

reason, the agenda must be sent to the Minister at the same time as to the members of the board.[83]

Any final balance of the relations between the government and the IAAs needs to take on board several distinctions. With respect to those IAAs which guarantee fundamental rights, there are significant differences between the universities, on the one hand, and the APD and RTVE on the other. The universities enjoy a considerable amount of autonomy from the government and parliament, and the only criticisms made of their legal order have to do with their economic dependence on the government and the financial difficulties they are facing at present.[84] In contrast, RTVE and the APD enjoy much less autonomy than the universities, and even than some of the 'independent regulatory authorities'. Legal opinion has been particularly critical of RTVE's dependence on the government, both in terms of personnel and economically. The guarantees that are in place are clearly insufficient to guarantee the autonomy of public broadcasting corporations from the government, especially bearing in mind the evident political interest the government has in controlling such a decisive shaper of public opinion.[85] As for the APD, government appointment of its director has been criticised, above all because the agency has to control not only private archives, but also those that are in the hands of the public administration.[86]

With regard to the 'independent regulatory authorities', although the government may exert considerable influence over them, there are also significant differences between them. These are usually illustrated through comparison of the CMT with the CNE since the CMT fits better the 'regulatory authority' model and enjoys greater guarantees of autonomy, whereas in practice the CNE acts almost exclusively in collaboration with government.[87] It should be remembered that the CNE is the fruit of the transformation of a former Commission, the *Comisión Nacional del Sistema Eléctrico*, and that its president resigned after a bitter confrontation with the government over aid to electricity companies to help with the costs of transition to open competition. Attention is usually also drawn to the CSN on account of the way in which its members' election and removal falls to the government but requires ratification by a three-fifths majority of Congress.

[83] Art 20.2 RCNE.

[84] Martínez Sospedra 'La reforma de la LRU. Algunas cuestiones políticamente poco correctas' op cit 156–9.

[85] For these guarantees see Juan González Encinar op cit 242 ff.

[86] JL Cascajo Castro 'Motivos de inconstitucionalidad de la Ley Orgánica 5/1992, de 29 de octubre, de regulación del tratamiento automatizado de datos de carácter personal' in *Estudios de Derecho Público. Homenaje a Juan José Ruiz-Rico*, vol. I (1997) 465 ff.

[87] Sala Arquer op cit 23 and elsewhere.

### *A. IAAs and Parliament*

For its part, parliament is free to determine the existence and status of the IAAs, except in those cases where a constitutional mandate forces it to set up and maintain a particular IAA. But even then, a certain reluctance has been detected on the part of politicians to accept the neutralisation of certain functions of clear political transcendence, such as the provision of the broadcasting service; as a result, the legislative working out of such constitutional mandates is debated amidst the contradictory principles of influence and governmental interference.[88] The best example of this is to be found in the legislation regulating RTVE.

For the rest, parliament takes part in the process of electing members to some IAAs, approves the budget of most IAAs, and exercises parliamentary control over all of them, except the universities.

With respect to parliamentary control, most IAAs are obliged to send annual or regular reports on their activity to parliament.[89] For its part, whenever it deems it necessary parliament may avail itself of the ordinary means of parliamentary control, namely parliamentary questions, interpellations and enquiry committees.[90] It is a moot point whether it is the government or the IAAs themselves that should answer directly to parliament. It would seem to be logical that parliament cannot hold the government accountable for what is beyond its control and that it is therefore the IAAs that account directly for their actions before parliament, while the government is only accountable for what is under its control, namely, in general terms, grave dereliction of duties and any specific activities whose control has been attributed to the government in particular cases. But two further points should be mentioned regarding the parliamentary control of IAAs in Spain: first, the limited nature of the so-called ordinary instruments of parliamentary control and secondly, the fact that most of the time the IAAs' members have been appointed by the government itself, which enjoys the support of the parliamentary majority.

[88] Sala Arquer op cit 417.

[89] Art 8 EAPD; Art 11 LCSN; Art 13 LMV; Disp. Adic. 11ª, tercera. 1, decimoséptima LSH; Art 1. Cinco LLT; Art 10 LABE; Art 26 ERTV.

[90] A specific parliamentary committee has been set up in Congress to control RTVE (Art 26 ERTV, and Art 46.2 and Disp. Final 5ª del *Reglamento del Congreso*). In this case, parliamentary control is a constitutional requirement (Art 20.3 CE: 'The law will regulate the organization and parliamentary control of the social communication media that depend on the state or any public entity . . .').

## VIII. JUDICIAL CONTROL (QUESTIONS 18, 19, AND 20)

As far as judicial control is concerned, both the Constitutional Court,[91] and the legislator and legal opinion[92] are of the understanding that the IAAs' qualified autonomy does not imply their exemption from judicial control. The judicial control over the IAAs is as follows:

(a) *Ordinary jurisdiction.* The judicial control of the IAAs is the same as that of the public administration. The administrative actions of these 'authorities', that is to say, those actions subject to public law, may be appealed directly, and only once, before the Contentious Administrative Court of the *Audiencia Nacional.*[93] Meanwhile, those actions of the IAAs subject to private law may be appealed before the pertinent ordinary jurisdiction: labour, civil, or criminal.[94]

(b) *Other forms of judicial control.* In some cases concerning particular IAA actions, the law provides for other forms of judicial control in addition to those mentioned above. Thus any decisions taken by RTVE during an electoral period in detriment of political and social pluralism or the neutrality of information may be appealed before the *Junta Electoral* (the body charged with overseeing the election process).[95] With respect to the *Banco de España*, the Court of Justice of the European Communities is competent to review any final decisions made by the bank regarding the imposition of sanctions, in line with the 'European Central Bank regulation on the powers of the European Central Bank to impose sanctions'; it may also rule in litigation concerning compliance with the 'Statute of the European System of Central Banks and of the European Central Bank'.[96]

As far as the actual exercise of judicial control over IAAs is concerned, in Spain the regulations regarding IAAs are quite precise in their establishment of the status of IAAs, which, for the most part, have no discretionary powers in the strict sense of the word;[97] as a result, the judges encounter no

[91] With regard to the Tribunal de Defensa de la Competencia, the STC 80/1983, in FJ 1°, declared derogated certain provisions of the *Ley de Defensa de la Competencia* of 1963 which prohibited the judicial control of that Tribunal.

[92] See, among others, García Llovet op cit 113–14; Betancor *Las administraciones . . .* op cit 272.

[93] It should be remembered that some decisions of the CNMV, the *Banco de España* and the CNE are not appealed directly before the contentious administrative court, must be appealed before at the hierarchically superior administrative institution (the Ministry with competence in the matter).

[94] Thus it is established in the acts setting up the IAAs (Art 16.2 ERTV; Art 2.4 EAPD; Art 6.4 LOU; Art 2.3 LABE; Art 1. ocho LLT; Disp. Adic. 11ª. tercero. 5 LSH; Art 49 LDC); and also in the LJCA, Disp. Adic. 4ª.

[95] Art 12 ERTV.

[96] Art 16 RIBE.

[97] As pointed out by M Sánchez Moron 'Siete tesis sobre el control judicial de la discrecionalidad administrativa' in AAVV, *Eficacia, discrecionalidad y control judicial en el ámbito administrativo* (1995) 158. See also Magide Herrero op cit 308 ff.

special difficulties when it comes to overseeing their activity. However, with respect to the exercise of the so-called 'technical' powers, there are few jurisdictional conflicts since the bodies that exercise such powers have been granted a generous margin of appreciation.[98]

## IX. IAAS AND THE CONSTITUTIONAL FRAMEWORK (QUESTIONS 7, 8, 9, 10, AND 11)

The Constitution defines Spain as a 'social and democratic state' and establishes the 'rule of law' and the parliamentary form of government, whereby the government is appointed by parliament, directs the administration, and is accountable for its activity to parliament. That being the case, it is easy to understand the main constitutional problems posed by the IAAs.

### *A. IAAs and the powers of the government to direct the administration*

According to the scholarship on administrative law, the main problem posed by the IAAs concerns the powers that correspond to the government *qua* paramount executive body, among which is the power to designate to and remove from administrative office and to direct (in the strict sense of the word) the administration.[99]

Concerning the free designation and removal of administrative officers, the Constitutional Court recognizes the legislator's freedom to regulate the election and removal of the members of public bodies, and even to attribute to itself such powers.[100]

As for the powers to direct (in the strict sense), while it is accepted that legislation may limit the government's powers to direct particular bodies, for such limitation to be enacted it is necessary for grounds to exist that justify that limitation. In this regard it should be remembered that two kinds of IAA exist:

With respect to the IAAs called for by the Constitution to guarantee a fundamental right, it is claimed that 'independence' is required by a special rule which prevails over the general rule establishing government competence in matters of political direction.[101]

[98] Malaret 'La Comisión Nacional del Mercado de Valores' op cit 559, n 13. For a similar argument see FJ Rodríguez Pontón 'Gobierno, política y Administración: elementos de debate para las administraciones independientes' Autonomies nº 24 (1999) 205.

[99] Parada Vázquez *Derecho administrativo II* op cit 320 ff. For a similar argument see García Llovet 'Autoridades administrativas . . .' op cit 117; A. Betancor Rodríguez, *Las administraciones independientes* (1994) 186–7.

[100] STC 108/1986, FJ 12º.

[101] Sala Arquer op cit 417.

With respect to those IAAs created to discharge a technical economic function, given that there are no grounds in the Constitution that justify any restriction of government powers, administrative legal doctrine has relativized the problem, indicating that, because the degree of government direction may be greater or lesser, it is a matter of striking the right balance between direction and functional autonomy, of making government direction compatible with the autonomy necessary for the accomplishment of the regulatory function. The IAAs may be attributed an ambit of autonomy, while the relationship between them and the government may be defined as a relationship of inspection, tutelage, or of low intensity direction.[102] As the IAAs are not subject to any strategic direction, evaluation or control of results on the part of the government (being subject only to governmental control in the event of grave dereliction or exceedingly deleterious working on the part of the 'authorities'), there is no problem when it comes to defining the relationship between the authorities and the government in the manner indicated. As will be apparent, the debate over the limitation of government powers with respect to IAAs is bound up with a reappraisal of the government's position and of the model for the administration, in which the IAAs have emerged as a new method of decentralising executive activity functions.[103]

### *B. Lack of control and political accountability*

Leaving aside the debate over the restriction of government powers, the fact that the IAAs are not directed or controlled by the government also poses a problem for democracy. To say that there is a relationship of low intensity direction or of tutelage may well solve the problem regarding government powers, but another problem remains unsolved, namely that of the lack of control and the political accountability of these 'authorities'.

In the first place there is some doubt as to whether one of the characteristics of the legal status of the IAAs is the limited political control exercised over them. Nevertheless, if there is any reason which justifies these 'authorities' enjoyment of qualified autonomy ('independence') from the State's political institutions in the discharge of particular functions, that autonomy must necessarily take the form of a restriction on ordinary political controls. In this regard, it should be borne in mind that the creation of some

[102] Betancor Rodríguez *Las administraciones independientes* op cit. 209; Jiménez de Cisneros Cid op cit 310 ff; García de Enterría and Fernández Rodríguez *Curso de Derecho Administrativo* vol. I (2000) 428–9.

[103] García Llovet op cit 66 ff; and Rodríguez Pontón op cit 189 ff; Betancor op cit 243–4; Ariño Ortiz 'Regulación económica y modelo de Administración' in A Pérez *Administración Instrumental* vol I op cit 27 ff (p 68).

IAAs is regarded as a constitutional requirement, in which case, logically, the non-existence or insufficiency of political controls would be justified. As for the other IAAs, that is to say, the 'regulatory authorities' set up to perform a technical-economic function, the opinion seems to be growing that the scant level of political control is the price that has to be paid if these 'authorities' are to discharge their functions effectively, although legal opinion is divided on this point.[104] In any case, it seems that some sort of balance between autonomy and control needs to be struck, a balance which would guarantee respect for constitutional principles; such a balance would rely on legislation defining with sufficient precision the IAAs' functions, competences and room for manoeuvre and on the strengthening of the mechanisms of political control.

Nor are the problems solely theoretical. There are practical problems too, for when it comes to controlling the activity of a particular IAA, it is often not sufficiently clear for what the government on the one hand and the 'independent authority' on the other are accountable to parliament, as a consequence of which any control that is finally brought to bear yields unsatisfactory results. Accordingly, the solution should be sought in the strengthening of parliamentary control once the spheres of government and 'independent authority' has been clarified.[105]

The problem of lack of control and political accountability has come in for particular criticism in those cases where the 'independent authority' takes part in, or is responsible for, the definition of a public policy, as is true of the *Banco de España*.[106] However, in this particular case the Bank's autonomy is required by the European Community Treaty, within the framework of the process of economic and monetary union; accordingly the problem in this case is posed within different parameters.[107]

### *C. The problem of legitimization*

The non-existence or insufficiency of democratic political control has led to recognition that the IAAs suffer from a deficit in respect of democratic legitimacy. Logically, there will be a deficit in the IAAs' democratic legitimization in proportion to the non-justified insufficiency of political control. To

[104] L Parejo Alfonso *Crisis y renovación en el Derecho Público* (1991) 37; Parada Vázquez *Derecho administrativo II* op cit 321; S del Saz Cordero 'Desarrollo y crisis del Derecho administrativo. Su reserva constitucional' in AAVV, *Nuevas perspectivas del Derecho administrativo. Tres estudios* (1992) 186.

[105] Salvador Martínez *Autoridades independientes* op cit 332–3 and 380–1.

[106] Bilbao Ubillos op cit 179; J Tajadura Tejada 'El Banco Central Europeo: su estatuto jurídico' in *La introducción de la moneda única en España, Dirección del Servicio Jurídico del Estado* (1999) 91 ff.

[107] For an extensive treatment see Magide Herrero op cit 457 ff.

solve this problem, attempts have in some cases been made (under the influence of French legal opinion) to compensate for the deficit in democratic legitimisation by appealing to so-called 'technocratic legitimacy'; in other cases, the participation of affected citizens has been requested.

In the first cases, the claim is made that the IAAs activities may be understood as legitimized because their members are specialists in the field and make all their decisions objectively, on the sole basis of technical criteria, and in complete freedom from any kind of political interference.[108] This line of argument rests on the premise that politically neutral technical management is possible and on the claim that the decisions made by these 'authorities' are technical decisions with no room for political judgements.[109] But the opponents of this argument claim that the scope for action of these IAAs is actually rather larger than we are sometimes led to believe and that no such thing as a purely technical decision exists.[110] Fiercer still are the criticisms formulated by constitutionalists who have dealt with the matter; they draw attention to the risks associated with 'technocracy' (risks already identified in Spain by García Pelayo)[111] and to the belief, at once sterile and fallacious, that an expert will be a more efficient manager in the public sector if cut off from any ideological position. They also point out that what lies behind the defence of the technicians is nothing other than a mistrust of political parties, and that it is a way of escaping the State's mechanisms of democratic control.[112]

In the second cases, the entrance of representatives of citizens affected by the institution's activity into some IAAs has been proposed as a means of compensating for the deficit of democratic legitimacy.[113] Something of the kind happens in the universities, whose legitimacy derives from the participation of all members of the university community.

[108] For all of which see Betancor Rodríguez op cit 29.

[109] For an extensive treatment see Magide Herrero op cit 247 ff.

[110] Malaret, 'La Comisión Nacional del Mercado de Valores' op cit 559, n 13. For a similar argument see Rodríguez Pontón op cit 205.

[111] Criticism of 'technical neutrality' is to be found in M García Pelayo's classic *Burocracia, tecnocracia y otros escritos* (1974) 52, and his *Las transformaciones del Estado contemporáneo* (1977) 132.

[112] Rallo Lombarte *La constitucionalidad de las administraciones independientes* op cit 240–1; Bilbao Ubillos op cit 180–1, where the author states that the solution 'consists in more and better democracy, not in embracing, consciously or otherwise, alternative legitimacies'.

[113] See, eg, G Ariño 'Regulación económica y modelo de Administración' in A Perez *Administración instrumental. Libro homenaje a Manuel Francisco Clavero Arevalo* vol 1 (1994) 27 ff. (p 67–8); and in 'Perspectiva actual y futuro de la Administración institucional del Estado' in *Constitución y el nuevo diseño de las Administraciones estatal y autonómica* (1998) 498–501. Of the contrary opinion are Magide Herrero op cit 132 ff.; and Parada *Derecho administrativo II* op cit 318.

## X. CONCLUSIONS

The problems associated with the IAAs are posed differently in accordance with the grounds which justify each IAA. In Spain it is evident that those institutions that serve to guarantee particular fundamental rights respond to a constitutional requirement. In these cases, their 'independence' is justified and the only problems that arise stem from the reluctance of the political arena to accept that independence. But these cases are the exception rather than the rule.

The so-called regulatory IAAs are a different kettle of fish. They have no constitutional justification and have been imposed by European community law in line with a blueprint for relations between State and market which is very similar to that in place in the USA. This means that as a matter of course constitutional problems attach to getting these IAAs to fit our form of state. At present there are only a small number of regulatory authorities; the legislation regulating them is crystal clear, their competences are limited, and their independence relative. As we have seen, all of this has led the burden of legal opinion to minimize the problems associated with these authorities too. However, they should still be given some attention since, quite apart from the specific constitutional problem the existence or praxis of one, or some, of the IAAs, may pose, the broader problem lurks in the shadows, waiting to make its appearance if the formula of the IAA is given the definitive thumbs up and, little by little, the functions and competences of the traditional institutions of the 'social and democratic State' and of the 'rule of law' continue to be eroded.

# 7. PRAGMATISM OR PRINCIPLE? THE USE OF AGENCIES IN PUBLIC SERVICE PROVISION IN THE UNITED KINGDOM

*Duncan Fairgrieve**

## I. INTRODUCTION

The constitution of the United Kingdom is a product of a long history of incremental development. Indeed, one of the striking features of the British system of government is the remarkable degree of historical continuity with the principal institutions of rule-making. The lack of a decisive rupture, such as a broad Revolutionary settlement, has meant that the formation of public service-provision in Britain has been a fairly slow process of adaptation of the governing apparatus to the exigencies of the moment. As has been pointed out:

> we have always had a somewhat messy system of administrative institutions. Bodies would be created to deal with particular problems as they arose with little thought being given to any rational allocation of decision making.[1]

The pragmatic approach to the Constitutional development of the State has had a variety of consequences. It has had an impact on the core notions of the Constitutional architecture of the United Kingdom. There has been a certain degree of confusion surrounding the notion of the State, a term which in continental systems is considered as central and which is thus subject to a corresponding detailed conceptualization.[2] In the United Kingdom, the notion has in fact no precise legal definition.[3]

This has evidently had an effect on the provision of public services. In modern times, the structures for providing public services have undergone rapid changes in all European countries. The United Kingdom is no

* I would like to thank Emanuela Lecchi for her comments on, and assistance with, a previous draft of this chapter.

1 See Paul Craig, *Administrative Law* (5th edn London 2003) 47.

2 French text books on Constitutional law often take the conceptualization of the State as a starting-point for analysis: D Turpin *Droit Constitutionnel* (4th edn PUF Paris 1999) 12 *passim*.

3 See C Harlow and R Rawlings, *Law and Administration* (2nd edn London 1997) ch 1.

exception. An emerging trend of the last 25 years is the reduction of the purview of the administrative state, and a radical re-thinking of the manner in which public services are provided.[4] These developments have been underpinned by the need to improve the efficiency of public service delivery, by hiving off tasks formerly executed by the State. The financial burden on the State has thus been reduced by obtaining competitive services at a lower price. In order to facilitate this process, a distinction has been made between the function of policy-making, on the one hand, and the actual application or implementation of policies, on the other, with solely the former considered to be within the natural attribution of central government.

This process of evolution has been undertaken in a heterogeneous manner, leading to a surprising variety of formats. One format, reminiscent of Victorian franchise contracts, which were a feature of the early development of railways and electricity in the UK,[5] has been the entire separation of services, by means of the complete contractualization of certain public services (in sectors sufficiently competitive and therefore in situations more favourable to contracts)[6] such as street cleaning, road repairs, and highways construction, or even prisoner escort services. Another such format is that of the agency,[7] which has enjoyed considerable success.

## II. ADMINISTRATIVE DIVERSITY: THE AGENCY FORMAT IN THE UNITED KINGDOM

The agency format has been an increasingly common method for public service provision in the United Kingdom, but the model adopted has not been uniform. Certain categories can be identified, though these subsets are by no means mutually exclusive.[8]

The major drive in favour of the agency format can be traced back to the creation of so-called Next Steps Agencies. This is an appropriate starting-point for the analysis.

[4] The concept of a unified and uniform civil service in the United Kingdom, with Governmental functions organized around distinct departments no longer holds true: see Craig, *Administrative Law* ch 4.

[5] See Jon Stern *Regulation and Contracts for Utility Services: Substitutes or Complements? Lessons from UK historical experience* London Business School Regulation Initiative Working Paper No 54, available via <http://www.london.edu/ri>.

[6] José A Gómez-Ibáñez *Regulating Infrastructure Monopoly, Contracts and Discretion* (Harvard University Press 2003) 186.

[7] The actual *names* of the particular institutions in question differ markedly, being indifferently called, eg, 'agencies', 'directorates', 'offices', 'commissions', 'inspectorates', 'directorates', 'services.' See Craig *Administrative Law* 96

[8] Generally, see ibid ch 4.

## III. NEXT STEPS AGENCIES OR EXECUTIVE AGENCIES

### A. *Overview*

Next Steps Agencies originated from an influential report compiled by Sir Robin Ibbs entitled '*Improving Management in Government: The Next Steps*' and published in 1988. This report concluded that there was insufficient focus on the delivery of government services (as opposed to policy and ministerial support), even though the vast majority of civil servants worked in service delivery functions. The report thus advocated the implementation of a divide between policy-making and service-delivery, which was inspired in some respects by the influential Scandinavian model. Agencies should thus be established to carry out the executive functions of government within a policy and resources framework set by a department. This would then enhance the service-delivery functions, to be undertaken by separate bodies, with parent departments to concentrate on policy development.

As a direct consequence of the Ibbs report, public service delivery was subject to scrutiny with a view to deciding whether the most effective structure should be preserved, or abolished, privatized, contracted out, or carried out by means of an executive agency.[9]

As part of this process,[10] a large number of so-called 'Next Steps Agencies' were duly formed. So successful was this that large parts of the provision of public service now take place within the structure of this agency format. As an idea of the importance of these agencies, over three-quarters of civil servants now work in such an organization.[11]

In public sector terminology, Next Steps Agencies are also commonly referred to as Executive Agencies. As of May 2002, there were 127 Executive Agencies, covering a diverse sphere of activities, including the Prison Service; Land Registry; Passport Office. The Inland Revenue, the Crown Prosecution Service, and the Serious Fraud Office also operate along these lines.[12] The first preliminary phase of large-scale creation of these agencies has now ended, and the main focus of government policy has shifted away from creation of agencies towards improving their performance.[13]

[9] See ibid 94.

[10] The Agency structure is by no means a result of one piece of reform. There have indeed been a series of initiatives and reviews since the implementation of the Ibbs report, which limits on space precludes us from examining in great depth. See, however, *Next Steps Report 1998* (Mar 1999, Cm 4273); *Better Government Services*: Executive *Agencies in the 21st Century* (July 2002).

[11] Agencies and Public Bodies Team, Cabinet Office *Creation, Review and Dissolution of Executive Agencies* (Apr 2004).

[12] See Craig, *Administrative Law* 94.

[13] Agencies and Public Bodies Team, Cabinet Office *Creation, Review and Dissolution of Executive Agencies* (Apr 2004).

A Chief Executive is responsible for the day-to-day running of the agency, and can be removed if the objectives set out in the agreement are not met. In several cases, executives have been recruited from outside the standard civil service career-pattern.[14] The main role of Next Steps Agencies is service-delivery, but it is also clear that the Chief Executive will generally have some input in the policy-making retained by the central government department. Chief Executives do speak in public about the performance of their agency, though they are expected to cover essentially operational-matters.

Next Steps Agencies are based upon framework documents, which are intra-public sector agreements entered into between the sponsoring department and the agency, with the Treasury often also being a party. This sets out the key elements of the policy and resources framework for the agency and the relationship and respective responsibilities of the Chief Executive, the relevant Minister, the departmental permanent secretary, the appropriate HM Treasury expenditure team and other departments, agencies and other organizations. The framework document thus defines the functions and the goals of the agency, its responsibilities and budget. The performance of the agency is regularly reviewed on the basis of the targets and objectives set.

Whereas the traditional approach has been for each agency to have a separate framework agreement, a recent trend has been for government departments to develop broader horizontal guidelines in the form of a departmental framework setting out the governance arrangements for the whole department, including its agencies.[15]

Next Steps Agencies do not have a corporate legal personality, and thus operate under powers that are delegated from Ministers and Departments. It has been held that as a matter of law decisions taken by officials within these agencies are to be regarded as decisions of the Secretary of State.[16]

### *B. Accountability of 'Next-Steps Agencies'*

#### *1. Appointment process*

The Chief Executive of an Agency is normally appointed by open competition by the relevant Minister. In line with the objective-related set-up of agencies, there is usually an element of performance-related pay included in the employment contract with the Chief Executive. [17]

[14] See A Le Sueur 'The Nature, Powers and Accountability of Central Government' in *English Public Law* (OUP Oxford 2004) paras 3.64.

[15] The Department of Work and Pensions has developed this approach.

[16] *R v Secretary of State for Social Security ex p Sherwin* (1996) 32 BMLR 1.

[17] Agencies and Public Bodies Team, Cabinet Office *Guidance on Framework Documents* (Dec 2002, updated Apr 2004) para 30.

As regards the recruitment and retention of the agency staff, the right to pay, promote and manage staff is delegated to the Chief Executive of the Agency. As part of the flexibility contained within the Agency structure, terms and conditions are often varied in order to adapt to local employment market conditions.

Where appointments are made to the senior civil service, then the requirements and processes laid down by the Civil Service Commissioners must be abided by.[18]

### 2. *Mission accountability*

Framework documents play an important part in ensuring that the necessary accountability is achieved. Indeed, one recent government policy document states that:

> Framework Documents set out the key accountability relationships between Agency Chief Executives and key players in their parent department including the Permanent Secretary, agency sponsors and the responsible Minister.[19]

Clearly, much depends upon the relationship between the Agency Chief Executive, on the one hand, and the Sponsor Department and Minister, on the other. There is a division of responsibilities. The relevant Secretary of State is responsible for establishing the policy framework within which each agency operates and for determining its strategic objectives and annual key performance targets. On the other hand, the Agency Chief Executive is responsible for the day-to-day management of the agency.

It should however be noted that the Constitutional paradigm of Parliamentary scrutiny has been subject to a certain degree of tension in respect of the establishment of executive agencies. In particular, controversy has arisen regarding the extent of ministerial responsibility. In a nutshell, how can a Minister be effectively held accountable to Parliament in respect of activities of bodies which, under the Next Steps initiative, have been granted operational independence?[20] Moreover, there is a recognized difficulty in dividing clearly between policy considerations, the responsibility of the government department, and service delivery, undertaken by the agency.[21]

A recent government publication gives an indication of official policy. It is stated that Ministers are accountable to Parliament on all matters

[18] See Civil Service Commissioners' Recruitment Code (5th edn Mar 2004).

[19] Agencies and Public Bodies Team, Cabinet Office *Guidance on Framework Documents* (Dec 2002, updated Apr 2004) para 1.

[20] See Craig *Administrative Law* 104–5.

[21] See ibid 104.

concerning their agencies.[22] However, this is tempered by the suggestion that the relevant Minister may ask a Chief Executive to *reply direct* to correspondence and written Parliamentary Questions that concern issues delegated to the Chief Executive.[23] Similarly, in respect of the work of Select Committees, it is stated that: 'At Select Committee hearings, Ministers will normally ask the [Chief Executive] to represent or accompany them if the Committee is concerned with the day to day operations of the agency.'[24]

It would thus seem that in the light of the increasing importance of the work of agencies, the notion of ministerial responsibility has evolved. As Craig has observed:

> This 'compromise', reflecting as it does traditional British pragmatism, may be no bad thing. The Minister will still be there and responsible, in theory at least, for matters of principle or general policy. In addition to this, the chief executive will, under the new regime, be visible and the objectives of the agency will be publicly known. In this sense there will be a new figure, who can be called to account for operational agency failure and this is to be welcomed. [25]

This new approach must also be placed within broader developments impacting on the issue of accountability, through the use of performance targets.[26] Annual performance targets appear in the Agency's annual report and accounts, and are submitted to Parliament by means of a Ministerial statement before the start of the financial year.[27] The Chief Executive is held accountable to the relevant Minister and the Accounting Officer for both the financial management of the agency and for the performance of the Agency in respect of key targets. Most agencies receive funding from their parent department and, although they are required to publish and lay before Parliament separate accounts, these accounts also form a constituent part of their parent department's accounts.

Other mechanisms should also be referred to here. MPs may refer complaints from the public to the Parliamentary Commissioner for Administration where an individual claims to have suffered injustice through maladministration on the part of these Agencies. In line with

[22] Agencies and Public Bodies Team, Cabinet Office *Guidance on Framework Documents* (Dec 2002, updated Apr 2004) para 17.

[23] Ibid.

[24] Ibid para 31.

[25] See Craig *Administrative Law* 105.

[26] Departments increasingly have objectives laid down in Public Service Agreements (PSAs) or Service Delivery Agreements (SDAs). See further Paul Craig, *Administrative Law* (London, 5th edition, 2003), page 131.

[27] Agencies and Public Bodies Team, Cabinet Office *Guidance on Framework Documents* (December 2002, updated Apr 2004) para 10.

general developments in central government,[28] agencies have also been encouraged to develop an effective internal complaints procedure.[29]

## IV. AGENCIES OTHER THAN NEXT STEPS AGENCIES

Agencies established outside the Next Steps initiative are generally based upon statutory authority.[30] Unlike Next Steps Agencies, where the powers and composition of the body is generally detailed in the framework agreement, other agencies are thus governed by the implementing legislation.

### *A. Non-Departmental Public Body (NDPB)*

It is important to distinguish the Next Steps Agencies or Executive Agencies from other types of body, created outside the ambit of the normal departmental framework of government activity.[31] These are sometimes referred to as a Non-Departmental Public Body (NDPB).[32]

The term 'Non-departmental public body' is officially defined as:

> A body which has a role in the processes of national government, but is not a government department or part of one, and which accordingly operates to a greater or lesser extent at arm's length from Ministers.[33]

NDPBs are typically set up where a function needs to be carried out at arm's length from ministers such as regulatory functions or funding decisions, where expert advice is required by ministers on technical issues or body needs to be set up to deal with appeals.

It is difficult to calculate accurately the number of extant NDPBs. In March 2003, it was estimated that there were a total of 811 non-departmental public bodies.[34] This group of public bodies may in turn be divided into various categories:[35] Executive NDPBs; Advisory NDPBs; Tribunal NDPBs and Boards of Visitors.

28 D Fairgrieve, *State Liability in Tort : A Comparative Law Study* (OUP Oxford 2003) 250.

29 Agencies and Public Bodies Team, Cabinet Office, *Guidance on Framework Documents* (Dec 2002, updated Apr 2004) para 18.

30 Although sometimes the prerogative may be invoked.

31 See Craig, *Administrative Law* 97.

32 Or alternatively referred to on some occasions as a 'Quango'. 'Quango' means 'Quasi-autonomous non-governmental organization.' This terminology is criticised as these bodies are rather non-departmental, than non-governmental, organizations.

33 Cabinet Office *Opening up Quangos, a consultation paper* (Nov 1997) ch 1, §1. See more recently Cabinet Office *Non-Departmental Public Bodies: a Guide for Departments—policy and Charatceristics of an NDPB* (Sept 2004).

34 Cabinet Office *Public Bodies 2003* (2003).

35 A Bradley and K Ewing *Constitutional and Administrative Law* (12th edn London 1998) 332. See also Cabinet Office *Public Bodies 2003*.

Executive NDPBs are established in order to carry out administrative, commercial, executive, or regulatory functions on behalf of the Government. They are legally incorporated and thus have their own legal identity. These bodies normally employ staff and have their own budget. As to appointments, there is no fixed policy as these agencies have often been created ad hoc, but generally speaking the relevant Minister will make the appointments, in accordance with the Appointment Unit of the Civil Service Department and the Commissioner for Public Appointments.

Examples of these bodies include the Advisory Conciliation and Arbitration Service (ACAS), Commission for Racial Equality (CRE), and the Equal Opportunities Commission (EOC). An important element is that the legislation creating those bodies may define the role to be played by the Minister, who may be allowed to give statutory directions, or may be required to give prior approval to certain courses of action.[36]

Advisory NDPBs are generally set up by Ministers to provide independent and expert advice on particular topics of interest. However, these bodies generally do not employ staff or incur expenditure on their own account. In this category of bodies are the Council on Tribunals[37] and the Football Licensing Authority.[38]

Another category is that of tribunals, which have jurisdiction in specialist areas of the law, such as the Mental Health Review Tribunal, Lands Tribunal, and Special Educational Needs and Disability Tribunal. They are usually supported by staff from their sponsoring department and do not have their own budgets.

Finally, there are Boards of Visitors who are the 'watch dogs' of the prison system, supervising the state of the prison premises and the treatment of prisoners.[39]

### *B. Regulators*

As seen above, some of the Next Steps Agencies perform regulatory roles. NDPBs such as the Board of Visitors also clearly have a regulatory remit. However, over and above the categories of Next Steps Agencies and the NDPBs, there are a number of other agencies, known as regulatory agencies which are primarily concerned with regulating previously privatised industries. Examples of these include the Office of

36 See Craig, *Administrative Law* 95.

37 <http://www.council-on-tribunals.gov.uk>. The Council on Tribunals supervises the constitution and working of Tribunals and Inquiries in England, Scotland and Wales as listed in the Tribunals and Inquiries Act 1992.

38 <http://www.flaweb.org.uk>. The FLA is an independent public body set up under the Football Spectators Act 1989 to (1) license league and international football grounds in England and Wales; and (2) oversee the control of safety at these grounds by local authorities.

39 See Cabinet Office *Public Bodies 2003*.

Communications (Ofcom),[40] Office of Gas and Electricity Markets (OFGEM),[41] and Office of Water Services (OFWAT).[42]

The great majority of these bodies have been set up by an Act of Parliament from where they gain their authority, powers and structures.[43] However, this is not always the case, and it is clear that the status of regulators and regulator bodies is distinctly heterogeneous.[44] The regulatory model is unusual in the United Kingdom and is somewhat of a Constitutional hybrid. If one of the main reasons behind the creation of Next Step Agencies was the perceived need to implement a split between the functions of policy-making and service delivery, in the case of formerly public owned industries there was a perceived need to separate out the policy-making function (which remained with the Government), the management and delivery function (which was attributed to the newly privatised companies) and the regulatory function (this is the function to be performed by the regulators). The regulatory function is particularly important in the case of sectors characterised by elements of natural monopoly in service delivery, to ensure that the newly privatised companies do not abuse their position in the markets. The regulators perform very complex functions of economic regulation and in the UK have been granted concurrent jurisdiction with the Office of Fair Trading (the main antitrust authority) to deal with potential breaches of the competition rules in the particular sector.

## V. ACCOUNTABILITY OF 'NON-DEPARTMENTAL PUBLIC BODY' (NDPB)

### *A. Appointments*

One of the key earlier considerations in respect of these bodies, and which

40 <http://www.ofcom.org.uk>. Ofcom was created at the beginning of 2004 and replaces a number of formerly separate regulators, namely OFTEL (the Office for Telecommunications), the ITC (Independent Television Commission); the BSC (Broadcasting Standards Commission) the RA (Radio Communications Agency) and the Radio Authority.

41 <http://www.ofgem.gov.uk>. Ofgem is the regulator for Britain's gas and electricity industries. Its role is to protect and advance the interests of consumers by promoting competition where possible, and through regulation only where necessary.

42 <http://www.ofwat.gov.uk>. Ofwat is responsible for making sure that the water and sewerage companies in England and Wales gives a good-quality, efficient service at a fair price.

43 See the Competition Commission, established by the Competition Act 1998.

44 Two examples will be given in the sphere of financial services. The Financial Services Regulator, the Financial Services Authority is in fact a company limited by guarantee established under the Companies Act 1985. It has however had functions conferred upon it by Statute due to the Financial Services and Markets Act 2000 which also requires it to comply with requirements as to its constitution and procedures. Another unusual example of regulatory architecture is the Panel on Take-overs and Mergers, established by the Stock Exchange in the 1960s, and is in effect a private regulatory body. It is an unincorporated assocation with no legal personality.

plagued the existence of Quangos,[45] was the procedure for the appointment of staff and the supervision of that process. This is a crucial question and is of considerable importance. More than 22,000 people are currently members of the boards of public bodies, including NDPBs.[46] One major department was said to be responsible for nearly 1,000 appointments of which 30 carried a salary or entitlement fee.[47]

Normally, responsibility for appointment rests with the Minister of the department responsible for the organization. Various control mechanisms do exist. The Minister is accountable to Parliament for Appointments. Following the Nolan Report,[48] an independent Commissioner for Public Appointments has been appointed.[49]

The Commissioner for Public Appointments monitors and advises on ministerial appointments to public bodies, including executive and advisory NDPBs, NHS Bodies, public corporations, nationalized industries, and utility regulators. The Commissioner has put together a Code of Practice setting out the principles and practice of selecting and appointing board members to public bodies. The Commissioner monitors the process to ensure those appointments are made on merit after fair and open competition, and can undertake investigations and complaints about the public appointments process.

### *B. Mission Accountability*

The system of accountability in the British governmental system has traditionally been premised on the concept of answerability of a minister to the House of Commons. Although the effectiveness and adequacy of this traditional means of accountability have subject to doubt,[50] governmental policy still sets great store by this mechanism. In a recent Cabinet Office Publication, the role of parliamentary scrutiny in respect of agencies was stated in unambiguous terms:

[45] See n 32 above.

[46] Cabinet Office, *Public Bodies 2003*.

[47] See Craig *Administrative Law* 98.

[48] First Report of the Committee on Standards in Public Life, Cm 2850-I (1995)

[49] <http://www.ocpa.gov.uk>. The Commissioner monitors, regulates, reports and advises on 12,000 Ministerial appointments to public bodies. Government departments are required to follow the Commissioner's *Principles* and detailed *Code of Practice* when processing these public appointments. The Commissioner is also responsible for investigating *complaints*.

[50] Ministerial responsibility is a model of accountability which is now generally no longer viewed as effective: 'The doctrine of individual ministerial responsibility has been significantly weakened over the last ten years or so, so that it can no longer be said, in our view, that it is a fundamental doctrine of the constitution' (J Jowell and D Oliver (eds) *The Changing Constitution* (4th edn OUP Oxford 2000) viii.

> Whilst NDPBs are distanced from government, the responsible minister is accountable to parliament for the degree of independence which an NDPB enjoys; for its usefulness as an instrument of government policy; and so ultimately for the overall effectiveness and efficiency with which it carries out its functions. Ministers also remain accountable to Parliament for public money spent by an NDPB, even though bodies operate at arm's length with their own designated accounting officers.[51]

This is not a very satisfactory solution for a number of reasons, and to some extent echoing our earlier discussion concerning Next Steps Agencies. The indirect nature of accountability described in the previous citation does little for efficiency. The arm's length relationship of the agency with the Minister evidently reduces the potency of this control.

Other routes of accountability have been honed. Improved financial accountability has been a focus of recent government initiatives.[52] Most NDPBs are under an obligation to establish combined Annual report and accounts.[53] The latter is subject to internal and external audit by inter alia the Comptroller and Auditor General.[54] This ties in also with the recent preoccupation with target-setting and monitoring. The bodies are required to publish, in agreement with the sponsor department, the key financial and quality targets before the start of the period they are intended to cover. Annual Reports are designed then to provide full details of the extent to which financial and other performance targets have been achieved.[55]

The Parliamentary Commissioner for Administration (PCA),[56] with its ombudsman functions, has also played an important role in ensuring the accountability of the agency to members of the public. Although the PCA mainly covers central government departments, its jurisdiction has vastly increased over the last few years and now extends to many agencies.[57] The Parliamentary Ombudsman deals with complaints from members of the public who consider that they have suffered injustice because of maladministration by government departments or other public bodies within the Ombudsman's jurisdiction.

The work of select committees has had a particular perspective in respect of regulatory agencies.[58] Select Committees are empowered to look at the expenditure, administration and policy of 'associated public bodies' of the

[51] Cabinet Office *Non-Departmental Public Bodies: a Guide for Departments—policy and Charatceristics of an NDPB* (Sept 2004) 4.

[52] See, eg, ibid.

[53] Note however that Advisory NDPBs do not prepare separate accounts.

[54] Ibid.

[55] Ibid.

[56] Parliamentary Commissioner Act 1967.

[57] Eg Equal Opportunities Commission, Commission for Racial Equality, OFCOM, OFWAT, Office of the Rail Regulator and International Rail Regulator, Acas.

[58] See T Prosser 'The Powers and Accountability of Agencies and Regulators' in D Feldman (ed) *English Public Law* (OUP Oxford 2004) para 5.19.

relevant government department.[59] The role of parliamentary select committees has been significant, with inquiries undertaken on a sectoral[60] or agency-specific basis.[61]

In terms of the regulatory agencies, it has already been noted that they have generally been established by statute. This has evidently had an impact on issues of accountability. The powers and duties of the body and its officers are laid down in the statute. The relevant procedural safe-guards are spelled-out.[62] Recourse against the decisions of the body is thus facilitated, and in some circumstances addressed in the enabling statute itself.[63]

## VI. LEGAL ACCOUNTABILITY

### *A. Judicial review*

Where agencies are founded on statute, then the bringing of judicial review is facilitated by the fact that the agency's powers and responsibilities are laid down in the relevant legislation. So, applications have been brought in the case of Non-Departmental Public Bodies, such as the Commission for Racial Equality. Similarly, it has been not uncommon for regulators also to be subject to the rigours of judicial review. However, it should be noted that the courts have in practice tended to very reticent to second-guess regulatory decisions, and thus have granted considerable latitude to the economic and utility regulators.[64]

On the other hand, we have already noted that Next Steps Agencies do not have a corporate legal personality. This lack of a formal legal status has had an impact on judicial review. Actions for review will generally have to be brought against the relevant responsible Minister.[65]

### *B. Damages Liability*

Agencies may be held accountable before the courts in actions for monetary

[59] See Standing Orders of the House of Commons Public Business 2003, s 152.

[60] Eg Treasury Committee *Financial Services Regulator* (1998–9 HC 73).

[61] Prosser, 'The Powers and Accountability of Agencies and Regulators' para 5.20.

[62] See, eg, Postal Services Act 2000 establishing the Postal Servicies Commission as a body supervising the provision of postal services. It has the power to license providers of postal services, subject to a variety of procedural requirements.

[63] See, eg, the Competition Act 1998, establishing the Competition Commission, in which the issue of appeals against the relevant decisions is addressed in the Statute (see s 46).

[64] For instance, the Competition Commission did not lose a judicial review challenge until 2001: *Interbrew SA v Competition Commission* [2001] EWHC Admin 367.

[65] See Craig *Administrative Law* 111. See *also R. v Secretary of State for Social Security Ex p. Sherwin* (1996) 32 BMLR 1 1996 WL 1090140.

claims.[66] This question has arisen most recently in respect of the damages liability of regulators, both from a domestic and comparative law perspective.

Traditionally, negligence actions against regulatory authorities have met with resistance,[67] thus providing protection for bodies acting in the sphere of health and safety,[68] control of financial institutions,[69] and the supervision of compliance with building regulations.[70]

However, recent developments have suggested a shift in approach of the courts both in terms of the general application of negligence in actions against public authorities,[71] but also in the development of the public law tort of misfeasance in public office. In the case of *Three Rivers District Council v Bank of England*,[72] litigation arose from the alleged wrongdoing by the Bank of England in supervising the Bank of Credit and Commerce International (BCCI). Following the liquidation of BCCI, depositors brought damages claims against the Bank of England for alleged failures in its supervisory role. These claims were struck out in the High Court and Court of Appeal.[73] But the House of Lords delivered two later judgments in which the elements of the tort of misfeasance in public office have been broadened considerably, thereby increasing the utility of this tort in claims against regulators. Similar developments have occurred in other jurisdictions.[74]

[66] With the exception again of Next Steps Agencies which, as they do not have a corporate legal personality, will incur the liability of their parent Department.

[67] C Hadjiemmanuil *Banking Regulation and the Bank of England* (LLP London 1996) ch 5; H McLean 'Negligent Regulatory Authorities and the Duty of Care' (1988) 8 OJLS 442.

[68] *Philcox v Civil Aviation Authority* The Times, 8 June 1995; *Reeman v DoT* [1997] 2 Lloyd's Rep 648; *Harris v Evans* [1998] 3 All ER 522. Liability arose exceptionally for negligent misstatement in *Welton v North Cornwall DC* [1997] 1 WLR 570. For a more liberal approach see also *Perrett v Collins* [1998] 2 Lloyd's Rep 255 (concerning personal injury) and *Watson v British Boxing Board of Control Ltd* [2001] QB 1134 (concerning personal injury; BBBC is a regulatory, but not a public, body), analysed by J. George (2002) 65 MLR 106.

[69] *Yuen Kun Yeu v Attorney General of Hong Kong* [1988] AC 175; *Davis v Radcliffe* [1990] 2 All ER 536.

[70] *Murphy v Brentwood DC* [1991] 1 AC 398; *Tesco Stores v Wards Constructions Ltd* (1995) 76 BLR 94.

[71] See generally, D Fairgrieve *State Liability in Tort: A Comparative Law Study* (OUP Oxford 2003).

[72] *Three Rivers DC* [2000] 2 WLR 1220 (House of Lords' first decision); *Three Rivers DC* [2001] UKHL 16 (House of Lords' second decision).

[73] At first instance, after initial proceedings concerning various preliminary issues of law, Clarke J acceded to the Bank of England's application to strike out the action (Judgment of 30 July 1997 (unreported)). The Court of Appeal upheld Clarke J's decision in a joint majority judgment of Hirst and Robert Walker LJJ; Auld LJ dissented: *Three Rivers DC v Bank of England* [1999] EuLR 211.

[74] M Andenas and D Fairgrieve 'Misfeasance in Public Office, Governmental Liability and European Influences' (2002) 51 *ICLQ* 757.

[75] See *Better Government Services*: Executive *Agencies in the 21st Century* (July 2002).

## VII. CONCLUSION

The use of the Agency format in the United Kingdom has been declared to be a success.[75] However, the pragmatic way in which these reforms have been ushered in has created tensions and ambiguities, all of which have not been resolved.

We have seen that difficulties have stemmed from attempts to square the new institutional make-up with traditional concepts of accountability. On the one hand, Next Steps Agencies and NDPBs are clearly intended to be run with a good deal of autonomy. The aim is thus to confer responsibility for a particular area to a body which will then ultimately be judged on its performance in attaining its set objectives. On the other hand, traditional doctrines mean that Ministers are ultimately responsible to parliament for the agencies' effectiveness and efficiency.

We have seen that this issue has been partially resolved by an acceptance that the traditional means of control, that of ministerial responsibility, is no longer compatible with both the new structures, and the heightened desire for efficient means of accountability. Other avenues have thus been developed and honed to come to terms with this, with the development of target-setting and monitoring, external and internal audits and the important role of bodies such as Ombudsmen and Parliamentary Committees.

Another ambiguity that is recurrent arises from the fact that the distance between government and these bodies is to some extent relative. In respect of Next Steps Agencies, we have already seen that there is a continued legal responsibility of the parent department. This is of particular importance in the context of judicial review and damages actions. Framework documents present many advantages as a legal tool, as they are both flexible and objective-orientated. But as Craig has pointed out, the reliance on this basis for the agency-department relationship has meant that legal responsibility has remained with the department, thereby undermining the concept of heightened responsibility which has underpinned the development of the agency format.[76]

[76] Craig, *Administrative Law* 112.

# 8. TOWARDS A MODEL OF INDEPENDENT EXERCISE OF COMMUNITY FUNCTIONS?*

*Edoardo Chiti*

## I. PURPOSE

Surprisingly enough, while a great deal of attention has so far been devoted to the various sectorial developments in European law involving the establishment of supranational bodies provided with independence,[1] legal science has not shown any specific interest in the possibility of building upon the analysis of the single sectors with the view of elaborating an overall scheme of Community independent authorities.[2]

The present work has much more limited aims than filling this lacuna. Its main purpose is to discuss certain elements around which a legal model of a Community independent authority seems to be in the process of developing. Thus, the core of this essay lies in the assessment of a general orientation toward the emergence of such a legal model, in the perspective of drawing some interim conclusions which should be both further developed and made subject to the test of future evolutions of European law.[3]

* Study for a paper delivered at the meeting on 'Independent Authorities in Comparative Administrative Law' University of Turin, 16–17 Apr 2003.

[1] Undoubtedly, the traditional focus of European legal science has been on the case of the European Central Bank: ex multis, R Smits *The European Central Bank* (The Hague Kluwer 1997); C Zilioli and M Selmayr *The Law of the European Central Bank* (Oxford Hart Publishing 2001); and S Cafaro *Unione monetaria e coordinamento delle politiche economiche* (Milano Giuffrè 2001) 187 ff. More recently, the establishment of the European Food Safety Authority has caught lawyers' attention: S Cassese 'La nuova disciplina alimentare europea' in Cassese (ed) *Per un'autorità nazionale della sicurezza alimentare* (Milano Il Sole 24 Ore 2002) 13 ff; and, id 'Proposte per un'Autorità nazionale per la sicurezza alimentare' in (2002) Giornale di diritto amministrativo 799 ff.

[2] It is interesting to note that the goal of a unitary interpretation of the phenomenon is typical of the political science literature: see, in particular, G Majone and M Everson 'Institutional Reform: Independent Agencies, Oversight, Co-ordination and Procedural Control' in O de Schutter, N Lebessis, and J. Paterson (eds) *Governance in the European Union* (Luxembourg Office for Official Publications of the European Communities 2001) 129 ff; and A La Spina and G Majone *Lo Stato regolatore* (Bologna, Il Mulino 2000) 61 ff; such a reflection, however, is somewhat detached from legal analysis, in that neither is it based on the relevant legal notions and concepts, nor does it aim at the reconstruction of a legal model of European independent authority.

[3] Those developments obviously include the constitutional framework envisaged by the

This operation requires an essential clarification.

Arguably, the establishment and functioning of Community authorities provided with independence can acquire full meaning only within the context of a wider regulatory scheme, namely the regulatory scheme laid down by the European legislator in order to define the modalities of exercise of the relevant Community function. As a matter of fact, the setting up of European independent bodies usually takes place within a more general organizational framework, characterized by the allocation of the administrative competences necessary to carry out the Community function among a variety of different offices, both national and supranational. Moreover, various instruments for cooperation and coordination are normally prescribed by European law, in order to ensure the integration of the various competent offices in a coherent administrative system. These phenomena are in line with the general features of European administrative law, whose progressive construction—resulting from the growing political and institutional maturity of the Community order—corresponds not so much or not only to the development of the supranational administrative level, as to an increasingly intense administrative integration between the European and the national systems,[4] according to schemes that are differentiated and at times innovative with respect to the traditions of the Member States.[5]

In this perspective, the assessment of the orientation toward the emergence of a legal model of Community independent authority implies addressing two different but intertwined questions: on the one hand, whether the supranational administration is in the process of being enriched by a new organizational figure provided with a number of distinctive features; on the other hand, whether this possible development in European law coexists with other legal institutes in combination with which it might determine the devising of an overall model of 'independent exercise' of Community functions.

Following this approach, the inquiry will focus on the setting up of supranational independent authorities, but will also extend, where necessary, to those institutional arrangements which are potentially able to found, together with the provision of a Community independent body, a

'draft Treaty establishing a Constitution for Europe' adopted by the European Convention on 13 June and 10 July 2003 and subject to discussion within the context of the current intergovernmental conference. Given its proposal status, the text will not be considered in this chapter.

[4] For a review of the main hypotheses of administrative integration between national and supranational authorities, see E Chiti and C Franchini *L'integrazione amministrativa europea* (Bologna Il Mulino 2003).

[5] An enlightening theoretical framework for the legal analysis and the interpretation of the various developments of European administrative law is provided by Cassese 'Il diritto amministrativo europeo presenta caratteri originali?' in (2003) Rivista trimestrale di diritto pubblico 35.

new scheme of exercise of European functions. These include, as previously mentioned, the 'pluralization' of the function, which is distributed at two or more levels, none of which is able to handle it autonomously, as well as the establishment of a number of tools for the administrative integration of the various competent bodies.

The investigation will be articulated as follows. First, the regulatory frameworks within which the organizational relationship of independence can be registered will be examined (Section II). Next considered will be the objectives and goals connected with the establishment of European authorities identified as independent, for the purpose of reconstructing the functional foundations of independence (Section III). Finally, the possibility to identify a number of essential features of an emerging model of independent authority in the European system will be discussed (Section IV).

## II. INDEPENDENCE

Contrary to what one might think, in the European system the element of independence recurs in a plurality of distinct regulatory frameworks.

These legal schemes cannot be easily typified, as the solutions provided by the Community legislator to the manifold problems raised by the construction and proper functioning of the internal market tend to produce remarkable differentiation, instead of giving rise to general patterns, if not to true and proper legal institutes.

Yet, at the present state of evolution of Community law, the emergence of two main regulatory frameworks based on the organizational formula of independence can be registered within the European legal order.

The *first* regulatory scheme includes the disciplines for monetary policy, data protection and food safety, as well as the regime establishing the European Ombudsman.

In consideration of the functions at stake, each of these areas of law set up a Community office granted with independence (respectively, the European Central Bank, the European Data Protection Supervisor, the European Food Safety Authority, and the European Ombudsman), not only *vis-à-vis* the national and supranational political power, but also with respect to economic and bureaucratic power. This has been realized through the recognition of certain peculiar organizational features, which make it possible for these supranational independent bodies to act as a neutral third party vis-à-vis whatever interests capable of conditioning their final decisions, normally with a view to guaranteeing the proper functioning and balanced development of the sectors they are responsible for. From this standpoint, no particular differences can be registered compared to what is found in most national systems, where the peculiar arrangement of such authorities was made necessary in order to allow them to exercise their proper functions effectively with the maximum detachment, in a position extraneous and indifferent to the interests involved.

This objective is pursued, in some instances, by means of a relatively simple legal design. This is the case, for example, with the European Ombudsman, which constitutes a monocratic body that exercises control functions in a completely independent and impartial fashion.[6]

In other situations a similar effect is instead pursued through a more complex legal scheme characterized, on the one hand, by the establishment of a Community independent authority having a complex internal organization, on the other, by the circumstance that the Community body does not exercise the function autonomously, but rather in combination with its national counterparts.

The most obvious example is represented by the establishment of the European System of Central Banks (ESCB), which is composed of the European Central Bank and the national central banks of all Member States, and is responsible, as a whole, for maintaining price stability.[7] As neither the European Central Bank, nor the national central banks in the Eurosystem, nor any member of their decision-making bodies are allowed to seek or take instructions from any other national or supranational body, the ESCB is a true and proper transnational network of independent authorities, governed, according to the Treaty provisions, by the two collegiate bodies of the European Central Bank, that is the Governing Council and the Executive Board. The Governing Council, moreover, comprising all the members of the Executive Board and the governors of the national central banks of the Member States, is envisaged as an office intended to create and manage a plurality of relationships involving the national independent administrations as well as, at least indirectly, the governments of the Member States and the European Parliament.[8]

Among the more recent examples, the new European food safety regime

[6] For an administrative analysis of the European Ombudsman, see MP Chiti 'Il Mediatore europeo e la buona amministrazione comunitaria' in (2000) Rivista italiana di diritto pubblico comunitario 303 ff; for a more general approach, P Bonnor 'The European Ombudsman: A Novel Source of Soft Law in the European Union' in (2000) European Law Review 39 ff; J Söderman 'The Role and the Impact of the European Ombudsman in Access to Documentation and the Transparency of Decision-making' in V Deckmyn and I Thomson (eds) *Openness and Transparency in the European Union, Maastricht, European Institute of Public Administration* (1998) 79 ff.

[7] The ESCB has to be distinguished from the Eurosystem, which constitutes a sub-system of the ESCB, composed of the European Central Bank and the national central banks of the twelve countries in the euro area.

[8] For a recent analysis of such regulatory framework, see M Pacini 'La "vigilanza prudenziale" tra banche centrali nazionali e banca centrale europea' in (2003) Banca Impresa Società, forthcoming; see also A Malatesta *La Banca centrale europea* (Milano Giuffrè 2003).

seems to be of particular interest.[9] In addition to establishing principles and general requirements for the sector, the relevant Regulation sets up a European Food Safety Authority which, however, is not responsible for all types of public intervention provided for by Community legislator, but only for the evaluation of risk, while the Commission is charged with the management thereof and the national supervisory authorities are responsible for the observance of the obligations arising from the Community discipline for the safeguarding of food security. The relations among the various offices that compose this complex apparatus differ in nature. *Vis-à-vis* the Commission, the European Food Safety Authority acts as an 'independent scientific reference point', albeit functionally linked to the central Community administration. In relations involving the European Food Safety Authority and the official systems of national control, what is instead provided for is functional and structural integration in a network coordinated by the Authority itself. Moreover, the integration of the supranational and national systems is also realized within the Authority, where an 'Advisory Forum' is set up composed of representatives of the competent bodies which carry out in the Member States functions analogous to those of the Authority.

In this way the establishment of an independent Community authority is connected with the provision for a complex apparatus that integrates national authorities and Community bodies on a permanent basis, according to a design for a system that is 'doubly composite, national and Community, and, at the Community level, direct and indirect (involving the Commission and a related but independent body)'.[10]

In these cases, moreover, Community discipline affects not only the function of the national administrations, but their organization as well, favouring or requiring the creation of independent authorities by the Member States.[11]

Considering the increasing resort on the part of the Community legislator to the regulatory design described—essentially characterized by the establishment of an independent Community administration and by the integration, in a complex administrative system, of the corresponding national authorities[12]—we should ask ourselves whether it cannot be stated

[9] European Parliament and Council Regulation 178/02; cf Cassese 'La nuova disciplina alimentare europea' op cit; and id 'Proposte per un'Autorità nazionale per la sicurezza alimentare' op cit.

[10] As observed by Cassese 'La nuova disciplina alimentare europea' op cit.

[11] Which, owing to the Community nature of their functional and organizational discipline, evolve from independent national authorities into independent federal authorities, as observed by F Merusi 'Le autorità indipendenti tra riformismo nazionale e autarchia comunitaria' in FA Grassini (ed) *L'indipendenza delle autorità* (Bologna Il Mulino 2000) 19 ff.

[12] And in consideration of the 'imitative effects of the organizational federalism of the ECB', as notes F Merusi op cit 28.

that the development of positive Community law gives rise to a true and proper model, though still in the process of being formed, of joint exercise of Community functions.

And yet, at the present state of evolution of European law and of corresponding theoretical reflection, a like hypothesis of reconstruction turns out to be premature. While it is without a doubt possible to identify a clear legislative orientation, the limited number of actual cases to date where the Community legislator has resorted to the design examined, coupled with the existing differences between the various legal regimes, does not permit the discerning of a true and proper legal institute capable of functioning as a synthesis of a discipline. More simply, what can be discerned is a new direction in Community law whose effective consistency will be subject to full evaluation only in the coming years.

A *second* legislative trend characterized by the independence of the Community public powers should be added to the legal scheme reconstructed above.

This involves an approach which has emerged only recently in positive European law: the trend to the structural and functional integration of independent national authorities according to the design defined, with reference to the new directive providing the framework in the area of telecommunications, as the 'European concert of regulators'.[13]

More than a stable design of relations between domestic administrations and Community authorities, what is at stake is a mechanism of administrative integration still in the process of being formed, but susceptible to interesting developments.

Consider, for example, the second generation of Community directives in the sector of telecommunications and the European regime of privacy protection previous to the partial reform of 2001.[14] In both cases the Community legislator sought to lay down a design for the structural and functional integration of the competent national regulatory authorities. First and foremost, the design provides for some strictures to be placed on

[13] The definition is by Cassese 'Il concerto regolamentare europeo delle telecomunicazioni' in (2002) Giornale di diritto amministrativo 689 ff.

[14] As is very well known, the first generation of Community directives in the matter of telecommunications were issued between 1990 and 1997 and were aimed at deregulating the market and establishing a common system of regulation; the second generation dates to March 2002 and was aimed at establishing a convergence of the sectors including telecommunications, the mass media and information technologies within a unitary regulatory framework, as well as the convergence of the organizational arrangements. As for the discipline of privacy, it was originally based on Directive 95/46, as modified by the subsequent legislation; however, the Treaty of Amsterdam included a new article which allows the Council to establish, according to procedure pursuant to Art 251, an independent control body charged with overseeing the enforcement of Community standards for specific sectors on Community institutions and bodies; it was in fulfilment thereof that the Council and the European Parliament adopted Regulation 45/2001, establishing the European Data Protection Supervisor.

the autonomy of the States with respect to the choice of organizational arrangement of the regulatory authority. Thus, for example, Directive 95/46 on the protection of personal data requires that 'full independence' be granted to the national authorities which the various Member States are obliged to entrust with the activity of the overseeing of the enforcement of the national provisions for the implementation of the directive; while the recent 'framework directive' in the matter of telecommunications provides that the tasks assigned to the national authorities by the European norms shall be entrusted to a competent body, legally distinct, and functionally independent of the operators, and that it shall exercise its powers impartially and in a transparent manner. Furthermore, the autonomy of the Member States is also subject to stringent limitations as regards the functioning of the national regulator. In particular, it was the Community that defined the goals that the national regulator shall pursue (for example, the promotion of competition and the development of the domestic market), the basic principles of the administrative proceedings where the national regulator is called into play (eg participation and cross-examination according to the notice and comment model) and the lines of conduct of its activity. In addition, the national regulators are themselves integrated in a unitary administration by means of a lateral opening of the national administrations, as well as, in certain specific cases, by the unitary configuration of the 'network' of the various regulators *vis-à-vis* third parties: a legal situation that is particularly clear in the 'framework directive' in the matter of telecommunications, but already anticipated by Directive 95/46, which imposes a number of different obligations on the relevant national authorities, thus giving rise to relations of mutual assistance. Finally, the architecture elaborated by the Community regimes provides for the establishment of a composite organization—in part national and in part Community, but defined in both cases as 'European group'—to which independent status is sometimes expressly recognized (*vis-à-vis* the national governments and the central Community administration)[15] and which holds a plurality of functions (ranging from providing assistance to the Commission and to the Member States, to the promotion of codes of conduct and control over the enforcement of Community law).[16] On the other hand, the establishment of

[15] Eg, such is the case with Directive 95/46, Art 29/1; while the Commission decision 2002/627, which establishes the 'European Regulators Group for electronic communications networks and services', limits itself to providing that the group 'shall provide an interface between the national regulatory authorities and the Commission in such a way as to contribute to the development of the internal market', also facilitating 'cooperation between national regulatory authorities and the Commission in a transparent manner so as to ensure the consistent application in all Member States of the regulatory framework for electronic communications networks and services' (cf the sixth whereas).

[16] Eg, the so-called Group 29 is assigned five main tasks. First of all, it examines any question pertaining to the enforcement of the national norms in fulfilment of Directive 95/46,

a like collegiate body composed of representatives of the national regulators and the Commission is compensated by the attribution to the central Community administration of a position of functional pre-eminence, particularly evident in the telecommunications sector.

In short, the legal distinguishing features of the scheme under examination turn out to be four in number. First of all, the achievement of the purposes identified by the Community provisions is assigned to a plurality of structurally distinct administrations. To avoid the risks of fragmentation connected with such an organizational pluralism, Community law then goes on to the regulate the organization and functioning of the national regulator, which, by virtue of such conditioning, is transformed from being a national authority into an autarchic institution of the European federation.[17] Furthermore, a collegiate body is set up at the Community level, composed of representatives of the national bodies and a representative of the Community, and independent of the national governments and of the central Community administration. Finally, the various competent national administrations, the collegiate body and the central Community administration are integrated in a unitary organization in terms of both function and structure.

It is interesting to note how many of these elements are not truly original. Thus, the choice to assign the carrying out of the Community function to a plurality of structurally distinct national and supranational administrations constitutes a typical characteristic of the regulatory scheme based on the establishment of a European agency.[18] Not even the fact of having conditioned through the Community the discipline of the organization and of the functioning of the national regulator represents an original element, inasmuch as the same effect can be determined also within the context of the legal regimes setting up a European agency. Analogous considerations can be made with reference to the integration of the various administrations in an organization that is unitary in terms of structure and function. The

informing the Commission of any eventual divergences that might jeopardize the equal protection of individuals in the matter of the handling of personal data within the Community. Secondly, it expresses opinions addressed to the Commission on the degree of safeguarding within the Community and in other countries, as well as on any planned change in Community law in the matter of privacy. Thirdly, it gives an opinion on the codes of conduct elaborated at the Community level. Fourthly, on its own initiative it makes recommendations on whatever questions regarding the safeguarding of individuals in the handling of personal data within the Community. Finally, it prepares an annual report on the state of individual safeguards in the handling of personal data within the Community and in other countries, which it has published and delivered to the Commission, the European Parliament, and Council.

[17] F Merusi 'Le autorità indipendenti tra riformismo nazionale e autarchia comunitaria' op cit; id 'Democrazia e autorità indipendenti' Bologna (2000) 75 ff.

[18] Chiti *Le agenzie europee. Unità e decentramento nelle amministrazioni comunitarie* (Padova Cedam 2002).

matter of the establishment at the Community level of a mixed and independent body is less clear-cut. On the one hand, in terms of structure a number of precedents can be found in the institutional practice of comitology and in the internal organization of the independent Community authorities, based on numerous mixed organs. On the other hand, however, it differs from such entities both as regards the element of independence (which is excluded in the case of comitology) as well as for the greater simplicity of its organizational design (which is incomparable to the complex internal architecture of the independent authorities).

To this it must be added that the 'European concert of regulators' is designed as a variant of the above mentioned trend to establish independent Community authorities with an internal organization made up of mixed offices composed of the representatives of national bodies and the representatives of Community institutions, and responsible for the implementation of the relevant European discipline together with the competent national authorities. The functional and structural similarity of the two regulatory structures is exemplified by the evolution of the European privacy regime, originally based on the so-called 'Group 29', and later flanked by an independent Community authority complementary in function to it.

Nonetheless, the overall combination of the elements upon which the regulatory structure of the 'European concert of regulators' is based is peculiar in so far as the objective of the putting into place of an organizational complex, in part common (being based on the involvement of the national regulatory authorities) and in part Community (being disciplined at the European level and providing for the establishment of a Community office), is pursued through a scheme distinct from those previously reconstructed. Moreover, the legal scheme maintains its own functional specificity, as an alternative to the establishment of independent Community authorities integrated with the national authorities and as a relatively flexible instrument for interaction, coordinated at the Community level, among the national authorities.

Such an interpretation is confirmed by the latest developments in competition law, where Council Regulation 1/2003 has substituted the traditional centralized arrangement for applying the exception from the prohibition on agreements with a system of exceptions directly applicable by competition authorities and courts in the Member States: a regulatory design aiming at establishing a network of public authorities cooperatively responsible for the implementation of the Community competition rules.[19]

[19] On the process which has led to the new Community regime, A Bonomo *Administrative Enforcement of Community Competition Law* (London Esperia Publications 2002); see also CD Ehlermann 'Il dibattito sulla sussidiarietà nel diritto della concorrenza; B Hawk and

From the foregoing observations, it follows that in the European system independence is configured as an organizational relation endowed with a plurality of meanings and implemented in a variety of schemes.

As for its meanings, the formula is designed not just as neutrality from Community political power, understood as a capacity to block the decisions of the political majority present in that system, but also as independence as regards the governments of the Member States and with respect to private power. Independence is therefore meant in its widest scope and designed to apply in a multi-level legal order.[20] As has been observed, however, such an arrangement does not imply an exclusive competence of the European independent authority in the carrying out of a certain function; rather the involvement is envisaged of a number of other national and supranational bodies, including the Commission, which is usually put in a position of functional pre-eminence.

As for the regulatory frameworks by means of which the element of independence is applied in the European administrative system, two have been identified. The first is characterized essentially by the setting up of transnational 'networks' of independent authorities coordinated by a Community authority endowed with independence. The second, which can be defined as the 'European concert of regulators', hinges on the institution at the Community level of an independent board and on the collaboration of a variety of independent national authorities. In both cases, Community administrative law operates not only with reference to the supranational authorities, but bears both directly and indirectly on administrative law in the national legal systems.

The reconstruction of the two regulatory frameworks through which independence is implemented raises the uneasy problem of differentiating such schemes from certain contiguous figures.

L Laudati 'Federalismo antitrust negl Stati Uniti e decentramento nell'applicazione del diritto della concorrenza nell'Unione Europea: un esame comparativo', V Korah 'Sussidiarietà e decentramento nell'applicazione del diritto della concorrenza europeo', M Siragusa 'Il ruolo delle autorità nazionali antitrust nel promuovere un'applicazione convergente delle norme sulla concorrenza in Europa: opportunità di un'applicazione decentrata della normativa dell'UE sulla concorrenza', A Tizzano 'L'applicazione decentrata degli articoli 85 e 86 del Trattato CE in Italia', K Van Miert 'Sviluppi e prospettive dell'applicazione decentrata del diritto della concorrenza europeo' in *Autorità garante della concorrenza e del mercato, La tutela della concorrenza: regole, istituzioni e rapporti internazionali, edizione speciale di 'Temi e problemi* (1996) respectively at 17 ff, 25 ff, 51 ff, 61 ff, 95 ff, and 113 ff. Analogous developments, though usually implying a lower level of institutionalization, can be registered in the field of public procurements (COM (98) 143), insurance (see Iais, Compiled Version of All IAIS Principles, Standards and Guidance Papers Approved by the Association, October 2002) and energy (where a Florence Energy Forum has been set up; see A Héritier 'New Modes of Governance in Europe: Increasing political efficiency and policy effectiveness?' in T Boerzel and RA Cichowski (eds) *State of the European Union* vol VI (Oxford OUP 2003) ch 5.

[20] On the (obvious) boundaries of independence see the recent judgments of the Court of Justice, 10 July 2003, case C-11/00, *Commission v European Central Bank*, and case C-15/00, *Commission v European Investment Bank*, not yet reported.

This is especially true as regards the 'decentralized integration' model,[21] which presents various affinities with those previously illustrated, but which differs from them essentially in terms of independence.

More precisely, the term 'decentralized integration' is used to refer to a new legal model of the joint exercise of supranational functions. Its novelty is, of course, relative, as it borrows from previous Community and national legal institutions and experiences.

The regulatory structure that emerges is first of all characterized by the shared allocation of powers to the Community and to the Member States' administrations. This is the result of the conferral of administrative competencies concerning the same Community function to a plurality of offices, so that the Community function is distributed at two or more levels, none of which is able to handle it autonomously.

Secondly, as a consequence of the various tools for coordination and cooperation prescribed by Community law, the competent offices must be seen, from a legal standpoint, as parts of a broader administration by sector. This broader administration can be identified both with the whole set of activities aimed at reaching the objectives singled out by Community law, as well as with the public authorities responsible for the exercise of the said function.

Thirdly, this regulatory structure presupposes the establishment of a Community body granted specific powers under Community law and informed by the organizational formula of representativeness. The purpose of creating the body is at once to realize a decentralization of the matter and an integration of distinct authorities, according to the modalities and within the limits provided by Community law.

Fourthly and finally, it should be noted that such a legal framework is not used in order to ensure the achievement of any Community goal. It is rather aimed at carrying out a specific regulatory administrative function, with a view to satisfying economic and social purposes, in relation to which the public authorities are conferred conditional regulatory tasks and teleologically prescribed regulatory tasks.

From the standpoint of this work, such a structure is peculiar in two respects.

First, this regulatory structure is characterized by its peculiar combination of decentralization and integration. As a matter of fact, the joint exercise of the Community function in this case requires a structure which is at the same time decentralized—through the establishment of a supranational body which excludes or restrains the administrative powers of the Commission—and integrated—through the provision by Community law of organizational and procedural tools for cooperation among the plurality of competent public bodies.

[21] E Chiti and C Franchini *L'integrazione amministrativa europea* at 72 ff.

Secondly, a Community body is set up that lacks independence from political power (whether Community or national), just as from private power.

As has been observed, the model of decentralized integration in fact presupposes the establishment of a Community office endowed with legal status and with legal tasks conferred upon it by the supranational legislation. Such an office is auxiliary to the establishing body, being subject to the central Community administration. As a matter of fact, accurate legal analysis reveals that some form of power of the Commission over the body is established in all the regulations by sector, albeit in varying degrees. This circumstance rules out the possibility of singling out any one specific form of expression of the power relationship, as it takes different forms in each case.

The identification of such legal traits characterizing the Community body makes clear the inaccuracy of the statement that European agencies fall under the category of independent authorities. This is argued quite frequently in theories advanced by political scientists who regard the Community as a 'regulatory State'.[22]

This is crystal clear in cases where the powers of the central Community administration are exceptionally great. An example is found in the agency for pharmaceutical products, whose official duties are limited to advising the Commission. The latter is responsible for the adoption of a provision concluding the various administrative procedures pursuant to Community legislation by sector. However, even when the powers of the Commission are not so great, the auxiliary body never enjoys independent legal status *vis-à-vis* the central Community administration in order to safeguard it against political or bureaucratic interference, as would be the case with fully independent entities.

Besides, the decision to establish a body auxiliary to the Commission is not so much to be attributed to a need to guarantee such bodies a certain degree of independence from political, bureaucratic and economic power, as to a desire to discipline the matter in decentralized fashion.

The aim is not really to establish certain organizations capable of acting

[22] Eg, cf R Dehousse, FG Snyder, C Joerges, and G Majone *Europe After 1992. New Regulatory Strategies*, European University Institute Working Papers, Law, 92/31. A more problematical treatment is found in M Everson 'Independent Agencies: Hierarchy Beaters' in (1985) European Law Journal 180 ff. In a normative perspective, but based on the consideration of positive law, a model for the European independent agencies is organically presented in G Majone and M Everson 'Institutional Reform: Independent Agencies, Oversight, co-ordination and Procedural Control' op cit, where existing European agencies are considered as offices deriving from the US notion of agency: 'an agency is a part of government that is generally independent in the exercise of its functions and that by law has authority to take a final and binding action affecting the rights and obligations of individuals, particularly by the characteristic procedure of rule-making and adjudication.'

independently of outside interests able to influence their final decisions, as independent authorities are typically meant to do. Rather, the attribution of legal personality to an office is intended to ensure the performance of an activity which, for political or technical reasons, cannot be directly carried out by the central administration, even though decentralisation could be accomplished in different ways according to the various hypotheses (eg by means of a partial decentralisation or a full devolution of decision-making powers to peripheral or non-central Community offices).

In conclusion, the model of decentralized integration constitutes a scheme comparable to those reconstructed above insofar as it pertains to the pluralization of the function and to the integration of a plurality of authorities (supranational, national, and mixed), but is radically differentiated from them under the profile of the lack of independence of the European agency that is established.

## III. REGULATION AND COMPETITION

Having reconstructed the regulatory frameworks wherein the element of independence recurs, we shall now proceed to a briefer examination of their functional foundations.

These are to be recognized in the activities of competition and of regulation (both economic and social).

As a matter of fact, some of the legal regimes mentioned in the previous section, such as the European system of central banks and the European Central Bank, aim at assuring that appropriate measures are taken to place competitors on an equal footing, in order to make possible the dialectical encounter that is competition among competing parties, meant as the 'option concerning how to manage the economy, horizontally rather than vertically, through the free play of competitors and not through rational heteronymous decisions; through the exercise of a right, the right of economic freedom, and not through the exercise of a public power'.[23]

In other instances, the institutional arrangements based on independence respond to the exigency to carry out a regulatory function.

For the purpose of the present study, the term 'regulation' is used in reference to 'those forms of interference that are part of the market, in the sense that they contribute to conform it, establishing equilibria that activate

[23] Cf F Merusi *Democrazia e autorità indipendenti* (Bologna Il Mulino 2000) 26, whose notion, elaborated with reference to the Italian system, but taking into account the Community legal framework, can prove most useful for the purposes of the present work. See also F Merusi and M Passaro *Autorità indipendenti, in 'Enciclopedia del diritto'* (Milano Giuffrè VI update, ad vocem); and F Merusi and M Passaro *Le autorità indipendenti. Un potere senza partito* (Bologna Il Mulino 2003).

interests, which then take advantage of regulation as an opportunity to exploit'.[24] Therefore, in contrast to the discipline of competition, which is inspired by the need to correct the undesired results of the market (such as, for example, agreements detrimental to competition or the abuse of dominant position), regulation is based on the premise that the market does not exist and that the principles that aim at the same ends or that imitate it must be affirmed (economic regulation), or else that it is necessary to guarantee results that the market, even if it does exist and function, does not succeed in guaranteeing (social regulation).[25]

In this perspective, the difference is evident between a like notion of regulation and that typical of North American studies. In the latter, in fact, the expression is used with the meaning of 'sustained and focused control

[24] Cassese 'Regolazione e concorrenza' in G Tesauro and M D'Alberti (eds) *Regolazione e concorrenza* (Bologna Il Mulino 2000) 11 ff; the excerpt is from p 12. Also see B Eberlein *Regulating Public Utilities in Europe: Mapping the Problem*, European University Institute Working Papers, RSC, 98/42; and, id 'L'Etat régulateur en Europe' in (1999) Revue française de science politique n 2, 205 and ff. For an early systematic treatment of the problems related to administrative disciplines connected with the functioning of the market, cf M Libertini 'La regolazione amministrativa del mercato' in F Galgano (ed) *L'azienda e il mercato, in Trattato di diritto commerciale e di diritto pubblico dell'economia*, III (Padova Cedam 1979) 469 and ff. Also see S Cassese and E Gerelli (ed) *Deregulation. La deregolamentazione amministrativa e legislativa* (Milano Franco Angeli 1985); as well as G Corso 'Lo stato come dispensatore di beni. Criteri di distribuzione, tecniche giuridiche ed effetti' in (1990) Sociologia del diritto 109 and ff.

[25] The distinction between regulation and competition, not commonly made in American literature, is outlined by Cassese, 'Regolazione e concorrenza' op cit 12–13; for an analogous differentiation in the field of economics, cf L Prosperetti 'I rapporti tra regolazione e tutela della concorrenza' in (2002) Mercato concorrenza regole 277 and ff; according to Prosperetti, 'public policy must therefore unfailingly safeguard competition, preserving it and limiting the distortions it may suffer from, and this is the task of the antitrust authorities; when competition is impossible, or when there are serious reasons for believing that it might lead to results that do not coincide with social welfare, it becomes necessary to somehow stimulate the desired effects: this is the task of ex ante regulation' (p 177). Also see G Marzi *L Prosperetti* and E Putzu *La regolazione dei servizi infrastrutturali* (Bologna Il Mulino 2001) esp ch II; as well as A Pera 'Appunti sulla riforma delle autorità: regolazione e concorrenza' in (2002) Mercato concorrenza regole 329 and ff, esp p 332 and ff. For that matter, the relation between the discipline of regulation and the discipline of competition is highly problematic and complex, as testified by the variety of the normative solutions devised in Italian and in other systems, and as recognized in both legal and economic theory. A concise treatment of the various issues pertaining to the relationship between the two disciplines, and to the relationship between the authorities that preside over regulation and the authorities that preside over competition is offered by Cassese 'Regolazione e concorrenza' op cit. In addition, cf the observations of M De Vita 'Regolamentazioni pubbliche: principi comunitari e disciplina italiana antitrust' in (1997) Il diritto dell'Unione europea 707 and ff; as well as L Di Via 'Appunti sulle 'frontiere mobili' del diritto della concorrenza', and G Fonderico 'Concorrenza e fini sociali nei servizi di pubblica utilità', both in *Liberalizzazione e concorrenza*, ed G Vesperini and G Napolitano 'Quaderni dell'Istituto Giuridico della Facoltà di Economia dell'Università degli Studi della Tuscia, Viterbo' (1999) 31 and ff and 79 and ff, respectively; M Monti 'Concorrenza e regolazione nell'Unione europea' *Regolazione e concorrenza*, ed G Tesauro and M D'Alberti op cit 75 and ff; and M D'Alberti 'Riforma della regolazione e sviluppo dei mercati in Italia' ibid 171 and ff.

exercised by a public agency over activities that are socially valued'.[26] So used, however, the notion embraces every sort of public interference in the economy, with the result that it ends up being of scarce explicatory value.[27]

If the functional foundation of independence is that defined by the legal notions of competition and of regulation, it must be noted that the relationship that is formed between these two activities varies according to the single sectors of intervention by the Community.[28]

In certain areas falling within the scope of the internal market, in particular public utilities, European law expressly establishes the principle of the prevalence of the discipline of competition, providing that this also shall be applied to public undertakings and to companies to which Member States grant special or exclusive rights, with the exception of the specific tasks assigned to undertakings entrusted with the operation of services of general

[26] In particular, cf P Selznick 'Focusing Organizational Research on Regulation' in RG Noll (ed) *Regulatory Policy and the Social Science* (Berkeley and Los Angeles University of California Press 1985) 363 and ff, as well as an earlier work by RG Noll *What is Regulation?* Social Science Working Paper no 324 (Pasadena California Institute of Technology 1980). The principal general works that use this broad notion of regulation include JQ Wilson (ed) *The Politics of Regulation* (New York Basic Books 1980); S Breyer *Regulation and Its Reform* (Cambridge MA Harvard University Press 1982); TK McCraw *Prophets of Regulation* (Cambridge MA Belknap Press 1984); KJ Meier *Regulation. Politics, Bureaucracy and Economics* (New York St Martin's Press 1985); and CR Sunstein *After the Rights Revolution. Reconceiving the Regulatory State* (Cambridge MA Harvard University Press 1990). Also see A Ogus *Regulation. Legal Form and Economic Theory* (Oxford Clarendon Press 1994); J Black 'Talking about Regulation' in (1998) Public Law 77 and ff; B Jessop 'The Regulation Approach, Governance and Post-Fordism: Alternative Perspectives on Economic and Political Change?' in (1995) Economy and Society 307 and ff; CR Sunstein 'Congress, Constitutional Moments, and the Cost–Benefit State' in (1996) Stanford Law Review 247 and ff; A Scalia 'Le Independent Regulatory Agencies nell'ordinamento statunitense' in *Rassegna giuridica dell'energia elettrica* (1996) 313 and ff. With reference to the English system, cf T Prosser 'Regulation, Markets, and Legitimacy' in J Jowell and D Oliver (eds) *The Changing Constitution* (3rd edn Oxford Clarendon Press 1994) 237 and ff; G Goldoni 'Il regolatore nel paese della concorrenza' in (1995) Energia n 2, 14 and following; M Thatcher 'Regulation, Institutions and Change: Independent Regulatory Agencies in the British Privatised Utilities' in (1998) West European Politics 120 and ff; R Baldwin, C Scott, and C Hood *A Reader on Regulation* (Oxford OUP 1998); and finally, concerning the French experience, cf AM Frison-Roche *Le droit de la régulation* (Dalloz 2001) 610 and ff. For a comparative approach, cf JG Francis *The Politics of Regulation. A Comparative Perspective* (Oxford Blackwell 1993). Certain Italian studies also subscribe to this broad notion of regulation (see N Longobardi *Il sistema politico-amministrativo e la riforma mancata* (Torino Giappichelli 1999) 86 and ff), as is the case with a number of investigations into the Community system (among them G Majone *La Communauté européenne: un Etat régulateur* (Paris Montchrestien 1996); and R Dehousse, FG Snyder, C Joerges, and G Majone 'Europe After 1992. New Regulatory Strategies' op cit). Finally, for a recent discussion of the existing literature, cf M Moran (review article) 'Understanding the Regulatory State' in (2002) British Journal of Political Science 391 and ff.

[27] Cassese 'Regolazione e concorrenza', op cit 11.

[28] For a general discussion expressly referred to the Community experience, M Monti, 'Mercato Unico Europeo, regolamentazione e concorrenza', C Babusiaux 'Liberalizzazione, regole e tutela della concorrenza', A Fornalczyk 'Quanta concorrenza, quanta regolamentazione?' in *Autorità garante della concorrenza e del mercato, La tutela della concorrenza: regole, istituzioni e rapporti internazionali*, cit, respectively at 199 ff, 207 ff, and 237 ff.

economic interest.[29] In this context, regulation constitutes an imperfect but necessary instrument, at first for leading the passage from monopoly to competition, then for disciplining universal service and the other social obligations of public service. This modality of the relationship between competition and regulation is the one traditionally most studied in legal theory, which, in the reflection on regulation, has often given preference to the analysis of the public utilities sector.

However, it would be erroneous to consider this model of relations as the only one possible. As a matter of fact, in a number of sectors contiguous but external to the internal market, such as consumer protection and public health, a different legal arrangement can be registered, in which the relationship between regulation and competition is realised in a quite different manner.

Such a framework is characterized under two profiles.

First, it is based on a notion of regulation that is fundamentally social. It might be objected that the sectors previously illustrated (that is to say the public utilities sectors) also are characterised by the co-presence of economic regulation and social regulation. Nevertheless, it cannot be ignored that in the public utilities sector the public authorities are called upon to assure the reaching of objectives of a distributive nature, albeit by means of market mechanisms. In this second possible model, instead, the social ends of regulation find their conceptual foundation not so much in the principle of substantive equality, as in the right to certain profiles related to the quality of life that the functioning of the market might not succeed in guaranteeing.

Secondly, an integration of (social) regulation within competition is realized, in the perspective of a redefinition of the notion of competition in view of the principle of harmonious, balanced, and sustainable development. Such integration, moreover, is not temporary, but permanent, so that regulation does not have an interim nature, there being no provision stating that regulation must give way to competition once certain specific objectives have been achieved; on the contrary, it must be a stable component of competition itself.

[29] On Art 86 (ex Art. 90) of the EC Treaty see G Cartei *Il servizio universale* (Milano Giuffrè 2002) 125 ff; on the interpretation of Art 16 of the EC Treaty, J Pielow 'Il 'service public' e l'art 16 del Trattato Ce da un punto di vista tedesco' in E Ferrari (ed) *I servizi a rete in Europa—Concorrenza tra gli operatori e garanzia dei cittadini* (Milano Giuffrè 2000) 53 ff; L Radicati di Brozolo 'La nuova disposizione sui servizi di interesse economico generale' in (1998) *Diritto dell'Unione europea* 273 ss; M Clarich 'Servizi pubblici e diritto europeo della concorrenza: l'esperienza italiana e tedesca a confronto' in *Rivista trimestrale di diritto pubblico* (2003) 91 ss; on Art 36 of the Charter of Fundamental Rights, MP Chiti 'I caratteri della Costituzione economica europea alla luce della Carta dei diritti fondamentali' in C Franchini and L Paganetto (eds) *Stato ed economia all'inizio del XXI secolo* (Bologna Il Mulino 2002) 49 ss.

This is what occurs, for example, in the case of the Community regulation establishing the European Food Safety Authority. As a matter of fact, over the years the role of the discipline of public health has progressively changed in the socio-economic constitution of the Community: from the original provision as an exception to the free circulation of goods to the current provisions of the Community Treaty, which establish that, in the definition and implementation of all Community policies and activities, a high level of protection of human health shall be guaranteed.[30] In this sector, then, the public discipline has assumed the characteristic features of the forms of intervention in the economy aimed at the conformation of the market, here in the specific sense of the achievement of results that the free functioning of the market might not be able to guarantee. As for that, the deepening and redefinition of the internal market is evident in the same legal standards specifically pertaining to food products, which do not aim at a limitation of the exercise of economic freedoms provided under Community law, but are oriented toward the protection of individuals from the risks inherent in industrial activities.

Interestingly enough, the scheme illustrated is not proper just to the legal frameworks characterized by the independence of the public powers. It is also recognizable in the standardization system[31] and in the above-mentioned 'decentralized integration' model.

The observations made thus far make it possible to draw four conclusions about regulation and competition in the European legal order.

In the first place, competition as such cannot be considered the unifying factor of the models centred upon the organizational formula of independence. Competition coexists with regulation, both economic and social, which is endowed with its own conceptual and functional autonomy.

In the second place, the terms of the relation that exists between competition and regulation are not limited to just one legal scheme. On the contrary, it is possible to identify at least two distinct types of relationships based, respectively, on the prevalence of competition and on the integration of social regulation within competition. Yet, other schemes could be brought into being by the European legislator on the basis of the cues offered by the Treaty.

30 Art 152/1 (former Art 129) of the Community Treaty; the distinction is to be observed between this and the homologous provision in the matter of the safeguarding of consumers, according to which the exigencies pertaining to consumer protection are to be merely 'taken into consideration' (Art 153, former Art 129A). Instead, the fact that the provision regarding environmental matters—unlike the provision regarding public health—is placed among the 'principles' of the Treaty rather than among the provisions by sector, does not appear relevant from the legal standpoint.

31 For a concise account of which see E Chiti 'La normalizzazione' in Cassese (ed) *Trattato di diritto amministrativo, Diritto amministrativo speciale* (Milano Giuffrè 2003) vol IV, 4003 and ff.

In the third place, as a consequence of what has just been pointed out, a pluralistic, problematic approach becomes necessary for an analysis of the relation between regulation and competition, in contrast to the more common approaches of legal and economic theory.

Finally, the 'competition/regulation' pairing is not exclusively proper to the figures characterised by the element of independence. The most striking example is the circumstance that the implementation of the Community competition provisions has been traditionally attributed to the Commission, rather than to an independent authority, as happens in the great majority of the Member States. A second example relates to the institution of European agencies for the purpose, along with national authorities, of performing the Community function of regulation: in several instances these agencies in fact give rise to a scheme for the integration of social regulation within competition. This prevents associating the element of independence with regulation and competition on an exclusive basis. If it is true that the models characterized by independence find their functional foundation in the 'competition/regulation' pairing, it does not follow that this activity of competition and regulation is always performed by independent Community figures.

To these observations one should add that such an articulation of the objectives and sectors of the function is not corresponded by a typology of the tasks assigned to the competent administrations. As a matter of fact, the general patterns which have been illustrated are implemented through several different methods and the tasks granted to the European independent authorities range from the adoption of a technical opinion on certain scientific issues to true and proper powers of control requiring more complex procedural solutions. Analogously, it is not possible to identify a recurrent scheme of allocation of powers among the various competent administrations: that is the central Community administration, the European independent body and the national relevant authorities. What does not change in the various sectors is the nature of the public interest at stake, which can be interpreted as a Community public interest, being independent of possible peculiar situations that could arise in national law and being provided for by Community regulations and achieved through the action of a plurality of different administrations coordinated by a supranational body.

## IV. TOWARDS A MODEL OF THE INDEPENDENT EXERCISE OF COMMUNITY FUNCTIONS?

At the conclusion of our analysis, it is necessary to return to the question forming the object of the investigation: the possibility of reconstructing a model of 'independent exercise' of European functions.

On the basis of the data gathered, it must first be observed that the element of independence is implemented through two distinct legal schemes. The first is essentially based on the institution of transnational networks of independent authorities, coordinated by a Community body endowed with independence. The second, defined as the 'European concert of regulators', is characterized by the institution at the Community level of an independent board and by the collaboration among a variety of independent national authorities. In both cases independence is designed as neutrality *vis-à-vis* Community political power, but also as independence as regards the governments of the Member States and as a third-party position *vis-à-vis* private power. Furthermore, the reconstructed models do not limit themselves to setting up a Community organizational figure (simple or complex) endowed with independence, but rather give rise to a true and proper transnational network of public powers variously articulated in the two cases.

This two-tiered regulatory structure based on independence tends to answer to the same functional foundation, identified by the regulation/competition pairing. However, as is true of the organizational element, the functional element does not present itself in a unitary manner. In fact, the relation that exists between competition and regulation is configured in two distinct manners according to the sectors of Community action: one is based on the prevalence of competition, while the other is based on the integration of social regulation within competition.

These observations are not such as to make it possible to register the emergence of a true and proper model of Community independent authority based on peculiar, significant features. They do, however, make it possible to identify a general orientation towards the elaboration in Community law of a model of independent exercise of Community functions, internally articulated in the ways described above.

As an emergent regulatory framework of exercise of a Community function, the scheme reconstructed is based not only on the elements of independence and of the performance of an activity of competition and of regulation. It also presupposes other elements, foremost among them being the pluralization of the function and the distribution of the tasks necessary for the performance of the activity among a variety of supranational, national and mixed offices. Independence, however, is the main differentiating feature, which influences the other aspects of the model and distinguishes it from contiguous models of exercise of a Community function, such as the decentralized integration model.

Moreover, the outlined regulatory scheme constitutes not just a new level of action and of administrative organization, but also a mechanism able to bear on the administrative law of the Member States. On the one hand, in various circumstances it imposes the institution of national independent authorities on the Member States. On the other hand, it determines an evolution of the national independent authorities already existing into federal independent authorities. However, it must be observed that the influence on national administrative law is realized according to the specific modalities and for the purpose of achieving the special aims set by the regulatory schemes illustrated earlier.

In conclusion, it must be recognized that the reconstruction proposed limits itself to sketching a number of essential features of an emerging regulatory framework of independent exercise of Community functions. Even though containing a set of typifications of the legal relationships that exist among the various competent activities and of the functions performed, the legal scheme identified lends itself to further specification and clarification. While going beyond the scope of the present work, such an in-depth examination would make possible further differentiation between the various figures referring to the general model illustrated in relation to the nature of the independence, to the organization of the authorities endowed with independence, to the function exercised and to the modalities of the administrative action.

# 9. THE EVOLVING CONCEPT OF SEPARATION OF POWERS AND INDEPENDENT ADMINISTRATIVE AGENCIES

*Mario Comba*

## I. INDEPENDENT ADMINISTRATIVE AGENCIES AND THE 'CLASSICAL CONCEPTION OF SEPARATION OF POWERS': AN UP-SIDE DOWN APPROACH

One of the problems most frequently faced in the study of Independent Administrative Agencies is to see how they can be reconciled with the constitutional principle of Separation of Powers. It is commonly perceived that the typical IAA—if ever it is possible to identify one typical IAA—is a single legal entity empowered with executive, regulatory and judicial duties (or at least two of the three), which may be at odds with the 'classical theory of separation of powers'. One can ask oneself if the 'classical conception of separation of powers' is set aside or derogated from to make room for IAA or, on the other hand, whether IAA may themselves be adapted to the exigencies of the separation of powers.

The logical scheme of this reasoning takes as granted the 'classical conception of separation of powers' and focuses on the various forms of IAAs in the context of different legal orders. This kind of comparative analysis usually tries to find out what are, if any, the common features of IAAs in different States, in order to appreciate and compare how they perform their tasks; the 'classical conception of separation of powers' is left as a background and is used in order to give a better relief to the models of IAAs.

Of course, every cautious scholar of public (comparative) law is well aware that a unique 'classical conception of the separation of powers' does not exist and, in fact, she usually disseminates *caveats* in the first paragraph of her study, in order to inform the reader that she is sophisticated enough to know that modern Constitutions do not incorporate Montesquieu literally (and that he, alas, is not just a dull 'tripartitist'). However, the cautious scholar usually goes on to state (or leave to the reader to understand) that for the purposes of the study, it is not possible to deepen the analysis and therefore a paradigmatic conception of separation of powers has to be taken into account, in order to concentrate on the study of IAAs.

The approach of this study will be up-side down. The 'classical conception of Independent Administrative Agency' will be taken for granted and used as a background against which to place the different theories of separation of powers in relief. Of course, I am well aware of the extreme complexity of the structures and tasks of what is commonly considered as IAA, but for the purposes of this study it is not possible to deepen the analysis and therefore a paradigmatic conception of IAA has to be taken into account, as a single legal entity empowered with executive, regulatory and judicial duties (or at least two of the three).

In reality, this study cannot provide an exhaustive picture of the different theories of the separation of powers and of their application to constitutional systems, due to the vastness of the problems implied and by consequence, to the endless legal literature on the subject.[1] However, it will try to provide a general idea of the evolution of the concept, from its liberal origin to its present adaptation to the Welfare State. It is in fact the intention of this paper to demonstrate how the theory of Separation of Powers is not a neutral device, good for all seasons, and for any form of State.

On the contrary, the model of Organization of Powers and State functions, within the framework of the State, is functional to the aims pursued by the State and, therefore, has to adjust itself with the changing of the scope of public powers.

This *functional* methodology will make it easier to perform our task, that is to verify the compatibility of the 'classical conception of Independent Administrative Agency' with the different forms of the Separation of Powers. Special attention will be given to the relationship between the Judicial and the Administrative Power.

First, it is necessary to describe briefly the role of the discourse on Separation of Powers principle in modern Western constitutionalism, in order to appreciate in what terms and with what changes it is still a central issue, more than 250 years since l'*Esprit des Lois* has been published.

[1] Separation of Powers is the subject of a very high number of specific studies and is at least mentioned in every handbook of Constitutional law. The following is a limited selection of books dedicated exclusively to separation of powers, by scholars in the main Western legal tradition. MJC Vile *Constitutionalism and the Separation of Powers* (Oxford Clarendon Press 1967); M Troper *La séparation des pouvoirs et l'histoire constitutionnelle française* (2nd edn Paris LGDJ 1980); G Silvestri *La separazione dei poter* 2 vols (Milano 1979–84); G Bognetti *La divisione dei poteri* (Milano Giuffré 1994); D Tsatsos *Zür Geschichte und Kritik del Lehre vor der Gewatenteilung* (1968).

## II. THE 'LIBERAL' SEPARATION OF POWERS DOCTRINE OF MONTESQUIEU: A DOUBLE MISCONCEPTION

### *A. Montesquieu and the English Constitution: The First Misconception*

The elaboration of the Separation of Powers, in its Montesquieu version, and the following incorporation in the constitutional documents of last two centuries by Western countries is not straightforward but rather a very much mixed-up process, somehow like a kind of chain of misconceptions.

It is well known that Montesquieu described the English separation of Powers without being very accurate about what was, in effect, the real situation on the other side of the Channel: 'La Constitution d'Angleterre selon les Anglais' is not the same thing as 'La Constitution d'Angleterre selon Montesquieu'.[2] The difference lies mainly in the fact that the English Constitution is based upon the 'Gouvernment mixte', with the Power exercised by the King in Parliament, that is the King together with (and hence not separated from) the Nobles (House of Lords) and the People (House of Commons). As for the Judiciary, it is still now 'subservient to Parliament', even if Judges are a group 'with which Parliament does not like to interfere'.[3] In other words, it is true that the English Constitution managed to guarantee liberty by means of a 'moderate Government', but this moderation was not reached through the Separation of Powers; it was instead the result of a mixed form of interaction between the Powers.

Montesquieu used therefore the English Constitution as an *argumentum quoad auctoritatem*, since he did not refer to a real model, but to a representation (an ideologization) of a real model.[4] However, his originality lies in the identification of three functions of the State, whereas at the time the State was thought to perform only two activities: it is the dual power of the King—well known to Medieval constitutional lawyers—consisting in *Gubernaculum* and *Jurisdictio,* coming from the Roman Law distinction between *Imperium* and *Jurisdictio*:[5] there was not any separation, inside *Jurisdictio*, between regulatory and judicial function, since both activities

[2] See E Zoller *Droit Constitutionnel* (2nd edn Paris PUF 1999) 287–90; see also C Grewe and H Ruiz Fabri *Droits constitutionnels européens* (Paris PUF 1995) 360–1.

[3] See R Stevens *The English Judges. Their Role in the Changing Constitution* (Oxford and Portland, Hart Publishing 2002) 89. In the following pages, Stevens describes the triple role of the Lord Chancellor, the dual role of the Law Lords and of their appointment procedure, trying to reconcile Parliamentary Sovereignity and Judicial independence, ending up by saying that judicial independence 'is not a legal concept in England' (97).

[4] Which is not uncommon in public comparative law, expecially since the eighteenth century: see G Lombardi *Premesse al Corso di Diritto pubblico comparato* (Milano Giuffré 1986) 100.

[5] See CH McIlwain *Constitutionalism: Ancient and Modern* (New York Cornell University Press 1947) ch IV. See also Zoller op cit 290–2.

were perceived, in opposition to *Gubernaculum*, or *Imperium*, as limited by the principle of reason.[6]

In the French *Ancien Régime* (starting from the reign of Louis XIV), the King governed with the stable help of his Councils: one of them was the *Conseil d'Etat privé, finances et direction*, which dealt with justice and administration together: on Monday mornings, in Versailles, the Councellors decided the litigation questions submitted to the King; on Monday afternoons (but fortnightly) they decided fiscal litigation and on Tuesdays they were occupied with non-litigatious fiscal matters.[7] The same mixing of functions can be traced in the competences of the Intendents, who represented the King in the provinces, and whose exact denomination was: 'Intendant de justice, police et finances, commissaire départi en telle généralité pour l'execution des ordres du Roi.'[8]

The first merit of Montesquieu was thus to have distinguished between the judicial and the executive function and to have 'invented' adjudication as a separate State activity from administration.

Of course, one has to notice that the solemn *incipit* of the famous Chapter VI, Book 11 of the *Esprit des Lois* does not refer to these three functions, but to the three functions of the State in the Lockean meaning: the legislative power, the executive power and the federative power, that is the power to conduct external relations.[9] But the same chapter goes on referring to the legislative/executive/judicial function triad, as if it was mentioned like that at the beginning of the Chapter: another (minor) misconception.

Once the three functions have been identified, the theory of Montesquieu is completed with the attribution of each function to a separate and independent organ, and by assuring that they are kept separate, by giving specific prerogatives to each legal entity. Those prerogatives should guarantee that each Power can stop the other, whenever it tries to expand its competence to another function: hence the famous sentence 'il faut que pour la disposition des choses le pouvoir arrête le pouvoir'.[10] The Montesquieu theory does not include, however, the concept of specialization of the organs; it is not said that each organ has to fulfil one and only

[6] For an accurate reconstruction of what they call the 'Jurisdictional State', see: L Mannori and B Sordi *Storia del diritto amministrativo* (Roma-Bari Laterza 2001) 36–71; for a contrary opinion, according to which the distinction between judicial and administrative functions was already existing in the *Ancien Régime*, albeit not developped, see F Burdeau, *Historie du droit administratif* (Paris PUF 1995) 29–40.

[7] F Olivier-Martin *Historie du droit français des origines à la Revolution* (Paris CNRS 1995) (1st edn 1948) 433–66.

[8] See F Olivier-Martin op cit 571.

[9] See Montesquieu *L'esprit des Lois* (1st edn 1748) Chapter IV, Book 11

[10] Grewe and Ruiz Fabri op cit 364–6, insists very much that the 'classical doctrine', with the specialization of functions, was not the Montesquieu doctrine.

one function, with exclusion of the others: that will be the 'exaggerations' of the Montesquieu theory as interpreted by the French Revolution

### *B. Montesquieu as Perceived by the American and the French Constitutions: The Second Misconception*

The first historical applications of the 'new' theory of Separation of Powers are the American Constitution of 1787 and the French Déclaration des droits de l'Homme et du Citoyen of 1789, along with the Constitution of 1791.

The American Constitution is the more strictly adherent to the theory of Montesquieu: even without formally declaring the Separation of Powers, it is based on a textual architecture that patently presupposes that principle: the first three articles deal respectively with the Legislative, the Executive and the Judiciary. In addition, in the Federalist, Madison translates Montesquieu almost literally, when it says that 'Ambition must be made to counteract ambition. The interest of the man must be connected with the constitutional rights of the place',[11] which is very close to 'Le pouvoir arrête le pouvoir'. It is clear that the constitutinal design of the Founders was to achieve a 'play of deliberately fragmented centers of countervailing power, almost Newtonian in its inspiration'.[12]

Another strict adherence of the American Founders to the thought of Montesquieu is the role played by the Judiciary: it has to be independent, but since it can only 'declare' the content of the law, it is 'en quelque façon nulle', for Montesquieu,[13] and 'the least dangerous' for Hamilton.[14]

It is precisely in relation to the role of Judiciary that the American Constitution begins to depart from the original principle of Separation of Powers: with the *Marbury v Madison* decision, in 1803, the Supreme Court of the United States nullifies a law of the Congress, thus breaking one of the first prerogatives of the Legislative and beginning the long march to become

[11] J Madison, A Hamilton, and J Jay *The Federalist Papers* (London Penguin Books 1987) (1st edn New York 1788) paper 51 (attributed to Madison), 319. In paper 47 (302), Madison accurately examines the theory of Montesquieu and, recognizing that it was grounded on the English Constitution, rejects the more radical application of Montesquieu Separation of Powers, thus showing a better understanding of the *Esprit des Lois* than a lot of French interpreters.

[12] LH Tribe *American Constitutional Law* vol 1 (3rd edn New York Foundation Press 2000) 7.

[13] Montesquieu op cit Ch VI, Book 11.

[14] Madison, Hamilton, and Jay *The Federalist* op cit paper 78 (attributed to Hamilton), which says: 'Whoever attentively considers the different departments of power must perceive that, in a government in which they are separated from each other, the judiciary, from the nature of its functions, will always be the least dangerous of the political rights of the Constitutions; because it will be the least in a capacity to annoy or injure them' (437).

the Third Chamber of the Congress.[15] The other turning point in the American Separation of Powers doctrine dates back to the New Deal and the birth of the Administrative State, when the Executive Power undergoes a huge expansion thus limiting the Legislative, after the dismissal of the non-delegation doctrine,[16] but this is a feature common to all other Western democracies and will be dealt with later.[17]

Article 16 of the Déclaration of 1789 contains what can be considered a formal constitutionalization of the Separation of Powers: 'Toute Societé dans laquelle la garantie des Droits n'est pas assurée, ni la Séparation des Pouvoirs déterminée, n'a point de Constitution' as does the French Constitution of 1791, which creates the Legislative, Executive and Judiciary Power.

But these are only illusions,[18] since the real position of the revolutionary Framers, influenced by Rousseau much more than by Montesquieu, was in favour of only one, indivisible Power, 'la Souveranité', belonging to the Nation. The distinction of functions is thus recognized, but not of Powers, the only real Power being the Legislative, which is monopoly of the Parliament, while the executive and the judicial functions are exercised by Authorities (the Government and the Judiciary), subject to the Legislative Power.

The Separation of Powers is replaced by the specialization of functions, so that the 'conception révolutionnaire de la séparation des pouvoirs débouche sur une hypertrophie de l'organe législatif et la confusion des pouvoirs'.[19] The Separation of Powers only plays in favour of the Parliament, because the Executive and the Judiciary are subordinate to it and canot contradict it, nor participate in its activity. In particular, in the idea of French revolutionary constituents and legislators, the Separation of Powers is construed in order to *limit* , not to increase, the autonomy of the Judiciary, because it was perceived as a dangerous power, due to the behaviour of the *Parlements* in the *Ancién Régime*, against the King and his Administration.[20] This is why the Law of 16–24 August 1790 was so strict in defining the boundaries of the judicial power against the legislative and the executive: Article 10 said: 'Les tribunaux ne porront prendre directement ou indirectement aucune part à l'exercice du pouvoir législatif, ni empêcher ou suspendre l'exécution des décrets du corps législatif, sanction-

[15] For the increasing power of American judiciary, see the classic AM Bickel, *The Least Dangerous Branch* (Indianapolis 1962).

[16] For the constitutional upheaval of the New Deal period, in the context of the evolution of American constitutional regimes, see B Ackermann *We, The People*, vol. I, *Foundations*, Cambridge, 1991; see also G Bognetti *Lo spirito del costituzionalismo americano* vol. II, *La Costituzione democratica* (Torino Giappichelli 2000) esp 1–53.

[17] The evolution of the US Separation of Powers from the original Madison–Montesquieu model to the Judicial–administrative one is accurately described by Zoller op cit 297–301.

[18] Ibid 311.

[19] Ibid 314.

[20] Ibid 186–7.

nés par le roi, à peine de forfaiture', and Article 13, in relation to the executive, was not less explicit: 'Les fonctions judiciaires sont distinctes et demeurent toujours séparés des fonctions administratives; les juges ne pourront à peine de forfaiture troubler de quelque manière que ce soit les opérations des corps administratifs, ni citer devant eux les administrateurs en raison de leur fonctions.'

In conclusion, it can be said that Montesquieu, having proposed a misleading version of the English Constitution, found far more faithful followers in Washington DC than in Paris, where his theory was formally adopted in solemn declarations, but substantially distorted, by exalting the idea of separation and losing the implicit reference to moderation.

### *C. Dicey: A Third Misconception?*

As we have seen, one of the great merits of Montesquieu was to divide the *Jurisdictio* into administrative and judicial functions while at those times the two activities were both performed by the King without any distinction between them. Rendering justice was the same thing as—or, was a part of—administering. We have also seen that the application of Montesquieu theories by the French Revolution was quite exaggerated, in the sense that it lost the moderate flavour which characterized it in the *Esprit des Lois*.

On the other side of the Channel, on the contrary, the pacific coexistence of administration and adjudication was the rule (or, at least, was not perceived as a problem),[21] neither troubled by Montesquieu theory, nor by Revolutionary exaggerations of that same theory, and it is still now quite like that.[22] This can help to explain the position of Dicey[23] when, between the end of the nineteenth and the beginning of the twentieth century, he

[21] In the sense that Administration is also charged with judicial functions: it is the case of Administrative Tribunals, or Commissions, which were already numerous in the first half of the eighteenth century. For example, the Commissioner for Income Tax was created in 1798, when the Income tax was introduced in England, and it is still now one of the most active. Other Commissions were that on Industry (1833), Railways (1840), Public Education (1840), Health (1848) and so forth: see S Cassese *La costruzione del diritto amministrativo: Francia e Regno Unito* in Cassese (a cura di), *Trattato di diritto amministrativo* (Milano Giuffré 2000) 26 (translated into French: see *La construction du droit administratif: France et Royaume Uni*, translated by J Marvillet-Maigret (Paris Montchrestien 2000).

[22] The English Tribunals and Commission were multiplied with the birth of the Welfare State. For a recent review of all existing Tribunals, see the Report of the Royal Commision on Tribunals (Leggatt Report), 2001, at <http://www.tribunals-review-org.uk>.

[23] AV Dicey *Introduction to the Study of the Law of the Constitution* (8th edn London Macmillan 1915), (the 1st edition was published in 1885; the 8th edition is the last that Dicey himself prepared. The quotations are from the reprint of Liberty Classics Indianapolis 1982). Chapter XII of Part II is about *The Rule of Law Ccompared with Droit Administratif*. In order to understand the evolution of Dicey's position in the different editions of his *Introduction*, see S Flogaïtis *Administrative Law et Droit Administratif* (Paris LGDJ 1986) 33–8, but, in actual fact, the whole chapter I 'Dicey et le droit administratif' continuously refers to the evolution of the position of Dicey in relation to the French administrative Law.

launched his famous critique against the *droit administratif*, which, according to him, was a danger for the liberty of citizens since it did not admit a judicial review of administration nor—and this was considered the 'most despotic characteristic of *droit administratif*'[24]—the liability of administrative officers.

The Dicean position has been widely criticized: it has been demonstrated that he was not aware (at least until the last editions of his *The Law of the Constitution*) of the real evolution of the French administrative sytem, which had, by the end of the nineteenth century, admitted the liability of public officers and the judidical review of the Administration, nor of the newest tendencies of the English system itself,[25] but the main point is, perhaps, that Dicey was right when he said that England did not have a *droit administratif*, since the existence of a *droit administratif* presupposes a well-established separation between administration and adjudication, and in England such a separation was not developed as it was on the Continent.

To be sure, Dicey does realize very clearly that the principle of Separation of Powers is at the basis of the distinction: in describing the 'two leading ideas alien to the conception of modern Englishmen',[26] he enumerates the privilege of the State and the Separation of Powers. Even if he does not complete the reasoning, showing how the former (the privilege of the State) is a by-product of the latter (the Separation of Powers), he points out that the French version of that principle means that government officials ought to be independent of and to great extent free from the jurisdiction of the ordinary courts, while the English meaning relates to independence of the judges.

Further, in the chapter dedicated to *droit administratif*, Dicey comes again to the different meaning of the Separation of Powers. When exhalting the merits of the rule of law, as opposed to the *droit administratif*, he notes that in England 'an extension of judicial power which sets at nought the dogma of the separation of powers, happily combined with judicial independence, has begotten reverence for the bench of judges. They, rather than the government, represent the august dignity of the State or, in accordance with the terminology of English law, of the Crown'.[27]

At this point, the reference to Montesquieu is inevitable, in order to explain the 'curious' historical growth of the Separation of Powers, Dicey says that it: 'rests apparently upon Montesquieu's *Esprit des Lois*, Book XI, c. 6, and is in some sort the offspring of a double misconception; Montesquieu misunderstood on this point the principle and practice of

[24] Dicey op cit 225.

[25] See Cassese op cit. paras 4, 4.1, and 4.2 describe the Dicey position, reconstructing his interplay with French writers and, in particular, para. 4.2 enumerates 'Dicey's errors'.

[26] Dicey op cit 219.

[27] Ibid 259.

English constitution, and his doctrine was, in turn, if not misunderstood, exaggerated and misapplied by the French statesmen of the Revolution'.[28]

It is exactly in that 'double misconception' that the apparent failure of Montesquieu can be traced both in describing the English Constitution and in influencing the French constitutional process at the end of the eighteenth century. As we have seen, his theory was perhaps most successful in the United States, through the thought and the practical intervention of Madison, but there too it was deeply modified by the introduction of judicial review of legislation, in 1803.

In a certain sense, Dicey was also mistaken about the Separation of Powers. First, from a systematic point of view, he did not realize that the privileges of the State are nothing else than another face of the French Separation of Powers: the two things can not be separated, because the first is a consequence of the latter.[29] But the absence of a French-style Separation of Powers in England leads to other and more relevant consequences: since the Administration and the Judiciay are mixed together, the latter cannot see and appreciate the specific and peculiar characteristics of the former and, in fact, single officers only have relevance in front of English Judges as private persons. But specificity does not mean only having privileges: treating the Administration differently from the citizens can also, potentially, lead to endowing it with specific duties and responsibilities, from which private citizens are exempt.

Not recognizing the Administration as such, but only the single government officers, prevents the Judiciary from condemning the Administration, and hence leads to the immunity of the Crown, which can be sued only with its own permission. But, in particular, it excludes the possibility for the citizen to have a guarantee against the *acts* of the Administration, in the same manner as he cannot have a judicial remedy against *acts* of other persons, but only against their behaviour. Recognizing the special status of the Administration, in other words, also means recognizing that it has special powers and therefore has to be treated differently from other persons because it requires a stricter control.

Dicey cannot deny that the Administration is given, also in England, special powers; he also admits that the number of these special functions imposed by law upon government officials 'has of late vastly increased', but the difference with the *droit administratif* is that while in England there are only many single laws conferring specific powers and duties upon government officials, the French *droit administratif* is characterized, on the contrary, by 'the sum of the principles which govern the relation between

[28] Ibid 220.

[29] Ibid 219, says that the two leading ideas alien to the conceptions of modern Englishmen are the special rights and privileges accorded to the State against private citizens and the Separation of Powers, as already mentioned in the text.

the French citizens, as individuals, and the administration as representative of the State'.[30]

And here comes the point, which is not dealt with by Dicey: in England, every law conferring upon government officials special powers and duties can also provide (and usually does provide) for the creation of a special organ (usually named Commission, Inspectorate or Tribunal) having the jurisdiction to administer those powers but also, quite often, to judge in first instance citizens' complaints. It is true that the dissatisfied citizen can always file a petition with the ordinary judge against the decision of the administrative organ, but that means that English judges do not have the monopoly of all litigation between citizens and government officers, because such litigation, at the first level, is dealt with by the same administrative organ upon which the law has imposed the power itself.

Therefore, it can be said that in the United Kingdom there is not administrative law, but not because there is a stricter control of the Judiciary over the Administration; rather because judiciary and administration are often closely mixed together, without any possibiity of distinguishing between them.

From this point of view, Montesquieu has to be reappraised, not so much for the his 'classical theory of the Separation of Powers', which gave rise to so many misunderstandings, but for its logical presupposition, which was a real expression of his genius and originality: the recognition of the difference between the administrative and judicial functions as the sole method to conceive complete mutual control.

## III. THE SEPARATION OF POWERS IN THE WELFARE STATE

The Separation of Powers is still today one of the fundamental elements of the modern Constitutional State. In his *Europäische Verfassungslehre*,[31] Häberle states with emphasis—and perhaps not without a certain dose of irony—that: 'Im ganzen erweist sich die Gewaltenteilung als Herzstück jedes Verfassungsstaates. Sie ist eine des glücklichsten 'Erfindungen' des Geistes—bzw. Kulturgeschichte und gleich einem del 10 gebote der Bibel—neben Menschenwürde und Demokratie, Menschenrechten und sozialem und ökologischem Rechtstaat, auch Kukturstaat, Föderalismus bzw. Regionalismus, Rechtsschutz durch unabhängige Gerichte und Verfassungsgerichtsbarkeit'.[32]

[30] Ibid 254–5.

[31] P Häberle *Europäische Verfassungslehre* (Baden-Baden Nomos Verlagsgesellschaft 2001–2).

[32] Ibid 408.

In fact, Häberle puts the *Gewaltenteilung* among the 'Wesentliche Verfassungsthemen und Textformen des sich konstituirenden Europa': he indicates the three 'klassischen Funktionen' as the Leglislative, Executive and Judiciary[33] and the 'typischen verfassungsstaatlichen Organe' as the Parliament, the Head of State, the Executive (that is Government and Administration) and the Courts, particularly the Constitutional Courts,[34] while other independent subjects, like the State Banks, are considered only 'Merkposten'.

Of course, the State functions are only instruments by which every State can reach its own goals, and since the variability of models in European Constitutions is very great, the comparatist can only proceed by generalizations. However, and notwithstanding the privatization process seems to have given to States new instruments in order to achieve their goals, the tripartition of functions is still valid, for Häberle, 'nach wie for',[35] in the panorama of contemporary European Constitutions.

Almost the same conclusion is reached by the (few) other scholars who have tried to describe the contemporary common principles of European constitutional law or theory, even if some doubts arise, here and there.[36]

A radically different approach is proposed by Bognetti, in his studies on the modification of the classical (liberal) idea of Separation of Powers in the Welfare State.[37]

According to Bognetti, the original model of Separation of Powers, elaborated by Montesquieu in its 'grande, elegante semplicità',[38] was suited to the liberal form of State, because it was aimed at granting the protection of liberty of the single person. In order to guarantee the protection of fundamental rights, the organization of the State should prevent any concentration of power, which was the rule in the absolute State. In order to avoid the concentration of power, the three functions of the State—legislative, executive and judiciary—were identified and, as we have already seen, that was a very sophisticated operation, in a period when administration and adjudication were the same thing and the activities of the State were in fact divided according to different subjects (and not functions).

The introduction of the Separation of Powers in the Constitutions of the nineteenth century—after the first experiences of the United States and of Revolutionay France—produced a great simplification in the organization of the State, as compared to the *Ancien Régime* models and in the creation

[33] Ibid 409. [34] Ibid 410. [35] Ibid.

[36] For example, Grewe, Ruiz, and Fabri op cit 366, says that 'on est en quête d'une nouvelle qualification des fonctions, avec une distinction entre fonction gouvernementale et foncion délibérante'. See also A Pizzorusso *Il patrimionio costituzionale europeo* (Bologna Il Mulino 2002) 139–42.

[37] G Bognetti *La divisione dei poteri* (Milano Giuffré 1994); id *La divisione dei poteri, oggi,* in 'Diritto e società' (2003) 219.

[38] Bognetti *La divisione dei poteri, oggi* op cit 219.

of the rules, which were reserved, with some limited exceptions, to Parliament, while in the *Ancien Régime* they were in the hands of a heterogeneous number of bodies.[39]

These elements could be found, according to Bognetti, in all the Constitutional systems of Western democracies—even if England and the United States had a different conception of the distinction between the administrative and judicial function. All those countries, in fact, shared the same idea of the liberal State, that is of the limited State, whose main preoccupation was not to get over the boundary which separated the public from the private area.

But when the structure of the Western State changes, due to the evolution of the liberal State towards the social State, or welfare State, the classical principle of Separation of Powers cannot stand the new and huge activities the State wants to perform. The social State, in fact, is an 'active' State, in the sense that it wants to intervene in the area so far scrupulously reserved to private activity. In order to do so, it needs newer and more flexible tools than the 'old' Law of the Parliament.

Therefore, the first structural change in the organization of the State is the shifting of the legislative function from Parliament to Government. Of course, the classical Separation of Powers theory also admitted the performing of a limited number of normative functions by the Government, but the change imposed by the new form of State modifies the nature of the function itself (hence the phenomenon of delegated legislation). The Parliament keeps a role of control over the legislative activity of the Government, but it is the Government which takes the lead and thus performs a new function, mixing legislative and administrative activities.

At the same time, the judicial function also undergoes inevitable changes, due to the rise of the social State. As can be easily understood, these changes, consisting substantially in a mixing-up (or *re* mixing-up) of administrative and judiciary functions, are crucial for the purposes of this paper and therefore would need a particularly accurate examination, which is not possible here, if not in very concise terms.[40]

The huge increase of litigation between citizens and the State due to the increase of the activities of Government and other public bodies, made it impossible for the Judiciary to keep deciding all the cases filed, which, in turn, led to the creation of specific organs, of a substantially administrative nature, aimed at solving in first instance the bulk of administrative litigation. This development had different features in the Common Law systems, which already had similar experiences, and in Civil Law systems, where the

[39] The effort to unify the production of norms was already initiated under the *Ancien Régime*, but apparently without much success: see F Olivier-Martin *Les lois du Roi* (1st edn Paris LGDJ 1997) 1988.

[40] It is treated at length in Bognetti *La divisione dei poteri* op cit 61 ff and 86 ff.

Separation of Powers principle—applied in its version of specialization of functions—was a great obstacle to mixing administration and adjudication. But it has however been a strong common tendency, whose characteristics can be clearly seen in all Western democracies,[41] perhaps with the only exception of Italy.[42]

The performing of judicial functions by the Administration is not final: in all countries the last word is left to the Judiciary (be it ordinary Judiciary, or specialized Judiciary), in the sense that the decision of the administrative body can almost always be challenged in a Court, but that means that the Judiciary has lost its monopoly in the solving of all litigation, changing it into a role of final and impartial control over adjudication-making performed by the administration. In addition, or—perhaps—as a consequence of this new role, the judicial function is no longer, as it was conceived by Montesquieu and as it was beleived to be during the liberal constitutionalism of nineteenth century, that of applying the Law to single cases. This is only a part of the judicial funtion, which is now also called to intervene in the legal system fostering the process of the development of Law.

The radical change of the State functions has caused a modification of Powers, that is of organs upon which the different functions are conferred (not exclusively, but as a major activity). In particular, the former Executive Power is now divided into the Governmental Power and the Administrative Power. The first is no longer the mere executer of the will of Parliament but is, on the contrary, the engine of the political activity, having the task to create and maintain the fundamental political choices of the State. The Administrative Power, in its turn, is formed by the bureaucratic apparatus of the State and of the other public bodies: it is no longer a mere 'belt of transmission' of the will of the Government because, as we have seen, it had grown enormously not only in quantitative terms, but especially in its funcions. Currently, the Administrative Power performs its duties by regulating, adjudicating and also, finally, applying legislation to single cases: all this implies the exercise of autonomous (political) decisional power.

41 A good example can be that of tax litigation, where a previous administrative recourse is required, in France and Germany, before filing a petition before the *Tribunal administratif* or the *Finanzgericht*. In England, the Commissioner for income Tax and the VAT Tribunals are two administrative bodies deciding tax litigation in first instance. In the United States the Tax Court is a legislative Court (or non-Art. III Court), ie its judges do not have the guarantees of ordinary federal judges. See M Comba *Lineamenti di giustizia tributaria comparata* in G Paleologo (ed) *La Commissione Tributaria Centrale e la giustizia tributaria in Italia. Storia e prospettive* (Milano Giuffré 2004) shortly to be published. But, of course, the best examples are Independent Administrative Agencies.

42 Bognetti *La divisione dei poter, oggi* op cit 225 ff; id *La divisione dei poteri* op cit 125 ff, notes how the Italian Constitution still assumes, in its Part II, a classical Separation of Powers model, presupposing a neutral role for the Judiciary, while, *de facto*, the Judiciary is, like in all other western countries—and perhaps even more—inevitably also performing a political role in participating in the evolution of Law.

If this distinction sounds new to the ears of a constitutional lawyer, one has to realize that, in reality, the recognition of a different role between the Governmental and the Administrative Powers—under the perspective of the relationship between politicians and bureaucrats—is nothing new for political scientists, who have considered it as a classical theme of analysis of modern bureaucracies since at least 50 years ago.[43] It can therefore be said that the phenomenon is not new, but perhaps constitutional lawyers were not so quick to perceive and analyse it, which increases the merits of those who first described and rationalized it.

It would be too easy and superficial to say that this new model of Separation of Powers, with a strong, central Governmental Power which is surrounded by the other Powers, directed by it but, at the same time, acting as brakes to its activity, reproduces the *Ancien Régime* model, with the central power of the King potentially absolute but *de facto* subject to the limitations of the various elements of the organic society.[44] Nor has it reproduced the ancient English idea of the mixed government, translated from Montesquieu, even if in a misleading way, in the *Esprit des Lois* and then applied in France and in the whole Continent with the misconceptions seen earlier, because the essential scope of that model was to mix the functions, in order to limit the activities of the State. With the new model, on the contrary, the mixing of functions (for example of administrative, regulatory and judicial functions in the Administrative Power) is a consequence of the huge growth of State activities, not a device in order to prevent it.

It is therefore a model which is not a return to that existing before Montesquieu, but nor is it the 'classical separation of Powers' as we have become used to thinking of, in its different versions as realized in continental Europe, in the United Kingdom or in the United States.

And it is curious to see how in the United States, where perhaps the Montesquieu model was most faithfully reproduced, even if soon disregarded, and where this same model is now still more resistant,[45] one of the most prestigious constitutionalists is harshly critical of the 'ritualistic incantation of Madison and Montesquieu',[46] proposing a form of government with a central power represented by a monocameral Parliament, surrounded by subordinated special-purpose branches acting as brakes to the 'bounded Parliament' and limiting it in the name of democratic legiti-

[43] Starting with behaviourist studies on the Administration: D Easton *The Political System* (New York Knopf 1953) and coming to the classical study of JD Aberbach, RD Putnam, and BA Rockman *Bureaucrats and Politicians in Western Democracies* (Cambridge Harvard University Press 1981). Among the most recent studies, see: H Bekke, and F Van der Meer (eds) *Civil Service System in Western Europe* (Cheltenham Edward Elgar 2000).

[44] Bognetti *La divisione dei poteri* op cit 94–5.

[45] The presidential form of government is in fact the most evident model of a dual government.

[46] B Ackerman *The New Separation of Powers* in (2000) Harvard Law Review 633.

macy, functional specialization, and protection of rights. The anger against Madison and Montesquieu is surely unjustified, since they should rather inspire 'quel sentimento misto di riconoscenza e di malinconia, che sempre accompagna, negli animi pensosi, la visione del tramonto di qualcosa di grande la cui ora purtroppo è venuta';[47] but the idea that the 'classical Separation of Powers' should be revised is in anycase correct, because it cannot be matched with the Welfare State.

Of course, the Welfare State also is now under reconsideration in Western countries, since the big party realignment which began in the United States and in the United Kingdom in the 1980s. We still do not know where this process will lead us—perhaps to a regulatory State after the positive, or welfare, State[48]—but what is sure is that the theory of separation of powers will follow those changes, since it is not a neutral mechanism good for any underlying constitutional value.

## IV. INDEPENDENT ADMINISTRATIVE AGENCIES IN THE WELFARE STATE'S MODEL OF SEPARATION OF POWERS

The Separation of Powers model developed with the Welfare State is therefore characterized by particular features, which do not in any way allow an identification with the 'classical conception of Separation of Powers' which, in its turn, did not exist as an homogeneous theory, being the result of at least a double (if not triple) misconception.

For the purpose of this study, the most important innovation is, of course, the expansion of the (former) Executive Power which, following the definition proposed by Bognetti, is now split into Governmental Power and Administrative Power, each performing a different function.

The first important element to be examined is the relationship between these two powers: they are somehow respectively autonomous, in the sense that the Administrative Power is endowed with such an enormous number of activities which it cannot be controlled by the political power in all that it is doing. This is why it has a wide range of discretion in performing its tasks: the delegation doctrine, developed in the relationship between the Legislative and the Executive, is now fully applied inside the (former) Executive Power in order to justify the increasing autonomy of the Administrative Power.

[47] Bognetti *La divisione dei poteri* op cit 101.

[48] A La Spina and G Majone *Lo Stato regolatore* (Bologna Il Mulino 2000), whose first chapter is titled: 'dallo Stato gestore allo Stato regolatore'; see also G Majone *From the Positive to the Regulatory State: Causes and Consequences in the Mode of Governance*, in 17.2 Journal of Public Policy 139–67.

It is therefore not in contrast with the model, that the Administrative Power be autonomous in relation to the Governmental Power: in the end, they are two Powers, performing two different functions even if, of course, the two functions are very closely connected. Under the perspective of the study of bureaucratic systems, it has been noted that, from the 1980s, the bureaucratic systems of Western countries have undergone, with different times and procedures, a common process of 'agencification', that is the creation of agencies bound to Ministeries not with a hierarchical relationship, but with 'contracts' (therefore something different from Independent agencies), with the purpose of separating, from an organizational point of view, political and managerial activities.[49]

If the model is that of a central Governmental Power, entitled with the creation and maintenance of fundamental political choices, surrounded by a network of other Powers (Legislative, Administrative, Judicial, and Constitutional control) having a role of integrating and braking che central power,[50] then the position of Independent Administrative Agencies is much less difficult to justify, also from the point of view of political legitimation. This model, in fact, presupposes that the political legitimation is not the only acceptable justification of the exercise of a public function.[51]

If we emphasize the situation, bringing it to its extreme consequences, it is possible to say that the autonomy of Independent Administrative Agencies from all other Powers can be considered the necessary price to be paid in order for them to exercise at the same time the regulatory and the adjudicative, as well as the executive, function. If they were hierarchically dependent from the Governmental (political) power, their judicial activity would be much more problematic, because of the concentration of Powers; but since they are independent and have the integrating/braking role, then they can more easily be invested with the three functions.[52]

And here we come to the second question about the compatibility between Independent Administrative Agencies and Separation of Powers: how can the IAAs have at the same time perform the judicial and the regulatory function, as well as the executive one, and be consistent with the Separation of Powers?

[49] This phenomenon was recognized and studied by the so-called New Public Management movement (see C Hood *A Public Management for All Seasons?*, in 69 Public Administration n. 1 3–19); for a description of the development of this phenomenon in Western countries (United States, United Kingdom, France, Italy, Spain, and Germany), see E Gualmini *L'amministrazione nelle democrazie contemporanee* (Laterza, Roma-Bari, 2003), esp 31–79.

[50] In these terms, the Bognetti model is not so far from the Ackerman model, even if the former is descriptive and the latter is prescriptive (and the former, perhaps more realistically, puts the Governmental Power at the centre, instead of the Legislative).

[51] Eg, Ackerman *The New Separation of Powers* op cit recognizes, besides the democratic legitimation, also the functional specialization and the protection of fundmental rights.

[52] This is also the position of the Economic Analysis approach: see R Posner *Economic Analysis of Law* (4th edn Boston–Toronto–London, Little Brown 1992) 618–20.

The solution to this problem springs from the above description of the evolution of the Separation of Powers. In the Welfare State, the distinction between the judicial and the administrative functions follows a different line than that in the Liberal State: the Administrative Power—and hence, *a fortiori*, the IAAs—administers justice at the first instance, in order to let only the important cases filter up to the Judiciary. This is, tendentially, the normal scheme in the Administrative Power, and therefore it should not be surprising to find it also in the IAAs.

At this point, considering the 'network' model of the Separation of Powers in the Welfare State and, at the same time, the tendential organization of the Administrative Power by agencies, one should perhaps ask not so much whether IAAs are consistent with the Separation of Powers principle but, turning the question up-side down, what, if any, are the substantial particularities of IAAs as regards to the Administrative Power, at least in relation to the functions performed.

# 10. INDEPENDENT ADMINISTRATIVE AUTHORITIES IN COMPARATIVE LAW: SCANDINAVIAN MODELS

*Mads Andenas* *

This study of independent administrative authorities in the Scandinavian countries illustrates many of the problems of the topic in European and comparative law. The Scandinavian countries share traditions and core features of their legal systems[1] but there is at the same time important differences both concerning the organisation of state authorities and in the content of the independence concepts.

Denmark, Norway, and Sweden share long-established traditions as parliamentary democracies based on fundamental separation of powers doctrines.[2] The public administrations of the Scandinavian countries can be described as conforming to the ideal of a classical Weberian Civil Service that would faithfully carry out the preferred policies of the Government of the day irrespective of that Government's political complexion within a hierarchical system of decision-making.

The principle of legality and formalized administrative procedures are

* MA, DPhil (Oxford); PhD (Cambridge). Director of the British Institute of International and Comparative Law, London. Professor, University of Leicester and Senior Fellow, Institute of European and Comparative Law, University of Oxford.

[1] Because of their close interrelationship and their common 'stylistic hallmarks', Zweigert and Kötz attribute the Nordic laws to their own legal family, alongside the Romanistic and German legal families. Nordic laws form part of the larger Romanist Germanic legal family. See K Zweigert and H Kötz *Introduction to Comparative Law* trans T Weir (3rd edn OUP Oxford 1998). More in-depth studies on Nordic law accessible to scholars outside the Scandinavian linguistic community include G Ring and L Olsen-Ring *Einführung in das skandinavische Recht* (München 1999), Dahl, Melchior, Rehof, Tamm (eds) *Danish Law in a European Perspective* (Copenhagen 1996) and J Pöyhönen (ed) *An Introduction to Finnish law* (Helsinki 1993).

[2] These three countries' constitutions are all based on a constitutional monarchy, with merely symbolic functions left for the monarch. This symbolic nature of the monarchy is better reflected in the written Swedish constitution, whereas the Danish and Norwegian constitutions still maintain the fiction of a Monarch exercising personal discretion and influence in matters of state. See M Andenas and I Wilberg *The Constitution of Norway. A Commentary* (Norwegian Universities' Press Oslo 1987). If one includes the two further Nordic countries, Finland has a President with important (although recently somewhat curtailed) constitutional functions, and Iceland a President with symbolic, figure-head functions.

well entrenched. Procedural codes, access to information, and a range of remedies including administrative appeals and judicial review are highly developed. Traditionally, not only access to judicial appointments but also any senior civil service appointment was limited to holders of university law degrees.

This is also a Civil Service with an independence based on the continuity resulting from professional careers and constitutional guarantees for tenure of office. Legality and administrative procedures, promoting fairness and impartiality, are seen as further guarantees for independence from politically motivated interference in administrative decision-making. The emergence of agencies outside the traditional structures of the ministries or departments of state structure does not seem to have threatened the cohesion or central features or values of the system.[3] The ministries of state and the rest of the national administration are organized in different ways in the Nordic countries, and the relationship to local administration varies. Also the independence concepts within the traditional civil service structure vary between the countries. There are further differences in the judicial review of administrative action, to some extent as a consequence of the different organisation of the court system.[4] So any reference made in this chapter to 'Scandinavian law' is a reference to the different legal systems of Denmark, Norway, and Sweden.[5] Occasionally reference is made to the laws of the two other Nordic countries, Finland and Iceland.

Independent administrative authorities have been a topic of some constitutional controversy but also this discussion has followed different national paths. Recent European and international developments have made the independence issues topical in all the Nordic countries. In order to under-

[3] There is no parallel to the 'fragmentation of the public service, the privatization of whole swathes of previously public business' that is described in other countries such as in the United Kingdom.

[4] Finland and Sweden have a separate administrative court system, whereas Denmark, Iceland, and Norway have a unified court structure where the general courts undertake judicial review of administrative action. There are further differences in the court review of constitutionality of parliamentary legislation which have been established in Norway since the late 19th century and has emerged more recently, still disputed, in the other Nordic countries. None of the countries have separate constitutional courts.

[5] In public law, the public's right to access to the documents of public administration is one field with common Nordic traditions. Denmark, along with the Netherlands proposed to include such a right in the Maastricht negotiations. In the Amsterdam Treaty, the new members Sweden and Finland joined Denmark's efforts. The European ombudsman is an institution with Nordic origins. It originated in Sweden, where the appointment of an Ombudsman by the Parliament was part of a constitutional reform that took place in 1809. When Finland became an independent state, the ombudsman system was adopted in its first Constitution of 1919. Sweden and Finland remained the only countries to have Ombudsmen with a general remit until 1953. In that year, Denmark established an ombudsman, followed by New Zealand in 1962 and by Norway the following year. In the negotiations that led to the Maastricht Treaty on European Union, proposals to establish the office of European Ombudsman were closely linked to those for European citizenship.

stand the different systems of these countries and to enable a discussion of the reform issues in any meaningful way, one needs to study the systems, in some depth, and at a comparative level. This chapter can only provide some of the relevant perspectives.

The chapter shows how the present project on Independent Administrative Authorities in the Laws of Europe could not be more timely. There is a need for an analysis which includes the different European and national levels.

The next section of this chapter (Section I), on independent administrative authorities in comparative law, sets out some aspects of the topic in international, European and national law, and makes the case for further comparative law scholarship in the field. Independence concepts are developed at many old and new levels of administrative law. New regulatory tasks have brought the development of independent administrative authorities to the fore as a matter of national law. The challenge is to manage to combine these different perspectives. This task can only be undertaken with the use of a sophisticated comparative law methodology.

Section II addresses independence concepts in Scandinavian administrative law and their relationship to European concepts. 'Independent Administrative Authorities' is not any precise term of statutory language in the Scandinavian countries. The independence of an authority in Scandinavian law depends primarily on the limitations placed on the powers of the central government in parliamentary legislation. The use of delegation of authority in such legislation can create a high degree of independence. Different recent OECD and EU processes provide material for fruitful comparison between the Scandinavian countries and between them and the emerging EU concepts and OECD categorizations.

Section III, on 'Independent Administrative Authorities and the Constitution, Head of State, Parliament and the Government (Executive)' sets out some of the different approaches in dealing with separation of powers and parliamentary control issues in the Scandinavian countries. Section IV discusses the legitimacy issues and independent administrative authorities. Section V gives an overview of who are the independent administrative authorities and what are their tasks. Section VI sets out the procedural rules that apply to the independent administrative authorities. In section VII is an overview provided over remedies against decisions by the independent administrative authorities. Finally in Section VIII, Conclusions, several core meanings of the independence concepts are set out.

## I. INDEPENDENT ADMINISTRATIVE AUTHORITIES IN COMPARATIVE LAW

This section sets out the case for studying independent administrative authorities in comparative law. At several levels of international law, administrative law is developing into the beginning of coherent disciplines or doctrines. In European Union law, there is a well-developed discipline of administrative law for the EU institutions. International and European human rights law set standards for administrative law at all these levels and also for national administrative law. Independence concepts are an important component at all these new levels of administrative law. In national law, independence is among the most universally live issues. New regulatory tasks have brought the development of independent administrative authorities to the fore as a matter of national law. The challenge is to manage to combine these different perspectives, and this is a task that only can be undertaken with the use of a sophisticated comparative law methodology. This is challenging, as there is not such method ready and developed, and its development has to take place in parallel with the collection of data.

### *A. The International Level: independence standards in an emerging international administrative law*

At an international level there are several developments that require a thorough look at independent administrative authorities in national law along the lines of this book. Principles of administrative law are developing in different corners of international law. One type of such principles set standards for national laws. The first issue is to determine how far these concepts go, and the next issue is the relationship with national law concepts. Independent administrative authorities have become an issue in world trade law, where in the WTO system the GATS agreement for trade in services sets certain standards for national administrative law, relating to the national regulator (for instance for telecommunications) and access to judicial remedies. This can be seen as requiring a certain standard of legality and fairness, and the minimum level of independence to secure this. The International Monetary Fund and the World Bank advocate independent monetary and regulatory authorities in different sectors.[6] The independence can here be seen to promote certain broad policies. However, with the narrow definition of targets (for instance to promote stability), or setting

[6] The foundation for an independent monetary authority, usually in central banks, was laid by the analysis of the time consistency problem: if economic policymakers lack the ability to commit in advance to a specific decision rule, they will often not implement the most desirable policy later on. Kydland and Prescott's research (which brought them the 2004 Nobel Prize in economics) shifted the practical discussion of economic policy away from isolated policy measures towards the institutions of policymaking, a shift that has largely influenced the reforms of central banks and the design of monetary policy in many countries in the 1980s and 1990s. See F Kydland and E Prescott 'Rules rather than discretion: The inconsistency of optimal plans' (1977) 85 Journal of Political Economy 473–90 and K Rogoff 'The optimal degree of precommitment to an intermediate monetary target' (1985) 18 Journal of International Economics 1169–90.

even more precisely defined targets for monetary policy, this will have greater similarities with the legality principles in the previous example. The Basel Core Principles for Effective Banking Supervision require a structure for the organization of banking supervision that is 'politically independent'.[7] These principles do not require independence from central banks but from the political authorities.[8] The most extensive international standard is developed by the International Association of Insurance Supervisors (IAIS).[9] The 'third international core principle', 'ICP 3 Supervisory authority', requires that the supervisory authority: (1) has adequate powers, legal protection and financial resources to exercise its functions and powers, (2) is operationally independent and accountable in the exercise of its functions and powers, (3) hires, trains and maintains sufficient staff with high professional standards, and, (4) treats confidential information appropriately. In the Explanatory Note it is stated that the supervisory authority should be 'operationally independent from external political and commercial interference in the exercise of its functions and powers'. It is further stated that:

> It is important to define the relationship between the supervisory authority and the executive and judicial branches, including processes for sharing information, consultation or approval with the relevant ministry and the manner in which the supervisory authority could be subject to judicial review. This might include establishing what information should be provided, how each entity should consult on matters of mutual interest and when approval from relevant ministries is necessary.

The IAIS principles have as one starting point that

> the supervisory authority must be fully empowered to achieve its objectives. The principle therefore covers the following essential elements relating to a supervisory authority: its legal basis, independence and accountability, powers, financial resources, human resources, legal protection and confidentiality.

They then point out that '[i]ndependence, accountability, transparency and integrity interact and reinforce each other.' For instance '[t][ransparency is a vehicle for safeguarding independence, ensuring accountability, and establishing and safeguarding integrity.' There should be provisions for the legal

[7] Core Principles for Effective Banking Supervision by the Basle Committee on Banking Supervision (1997): 'Principle 1: An effective system of banking supervision will have clear responsibilities and objectives for each agency involved in the supervision of banking organisations. Each such agency should possess operational independence.'

[8] This is another independence discussion: do central banking and banking supervision have to be kept separate, see M Andenas and L Panourgias 'Applied Monetary Policy and Bank Supervision by the ECB' in JJ Norton and M Andenas (eds) *International Monetary and Financial Law Upon Entering the New Millennium* (BIICL London 2003) 119–70 and M Andenas 'Who Is Going to Supervise Europe's Financial Markets' in M Andenas and Y Avgerinos (eds) *Financial Markets in Europe: Towards a Single Regulator* (Kluwer Law International The Hague 2003) xv–xxvi.

[9] The International Association of Insurance Supervisors (IAIS) *Insurance core principles,* approved in Singapore on 3 Oct 2003.

protection of staff, by which is not only meant job security but protection against criminal and tort liability. The general institutional independence is developed in this way: the supervisory authority should be 'operationally independent from external political and commercial interference in the exercise of its functions and powers'. The argument is that '[i]ndependence enhances the credibility and effectiveness of the supervisory process.' This makes it important to define the relationship between the supervisory authority and the executive and judicial branches, including processes for sharing information, consultation or approval with the relevant ministry and the manner in which the supervisory authority could be subject to judicial review.

In addition to the adequacy of the funding, the principles require independent management of the agency, that includes freedom in the agency's management of its internal finances.

The standards of the International Organization of Securities Commissions[10] state among the principles relating to the regulator that it 'should be operationally independent and accountable in the exercise of its functions and powers'. The regulator should be 'operationally independent from external political or commercial interference in the exercise of its functions'. However it is added that '[i]n some jurisdictions, particular matters of regulatory policy require consultation with, or even approval by, a government, minister or other authority.' Here,

> [t]he circumstances in which such consultation or approval is required or permitted should be clear and the process sufficiently transparent or subject to review to safeguard its integrity . . . generally, it is not appropriate for these circumstances to include decision making on day-to-day technical matters.

The requirement of adequate funding includes that '[t]he level of resourcing should recognize the difficulty of retaining experienced staff who have skills that are valuable to the private sector.'

The standards for independent administrative authorities in national law can be studied on the background of the standards applying to a level between traditional public international law and national law. Legitimacy, independence, accountability, transparency, and management of conflicts of interests are among the core areas of concern. In a recent paper B Kingsbury, N Krisch, and R Stewart set out a programme for analysing the emergence of global administrative law.[11] They consider the emergence and the need for further development of administrative law mechanisms to promote greater accountability in decision-making and rule-making for the

[10] *The Objectives and Principles of Securities Regulation* the International Organization of Securities Commissions (IOSCO 2003).

[11] B Kingsbury, N Krisch, and R Stewart *The Emergence of Global Administrative Law* IILJ Working Paper 2004/1 (Global Administrative Law Series NYU New York 2004).

wide range of global regulatory structures including formal international organizations such as the WTO, the Security Council, World Bank, the Climate Change regime, and informal intergovernmental networks of domestic regulatory officials such as the Basel Committee of national bank regulators. It also includes domestic authorities implementing global regulatory law, hybrid public–private and purely private transnational regulatory regimes. These regimes and subjects, they argue, are part of a single global administrative space distinct from the domains of international law and domestic administrative law. They identify a number of structural mechanisms that have arisen to develop and apply global administrative law, including domestic courts and legislatures reviewing domestic implementation of global standards and national officials' participation in global administrative decisions, and new mechanisms developed at the global level for governance of international and transnational regulatory bodies. They conclude that the field of global administrative law is an important emerging phenomenon, distinct from international law and from domestic administrative law, that deserves systematic study and development.

### *B. The EU: standards of independence for EU institutions and for domestic law*

In the European Union there is an emerging administrative law that applies to the EU institutions. This emerging EU administrative law also applies to member state authorities when EU competences or rights are involved. The starting point for EU administrative law, as part of an EU autonomous legal order, remains in the national administrative laws. There is a new literature that responds to the challenges to scholarship created by this interaction between domestic law reform, European Union law and European human rights law.[12]

Independence concepts have been at the core of EU law. They form an important part of the constitutional balance of the Treaty of Rome that the Commission, the Court of Auditors and Court of Justice have independence from the Council and Member States.

The independence of the European Central Bank (ECB) which was one of the central features of the Maastricht Treaty takes this further, and here the independence of the member state central banks (NCBs) provide a rich field for comparison.[13] Building further on the EMI's 1995 Convergence

[12] The emerging scholarship is, as one could expect, focusing on the bilateral dimension between one of the national jurisdictions and the EU one, see for instance S Kadelbach *Allgemeines Verwaltungsrecht unter europäischem Einfluß* (Tübingen 1999).

[13] Chapter II of the Maastricht Treaty set out several statutory requirements to be fulfilled for National Central Banks (NCBs) to become an integral part of the European System of Central Banks (ESCB). Art 7 of the EMI Statute laid down further detailed requirements. See

Report, the EMI in its 1996 Report established a list of features of central bank independence, distinguishing between features of an institutional, personal, functional and financial nature. In doing so, the EMI made several basic assumptions: Central bank independence is required when exercising the powers and carrying out the tasks and duties conferred upon the ECB and the NCBs by the Treaty and the Statute and features of central bank independence should therefore be considered from that perspective. Such features should not be seen as a kind of secondary Community legislation, going beyond the scope of the Treaty and the Statute, but as tools to facilitate an assessment of the independence of NCBs. Central bank independence is not a matter which can be expressed in arithmetical formulae or applied in a mechanical manner. The independence of individual NCBs should therefore be assessed on a case-by-case basis given that the institutional context in which NCBs operate differs from country to country. Whereas some provisions of the statutes of NCBs were clearly incompatible with the Treaty and the Statute, others could require further analysis before a final assessment can be made. The EMI then established different core components of the independence concept. This is set out in some detail here as it provided the basis for the review of the Danish, Finnish, and Swedish central banks.

First, institutional independence: The requirement of institutional independence is laid down in Article 107 of the Treaty as reproduced in Article 7 of the Statute. These Articles prohibit the ECB, the NCBs and members of their decision-making bodies from seeking or taking instructions from Community institutions or bodies, from any government of a Member State or from any other body. In addition, they also prohibit Community institutions and bodies and the governments of the Member States from seeking to influence the members of the decision-making bodies of the ECB or of those decision-making bodies of the NCBs whose decisions may have an impact on the fulfilment by the NCBs of their tasks in the European System of Central Banks (ESCB). Against this background, the EMI was of the opinion that the following rights of third parties (eg government, parliament) were incompatible with the Treaty and/or the Statute and therefore required adaptation: (a) a right to give instructions, (b) rights of third parties to give instructions to NCBs or their decision-making bodies, (c) a right to approve, suspend, annul or defer decisions as far as ESCB-related tasks are concerned, (d) a right to censor, on legal grounds, decisions relating to the performance of ESCB-related tasks is incompatible with the Treaty and the Statute as the performance of these tasks may not be

the review of the independence of the central banks of the member states in the reports leading up to Economic and Monetary Union, The European Monetary Institute *Progress Towards Convergence 1996* (EMI Frankfurt 1996) and *Progress Towards Convergence 1997* (EMI Frankfurt 1997).

obstructed at a national level. This was seen not only an expression of central bank independence but also of the more general requirement of the integration of NCBs in the ESCB. The EMI added that the statutes of several NCBs provided for a right of the Governor to censor decisions on legal grounds and subsequently submit them to political authorities for final decision. This would be equivalent to seeking instructions from political bodies, which is incompatible with Article 107 of the Treaty.

Secondly, personal independence: The EMI set out the following features of personal independence. (a) The statutes of NCBs must, in accordance with Article 14.2 of the ESCB Statute, contain a minimum term of office for a Governor of five years. This, of course, does not preclude longer terms of office, whilst an indefinite term of office does not require the adaptation of statutes if the grounds for the dismissal of a Governor are restrictive in line with those of Article 14.2 of the Statute. (b) NCB statutes must ensure that Governors may not be dismissed for reasons other than those mentioned in Article 14.2 of the Statute (ie no longer fulfilling the conditions required for the performance of his/her duties or being guilty of serious misconduct). The purpose of this requirement is to prevent the dismissal of a Governor from being at the discretion of the authorities involved in his/her appointment, particularly the government or parliament. As from the date of the establishment of the ESCB, statutes of NCBs should contain grounds for dismissal which are compatible with the European standards.

Thirdly, functional independence: NCBs operate in a framework whose objectives are determined by Article 105(1) of the Treaty (the core element of which is the primacy of maintaining price stability) and statutes of NCBs should unambiguously reflect this situation. This aspect of functional independence is also closely related to the integration of NCBs in the ESCB in general. In addition, under Article 14.4 of the Statute, an NCB may perform tasks and functions other than those related to the ESCB, unless these are deemed, by the Governing Council of the ECB, to interfere with the objectives and tasks of the ESCB. This should also be regarded as a feature of functional independence protecting the integrity of the system.

Fourthly, financial independence: If an NCB is fully independent from an institutional and functional point of view, but at the same time unable to avail itself autonomously of the appropriate economic means to fulfil its mandate, its overall independence would be undermined. NCBs should be in a position to avail themselves of the appropriate means to ensure that their ESCB-related tasks can be properly.

In Section II below, we return to the reforms in the Scandinavian countries as a consequence of the assessment that took place in the process leading up to EMU.

The Treaty provisions about central bank independence at the European level have already been subject of litigation and the European Court of Justice has contributed to give a fuller meaning to the concept.[14]

Independence in competition law enforcement is one of the other areas where independence concepts have been developed, and where the establishment of an independent administrative agency have been considered at a European level. The establishment and strengthening of the post as Hearing Officer with an independent role is one way of meeting independence and conflict of interest concerns.[15] The modernization of competition law enforcement began in 1999 with the publication of a White Paper on the modernization of the implementing rules of Articles 81 and 82 of the Treaty, suggesting a fundamental reform of Regulation No 17, which dated back to the 1960s. The new Regulation (EC) No 1/2003 required amendments of several national laws. National courts and national competition authorities got a more important role. The process did however not focus much on the independence of the national competition authorities but it has encouraged a development in this direction that was underway in many of the Member States.

The Commission's 2001 White Paper on European Governance and *The Better Regulation Action Plan* focus on openness, effectiveness and accountability. The decisions the Commission adopted in 2002 also comprised proposals on regulatory agencies and a further development of independence concepts.

There is no legal competence for the EU to harmonise the public administration in the member states. Nevertheless European policies impact on the national administrations. The harmonizing effects on the administrative law of the Member States of the emerging EU administrative law are considerable. Despite the fact of community influence, the prevailing view is still that 'the distribution of administrative powers in the European Union rests on the presumption that EU law is administered by member states which act autonomously' and that 'interference into that organizational autonomy is either punctual or indirect'.[16] This is a view that is more and more open to challenge.[17]

[14] Case C-11/00 *Commission v European Central Bank* [2003] ECR I-7147 ; Case C-15/00 *Commission v European Investment Bank* [2003] ECR 7231, see also the opinions in both cases by AG Jacobs.

[15] See most recently, Commission Decision of 23 May 2001 on the terms of reference of hearing officers in certain competition proceedings.

[16] See S Kadelbach 'European Administrative Law and the Law of a Europeanized Administration' in C Joerges and R Dehousse (eds) *Good Governance in an Integrated Market* Vol. XI, Book 2 of the Collected Courses of the Academy of European Law (2004).

[17] See, P Birkinshaw 'Does European Public Law Exist?' Queen's Papers on Europeanisation No 9/2001 (Belfast 2001). Professor Birkinshaw assesses whether such a thing as European Public Law exists and what forms it takes. He focuses on the mutual influence and inter-penetration of EC Law, the ECHR and domestic laws. He finds that there are similar developments

The development of general doctrines of EU law, such as direct effect of EU law in national legal systems and tort liability for breach of EU law, may have some bearing on the independence issues in national administration. Direct effect may facilitate the functioning of independent administrative bodies. Tort liability for sufficiently serious breaches of EU law, may go the other way if the liability rests with the Member State and not with the independent authority.[18]

The independence issues have been at the forefront in the field of utilities regulation and more generally in public supervision of markets and actors in the different public markets.[19] The convergence of the telecommunications, media and information technology sectors and the progressive move away from state monopolies in domestic telecommunications and electronic communications infrastructure and related services posed a significant regulatory challenge both at the domestic and the European level. The response adopted at Community level, known as 'the new regulatory framework', is dependent for its effectiveness on national regulatory authorities established by each Member State (NRAs). The NRAs are intended to be independent bodies that perform the tasks assigned to them with complete impartiality.[20] Under the relevant Community legislation, the Member States are to confer upon the NRAs extensive powers ranging from general powers (such as the power to assess the market and determine whether or not an operator has significant market power) to specific powers (such as the powers to adopt interim relief in cases of urgency or to resolve a particular dispute between undertakings providing electronic communications networks or services in a Member State).[21]

occurring in all Member States concerning the influence of European Law and laws on domestic systems of law in Europe and vice versa. His conclusion is that such a phenomenon as European Public Law is emerging. His journal, *European Public Law* (Kluwer Law International), provides running documentation for this phenomenon at a high level. See also *European Principles for Public Administration* SIGMA Papers No 27 (OECD 1998) 5; and M Andenas 'The Common Law of Europe and the Public Law of the Common Law' in M Andenas *English Public Law and the Common Law of Europe* (Key Haven Publishing London 1998) 1–8, and M Andenas and D Fairgrieve 'Sufficiently Serious? Judicial Restraint in Tortious Liability for Public Authorities and the European Influence' in M Andenas *English Public Law and the Common Law of Europe* (Key Haven Publishing London 1998) 285–326.

18 See *Det allmännas skadeståndsansvar vid överträdelse av EG-regler* Justitiedepartementet, Betänkande av Utredningen med uppdrag att analysera frågan om det allmännas skadeståndsansvar, Statens offentliga utredningar (SOU) SOU 1997:194.

19 See Recommendation of the Council of the OECD on 'Improving the Quality of Government Regulation' (1995).

20 Directive 2002/21/EC of the European Parliament and the Council (OJ 2002 No. L108/33), Art 3.

21 See Directive 2002/19/EC of the European Parliament and of the Council (OJ 2002 No L108/7); Directive 2002/20/EC of the European Parliament and of the Council (OJ 2002 No L108/21); Directive 2002/21 (above); Directive 2002/22/EC of the European Parliament and of the Council (OJ 2002 No L108/51). Directive 2002/58/EC of the European Parliament and of the Council (OJ 2002 No L201/37), which is counted among the legislative measures form-

The package of rail transport directives from 2002 includes a directive that covers capacity allocation, charging and safety certification.[22] It is another example in European legislation of the use of independence requirements with address to national administrations. One of its main features is that it requires each member state to establish a regulatory body. This has to be independent of any infrastructure manager, charging body, allocation body or applicant. The directive requires that it is independent in its organisation, legal structure, funding and in its decision making. Decisions taken by the Regulatory Body shall be subject to judicial review.

There is presently a wider discussion of the transfer from a welfare state model to a regulatory state model where the establishment of an independent agency has become a standard institutional response in particular to dealing with the regulation of markets. There are two distinct literatures emerging, the analysis of regulatory regimes and the literature of Europeanization. A recent survey by M Lodge shows differences in European approaches where the British political process go further than any of the other countries in the survey in relying on the agency model, closely followed by Ireland and Sweden.[23] In Germany the dominating response, supported by the ordo-liberals, has remained highly sceptical of the value of more than temporary sectoral regulatory agencies. Independence issues were one of fields where the main differences were found. In Germany there was a far more hierarchical understanding of the role of the regulator (subordinate to the policy-making functions of the ministry). This was also expressed in the approach taken in Council working groups. In Britain, agencies took on, within political constraints, a more entrepreneurial role. In Britain the regulator still remained at the mercy of the individual minister, while in Ireland, the appointment procedure to some extent increased the distance between minister and regulator by relying on the civil service appointment commission. M Lodge argues that with regard to the Europeanization process, rather than studying change incurred due to the application of a single set of EU provisions or the shift of policy competence (in the legal sense) to the EU level, Europeanisation processes can also include broader shifts in policy instruments, which might be less related to 'EUisation' but occur through more diffuse processes of vertical 'Europeanization'. In line with institutionalist assumptions, Lodge's study did not reveal a convergence towards a single approach to establishing the 'consumer sovereignty' that underlies for

ing the new regulatory framework, is not concerned with the powers of the NRAs. The three powers referred to in the text are set out in Directive 2002/21: see Arts 14–16 (the function of analysing the market in order to decide whether or not an operator has significant market power is provided for in, for example, Art 6 of Directive 2002/19), 7(6) and 20, respectively.

[22] Directive 2001/14/EC.

[23] M Lodge 'From Varieties of the Welfare State to Convergence of the Regulatory State? The 'Europeanisation' of Regulatory Transparency ' Queen's Papers on Europeanisation, No 10/2001 (Belfast 2001).

instance US competition policy and is becoming more and more dominating in general EU competition policy. The initial differences both in the starting points of the 'welfare state', and in terms of domestic regulatory reform strategies, makes this unsurprising.[24]

### *C. European human rights law and independence concepts*

Another important European influence on administrative law derives from the European Convention on Human Rights. Article 6 ECHR requires that any determination of civil rights and obligations shall be by an independent and impartial tribunal. This has an impact on national administrative procedural law and on the availability and intensity of judicial review. The procedures before the European Court of Human Rights have developed the independence concepts and applied them on national laws. The administrative procedures of all the Scandinavian countries have been censured by the ECtHR, primarily in finding that the administrative procedures in place did not satisfy the independence requirements. Extensive Swedish reform of the administrative court system and of the powers of criminal courts has been undertaken to comply with the ECHR. The Norwegian system of review of psychiatric detention has also been censured and lead to reforms.

There is a rich ECtHR case law in different fields, for instance for planning procedures. The ECtHR has recognized the variation between the laws of the Member States but laid down certain minimum standards for compliance with Article 6 ECHR. The concern here was originally with private law rights but the case law has expanded the reach to cover regulatory intervention. An independent and impartial tribunal can be part of an administrative process. It can be remedied by the availability of judicial review. The requirements of this review are contested.[25]

### *D. OECD and regulatory policies*

OECD's work on regulatory policies has much interest, also because it has been accompanied by parallel studies in many of its member countries. It attempts to draw general conclusions and is of assistance in developing

24 See the overview in M Lodge 'Administrative Patterns and National Politics' in B Peters and J Pierre (eds) *Handbook of Public Administration* (J Sage London 2003); K Dyson and KH Goetz (eds) *Germany and Europe: A 'Europeanized' Germany?* (Oxford University Press/British Academy Oxford 2003); and M Lodge 'Explaining Institutional Choice and Policy Transfer: The Case of British and German Railway Reform.' (2003) Governance 16, no 2 159–78.

25 See *R (Alconbury Ltd) v Environment Secretary* [2003] 2 AC 295 where the English planning procedures were held by the UK House of Lords to comply with the ECHR. This is contested, see M Andenas and L Busch (eds) *Policy-Making and Decision-Taking: Administrative Law After Alconbury* (BIICL London 2005).

more general independence concepts. In the 2002 Report *Regulatory Policies in OECD Countries—From Interventionism to Regulatory Governance*[26] it is concluded that independent regulatory authorities represent progress compared with leaving the regulatory functions in the ministries or central government department.

The general argument in the 2002 Report is that in the rise of regulatory policies, explicit policies aimed at continuously improving the quality of the regulatory environment, early notions of 'deregulation' or 'cutting red tape' gave way to a central 'good governance' notion. This notion is based on an understanding of how regulatory practices can substantially improve market performance, public sector effectiveness and citizens' satisfaction, through a mix or deregulation, re-regulation and better quality regulation, backed up by new or improved institutions. Independence concepts are at the heart of the institutional reform process. Specialised and independent authorities enable quicker, more responsive and better decision making, with increased transparency and predictability.

The 2002 Report also raises the problems with sectoral regulatory authorities which may slow down structural developments. It points out the problems with regulatory capture and democratic accountability that must be remedied by procedures and transparency.

Denmark was among several OECD countries to request a broad review by the OECD of its national regulatory practices and domestic regulatory reforms. The OECD review[27] concluded that Danish regulatory reform had proceeded with many pragmatic steps that had contributed to solid economic performance, management of economic and social adjustment to changing conditions, and improved efficiency of government services. However, sheltered sectors, including service industries, still suffered from cooperation and price fixing, contributing to high consumer prices. The competition regime is weaker than in many other countries, and so were regulatory regimes in areas such as energy. The organisation of the regulatory authorities and their lack of independence were among the critical points made. The policy recommendations presented a plan of action for both short and longer-term based on best international regulatory practices.

OECD reporting on national regulatory practices and domestic regulatory reforms takes place in several other contexts. Finland has attracted criticism as in addition to having generally limited independence, the powers of Finnish regulatory agencies are seen to be too limited. This applies both to rule-making and enforcement. Regulation and policy development are also usually responsibilities of line ministries, though regulators may be consulted.

[26] OECD Paris 2002.

[27] *Regulatory Reform in Denmark* (OECD Paris 2000).

The different OECD documents contribute to the development of independence concepts but have not established any general concept of an independent regulatory or administrative authority. The three basic categories used in OECD work are helpful but not legally well defined. They are: (1) the ministerial department is a regulator established within a Ministry and without any substantial degree of independence. (2) A ministerial agency has a separate budget and operates at arms' length from the relevant ministry, but is ultimately subject to ministerial direction. (3) An independent regulatory body has a generally more substantial degree of independence from ministerial direction, although the extent of this varies considerably across different bodies.[28]

### E. *The Role of Comparative Scholarship*

In the emerging body of scholarship in European administrative law, the pioneer work of J Schwarze[29] has a special place. The insights of this work have been taken further in a broad range of studies, continuing the analysis of both national and European administrative law.[30]

There are highly disparate doctrines and conceptual frameworks in the different systems. Contrary to what is often stated, usually by private lawyers but sometimes even by public lawyers, comparative public law has rich traditions both as scholarship and its application in law reform.[31] Scholarship has generally been limited by its practical application, usually serving the domestic law reform process. So it should be surprising that when new needs require European concepts they are simply not there. For our purpose, looking at independent administrative authorities, it is significant that there is no concept of administration or administrative authority that can lay claim to any general validity in the member states of the European Union.[32] There is certainly no universal concept of independent administrative authority.

28 See PUMA/REG: PUMA/REG (2001)12 and another study by IEA, *Regulatory Institutions in Liberalised Electricity Market* (OECD Paris 2001).

29 J Schwarze *European Administrative Law* (Sweet & Maxwell London 1992) is perhaps the most important outcome of this pioneer work for our purposes.

30 G della Cananea *Beyond the State: The Europeanization and Globalization of Procedural Administrative Law* (2003) 9 Eur Pub L 563 See also the reference to S Kadelbach *Allgemeines Verwaltungsrecht unter europäischem Einfluß* (Tübingen 1999) above, focusing on the relationship between German administrative law and EU law.

31 M Andenas 'Amending Constitutions: An Introduction' in M Andenas (ed) *The Creation and Amendment of Constitutional Norms* (BIICL London 2001) ix.

32 See J Schwarze *European Administrative Law* (Sweet & Maxwell London 1992) 19–20. EU law has dealt with what constitutes public authority in the EC Treaty derogation allowing reserving certain kinds of employment to own nationals. This illustrated many divergences in the national systems and one kind of problems that follow from this. See J Schwarze *European Administrative Law* 20–1. It has however not contributed much towards the creation of a European concept of public administration for other purposes.

A study of independence concepts is of merit, not only as it will throw light on the concept of what constitutes administration or administrative authority. European Union law, European Human Rights law and national administrative law are dealing with problems of developing the legal framework for independent administrative authorities in many different contexts. As is often the case, comparison is limited to a binary or bilateral perspective (two countries, one country and the EU, etc) and the challenge is to capture the many different dimensions that form the legal reality.

## II. INDEPENDENCE CONCEPTS IN SCANDINAVIAN ADMINISTRATIVE LAW AND THEIR RELATIONSHIP TO EUROPEAN CONCEPTS

'Independent Administrative Authorities' is not a term of statutory language with any precise meaning in the Scandinavian countries. It is well known in the administrative law scholarship, and also in the social sciences but has not found its way into the statute book. In United States administrative law, the labelling by Congress of an agency as 'independent', has a number of consequences.[33] Other countries, such as in recent Italian practice, make use of terms such as 'independent authority' that is similar to that in the US.

That an administrative body is described as 'independent' may only signify that it is not part of the organization of a ministry of state. It may otherwise be fully integrated in the state administration, under the authority and control of the minister.

The independence of an authority in Scandinavian law, depends primarily on the limitations placed on the powers of the central government in parliamentary legislation. The central government's delegation of authority in such legislation can create a high degree of independence.

### A. *'Independence' in Scandinavian Administrative Law*

Under the Swedish Constitution, *Regeringsformen* (RF), Chapter 11, judicial authority is exercised by the courts, and administrative authority by state and local authorities.

[33] 'Independence' here signifies independence from the President and the Executive. It does not mean that there are no controls on the agency: numerous and powerful controls remain. Congress imposes other forms of control, and there would also be judicial review. In other contexts, independence would limit the forms of interference that the legislature can impose. See, for instance, the independence requirements for national central banks in the European System of Central Banks (ESCB) where for instance Sweden and Finland had to amend their legislation to secure the independence from the legislator. The separation of powers doctrine will in most countries also limit what the legislature can do in relation to the exercise of judicial powers, and now this is reinforced by due process requirements in international and human rights law.

They are the public authorities, 'myndigheter'. The Norwegian and Danish constitutions have similar provisions about the branches of government and about the executive branch of the government. The independence issues are dealt with in different ways.

One of the common features is that in all the Nordic countries there are extensive protections for civil servants. Irremovability or security of tenure for most categories of senior civil servants was established in the 18th century. It was entrenched in the Swedish Constitution of 1809 (RF Article 36) and is preserved in the present constitution. In the Norwegian Constitution of 1814, *Grunnloven*, a similar provision is found in Article 22 which still applies.

The nature of the hierarchical structure of the public administration varies between the Scandinavian countries. Their origins have much in common. By the middle of the 19th century, superior bodies for instance a ministry or department of state) could not in general direct inferior bodies about their exercise of discretionary powers, and the superior body could in general not revoke the decisions of the inferior bodies. There was no general right of complaint or appeal, for instance to the ministry or department of state. The hierarchical system of the present administration, and the general right of appeal, developed gradually.[34]

In Scandinavian administrative law are discussed these four distinctions between different ways that the superior authority can exercise its authority: (1) through rule making, (2) through instructions about decisions in individual matters (before they are made), (3) through overturning decisions on the initiative of the superior authority itself, or, (4) through overturning decisions on appeal from a party to the decision. The Swedish system differs from the others in that only rule making, (1), and overturning on appeal, (4), are open to the superior authority when an individual or local authority is party to the decision. In Swedish administrative law instructions about the application of the law, or decisions in individual matters, (2), and overturning decisions on the initiative of the superior authority itself, (3), are not open as ways of exercising authority which they are in Denmark and Norway. In Sweden, the way of administrative appeal is usually not open when there is a right of judicial review by way of complaint to the administrative courts.

The Swedish Constitution (Chapter 11, Article 7 § RF) provides that the administrative authorities—in this respect to be distinguished from the courts of law—are subject to the authority of the central government. The administrative authorities are the instruments of the central government in governing the country. The central government can therefore instruct other

[34] HP Graver *Alminnelig forvaltningsrett* (2nd edn Universitetsforlaget Oslo 2002) 176 on the Norwegian system.

public authorities about decisions, also in individual matters. This is the authority that is limited when an individual or local authority is party to the decision, or when it concerns the application of the law. (A parallel limitation applies in the relation to local representative bodies and local administrative bodies.) This is referred to as the independence of administrative authorities. It is seen as an important guarantee for the rule of law.

The independence of administrative authorities and its value as a guarantee for the rule of law in Sweden has been challenged both by political scientists and in administrative law scholarship.[35] The case has been made that although different in principle, the Swedish system and the other Scandinavian systems are not so different in practice. Governments hand over, by necessity, decision making without any effective supervision in all countries. At the same time, the Swedish government has undermined the freedom the Constitution provides for. The government's interpretation of the Constitution's provisions on independence has been increasingly restrictive (in disfavour of independence) in the last 20 to 25 years.

As mentioned above, that an administrative body is described as 'independent' may only signify that it is not part of the formal organization of a ministry of state. It may otherwise be fully integrated in the state administration, under the authority and control of the minister. At the same time, departments within a ministry of state, may have a high degree of autonomy. Legal advisers usually are seen to have a high degree of independence in the sense that their legal advice will not be overturned and usually acted upon. Other bodies with specialist competence may also have developed a similar position.

### *B. Testing Independence: due process under European human rights law*

In Section I above is already discussed the important European influence on administrative law deriving from the European Convention on Human Rights. Article 6 ECHR requires that any determination of civil rights and obligations shall be by an independent and impartial tribunal. This has an impact on national administrative procedural law and on the availability and intensity of judicial review. The procedures before the European Court of Human Rights have developed the independence concepts and applied them on national laws. The administrative procedures of all the Scandinavian countries have been censured by the ECtHR, primarily in finding that the administrative procedures in place did not satisfy the independence requirements.

[35] See critical assessments in T Bull 'Självständighet och pluralism' in *Festskrift till Fredrik Sterzel* (Stockholm 1999), H Ragnemalm in [1986] Förvaltningsrättslig tidskrift 1–13 and B Wennergren, Den svenska modellen och grundlagen in [1998] Förvaltningsrättslig tidskrift 97–119.

Extensive Swedish reform of the administrative court system has been undertaken to comply with the ECHR. These include bringing the administrative courts closer to the ordinary courts in terms of procedures, not dissimilar from the process in most other European countries with separate administrative courts such as France and Germany, and of the powers of criminal courts, bringing detention issues from the independent prosecutor to the courts.

The Norwegian system of review of psychiatric detention has also been censured and this has resulted in reforms.

### C. Testing independence: in the central banks

In Section I above is also the independence of the European Central Bank discussed. This was one of the central features of the Maastricht Treaty. The independence of the member state central banks provides a rich field for comparison. The Treaty provisions about central bank independence have already been subject of litigation and the European Court of Justice has contributed to give fuller meaning to the concept.[36] Chapter II of the Maastricht Treaty set out several statutory requirements to be fulfilled for National Central Banks (NCBs) to become an integral part of the European System of Central Banks (ESCB). The reports according to Treaty Article 109j assessed the Nordic EU member state central banks' compliance with the independence requirements.[37] This resulted in reform of the central bank legislation, and provides an interesting analysis of the different independence mechanisms in the European and national systems. Norway is not an EU member states, and it has maintained a system of central bank independence which clearly would not satisfy the convergence criteria. Denmark was in particular position having a derogation from joining the European and Monetary Union but was nonetheless subject to full review of the independence of its domestic central bank.[38]

The statute of *Danmarks Nationalbank* is contained in the National Bank of Denmark Act of 1936 with later amendments. The Bank is a self-governing institution, its profits after allocations falling to the State.

[36] Case C-11/00 *Commission v European Central Bank* [2003] ECR I-7147; Case C-15/00 *Commission v European Investment Bank* [2003] ECR 7231, see also the opinions in both cases by AG Jacobs.

[37] The European Monetary Institute *Progress Towards Convergence 1996* (EMI Frankfurt 1996) and *Progress Towards Convergence 1997* (EMI Frankfurt 1997).

[38] In relation to the application of Article 107 of the Treaty on central bank independence and Article 108 of the Treaty on the adaptation of national legislation and the statutes of NCBs, the Treaty and the Statute do not make a distinction between Member States with and without a derogation. A derogation implies that the respective NCB retains its powers in the field of monetary policy and participates in the ESCB on a restrictive basis until the date at which the Member State joins Monetary Union.

Authority for monetary policy rests with the Board of Governors, including setting interest rates and deciding on other monetary policy instruments. This includes the tasks of fixing the discount rate and rates on advances, folio account and current account, the issuing of bank promissory notes and the purchase and sale of securities. The Board of Governors has full freedom in formulating and implementing monetary policy.

In Finland monetary policy is determined independently by the Central Bank. The Act did and does not any longer impose any requirement on the Bank to negotiate monetary policy decisions beforehand with the Government. The Minister of Finance may not attend meetings of the Board nor veto any monetary policy decisions taken by the Bank. The Bank is independent in the use of its monetary policy instruments (open market operations, credit operations, minimum reserves). The decision-making procedure regarding changes in the external value of the *markka* is defined in the Currency Act. Under the Currency Act, the Council of State (Government) takes decisions on the external value of the *markka* on a proposal by the Bank. The Parliamentary Supervisory Council decides whether to make such a decision.

In Finland and Sweden inconsistencies with the Treaty and Statute required amendment of the central bank legislation. In Finland, the inconsistencies mainly concerned, as far as institutional independence is concerned, the role of the Parliamentary Supervisory Council. As far as personal independence is concerned, they concerned the security of tenure of the Governor and other members of the Board. Furthermore, as far as functional independence was concerned, the statute of the Bank did not unambiguously reflect the primacy of maintaining price stability. The Finnish legislator acknowledged the need for reform. Draft amending legislation was submitted for consultation to the EMI in 1996 and the EMI delivered its opinion on shortly afterwards.[39] The draft legislation mainly concerned the neutralisation of the role of the Parliamentary Supervisory Council in monetary policy matters and an explicit reference to the minimum term of office for the Governor and the grounds for his/her dismissal as laid down in Article 14.2 of the Statute. This security of tenure was extended to the other members of the Bank's Board as well. The draft legislation incorporated in the Bank's statute the prohibition on public financing laid down in Article 104 of the Treaty.

*Sveriges Riksbank* was also singled out for attention in the EMI 1997 Convergence Report. This was done in connection with the obligation under Article 108 of the Treaty to remove inconsistencies with the Treaty and the Statute also applies to legislation other than the statutes of NCBs if such other legislation has an effect on central bank independence. The

[39] 13 May 1996 (CON/96/5).

example taken was the Swedish Constitution which contained provisions on the status of *Sveriges Riksbank* and the members of its Governing Board 'which might have to be adapted to the requirements of the Treaty, or otherwise developed in ordinary legislation in a manner compatible with it'. In 1998 the new *Riksbank* legislation was approved. It was not uncontroversial.

The statute of *Sveriges Riksbank* is contained in the Constitution, the *Riksdag* Act and the *Sveriges Riksbank* Act (1988: 1385) as amended. The Bank is an institution organised under public law, with full responsibility for the formulation and implementation of monetary policy. The 1998 reform responded to EMI's objections.

The Riksbank Act specified the available policy instruments, but the use of these instruments was determined exclusively by the Bank. The major inconsistency in the Swedish Constitution and the Bank's statute with Treaty and Statute requirements for central bank independence pointed out in the EMI 1997 Convergence Report was the obligation for the Bank to consult the Minister of Finance on decisions of major importance. This provided for an explicit statutory mechanism to influence such decisions, thus infringing the requirement of central bank independence.

The EMI 1997 Convergence Report also had objections to the personal independence. The minimum term of office of five years should be extended to all members of the Governing Board. Also, grounds for dismissal should be brought into line with the Maastricht standard. A final controversial point concerning personal independence was the appointment of members of Parliament as members of the Bank's Governing Board. This, in the EMI's view, provided a clear potential for conflicts of interest between their duties vis-à-vis the Bank and the interests of their electorate. Simultaneous membership of Parliament and the Governing Board was deemed to be incompatible with the principle of central bank independence. Sveriges Riksbank had added, in a footnote to the EMI Report, a protest: it remained of the opinion that membership of Parliament does not in itself entail conflicts of interest and is therefore not incompatible with simultaneous membership of the Bank's Governing Board.

As far as functional independence is concerned, the statute of the Bank did not unambiguously reflect the primacy of maintaining price stability.

As amendments to the Constitution require the endorsement of two consecutive Parliaments, it took time, and it also requires a supermajority.

Norway has been left behind. In Norway a parallel system to the previous Swedish one is based the 1985 Act on *Norges Bank* and the Monetary System, and this remains in force. Norway is not an EU member state and is not required to reform as the other countries. Section 2, Relationship to the government authorities, provides that 'before the Bank makes any decision of special importance, the matter shall be submitted to the ministry. . . . The

King in Council may adopt resolutions regarding the operations of the Bank. Such resolutions may take the form of general rules or instructions in individual cases. The Bank shall be given the opportunity to state its opinion before such resolutions are passed. The *Storting* shall be notified of resolutions as soon as possible.' This means that instructions to the central bank can only be given by a formal government decision, made by the Cabinet of ministers, in the name of the King.

To the discussion of *Sveriges Riksbank* should be added that the Swedish National Debt Office is one of the oldest institutions with independence in the monetary field.

The Swedish National Debt Office was established in 1789 to give *Sveriges Riksdag*, the Swedish Parliament, control over the central government debt. Sweden was in the middle of a (yet another) war against Russia initiated by Gustav III. After a legislative amendment in 1786, the King could no longer order *Sveriges Riksbank* to print more paper money. To finance the war, the Swedish National Debt Office issued promissory notes called *riksgälds*. Despite the *Riksdag*'s attempts, the King continued to exercise influence over the Debt Office up until his death in 1792, when he was assassinated at the Opera.[40] The *Riksbank*'s *riksdaler* could be redeemed for silver and the Riksbank was obliged to keep an amount of silver equivalent to at least two-thirds of the amount of paper money in circulation. The Swedish National Debt Office had no such limitation. After Gustav's death, the Swedish National Debt Office was completely exempted from any formal influence by the King or the executive and put under parliamentary control.

### *D. Market supervision: OECD and EU review*

Independence for competition regulators and utilities regulators have been actively discussed in the all the Nordic countries. Competition regulation and enforcement has been reformed, partly in response to EU developments as discussed in Section I above. This also applies to utilities regulation and to some extent to market supervision in general.

As mentioned in Section I above, Denmark was among several OECD countries to request a broad review by the OECD of its national regulatory practices and domestic regulatory reforms. The OECD review[41] concluded that Danish regulatory reform had proceeded with many pragmatic steps that had contributed to solid economic performance, management of economic and social adjustment to changing conditions, and improved efficiency of government services. However, sheltered sectors, including service

[40] A romanticized version of the assassination is found in Verdi's *Un ballo in mascara.*

[41] *Regulatory Reform in Denmark* (OECD Paris 2000)

industries, still suffered from cooperation and price fixing, contributing to high consumer prices. The competition regime is weaker than in many other countries, and so were regulatory regimes in areas such as energy. The organization of the regulatory authorities and their lack of independence were among the critical points made. The policy recommendations presented a plan of action for both short and longer-term based on best international regulatory practices.

OECD reporting on national regulatory practices and domestic regulatory reforms takes place in several other contexts. Finland has attracted criticism as in addition to having generally limited independence, the powers of Finnish regulatory agencies are seen to be too limited. This applies both to rule-making and enforcement. Regulation and policy development are also usually responsibilities of line ministries, though regulators may be consulted.

All the Nordic countries have recently undertaken broader domestic reviews of their national regulatory practices. They develop the requirement of independent regulators and review the existing institutions. The Swedish review concludes that the existing regulators generally satisfy the requirements.[42] The Review does not consider any major constitutional challenges. It makes reference to a number of parallel reviews of different regulators in areas with EU requirements to independence. In a Norwegian 2003 Government White Paper with a similar remit,[43] there is a more extensive discussion of the constitutional issues that regulatory authority independence can give rise to (see below under the next section, section III, of this chapter).

## III. INDEPENDENT ADMINISTRATIVE AUTHORITIES AND THE CONSTITUTION, HEAD OF STATE, PARLIAMENT, AND THE GOVERNMENT (EXECUTIVE)

In this section independent administrative authorities are discussed in the context of separation of powers under the Constitution, and their relationship to the Head of State, the Parliament and the Government (Executive).

The separation of powers doctrine is expressed in all the Scandinavian constitutions. The Swedish and Danish constitutions are modern texts, and drafted so they to different degrees reflect a modern parliamentarian system. The text of the Norwegian Constitution of 1814 has not taken account of the introduction of a parliamentary system in the late 19th century. As an extension of the separation of powers, the independence of parliament and courts from the executive is guaranteed in different ways.

42 SOU 2004:100 *Tillsyn. Förslag om en tydligare och effektivare tillsyn.*
43 St meld nr 17 (2002–3).

Independence of civil servants is guaranteed in different ways as described in the previous section. There are no general provisions on independent administrative authorities.

The Scandinavian constitutions provide for certain independent administrative authorities of long standing, such as the Swedish Ombudsman and Foreign Debt Office. The Scandinavian constitutions have found different solutions in many respects. This also applies to the main national audit institution but after a recent Swedish reform all three countries have a parliamentary audit service.

The independence of the central banks are now reflected in the constitutions of Sweden and Finland.

### A. *Separation of powers, the Head of State, Parliament and the Courts*

The national audit services are the most important state agency reporting to Parliament and operating independently from the Executive. The Office of the Auditor General (established in 1816) is the Norwegian supreme audit institution and the supervisory body of the Norwegian parliament, the *Storting*, and has the status of an agency that is independent of the Norwegian government and public administration. The main task of the Office of the Auditor General is to monitor that public assets are used and administered according to sound financial principles and in keeping with the decisions and intentions of the *Storting*. The National Audit Office of Denmark is also organizationally placed under the *Folketing*. The new Swedish *Riksrevisionen* or National Audit Office replaced *Riksrevisionsverket* and the Parliamentary Auditors in 2003. All three Scandinavian national audit institutions are seen as a substantial part of the system of parliamentary control, the new SAI will have an important role in the democratic system. Their independence in the performance of their duties is clearly stated and linked to the goal of maintaining standards of impartiality and objectivity in their approach when undertaking examinations.

The Scandinavian parliaments have their own internal administration which is independent of the executive.

This has to some extent also been developed for the courts. The traditional focus on independence of courts has been in the exercise of judicial authority. Judicial appointments and discipline in relation to the judiciary bring up other issues. Recently the appointments system, but also the internal administration of the court system, including the financial management, has been reformed to secure judicial independence. Denmark (1999) and Norway (2002) have introduced new court services, organized as independent agencies. The Swedish court service agency, as established in the 1970, does not have any special status in the Swedish system. But as discussed under Section II above, Swedish agencies cannot be instructed in individual cases.

The independence issues have been a matter of some discussion in the prosecution service. This is seen as an administrative service with certain particular features. In all the countries the prosecution service enjoys a high degree of independence. In the Norwegian system, the prosecutors can only be given instructions by the political authorities in the form of a formal government decision, made by the Cabinet of ministers, in the name of the King. See a similar procedure for the central bank, *Norges Bank,* under Section II, above, but the prosecutor has no duty to submit any matter to the ministry in the way that *Norges Bank* has. Such a formal government decision has never been made. In Denmark, the Ministry of Justice can directly give instructions without any similar formal procedures. This is, however, supposed to have occurred very rarely if ever.[44]

The Monarch or Head of State has a separate court administration and is not subject to any formal review by the executive or legislature. The annual budget appropriations provide some measure of control. The Head of State has no role in appointments for independent administrative authorities or the judiciary as in some other countries.

### *B. Parliamentary control and independent authorities*

When the Swedish review concluded that the existing regulators generally satisfy the requirements to independence,[45] this can be understood on the background of the high degree of independence that the government authorities or agencies traditionally have had from the central government in Sweden. This also can account for the way in which the review did not consider any major constitutional challenges as a consequence of a further development of independence. This applies also to the approach taken to this issue in the number of parallel reviews of different regulators in areas with EU requirements to independence.

The Norwegian 2003 Government White Paper with a similar remit,[46] and its more extensive discussion of the constitutional issues that regulatory authority independence can give rise to, deals with a different tradition. Previous doctrine distinguished between general instructions and instructions about the decision in an individual matter. Current doctrine looks at whether the decision is made by a collegiate body with special technical or local competence or other qualities that can determine independence.[47]

The relationship to the Article 3 of the Norwegian Constitution,

[44] M Andenas *Independence and Efficiency: A Comparative Study of Prosecuting Services* (BIICL/Asian Development Bank London/Manila 2000).

[45] SOU 2004:100 *Tillsyn. Förslag om en tydligare och effektivare tillsyn.*

[46] St meld nr 17 (2002–3).

[47] See HP Graver *Alminnelig forvaltningsrett* (2nd edn Universitetsforlaget Oslo 2002) 178 and T Eckhoff *Forvaltningsrett* (6th edn by E Smith Tanum Oslo 2002) 180.

*Grunnloven (1814)*, about the King having the executive power, has been considered over the years on a number of occasions. The limitations that independence could have for parliamentary control is also discussed in all the Nordic countries. The modern hierarchical form of government administration is relatively new in Scandinavia. As mentioned above, by the middle of the 19th century, a ministry or department of state could not in general direct the authorities reporting to it in other ways about their exercise of discretionary powers, and the ministry could in general not revoke the decisions of the inferior bodies. There was no general right of complaint or appeal, for instance to the ministry or department of state. The hierarchical system of the present administration and the general right of appeal developed gradually. This hierarchical system provided the basis for parliamentary control. When this was established, independent authorities and other ways of organizing public administration, for instance trough state owned companies, could limit or circumvent parliamentary control.

In 1977 the Norwegian Parliament made a formal decision of principle that:

> The principle is that the King or the Ministries of State shall have the right to direct and control other public bodies. If in statute or other decision by parliament the right to direct and control other public bodies is limited, this must be justified in special considerations.[48]

In Norway, state owned companies and other forms of separate incorporation were critically reviewed in the aftermath of this decision. Usually the Minister of State would constitute the shareholders' meeting where the state owned 100 pct and this would satisfy the requirements of the parliamentary decision.[49] Large parts of public activity is organized through special state companies or companies incorporated under the general companies legislation, for instance mail services, telecommunications, railways and in Norway there is also the state oil company. I all these fields there are potential conflicts between the state's management of its direct involvement and the regulatory tasks.

In the Norwegian 2003 Government White Paper parliamentary control was however not considered to be any issue any longer for the forms of independent market regulation that was reviewed there.

A most recent discussion on independence of a market regulatory authority concerns the Norwegian Competition Authority. Here the

[48] Stort forh 1977 4077. This decision followed the recommendation of a commission, NOU 1972: 38 Stortingets kontroll med forvaltningen mv (Ingvaldsenutvalget), and the parliamentary committee, Innst S nr 277 (1976–7). See HP Graver Alminnelig forvaltningsrett (2nd edn Universitetsforlaget Oslo 2002) 178.

[49] J Andenas Statsforfatningen i Norge (8th edn Tanum Oslo 1998) 235.

Competition Act[50] decides that the Authority cannot be instructed about its decisions in individual matters. The political authorities can however order the Authority to review a matter but this instruction by the political authorities will have to be in the form of a formal government decision, made by the Cabinet of ministers, in the name of the King. See (A) about the similar procedures for the central bank, *Norges Bank,* under section II, above, and for the Norwegian prosecution authorities, under (A) above in this section.

One consideration has been that a government body may have specialist competence but that certain general considerations are better decided at a political level. Instances mentioned are mergers and the competition authority and discharges and the pollution control authority.[51] One view has been that it is more transparent if the specialist authority makes decisions on narrow grounds, based on its expertise and mandate, and that the general good or other general considerations are undertaken by the ministry or central government. This can clarify when politician discretion has been exercised, and allow for a more effective accountability.

The Stock Exchange Appeals Tribunal is a recent instance of the establishment of a judicialisation of the administrative process. The Appeals Tribunal's decisions cannot be overturned by or appealed to the Ministry which previously dealt with all appeals from the Stock Exchanges.[52]

## IV. THE LEGITIMACY ISSUES AND INDEPENDENT ADMINISTRATIVE AUTHORITIES

The legitimacy issues and independent administrative authorities were discussed in both the Swedish 2003 review[53] and the Norwegian 2003 Government White Paper.[54]

Due process and transparency were considered to remedy most objections. In the discussion about independence of the Norwegian Competition Authority leading up to the 2004 Competition Act,[55] the prevailing view was the Government would still be better placed to exercise a general discretion including broader general good considerations. That was one justification for refusing the independence that now has emerged as good European practice.

[50] Lov 2004-03-05 nr 12: Lov om konkurranse mellom foretak og kontroll med foretakssammenslutninger (konkurranseloven).

[51] See HP Graver Alminnelig forvaltningsrett (2nd edn Universitetsforlaget Oslo 2002) 179.

[52] See Lov 2000-11-17 nr 80: Lov om børsvirksomhet m.m. (børsloven).

[53] SOU 2004:100 *Tillsyn. Förslag om en tydligare och effektivare tillsyn.*

[54] St meld nr 17 (2002–3).

[55] Lov 2004-03-05 nr 12: Lov om konkurranse mellom foretak og kontroll med foretakssammenslutninger (konkurranseloven).

The ideals of Scandinavian public administration, legality and fairness, and that independent administrative authorities are seen to have specialist competence, have provided relatively limited concern about legitimacy.

## V. WHO ARE THE INDEPENDENT ADMINISTRATIVE AUTHORITIES AND WHAT ARE THEIR TASKS?

As mentioned under section II above, 'Independent Administrative Authorities' is not a term of statutory language in the Scandinavian countries. The independence of an authority in Scandinavian law, depends primarily on the limitations placed on the powers of the central government in parliamentary legislation.

A number of authorities have been discussed above. They include the central banks and different market regulatory authorities. A number of ombudsmen institutions have been established. The use of appeals tribunals is increasing.

The development of new forms of market regulation and supervision has provided a sector with a clear development towards the establishment of independent administrative authorities.

There are different independent authorities and appeals tribunals in the social security and pensions field. Patents, taxation, immigration and privacy are other core areas. In these fields individual rights are involved.

## VI. THE PROCEDURAL RULES THAT APPLY TO THE INDEPENDENT ADMINISTRATIVE AUTHORITIES

The general administrative procedural codes apply to the independent administrative authorities unless particular exceptions are made. In practice this would be in the form of more formalised, stricter and more court oriented rules.

The extensive transparency and access to information regimes of Scandinavian administrative law applies.

## VII. REMEDIES AGAINST DECISIONS BY THE INDEPENDENT ADMINISTRATIVE AUTHORITIES

Here again the full panoply of administrative or court remedies apply against decisions by the independent administrative authorities. The main exceptions are a cut off of administrative appeals in many cases, typically so that the agency's decisions cannot be appealed to the

Ministry/Department of state (this may be seen to be the core feature of 'independence').

There are no particular restrictions on judicial review. The review applications will in some instances start in a court of appeal and not in the usual court of first instance. This applies for instance to the decisions of the Norwegian Social Security Appeals Tribunal.

There are no special immunities from damages liability.

The Scandinavian legal systems offer several differences in the field of remedies. Swedish administrative law was complemented by criminal law to a higher extent than in the other countries. The Swedish catalogue of criminal offences committed by civil servants did include negligence offences. A widely defined personal damage liability for civil servants was another sanction. Criminal liability today plays much less of a role in the context of actions by civil servants than for instance in Italy and France. Damages liability is in effect transferred to the state or local authority.[56]

The question of damages liability can give rise to special issues in relation to independent authorities. Holding the independent authority and not the state liable can increase the accountability. This depends on procedural rules that again are different in the Scandinavian countries. Also *Francovich* liability under EU law can give rise to issues here but in general under the present law it is the member state that is held liable, but again procedural rules in member states may have an impact on the question.

## VIII. CONCLUSIONS

In Scandinavia, independent administrative authorities have lead to some constitutional controversy. The international and EU developments have to a large degree coincided with domestic goals for reform. Norway's staying out of the EU has provided a measure here and in terms of independence of the central bank it has not formalised this in the way that the Maastricht criteria require. This was a controversial issue in particular in Sweden who did give effect to its EU obligations. Also the Norwegian resistance to giving the Competition Authority and other authorities formal independence may be a consequence of its staying on the outside of the EU where the new international standards are coming into effect through EU mechanisms.

Independence concepts are an important component at the several new levels of administrative law that now come in addition to the domestic law. This chapter shows some of the difficulty in managing to combine these different perspectives. More active discussion can aid in the development of

[56] See N Herlitz 'Legal Remedies in Nordic Administrative Law (1966–7) 15 The American Journal of Comparative Law 687.

a more sophisticated comparative law methodology which is needed to resolve the issues of application and reform of administrative law.

The comparison between the countries, and with the different levels of international and European law, allow for making certain distinctions between the components of independence concepts.

The first meaning of an independent administrative authority is that of United States administrative law, and means independence from the President and the Executive.

A second meaning limits interference from the legislature. Here we have discussed the independence requirements for national central banks in the European System of Central Banks (ESCB) where for instance Sweden and Finland had to amend their legislation to secure the independence from the legislator.

A third meaning is organizational and financial independence. Here again the European Central Bank provides an example: it is not subject to organizational, budgetary, or other controls from other community institutions but uses the ESCB as the main control mechanism. For many national regulatory authorities, the possibility to set own pay scales, over those for civil service in general, is an important matter.

A fourth meaning is related to the mandate or purpose of an authority. If this is formulated in a narrow and technical way, not allowing for broad balancing of interests and policies, or for wide exceptions or derogations, this can increase the independence of the agency. This happens partly by the way in which this strengthens the legitimacy of the authority. There is also a potential for strengthening the transparency and accountability in this way without lessening the independence.

A fifth meaning is concerned with judicial review and court remedies. This has not been discussed in the Scandinavian countries. But extensive judicial review, invasive remedies and tort liability, have in other national and international contexts, been regarded as a threat to independence.

# 11. ANNEXE: INDEPENDENT ADMINISTRATIVE AUTHORITIES: THE EUROPEAN WAY(S)

*Framework of Questions*

## OVERVIEW

This research project is aimed at analysing the development of independent administrative authorities (IAA) at the European level as well as within the context of certain selected Member States.

The main aim of the project is to see how these independent administrative authorities fit within their respective constitutional frameworks, and how they may be contributing a shift in to the constitutional frameworks. More specifically, we will examine to what extent IAA are at odds with the so-called (tripartite) separation of powers.

These constitutional developments may result in various different outcomes:

- IAA may themselves be adapted to the exigencies of the separation of powers.
- The classic conception of separation of powers is set aside or derogated from to make room for IAA.

Further, IAA may perhaps be considered to be at odds with the principle of democratic legitimacy and accountability of the executive/administrative power. Here again various possible solutions to this dilemma may be envisaged:

- IAA are not totally excluded from the processes of democratic legitimacy (and accountability).
- Executive functions can be legitimised in ways which are different from the traditional democratic process.

The following questions are not supposed to be a straitjacket, but rather a suggested path to a comprehensive treatment of the subject matter; they may departed from if they do not really suit the specific features of the legal order under analysis.

It is hoped that the resulting reports will be published by an international publisher at the end of the project.

QUESTIONS

What is/are the meaning/s of IAA in the legal order you are dealing with; and also, is there just one types of IAA or they come in different fashions?

What is the position of IAA in relation to to the executive branch (the Head of State and/or the Government)?

Are public servants supposed to act impartiality in the discharge of their duties? If so, is independence in any way different from impartiality?

What is the position of IAA in relation to the legislative branch?

What is the position of IAA in relation to sub-national levels of Government (e.g. federated States, Regions and so on, according to which is applicable)?

Are there one or more specific provisions in the Constitution or in documents having constitutional value concerning IAA?

If not, how are IAA made consistent with the constitutional framework?

Are constitutional reforms concerning IAA being discussed or debated?

Are IAA accountable to anyone, and, if so, to which other organ? Or conversely, are they accountable to no one, not even to the people?

How do IAA derive their legitimacy?

More specifically, does (all or part of) their legitimacy derive from a higher law, such as for instance European Community law?

What authorities are considered independent under the criteria laid down in the previous points (please, give specific indications as to the statutes or other rules having set them up; since the paper or at least some part of it will go on internet, please give a complete list with the internet sites of the IAA concerned)?

How is independence sustained for each of the IAA considered (matters such as appointment, non revocability, budgetary autonomy and so on are to be considered)?

What are the (main) functions allotted to any of the IAA (whether advisory, adjudicatory, regulatory and so on)?

Are the rules applied to the functioning of / proceedings by IAA in any way different from those applying to:

Courts proceedings;

Administrative proceedings.

In what sectors do IAA operate (more specifically, are they concerned with market regulation only? Is fundamental rights protection one of their concerns)?

If (one or more) IAA is set up to protect fundamental rights, how is their role coordinated with that of the courts (the traditional guardians of fundamental rights)?

Is judicial review allowed against their decisions? If so, which courts (civil or administrative or other) are charged with reviewing decisions taken by IAA?

If judicial review is allowed, is it strict or rather bland, compared also with the attitude courts normally adopt concerning judicial review of administrative action

Are damages a remedy against IAA?

The United States of America, the European Union and some Member States of the European Union are to be covered by the research.

| Legal Order | Person Responsible | E-mail address |
|---|---|---|
| USA | Saskia Lavrijssen | askia.Lavrijssen@Kub.nl |
| UE | Edoardo Chiti | edoardo.chiti@libero.it |
| France | Jeanette Bougrab | bougrab@univ-paris1.fr |
| Germany | Anne van Aaken | nne.van.aaken@rewi.hu-berlin.de |
| Italy | Roberto Caranta | roberto.caranta@unito.it |
| Netherlands | Leonard Besserlink | L.Besserlink@law.uu.nl |
| United Kingdom | Duncan Fairgrieve | d.fairgrieve@biicl.org |
| Sweden (and Norway) | Mads Andenas | m.andenas@biicl.org |

DEADLINES

**End June 2002:** Dissemination of the first draft questions to the reports.

**July 2002:** Comments by the reporters and definitive draft of the questions; posting of the questions on the internet site of the research project.

**End February 2003:** Draft reports are circulated among the reporters and posted on the internet site of the research project;

**16 April and 17 April 2003:** Workshop in Turin to discuss the reports.

**End May 2003:** Definitive reports submitted to the editor.

**End 2003:** The book is published.